A CELEBRATION OF POETS

PENNSYLVANIA
GRADES 4-12
FALL 2011

creativeCOMMUNICATION
A CELEBRATION OF TODAY'S WRITERS

A Celebration of Poets
Pennsylvania
Grades 4-12
Fall 2011

An anthology compiled by Creative Communication, Inc.

Published by:

creativeCOMMUNICATION
A CELEBRATION OF TODAY'S WRITERS

PO BOX 303 · SMITHFIELD, UTAH 84335
TEL. 435-713-4411 · WWW.POETICPOWER.COM

Authors are responsible for the originality of the writing submitted.

Copyright © 2012 by Creative Communication, Inc.
Printed in the United States of America

ISBN: 978-1-60050-472-3

FOREWORD

In January of this year, I was watching the Miss America Pageant. I thought of all the accomplishments that culminate in this one ending competition. These outstanding women had decided what they wanted, paid the price and now were reaping the rewards of their hard work. While watching the pageant, the finalists were on stage and a few of their accomplishments were written across the screen. For Miss Arizona, Jennifer Sedler (who ended as 3rd runner-up), one of her accomplishments was having a poem published in 5th grade. In checking our records, it was our company, Creative Communication, that published her poem "Hawaiian Seas" in the Fall of 2002.

Jennifer wrote to us about the experience of being published:

> "I had a poem published by Creative Communication in 5th grade, and I will never forget how special and inspired it made me feel. I have since gone on to win numerous essay contests, many which earned me scholarship money for college, and I may have never believed in myself if it wasn't for Creative Communication. And as Miss Arizona, I write pages and pages of creatively-written updates for all of my followers. Now of course I still take time on my own to read, study, and write poetry. When you choose to be an active learner and writer, I think you will find, just as I did, that truly anything is possible."

When a poet enters our writing contest, they are students like everyone else. As they move on in life, talents are developed. A 5th grade student becomes Miss Arizona. Another student, novelist Angela Bishop, also wrote to me the following:

> "My name is Angela Bishop, and almost ten years ago you selected one of my poems to be published in the Southern edition of your book. I was 15 and it was the highlight of my young life. Although it has been nearly a decade, I just wanted to finally express the thanks I have felt all these years. I cannot thank you enough for accepting my work and publishing it. I have been writing since I was a child and have continued to write. I am currently working on my second novel. So, thank you, thank you, for the confidence you unknowingly gave me in 1999. I plan to keep writing for as long as I possibly can. Your poetry contest is a wonderful thing, and you open a window for tomorrow's great writers to find their way through and gain the confidence in their work. Keep it going, you are making dreams into realities."

To both Jennifer and Angela and the students in this anthology, I am glad that we are here for you. We helped you in creating an accomplishment that you can be proud of and add to your resume. When students wonder if they should enter a contest, I give a strong affirmative. You may not be accepted to be published, but if you don't enter, there isn't a chance of being published or being a Top Ten winner. Sometimes you have to take a risk and enter a contest. It may change your life. Just ask Jennifer and Angela.

I hope you enjoy the poems that are included in this anthology. We are pleased to help provide the spark that makes lifelong writers. Each of these students took a risk in entering and has the potential to achieve great things in their lives. Good luck.

Tom Worthen, Ph.D.
Editor

WRITING CONTESTS!

Enter our next POETRY contest!
Enter our next ESSAY contest!

Why should I enter?
Win prizes and get published! Each year thousands of dollars in prizes are awarded throughout North America. The top writers in each division receive a monetary award and a free book that includes their published poem or essay. Entries of merit are also selected to be published in our anthology.

Who may enter?
There are four divisions in the poetry contest. The poetry divisions are grades K-3, 4-6, 7-9, and 10-12. There are three divisions in the essay contest. The essay divisions are grades 3-6, 7-9, and 10-12.

What is needed to enter the contest?
To enter the poetry contest send in one original poem, 21 lines or less. To enter the essay contest send in one original non-fiction essay, 250 words or less, on any topic. Please submit each poem and essay with a title, and the following information clearly printed: the writer's name, current grade, home address (optional), school name, school address, teacher's name and teacher's email address (optional). Contact information will only be used to provide information about the contest. For complete contest information go to www.poeticpower.com.

How do I enter?
Enter a poem online at:
www.poeticpower.com
or
Mail your poem to:
Poetry Contest
PO Box 303
Smithfield UT 84335

Enter an essay online at:
www.poeticpower.com
or
Mail your essay to:
Essay Contest
PO Box 303
Smithfield UT 84335

When is the deadline?
Poetry contest deadlines are August 16th, December 6th and April 9th. Essay contest deadlines are July 19th, October 18th and February 19th. Students can enter one poem and one essay for each spring, summer, and fall contest deadline.

Are there benefits for my school?
Yes. We award $12,500 each year in grants to help with Language Arts programs. Schools qualify to apply for a grant by having 15 or more accepted entries.

Are there benefits for my teacher?
Yes. Teachers with five or more students published receive a free anthology that includes their students' writing.

For more information please go to our website at **www.poeticpower.com**, email us at editor@poeticpower.com or call 435-713-4411.

TABLE OF CONTENTS

Fall 2011
Poetic Achievement
Honor Schools

Teachers who had fifteen or more poets accepted to be published

The following schools are recognized as receiving a "Poetic Achievement Award." This award is given to schools who have a large number of entries of which over fifty percent are accepted for publication. With hundreds of schools entering our contest, only a small percent of these schools are honored with this award. The purpose of this award is to recognize schools with excellent Language Arts programs. This award qualifies these schools to receive a complimentary copy of this anthology. In addition, these schools are eligible to apply for a Creative Communication Language Arts Grant. Grants of two hundred and fifty dollars each are awarded to further develop writing in our schools.

Armstrong Middle School
  Fairless Hills
    Beth Clark*
    Carol Lorenz*

Aston Elementary School
  Aston
    Vivienne F. Cameron*

Bellmar Middle School
  Belle Vernon
    Carol Aten Frow*
    Karen Guseman*

Burgettstown Elementary Center
  Burgettstown
    Lorraine MacFarlane*

Charles F Patton Middle School
  Kennett Square
    Christina Sapyta*

Chichester Middle School
  Boothwyn
    Cynthia Bottomley*
    Susan Fitzgerald*
    Meaghan Wallace

Clearview Elementary School
  Bethlehem
    Amy M. Kravetz*

Eden Hall Upper Elementary School
  Gibsonia
    Gregg Somerhalder*

Fairview Elementary School
  Midland
    Donna Harn*

Faith Tabernacle School
  Mechanicsburg
    Sylvia Grove*

Foster Elementary School
  Pittsburgh
    Mary Hopkins*

Fred S Engle Middle School
  West Grove
    Karen Capone*

Good Shepherd School
  Camp Hill
    Carol McGrade*

Greencastle-Antrim Middle School
Greencastle
Ann Fague*
Beth Powers
Kelly Saylor

Holicong Middle School
Doylestown
Miss Ambrosini*
Monica DeMuro
Jason Hepler
Lisa Levin
Mrs. Mandes
Mrs. Schmitt

Holy Child Academy
Drexel Hill
Patricia McDaniel
Barbara Sherwood

Hopewell Memorial Jr High School
Aliquippa
Paula Battisti
Dawn Gailey*

Interboro GATE Program
Prospect Park
Kelly DiLullo
Joyce Faragasso

J R Fugett Middle School
West Chester
Elena Castilla*
Robin Dannehower

Jefferson Elementary School
Pittsburgh
Joy Buettner*
Jessica Zajac

Landisville Middle School
Landisville
Diane Anderson*
Scott D. Feifer*

Lincoln Elementary School
Pittsburgh
Cynthia Biery*
Stacy Maehling

Linville Hill Mennonite School
Paradise
Susan Homsher*

Middle Smithfield Elementary School
East Stroudsburg
Barbara Dahl*

Moravian Academy Middle School
Bethlehem
Bud Brennan
Cindy Siegfried*

Nazareth Area Intermediate School
Nazareth
Lynn Post*

Pennridge North Middle School
Perkasie
Melissa Plack
Petie Ritchie*

Pittsburgh CAPA 6-12 School
Pittsburgh
Mara Cregan
Lynn Marsico

Pittston Area High School
Pittston
Kathryn Conlon*

Reiffton School
Reading
Mrs. Dale
Erin Trostle

Richboro Middle School
Richboro
Dawn M. Donmoyer
Rebekah Lang*

Sacred Heart School
Oxford
Cara Grebner*

Sandy Run Middle School
Dresher
Mrs. Connelly
Danielle DiPasquale
Mrs. Parkin

Schuylkill Valley Middle School
Leesport
Codie Bender
Caitlin Overman*

Southern Lehigh Middle School
Center Valley
Lori Frasch*

St Anselm Elementary School
Philadelphia
Miss LaVerghetta*
Melissa Montag
Freda M. Tait
Joann Whartenby

St James School
Sewickley
Karen Scully*

St Joseph School
Mechanicsburg
Linda Connolly
Rosanna Ellis
Marie C. Vassey

St Jude School
Mountaintop
Marilyn Baran
Maralyn Mance

St Thomas More School
Allentown
Donna Davidson*
Stephanie Gaughan*
Margaret Herman*

Strath Haven Middle School
Wallingford
Mary Reindorp
Elaine Shipman*

The American Academy
Philadelphia
Dr. Sharon Traver*

Trinity East Elementary School
Washington
Denise R. Cummins*

Trinity Middle School
Washington
Denise R. Cummins*

Whitehall High School
Whitehall
Jessie Bucchin*

William M Meredith School
Philadelphia
Elizabeth Cieri*

Wissahickon Charter School
Philadelphia
Leslie S. Leff*

Language Arts Grant Recipients 2011-2012

After receiving a "Poetic Achievement Award" schools are encouraged to apply for a Creative Communication Language Arts Grant. The following is a list of schools who received a two hundred and fifty dollar grant for the 2011-2012 school year.

Annapolis Royal Regional Academy, Annapolis Royal, NS
Bear Creek Elementary School, Monument, CO
Bellarmine Preparatory School, Tacoma, WA
Birchwood School, Cleveland, OH
Bluffton Middle School, Bluffton, SC
Brookville Intermediate School, Brookville, OH
Butler High School, Augusta, GA
Carmi-White County High School, Carmi, IL
Classical Studies Academy, Bridgeport, CT
Coffee County Central High School, Manchester, TN
Country Hills Elementary School, Coral Springs, FL
Coyote Valley Elementary School, Middletown, CA
Emmanuel-St Michael Lutheran School, Fort Wayne, IN
Excelsior Academy, Tooele, UT
Great Meadows Middle School, Great Meadows, NJ
Holy Cross High School, Delran, NJ
Kootenay Christian Academy, Cranbrook, BC
LaBrae Middle School, Leavittsburg, OH
Ladoga Elementary School, Ladoga, IN
Mater Dei High School, Evansville, IN
Palmer Catholic Academy, Ponte Vedra Beach, FL
Pine View School, Osprey, FL
Plato High School, Plato, MO
Rivelon Elementary School, Orangeburg, SC
Round Lake High School, Round Lake, MN
Sacred Heart School, Oxford, PA
Shadowlawn Elementary School, Green Cove Springs, FL
Starmount High School, Boonville, NC
Stevensville Middle School, Stevensville, MD
Tadmore Elementary School, Gainesville, GA
Trask River High School, Tillamook, OR
Vacaville Christian Schools, Vacaville, CA
Wattsburg Area Middle School, Erie, PA
William Dunbar Public School, Pickering, ON
Woods Cross High School, Woods Cross, UT

Grades 10-11-12
Top Ten Winners

List of Top Ten Winners for Grades 10-12; listed alphabetically

Maria Capitano, Grade 11
Pittston Area High School, PA

Anna Daavettila, Grade 10
Houghton High School, MI

Anna Groeling, Grade 11
Arapahoe High School, CO

Arniecia Hinds, Grade 10
Germantown High School, TN

Sabrina Maus, Grade 10
Haynes Academy for Advanced Studies, LA

Erin McCune, Grade 10
Bellarmine Preparatory School, WA

Declan Routledge, Grade 12
Webber Academy, AB

Jacob Schriner-Briggs, Grade 12
Liberty High School, OH

Lianna Scott, Grade 11
Xavier College Preparatory School, AZ

Alexander Wimmer, Grade 10
Home School, GA

All Top Ten Poems can be read at www.poeticpower.com

Note: The Top Ten poems were finalized through an online voting system. Creative Communication's judges first picked out the top poems. These poems were then posted online. The final step involved thousands of students and teachers who registered as the online judges and voted for the Top Ten poems. We hope you enjoy these selections.

The Need to Remember

"God, my life is hard.
I'm hurting and all alone.
My heart has become hard like a pathway of stone.
I have dealt with much heartache and strife,
And I have faced many trials in life
While others seem to glide right through.
You are with me; I only wish I knew."

"My dear child, I am always near.
When you are hurt and lonely,
I have held your hand and have heard your every plea.
You have placed yourself in a prison,
And your pain has clouded your vision;
For others have suffered, too.
Remember, my son died on the cross for you."

"O heavenly Father, how much I have forgotten.
I have lost sight of Your love, mercy, and grace.
I allowed the Devil to take Your place.
How selfish I have been.
Discontentedness is my greatest sin.
May I always recognize Your goodness,
And know that You will continue to bless."

Megan S. Feaser, Grade 12
Faith Tabernacle School

Male Tide, Female Tide, Darkness Falls

Male Tide
He ROARS slamming his fists,
Yelling at the sky, storming the beach,
Spraying foam of white from his mouth.
He runs from himself only to return
Starving beasts he holds within.
He taunts the land dwellers.
His waters like liquid obsidian and his form omnipresent.
His mouth a gaping hole, ready to swallow you whole.

Female Tide
She swells with passion
Whispers, quietly, calmly
Calling to you, singing to you sweetly.
At dusk she feeds
Devouring the land imprisoning her
Allowing it to truly sleep.

Darkness Falls
Male tide has cleansed the beach
Female tide has laid it to rest.
Trickster moon is throwing his reflection on their bodies
While a hero lies in wait in the depths.

Quincy Atkins, Grade 11
Abington Heights High School

Joy

Joy is a blessing from God above,
Sent to all with lots of love.

The smallest smile has a way
Of brightening even the gloomiest day.

Joy can make your heart a song
Even when the path seems wrong.

Joy can be accomplishment done
Even if it is the simplest one.

Joy can bring a tear to your eye,
When you hear a newborn baby's cry.

Joy is the comfort of talking to a friend
That you know will be there 'til the very end.

Joy has a way of spreading about
Just when everyone begins to doubt.

Joy will always be there along the way
Just like God throughout each day.

Donald E. Witherow, Grade 12
Faith Tabernacle School

Watch, Listen, Call

I want to help,
Wish I could help,
But I watch, listen, and call.

I watch you pour your drink into your glass,
Watch you down it like a cup of water.
I watch you inhale, hold, breathe out,
Like you've done nothing wrong.
I watch you, even help you,
Try to escape the tug of war you're caught between,
But you are the rope.

I don't know where you do it,
But you showed me the slices in your wrist,
The thin, penciled scars,
The fresher, bleeding wounds,
As if your problems were inside of you,
And you were simply freeing them.

I want to help,
Wish I could help,
But I watch, listen, and call.

Elizabeth Shackney, Grade 11
The Ellis School

Bugs to a Light

Amassing more and more, attracted like bugs to a light —
They're angry, they're frustrated, and they're ready to fight.
To fight! Fight! Fight! Fight for what's right!
Changes are needed, and they must start tonight!
And so it begins.

They're moving as one, a fist swinging wildly at its foe;
They chant, and they shout, anger's all that they know;
The street's raining glass; hate's swirling like snow,
Chaos reigns king wherever they go.
And so it is.

Then shrieking knives slice the air, tearing the fist asunder
And the fingers clenched together, they don't know each other;
They can't tell foe from foe; brother fights brother
And to dismay, they start to fight against one another —
And so it collapses.

Hence the short battle's over, but the damage is done
As the injured bugs fly off the light, one by one.
The light had seemed so right, the battle already won,
But their voice has been heard! And the war, it's just begun!

…But — I suppose, as it is, a riot alone never solved anything…
Erin Feaser, Grade 10
Faith Tabernacle School

The Challenge

Climbing, climbing,
His expedition will never end.
He journeys up through this frozen, barren rock
With no one to help him, not even a friend.

Climbing, climbing,
Not even knowing why.
All he knows is to climb to the end,
And to him, that is all he needs to get by.

Climbing, climbing,
The wind whipping at his face,
He never dares to stop, never dares to cease,
For he must keep going if he wishes to win the race.

Climbing, climbing,
The challenge is almost won.
The man now moves quick as lightning,
Realizing that his task will soon be done.

Climbed, climbed,
The man has beaten them all.
But though no one will ever know,
This man has just answered God's call.
Timothy J. Umstead, Grade 10
Faith Tabernacle School

Wisdom Lost*

I sing of teeth and a man.
He who, condemned by fate,
First came to the oral surgery clinic.

Muse, tell me the cause: how offended in her divinity,
How was she grieved, that Fairy of Teeth, to drive four molars
Noted for size, so perpendicularly against their companions…
Can there be so much pain, at the hands of the dentists?

Such thought pondered, I await extraction
Of cursed teeth: led to the high throne and bestrapped tightly,
Pierced with IVs, machines measured my reaction
To blessed anesthesia, that struck not lightly.

Then, awakened from sweet painless bliss,
Sought I to express happiness:
Alas, joyful noise was blotted out
By gray, grim gauze that staunched the spout.

Led forth on a chair of wheels,
For six days ate I soft meals.
Sick of yogurt, Jell-O, and assorted cheese.
Madam Fairy, my money, if you please.
Sam Anthony, Grade 12
The American Academy
*Inspired by Virgil's Aeneid

Happily Ever After

I arrive on the scene to a pitiful sight:
A girl in rags with a heart full of light.
Through three little words, I changed her life.
After years of struggle, I end her strife.

I make her rich and pretty, and she seems rather chipper
As I grace her feet with two glass slippers.
But with magic comes rules; to this she did not fight:
"No one must know you are gone and be home by midnight!"

She danced the night away with the prince of her dreams,
But as time ticked on, the magic was bursting at its seams.
At the stroke of twelve, she left the ball with great care,
But in her rush, she left her shoe on the stair!

Our princess returned to her sorrowful life,
To chores and cleaning for her dead father's wife.
But her prince found her shoe, and was knocking at her door.
It was then she knew she would clean no more.

It was as if a light was shining down from above
As our princess at last, discovers true love.
The rest they say is history, with years full of laughter
And our princess finally gets her happily ever after.
Abby Shore, Grade 11
Eastern York High School

Perfection in My Eyes

She is perfection in my eyes
She is the sun in my skies
The water in my ocean
And the green in my eyes

She is the shampoo in my hair
The oxygen in my air
The truth to my dare
And the fun in my fair

She is the pep in my step
The faith in my leap
The dreams I have each night
And the wool to my sheep

She is the flight to my bird
She is every sound I've heard
She is the angels that sing
And she is my everything

Russell Orler, Grade 12
Methacton High School

Life Cycle

Opening its sky-blue eyes the first time
Hearing the new voices and sounds nearby
Smiling with a face as round as a dime
Having no voice, the baby is quite shy.

The baby is now living by itself
Going out in search of making new friends
It is working to obtain its own wealth
As it grows older, its adult phase ends.

Possessing a grin on its wrinkled face
Unable to hear sounds of its childhood
Searching everywhere for its glasses case
The baby lies there and is gone for good.

Melting away like a warm icicle
Life is an uncontrollable cycle.

Suraj Pursnani, Grade 11
Pittston Area High School

Loving You

Loving you is all I want to do
But you just don't want me to,
Your feelings are growing for me
Every day it seems.

You say you don't want to feel this way
But I want your feelings to stay.
I just hope your feelings don't delay,
There are so many things I want to do
Only if you let me love you.

Nahkia Galloway, Grade 11
Conestoga High School

The World Beyond Your Eyes

Angelic chorus has no effect on me unlike your voice,
Making my knees tremble with happiness,
Leaving me breathless with every word you say,
Your eyes lead me to a place I've never seen before,
A place of happiness and peace,
Where everything makes sense,
Where I'm invincible and nothing can break my spirit,
Catching me up in a life of sweetness,
So with these broken wings I will show you what I see,
To show you how beautiful you really are,
And how amazing you truly are,
Give me the opportunity to show you and I'll show you what I see through my eyes,
How truly beautiful you are the sweetness you show and the angel I see in you,
You're loving and compassionate,
Beyond anything of this world,
Making my heart race when we lay our hearts together,
Giving me the strength to be able to do what is impossible,
With you in my arms there is nothing that is going to stop us.

Brandon Downs, Grade 11
Fort Cherry Jr/Sr High School

Ode to LeBron James

Here's to my favorite athlete, hoping one day we shall meet.
Here's to a great leader, now a heat once a cavalier.
Hated by most of society, but to me still almighty.
On the court you're a legend, through media you get skewered to no end.
Despite your few bad decisions, you're a great man in my vision.
Twice you have been close, even though you helped the most.
Maybe next year is the year, just take it to another gear.
The Miami Heat are back for more, watch the big three own the floor.
I love it when you slam it down, or when you sink it from downtown.
Or when you stuff it in Kobe's face, putting him in his place.
Your career is far from over, becoming too old will take forever.
I started watching you from day one, and I won't stop until you're done.
You definitely have lived up to the hype, you became the player we thought you might.
Once again you are amazing, do not fall for all the doubt,
Show the world what King James is all about.

Justin Zweig, Grade 11
North Allegheny Sr High School

Life Changes…In the Blink of An Eye…

In the blink of an eye, your life can change.
In the blink of an eye, you life can get better.
In the blink of an eye, your life can fall apart.

In the blink of an eye, you can become sick.
In the blink of an eye, you can lose someone that you are close to.
In the blink of an eye, you can hit a home run.
In the blink of an eye, you can make a difference in someone's life.

In the blink of an eye, your life can change from silver to gold.
In the blink of an eye, your life can change from gold to dirt.

Your life can change, regardless if you think something good or bad can ever happen to you.

Stephanie Beregi, Grade 12
Brownsville Area High School

Lost Soul

With nothing left to fill the void,
She's left with all her dreams destroyed.
And walking through this world alone
She's descending into the dark unknown.
There hung about clouds of despair,
Too thick for even a knife to tear.
Depression wraps its cold arms around her,
And despite her pain no feelings stir.
That blank, emotionless, solemn gaze,
Unchanging as she disobeys,
Never gaining that concern she craves.
And on these pages she rants and raves,
Of these feelings which she's stuffed in caves.
And here in this desperate isolation,
She's lost among her own frustration.
Then she's off to save her stranded soul,
Alone at night on an endless stroll.

Kayla Groft, Grade 11
Eastern York High School

Our Song

Our poem is the blowing warm breeze
Walking out late with the vibrant sunset
With the seagulls flying in the background
And we're all alone talking with ourselves

Our poem is the blowing warm breeze
Riding the Ferris wheel looking down at roofs
And the city lights looking like the stars
The world's below and we're miles apart

Our poem is the blowing warm breeze
Running through your hair as we twist and sway
All night long dancing to the quick drum beat
A beautiful poem was this tale

Michelle Runkle, Grade 11
Eastern York High School

Long Gone

I wish I could go back to those easy summer days
Sitting with you, feeling more than a warm breeze
Now everything we had is a blurry haze
And I beg for you to remember me, please
I will never forget your deep brown eyes
Or the way those eyes looked into mine
How we stayed out to see the fireflies
Lying under the stars like everything was fine
You held my hand so tightly and didn't let go
Making promises to last as long as they can
Neither of us had a way to know
We would lose our hearts again
I wish I could return to my loving my best friend
But your love and my favorite summer have long come to an end

K. Riley Shenberger, Grade 11
Eastern York High School

Friday Night Lights

The final bell rings, I walk out of school
I head on over to the locker room
Outside, the November air feels so cool
And tonight we will go out with a boom!

The ball is kicked off, the crowd gives a roar
The different players run down and SMASH!
For us it's not just a game, it's a war
This is a battle where two teams will clash

The refs throw a flag and we get a call
We came in hot; hit them with our power
There's two minutes left and we have the ball
After all our work, victory is ours

Nothing can beat playing under bright lights
Lord knows I live for these great kinds of nights.

Stephen Starinsky, Grade 11
Pittston Area High School

The Way I See Things

If you could look through my eyes, you would see
The simple good in most everything
And the wonderful place our world can be,
Since people are mostly good, I believe.
Bad things may happen, things may turn out wrong
But don't get lost in the darkness and pain
Learn from suffering, let it make you strong
For there can be no flowers without rain.
So remember the light in your smile
And those that you touch with the love you show
Laugh with your old friends once in a while
And sing along with every song you know.
But what I wish the most for you to do
Is to see all the good I see in you.

Maria Capitano, Grade 11
Pittston Area High School

Two Young Girls

Two young girls, four years apart,
Sometimes share feelings of the heart.
The hardships of life have done them wrong,
But showed both they are capable of being strong.

One's hair is light, the other's dark,
But both share the same Mark.
Half different, half the same,
More time together, the closer they became.

The two of us have a very special bond.
When things get tough, I still love my sister of blonde.
Although sometimes our relationship gets blistered,
We must remember: "sisters forever," as we always whispered.

Mariah Swartz, Grade 11
Eastern York High School

A Gracefully Compact Guide to (Your) Day

add (we) a few hours to (our) day would be good
so never enough there are
to time (ourself) out stresses (our) day from the beginning
        wake up too early; or too late; messes the Zen of day

take time to look at the moon setting; the sun rising;
might ease (us) start (us) off on a good note
bygones be bygones; (we) shall let go
        in the street listen to the, not so, crazed women full still of wisdom

time (we) take to look at little things, not much so
starting might be good for (those) look only at big picture
no yell; no fuss; no moan; no cry
with what comes, go; roll with punches gracefully

no yelling useless at petty
yummy food so (no one) sticks tongue at (you) eating
head down with pillow upon darkness around consumes, no sound no light
        head matches (your) thoughts; pure to sleep free

Rose Roberts, Grade 10
Whitehall High School

You Are a Rainbow

Splattering the walls of my white room, you bring me my morning dose of laughter on a silver platter,
I give you the tricks to life as they come.
You are the same colors as me, but different shade, you are a smaller version of me, but you.
You are the color green, free and natural rolling down flower covered hills, just you and me.
You are the color purple, deep and mesmerizing, as mysterious as the dinosaurs, you roar and stomp.
You are the color pink, goofy and loving giggling at my jokes, giving me a hug when it is most needed.
You are the color black, troubled and confuse, full of land mines, being led out of the darkness by a light.
You are the color white, pure and new, innocent in every way, living in a safe cocoon.
You are the color orange, wild and energetic, always moving always dancing, never holding back.
You are the color red, fiery and fierce, standing up for yourself, against any threat
You are a rainbow, colorful and vibrant, shedding your light on the world, filling my life with meaning.

Meghan Veglia, Grade 12
Upper Saint Clair High School

The Start of the Race

Lined up one after the other,
Engines thunderously revving,
Each driver's heart beats rapidly,
Waiting for the wave of the black and white flag.

Sitting behind their steering wheels,
Black helmets strapped on tight,
Each driver is ready
To show off their skill.
Whoosh! Waves the checkered flag.

The cars speed off
Like stones from slingshots,
Leaving behind only
An audience holding their breath
And the bitter smell of burnt rubber.

Atalie Hiester, Grade 10
Faith Tabernacle School

Worship

The soothing water and sunset shore
Leave me longing to want you more
You created everything, beauty and strong
But still it is you I wish to belong
Your sacrifice was our bath
But we still do wrong and deserve Yhwh's wrath
I do long for the chance to be
Following you all eternity
You cast out demons and rose the dead
But the greatest are the words you said
The way of life you've given to all
To prevent another terrible fall
To all who listen their hearts are open
For it is you that they have chosen
To those who don't posit and don't obey
You might want to start…first step…pray

Aarron Teudhope, Grade 12
Conneaut Valley High School

Winter

Coldness has arrived,
Freezing the lakes
And killing the leaves,
Bringing them down
One by one.
Daylight is shortened,
And night is forever long.
The ground is frozen
Solid as a rock
While the wind roars
And does not stop.
Frost has approached,
Covering the ground
Like a blanket of ice crystals.
Snow has begun to appear,
Falling slowly and softly,
Laying inch by inch
Without a sound.
The snow has ceased
And life lies low and still
In this winter wonderland.
Lloyd A. Goodyear, Grade 10
Faith Tabernacle School

Misconception

The untrue cuts into routine
The monsters come through mist and trees
It was all a misconception
The part we all missed of the lesson

A twisted way to breathe in life
For someone else's broken eyes
Shocked defense in sudden truth
They're misconceived, but held aloof

A newborn, innocent and pure
Although bright blue has its allure
Red on white, in stripe and splatter
We didn't know, what does it matter…?
Katie Borne, Grade 11
Commonwealth Connections Academy

Without You

To do without doing
Is being still.

To speak without speaking
Is being silent.

To think without thinking
Is being forgetful.

To be without being
Is being without you.
Alexandra Nicholson, Grade 11
Commonwealth Connections Academy

No-Man's Land

The guns have been shot; the bodies have been blessed.
The troops have returned; the countries are at rest.

The smoke clears from the field; there are bodies everywhere.
Blood stands in puddles, but no one really cares.

As a little girl takes a step onto the warring field,
She feels the pain of loss, but her tears are concealed.

In her hands she holds a bouquet of bright white flowers.
They remind her of the winter, and the strive for peaceful power.

She closes her eyes for a moment, sending a quiet prayer.
She thinks of all the death and war, but her heart refuses to despair.

She knows there is a brighter future; she knows she has to try.
She knows there is another way where no one has to die.

And this girl, with her bright white flowers, might one day change the world,
Because she has hope and a dream,
And lives with her angel's wings unfurled.

Ana Turosky, Grade 10
Holy Redeemer High School

To Understand a Song

To understand a song
You could see the brain send a pulse through the nerves
Which carry the pulse over to the vocal cords
Which beat against each other to create a pitch
Which then gets channeled through the throat and face
To be sent as waves to the outside
Which is interpreted by the ear and is dissembled
Word by word, note by note, pitch by pitch, and eventually
Individual beat of the vocal cords by individual beat
Or you could see the spark in the brain
Which causes the eyes to twinkle
Which jump starts the heart to fluttering,
And this fluttering causes the soul to surge
To be sent out to the world as happiness
And then sends the ear into ecstasy
Which allows that heart to beat in tune and understanding with another
And connect with all that is trying to be said
Or individual beat of the vocal cords by individual beat
To understand the exact same song

Joshua Lewis, Grade 11
Eastern York High School

How Many Miles to Wonderland?

To Wonderland we go
Meet with Alice and friends.
Where all I can hope
Is adventure never ends.

Oh, little white rabbit
Please take me away,
I'll be waiting
All year, all month, and all day.

Curiouser and curiouser
I'll say when I'm there;
I'll meet with a hatter,
And maybe a march hare.

I can escape,
This world of terror and pain.
Where I cry in the sun,
And dance in the rain.

I don't mean to hurt you,
Or make anyone sad,
But now you can see,
I am most certainly mad.

Harley Brandstadter, Grade 11
Deer Lakes High School

My Brothers

I love them.
All four of them.
Two older, two younger.
But all the best.
Andy's funny.
Chris is special.
Hunter's optimistic.
Mordecai?
Well, you can't help loving him.

I love them.
I miss them.
All four of them.
Why can't they be here?
Why can't they be with me?
To stop the aching,
And hurt.
To say goodnight.
To say good morning.

I miss them.
All four of them.
But I need to trust God's plan.

Misty Clingerman, Grade 12
Union Valley Christian School

Toe Dancing and Butterfly Kisses

I watch you,
wide eyed and curious,
anticipating your next move.
I run to you,
arms wide open,
grinning ear to ear.
I lean toward you,
butterfly kisses,
fluttering from my eyelashes.
I laugh at you,
stepping on your shoes,
dancing while your feet move us.
Across,
Down, side to side.
I watch your blue eyes shine.
Flashback is over,
and I look at your face.
Your wrinkles from all those laughs,
the same shimmer in your eyes.
I know my Daddy will always be there,
no matter how old I grow.

Cheyenne Knight, Grade 11
Kennard Dale High School

Can't Be Stranded

Everything's been a drag now
Still I try to go through the motions
Struggling to make two ends meet
Mending 'n' looking to find my feet

Ref: Come rain come shine
For better for worse
I can't be stranded
In famine or feasting

Life is getting tighter all the time
Gotcha beat the grind in due time
Soon as I get the jinx off my back
Don't wanna go down the memory lane
To survive the jinx I can't be stranded

It goes around and comes around
Like the grind of the windmill of life
Trying to beat the cycle of the circus
From day to day as the swiss clock ticks
The world revolves and the years roll by

Uche N. Obianyo, Grade 12

Heavenly Affairs

See that little sun
Lusting up through the sky
To meet his earthly lover
To melt the snow that coats her eyes
And she relents, reluctantly
Until midday
When the sun's charm becomes too strong

She forgets the little sun
Has seven other lovers
All bathing in the same rays
To seven other lovers
He is the father of the day
Then he retreats, radiant
Until eventide
When he cannot see the earth turn her face

But before dawn comes
Under wings of darkness
Under cover, out of sight
The sun is just another star
Out of the millions the Earth dances with
Every night.

Luiza Lodder, Grade 11
State College Area High School

Swift Skirmish

Soldiers, fitted in much darkened armor,
Prepare for their day ahead.
They evaluate their precise weapons
As the mission objectives are said.

Soldiers move to the ammo depository
To pick up clips for the day.
They test their guns and gadgets;
Then they move to the hanger bay.

Soldiers mount up on their agile aircraft
And belt themselves to the seat.
The pilot introduces himself to the squad
And warns them of the battle's heat.

Soldiers land on the unknown terrain
To start their fight for survival;
The wounded men are identified
And taken to cover for revival.

Soldiers, buzzing bullets everywhere,
Start their triumphant walk.
They have won a glorious skirmish;
Their victory was swift like the hawk.

Derrick A. Notz, Grade 11
Faith Tabernacle School

Empty

My mind is disconnected from my body
It's locked in a state of despair
I don't know how to save myself
The thought is too much to bear

Loneliness consumes my heart
The pain radiates from my chest
I weep from fear of the unknown
If I'll ever pick myself up from this mess

I'm going crazy with silence
The voice inside my head has died
There's nothing left of me but pieces
Over every single piece I've cried

Will I ever escape this place?
A moment caught between pain and reality
My temper for hope is running short
There's not enough room in me for any more brutality

Kaitlin Griel, Grade 10
Conestoga Valley High School

A Typical Race

It is the morning of the district run
Each runner knows that the race will be tough
Teams get on the line and wait for the gun
The bang is heard and the jostling gets rough

Many legs are lifting and arms pumping
Lead runners start to break off from the pack
The crowd is loudly cheering and jumping
Even for the slower runners in back

The first runners near the end of the race
The tape is ahead waiting to be reached
The sprint begins and they pick up the pace
Legs are fatigued and the limits are breached

The feeling of victory is so sweet
Although the champ can't wait to rest her feet

Kristen Lombardo, Grade 11
Pittston Area High School

Fall

The fall season is here,
with scattering leaves and deer.
The weather is cold and trees are bare,
and families going to a harvest fair.
Falling snow is an unusual sight,
but when it hits the ground it melts in the light.
Thanksgiving vacation is what students wait for,
to hear that last bell and to run for the door.
It's a holiday all about being kind,
with friends and family having a good time.

Michael Twardowski, Grade 11
Pittston Area High School

7 Figures

"I feel like a million bucks, but my money don't really feel like I do."
   – Mac Miller

Seeing your reflection
It isn't always what you want
But there shouldn't be any correction
The way you are is the way you should be
You shouldn't have to travel far
To find out where you belong
All you need is your heart
And a really good song

It's hard you see
To believe you really can be
One of the best
When you have less than the rest
So think hard and have a breakthrough
Because they're not laughing at you
They're laughing with you

Takla Zaghtiti, Grade 10
Whitehall High School

The Flood

The rains came down in early September
What they left behind is unpleasant to remember.
The river rose and spread its wings
And on its way destroyed many things.
it sped along on its merry way
What it left behind is still not okay.

Homes and businesses covered in brown
Furniture, clothing, toys on the ground
And people in shock moving around.
Our basement was flooded to the rafters
We just experienced our first natural disaster.
Putting things on the curb was really tough
"We're lucky" Dad said
"We only lost some stuff."

Jim Ziobro, Grade 11
Pittston Area High School

Jeremy

Jeremy is my youngest,
Well-loved by many,
Taller day-by-day.
His dimple betrays his mischief.
His eyes, shining like diamonds,
Tell me he's just been picking on Jenna.
He is a very fast runner,
Sometimes even fast enough to out run trouble.
He runs like the wind,
Imagining, he's tall like Dad,
Mowing lawns and gathering wood.
There's no wonder he's spoiled;
He is my brother.

Elizabeth Thoman, Grade 10
Faith Tabernacle School

The Audition

Hours and days and weeks and months, what?
C#? What's that? What are those symbols hovering next
to that little black dotted text? Go up, up, up, No breath!

Then down, down, down, down, how far? And in another second they shout — Go! Tongued, or was it slurred?
And your eyes are just dying to look at that paper, just a glance; was that five flats or four? How many more?

Then they just say — Next! And no thank you for all those hours and days and weeks, months?
But before you have time to thank them for their time and "courtesy" they have already moved on to 4592,
the number that's right after you — Phew!

Oh for that short-lived relief!
That sigh, that deep breath at 120 because that's where you were at.
Now change that! Fast, fast, fast, rhythm, notes, tone, pitch!
Don't move, can't itch to play faster, but you already will with the nerves
Legs like Jell-o, notes a cup of pudding, bashing and smashing and mashing
into each other, but then you're on to — Room three, you're almost there!

Take a deep breath — Slow, slow, slow, musicality, technique, vibrato!
Don't let those butterflies take away your music and run
Focus, focus, focus — Done?

All those hours and days and weeks, months? Was it really worth it?
Will you come out on top — Stop!

Meghan Walsh, Grade 11
Lancaster Catholic High School

Red-Roofed Lullaby

Balmy June air floats through my open-screened window,
Penetrating my restless sleep and beckoning me to the haven.
The haven where hay is softer than my feather mattress
And the warm, tickling barnyard breath more comforting than flannel sheets.
The haven where slotted shutters shove the evil out,
And tall, whitewashed walls secure the serenity.

Warm breath radiates from the horses, lumbering with cocked hind legs in straw-padded stalls.
Black-and-white Bessies chew their cud,
And the piglets oink at their father for hogging the mud.
Three baby swallows chirp and flutter at attempted midnight flying lessons.
The goats in the corner grunt their protests.
Upstairs the hens squawk as they settle into their roost.

The rooster crows.
Dawn breaks.
Peace slithers away.
No more time for the peace of animals who do not know hate or evil.
Only time for the war of humans who do not know love or peace.
Until tomorrow night, Red Roof.

Cassidy L. Feaser, Grade 10
Faith Tabernacle School

Plumbing the Depths

About plumbing some people don't know that much,
Of reamers and augers and Sharkbite and such.
But I happen to have a Master Plumber father
So tools for me aren't so much of a bother.

When you walk in a house, the first thing you do
For those of you who do not have a clue
Is to get some important information:
Find the shut-off valve's location.

I know how to solder copper piper together
It can be done in good or bad weather
First clean the pipe with sandpaper slowly;
Then apply the flux to let the solder flow smoothly.

Use an acetylene torch to heat up the pipe
Then with pliers, cutters, wrenches,
Channel locks, you'll have no gripe.
Thus I've learned how to use many plumbing tools,
And I've also learned you must follow the rules.

Jim Mearns, Grade 11
The American Academy

Dance Away

What do you do when you have a good beat,
Or when you feel the rhythm in your toes?
You shake your body and move your fast feet.
Keep on moving, grab a friend or a foe.

You can take a breath just don't be stoppin.
How low can you go, drop it to the floor?
Go on jump, jump, clap, clap keep it poppin.
Whatever you do, don't be a real bore.

Move your own way or "Beat It" like MJ,
Your hips won't lie if you move them all night.
On the dance floor tell people to make way,
Because you're in the mood for a dance fight.

Dance with your heart and soul in every song,
With that advice you can do nothing wrong.

Miranda Warunek, Grade 11
Pittston Area High School

Dulling Down the Doldrums

Oh! Would I trace your name in the stars every night,
Had not the rain and fog clouded my vision of them.
I would bet the brightness of your eyes you feel the same.
Do you trace into mine and tell me I am right?

Or does a storm of silence overcome and dull your eyes,
Telling you how hate heals the heart?
It is a wonder how the sun is always chasing the moon.
As spring chases summer, the perceived prize.

Steve Rankin, Grade 12
Conneaut Valley High School

Wire the Amps

Take a deep breath,
slow, sinking,
drag your nails deep
into the cotton

Close your eyes
and spit
apple pit bullet holes
through the fuzz of the clouds

Fall!
Let the volume pierce
your bones

And ring
in your ears
for eternity.

Gloria Yuen, Grade 10
Julia R Masterman Laboratory and Demonstration School

Deception

The way one can have peace is through deceit
Some choose to live a lie but I will not
In this they find refuge, to me, defeat
Succumb with guilt and shame, their fame is bought

Money, reputation, filled with a gloom
When truth comes down onto a crowd, run far
For if you stay, only impending doom
Will greet your loves with harsh and cold, ill war

To go and be false first is not the best
But here in a world sewn together vile
The one and only choice is one depressed
To suppress the truth, to avoid exile

So here is to a better future life
Where we can be well off without much strife

Austin Kostelansky, Grade 11
Pittston Area High School

The Pack

They're the masters of the night.
They dart as dark silhouettes among the trees,
And with a deep, bone-chilling howl,
They stalk their prey
As swift and silent as the breeze.
They are the creatures in the dream
Who give the child fright.
They're the masters of the night.
They are a tight knit family
Who leave none of their own
Down or all alone.
They're the masters of the night.

Alan L. Carpenter, Grade 10
Faith Tabernacle School

The Room

I'm trapped in a room
and I'm all alone.
everything reeks of anesthetic fumes.
Whitewashed walls and sterile songs
are all what's Home to me…

So polished is this room, that
the very Walls glisten!
but with glee or contempt,
I wonder, do they glow?

I'm in a room,
it's an ugly place.
Not for what's inside,
but for the memories they hold.
carried in on the backs of
goblins and trolls.

I'm in a room,
and I'm here alone.
The door is locked,
and you swallowed the key.

It's okay.
Idon'teverwantoleave.
Ryan Hatch, Grade 10
Whitehall High School

Wilted Flower Child

Skipping through the lush fields,
Not a care in the world.
Bushes and trees like shields,
Through our heads happiness swirled.

This is the place,
Where the sun will always shine.
It kisses your face,
And it caresses mine.

Flowers blooming, both big and small,
In the meadow where the children play
Lonely little teardrops fall
But the sun will wipe them away

Flower child, flower child
Why do you weep
Flower child, flower child
The peace you must keep

This is the place,
Where the sun will always shine.
It kisses your face,
And it caresses mine.
Rachael Landis, Grade 11
Middletown Area High School

Hazel Eyes

Her hazel eyes
Like the stars, they shine
With wisdom beyond
The depths of time.
For the person I am,
They see me
Gazing into my soul,
They set me free.
Her hazel eyes,
Her beautiful face
I hope my memories
Will be kept safe.
For life is short
Though it may seem long
I try to keep my feelings
To a simple song.
Her hazel eyes
Have captured my life
And that day I asked her,
"Will you be my Wife?"
Jeremiah Lubawski, Grade 12
Kennard Dale High School

The Home

Built many years ago,
This two-century-old structure
Stands as the monument of my life.
My home is my rest.

Some may say it is shabby,
But even though the floor creaks,
And the furnace hums,
It is the image of inward beauty.

Its pallid siding, its rustic roof
Welcomes me home
This plain place
Is where I belong.
Christian B. Notz, Grade 10
Faith Tabernacle School

The Days Go By

Every day seems the same, passing
quickly and slowly,
not expecting anything different
(nothing matters) to me really
it all seems the same

On a schedule I wake up,
same day, same basis to me
quickly and slowly
it's always the same I see
The days go by like I don't even notice
slowly and quickly, it all seems the same
Toni DePinto, Grade 10
Whitehall High School

The Serpent

The Serpent takes to the ground
Where the others lie
Waiting — watching

He listens as they do
He sees as they do
He makes no sound

There were others before him
Who've lain where he is now
They've eaten their fill

This is the time
This is the moment
This shall not pass this way again

And there it is
Small and fleeting
Along the path it scurries

This is the time
This is the moment
This shall not pass this way again

Launch! Snap! Twist! Tear!
But he misses

This shall not pass this way again
Quinton Laurencio, Grade 11
William Penn Charter School

Life's a Dance

Life's a dance
That can be easy,
Hard, or confusing to
Learn because of all
The ruts that we need to
Jeté over with a large flying leap.

Life is a never –
Ending dance that
Twists and turns from
A memorable moonwalk to
A heart-wrenching jazz.

However, we know that
At the end of the song,
The dance must conclude.
Life will one day draw
To a close, and we
Will want it to keep playing
Forever, like one of our favorite dances.
But, no matter how much we hope,
The curtain must fall.
Lorinda Brenize, Grade 11
Faith Tabernacle School

Burnt

It's all on fire
A serious mess
The blazing continues
Regardless of the wet

We brace ourselves
For the bloody impact
That the raging fire
Will be our last

The screams of fright
As they run away
Into their deaths
At the brink of dismay

A few more short
To help us survive
This horrible blaze
That burned us alive
Haley Edsell, Grade 10
Northeast Bradford Jr/Sr High School

Love

When you see us together,
I guess it breaks your heart.
But that does not give you the right
To go and break us apart.

You say that you are over him,
But we all know that's a lie.
Because I see you watching us.
Like some kind of tricky spy.

I know you used to like him.
And he used to like you too.
And I'm truly sorry it didn't turn out
The way you planned it to.
Tiana Stull, Grade 11
Pittston Area High School

America

People weeping from increasing prices
People weeping from lost jobs
Wondering what to do
This is a recession

Hope is lost
Sadness grows deeper
People starving on the streets
This is a recession
Michael Stanley, Grade 10
Whitehall High School

The Wood Stove

The black dragon sits in the corner of the room,
Dormant as he awaits the winter.
Black and shiny, he sits motionless,
Yet is prepared to create heat to battle the cold.

As rolled paper and twigs are laid in his stomach,
He takes in air, slowly, ready to ignite with fury.
Suddenly, a tiny flame begins to consume the kindling,
Growing and jumping swiftly from stick to stick,
Lighting each one with his fiery touch.
The dragon continues breathing steadily, causing the flames to increase.
Larger logs are thrown in his glowing mouth.
He responds with delight, consuming them swiftly
And causing an intense heat that diffuses the cold air.

As the dragon slowly decreases his spark-spitting fury,
He begins to cough up white ashes — remains of his fiery fight.
He then settles contentedly; he has won the battle.
Laurie A. Gerberich, Grade 11
Faith Tabernacle School

With God as My Friend

My friends walk by my side each and every day.
With patience, kindness, trust, and joy, I know they're here to stay.
We share our secrets, have our laughs, and grow together too,
But most of all, I won't forget my greatest friend is You.

My greatest Friend walks by my side each and every day.
With patience, kindness, trust, and joy, He shows me His true way.
I confide in You, am brought to joy, and learn by Your love too,
But most all of, I won't forget my greatest friend is You.

This path of sorrow, suffering, and pain is never traveled alone,
For friends surround me every day, and a Friend who'll lead me home.
They've taught me patience, love, and kindness, as well as laughter too,
But most of all I won't forget my greatest friend is You.
Ashley E. Nellis, Grade 12
Faith Tabernacle School

Of Clay We Were Created

Of clay we were created.
Each one different.
Not a one the same.
Special because of our shape.
Of clay we were created.
Crafted by hands that are full of promise.
The graceful strokes of which resemble great meaning if interpreted.
Of clay we were created.
To create a closure within one's self.
Drawing out fears of uncertainty and unwelcoming thoughts.
Of clay we were created.
Waiting to drift into compromise, to smooth the rift the waves have created.
Of clay we were created.
Never to be defined, but to forever be quoted.
Jessica Ramey, Grade 11
Penn Foster High School

Freedom

Freedom is
going where you want.
Distant or proximate,
here or there.

Freedom is
going when you want.
Past or future,
now or later.

Freedom is
being what you want.
Sage or fool,
everything or nothing.

Freedom is
being who you want.
Everyone is different,
everyone is the same.

Freedom is
what you make it.
Shannon O'Hara, Grade 10
East High School

Falling

In a vortex of black.
With no way back.

In love with you,
but you haven't a clue.

Being tossed
down this hole of endlessness.

I'd give you my heart and soul.
But you are such a fool.

Tumbling down an abyss.
I'm having a nervous fit.
In a hole that hasn't been lit
by your kiss.
Kristen Grom, Grade 11
North Hills High School

Ultimate Battle

This is the ultimate battle
Taking place in Armageddon
Jesus Christ and Satan
Fighting with their fists
And only one will conquer
I think I know who it will be
This is the ultimate battle
For our unified destiny!
Jakub Anderskovich, Grade 10
Westmoreland Christian Academy

I Wish

I wish you thought I was your favorite girl,
I wish you thought that I was the reason you were alive,
I wish our love was real like a fairy tale,
I wish my smile was your favorite kind of smile,
I wished the way I dressed was your favorite kind of style,
I wish you couldn't figure me out but you wanted to know what I was about,
I wish you would hold my hand when I'm upset,
I wish you would never forget the face expression I had when we first met,
I wish we would be able to grow old together,
I wished we could cuddle all night,
I wish I knew you would never hurt me,
I wish I could actually say I trust you and mean it,
I wished I had lots of money; you would never leave or want anything else,
I wished that without me, you would spend the rest of your nights awake,
I wish you knew when I said I was cold to give me your coat,
I wish that without me your heart would break,
I wished that when it was storming you'd know to come over and hold me,
I wish that someday you will ask for my hand in marriage,
I wish I could have a million dollars to share with you,
I wish for peace in the world and that everyone got along,
But most of all what I wish is that you loved me the way I love you!
Samantha Smith, Grade 11
Lawrence County Career & Technical Center

The Ardennes Offensive

Cursing, throat raw, he ducks into his foxhole as the world explodes
In a flurry of snow and dirt and blood and pieces of his comrades.

Orders shouted in English and German, half-drowned by whistling mortars.
He swigs from canteen, grabs the aid kit, the knife, the bandages.
Down to two rolls after weeks in Belgium.

He hauls himself over the lip of the hole and runs
Against instinct, against all common sense, toward screaming death.

Trees crack and crumple as he runs, stumbles in the knee-deep snow,
And runs again, the Red Cross on his arm and helmet an unreliable beacon.
He slides when he stops to help, like
Playing ball, not losing momentum or time.

He's frozen down into his bones but his hands are steady
Wrapping the bloody leg of Jonesy, just a kid,
A stupid kid who thought war was all glory and no guts.

Why waste bandages on a dead man? The voice in his head intones.
He lies, "You're gonna be fine."
Kate Sheridan, Grade 12
Mount Saint Joseph Academy

Daddy's Hands

His callused palm
Tells the tale of the many hours worked
DAVID

His fingertips
Show the strength he holds
POPS

The soft back of his hand
Mirrors his loving heart
FATHER

The size of his hand
Is big enough to keep
His family together
DADDY

His fingerprint
Forms a smudge on my heart
That can never be concealed
DADDY'S HANDS

Brittany Peffley, Grade 10
Faith Tabernacle School

No School Today

No school today, hurray, hurray!
We can sleep in and do nothing all day.
I walk down the stairs, Oh no! No way!
My feet are all wet.
My house is a mess.
Boxes float by,
Bobbing like apples.
Sweaters are drenched,
The treadmill is under water,
My whole life just floating around,
Things around me are all falling down.
Personal possessions are all getting ruined.
My poor dad, his temper is brewin'
I try to clean, busy as a bee
Thanks a lot Tropical Storm Lee.

Aubrie Lutz, Grade 12
Kennard Dale High School

Clowns

A clown is the life of the party,
Center of attention,
Comedian of the show.
By entertaining audiences,
A clown fills the room with laughter.
His wild-colored wig and big red nose
Make him sure to be noticed.
Known for his big, baggy bibs
And goofy, yard-long shoes,
He is content to amuse the crowd.

Erica C. Feaser, Grade 11
Faith Tabernacle School

The Thrill of the Night

In the hallway I start to feel my stomach become uneasy
All of a sudden the lights go out and the lights over the mat are on
Running out to the familiar "Eye of the Tiger" I feel the crowd start to stare
After the warm up I return to our side of the mat to await my turn
The national anthem begins to play and I already can feel myself starting to sweat
As my match approaches I begin to stretch out in preparation
I look up to see my name next to my weight class one more time
As I feel my opponent start to stare I pace up and down the row of chairs
now it is my turn to go out so I run over to the score table
I say my name and weight class to check in while casually adjusting my headgear
Approaching the center I feel the thrill as everyone's gaze is on me
Knowing if I lose there will be shame in defeat, and if I win there will be stories of glory
After the match I feel a sense of pride when everyone sees the ref raise my hand in victory

Camden Stoops, Grade 11
Eastern York High School

True Rebellion

So we act like fools to you,
And we're nothing but rebels, true,
In my mind I'm just a survivor of thought,
From all the lies that you've taught,
Call me dumb and call me crazy,
But know this that I'm not lazy,
When it comes to my rights and the things I know,
You can't tell me that I'm just a joke, So
When will you admit to yourself that even though I don't have your years,
I'm already as smart as you and have overcome all your fears,
Age doesn't glorify anything except that you've managed to live through more,
And even though you say that, you never even remember the score.

Darren Baer, Grade 11
Owen J Roberts High School

Serenity

I had to find the side of me
That ignites the fight in me
I had to find the part of me
That's so tender and right
about me
Maybe we can work it out
Maybe we can work it out
Maybe we could fall in love
Baby you're the one I love
There's no one else
I'm thinking of
I had to find my piece of mind
To make space for love so divine
I try harder every day
for Serenity
What's serenity you say?
Beautiful lovebird sing me a note
To get me going, my serenity flowing
That's what I call serenity
My love…
Don't ya know?

Kara Clark, Grade 10
Pennsbury High School East

Mirror Mirror

Misty mirror and the image within,
Showing what is and what has been.
It has the would've, the could've,
And the should've, under the skin.

In swirling mists hide the sight,
Of an eye, aglow under the light.
Black with madness, with gladness,
And sadness within the white.

Under the cloudy surface lies,
Knowledge secret only to the wise.
Sacred to men living, men dying,
But not to those without such ties.

Within and behind the surface be
The same as those in front of me.
Be it terrible, great, or mundane:
In your mirror there is only thee.

Nothing less, and nothing more.

Ziyun Zhu, Grade 12
Upper Dublin High School

Wandering

Within the foggy haze
Through the dark shadows
A voice tries to speak out
But is unheard

A lost soul wanders
Looking for the reason to move on
A spooky figure moves like a snake
Through the snow-covered ground

Like a ghostly snowman
Seeable only in the dim light
In a saddened world it looks
But only to find bare trees

Moving slowly to his spot
In search of something
The cold wind blows as the
Figure disappears…
Frederick Gill, Grade 11
Elizabeth Forward High School

On a Park Bench

Two people sitting,
exchanging awkward glances,
strangers, not yet acquaintances.

They are shadows,
sitting silently together,
against the fading sun.

One lady, one man,
both pale, a hint of sunburn,
brushed onto their cheeks.

We don't know of their story,
light fading behind them,
quiet and mysterious.

They rise to part ways,
the darkness closing around,
exchanging a sweet smile.
Victoria Rosario, Grade 10
Whitehall High School

Rainy Day

One rainy day,
I was in dismay
As I found out
My hard-earned money
Had been stolen
By some clown.

I am not poor
But the money was for
New bolts and a doughnut
For my exhaust system
In my hooptie, which
Is now only hanging on
By a few wires.

Now my car will stay yucky,
Because of some clown
Who stole my car part money.
Lacy Anderson, Grade 11
Kennard Dale High School

Black Knights

Oh, we, the glitter lights
stayed in droplets and in nights
gold, we play, but not from day
reflect, we do, the lamplight's glance

Oh, we, the blackened knights
stayed in window panes, stayed in flight
downward hurtling, toward the gurgling
of the street, the stony black

I, the navy, open, still
full of mischief and goodwill
wind I carry ever, sunlight have I never
and content am I with the cool damp wet
Kate Kempf, Grade 11
Delaware County Christian School

Forgotten But Needed

Forgotten in the shadows,
Blocked by novels and articles.
All lonely, collecting dust on the back shelf.
We feel we do not need it.

But without it,
We would lack emotion
And expression.
Holding thoughts deep down inside.

It is forgotten,
But obviously needed.
This is,
The art of poetry.
Richard Stanley, Grade 10
Whitehall High School

You Don't Bother Me

people all around me,
but they make no difference
I don't see or hear their influence
on, the world I know

thoughts and ideas surround me
I could care less
although I enjoy their presence
I need nothing more, and nothing less

the world will try to judge
when my eyes are shut uptight
(and open the others are)
As I make my way

they say what they want to say
as do I, and even if I were to follow
it would make no difference
nothing would change
Jackie Haiem, Grade 10
Whitehall High School

The Maid of Orléans

She cuts a proud figure
Astride her horse.
Wisps of hair blow gently
In the western breeze.
Her sword hangs ready in its scabbard,
Her lance pierces
Sun-streaked clouds.
She glances toward the battlefield.
Perhaps its gory earth
Shall be her deathbed.
Perhaps not.
Perhaps she shall live to see
Another sanguinary field
Perhaps a thousand.
It matters not.
All is God's will,
And she but his earthly sword.
Joan of Arc at Clairvoix.
Nora Bryson, Grade 12
Mount Saint Joseph Academy

Christmas

I rev'l 'n Christmas, though you gotta wait for 't.
It's November, yet has already snowed.
Santa'll stop at someone's house, and exit 't.
'ave waited all the year; he never showed.

Putting up the tree and decking our halls,
Baking Christmas cookies; spreading bits o' cheer.
Doing shopping in local stores and malls,
But I would rather it be here and now.

December is icy, frosted, snowy.
Peaceful, quiet; gotta love snowy days.
Suscon winters leave you feeling lonely.
Highways, grasses; covered by the haze.

Icy winter holds the warmest season.
Christmas; hearts are warm as we are freezin'.

Austin Elko, Grade 11
Pittston Area High School

The Reasons for the Changing of the Seasons

Spring bursts out of the snow to give rebirth
You can hear many new noises happening
This season brings a new start to our Earth
Emotions came like the joy of living

Summer comes along to brighten our days
Everyone is lively thanks to the sun
Underneath the sun, plants and the world lays
it is distinct because the mood is fun

The one season that makes us lazy, fall
This time prepares everything for the cold
A day will shorten and a night will crawl
The colors brighten the moody, they are bold

Winter contradicts the other seasons
The time has to come, it has its reasons

Cassy Giarratano, Grade 11
Pittston Area High School

Zenyatta

When you hear her name you know
she is more than just an animal
More than just a horse
She's dark like clouds in a storm
Her coat shines like a new car,
when you look at her you see
Her strong, slender legs like black bars of steel,
a blaze that streaks across like a streak of lightning
She is quick like thunder
with the speed of an athlete
she runs like a winner,
And wins like a champion.

Brittany Ritenour, Grade 12
Westmoreland Christian Academy

No One Shines in a Closet

You're my light in the darkest of nights
You show me my way, never leading me astray
A shadow in day light
Glowing during the night
No matter what, you are a beautiful sight
I wish you'd joined me in the sky dusk to twilight
Possibly willing to let your true colors fly high
But I understand why you must stay away
The bravest of all can't always stand tall
For now I'll continue this waiting game,
To set a course across the sky and take aim
I've gone through the pain, you are not one to blame
But it only takes a step for progress to start
No one said the journey wouldn't be harsh
Then we could travel around the earth, side by side heart to heart
Finally expressing your inner art
Showing your true self with a fresh start
Even though during the day you are hiding afar
You will always be my shining star.

Brandon Hoy, Grade 11
Methacton High School

The Light Heaven Doth Shine Does Not Compare...

The light heaven doth shine does not compare,
To thy beauty and thy wholesome bright face.
Heaven hath lost its one angel, declare —
Thou doth sweep me away with thy love's grace.

Under the bridge, over the stars, knoweth
Thou wilt always be in mine heart, near me.
Thy soul is pure, kindness as white snoweth;
The warmth you radiate fills me with glee.

If love is blind, then I wilt be thine eyes.
I now realize, beloved, thou art the one.
And now my heart swells up, it multiplies;
I shalt give up my life, our love has won.

Mine eyes hath gazed on an angel so grand,
I shalt protect our love; give me thy hand.

Boratha Tan, Grade 12
Parkway Center City High School

Letters in the Sand

Have you ever written letters in the sand?
Some truth you hope will always remain true?
Have you ever written about love?
Or someone who loves you?
And you think it has to stay the same
Because they're now letters in the sand.
Until the water washes it away,
Until the water undoes all your truths.
And you think they were never really true at all.

Josephine Beck, Grade 10
Galeton Area School

Dad

If only I could remember anything about you
The smallest thing
From the way you smiled
Or even laughed
The days go by slowly
As I wonder why
Why did this happen to me
Why do I have to live without you
Why will I never get to know you
There will be many stories that I hear
But they do nothing for me
I miss you even more every day
It's hard to live without you
I wish I could tell you something
Anything at all
And even if I could see you
And just tell you one thing
That I'll never stop loving you

Taylor Stull, Grade 11
Pittston Area High School

The Cobblestone Streets

the cobblestone streets we walk
through snow and rain and sunshine days
on knowing days, we go our ways
we hear the chatter of the town,
in the air, the words, they drown

the cobblestone streets we walk
through smiling days and crying days
keep our pace, you and I
they emerge, the words from the water
and in our hearts they cut deep

the cobblestone streets we walk
today we run, and maybe far
myself dressed in white, I run
hearing, but not listening to the yells of the town
for today we run, and we are free

Michaela Pringle, Grade 10
Whitehall High School

The Stream

The water glistens
As it races down the stream
Running with the sun.

They are small crystals
As the white flakes fall gently
Covering the ground and landing on the running water.

The huge wave raged
As it engulfed the small town
Turmoil filled the air.

Julia Snyder, Grade 11
Dallastown Area Sr High School

Photographs

"Poetry is the opening and closing of a door,
leaving those who look through to
guess about what is seen during the moment."
—Carl Sandburg

Poems are photographs
The scene captured in words
Flowing on the parchment
Meant only for the poet

No one knows what is happening
Everyone wondering and questioning
Wishing to see the scene as well
Diversely interpreting the photograph

Poets stumbling upon their poems
Remembering the photographs taken
Desiring to go back in time
But knowing their memories will last

Angela Nguyen, Grade 10
Whitehall High School

Calling for Help

Bombs are falling
and crackling stone.
The people are calling,
but receive the dial tone.

No help to find
so death's the only way.
Half the world is being blind,
but it's not that hard to portray.

Lives are being killed
for no reason at all.
Graves are being filled.
Who's is going to answer the call?

Wars are like fights, they don't solve a thing,
so answer the call, can't you hear the ring?

Denise Gold, Grade 10
Chambersburg Area Sr High School

Walking Alone

As I walk along a barren field
That wild flowers align,
The wind brings nature's settling touch.
The solemn solitude tugs at an unfamiliar peace.
Thoughts run free;
Frustrations drain out.
It's my favorite time of day
When nothing seems to matter,
And all earlier disappointments fade
Like the sun that is now running towards the horizon.

Natalie Steele, Grade 10
Faith Tabernacle School

Trust

Heartache and pain weigh heavily on my heart
As I think about my dear son lost at war.
His vibrant smile and flaming red hair come to mind
And lightens my load,
As he always used to,
But then realization hits.
Who do I run to now that I'm all alone?

I go to my friends, and they are always there,
But what if one day they fade away like my child?
I need that one constant Friend that I can rely on,
To trust with all my heart, to be there whenever I am down.

Where will I find that person in this world
That will be there for me for certain?
The answer is nowhere because He is not on this earth
But in the most glorious place called Heaven.

As I meander down life's road
Wandering through the heartaches and pains
That are tossed my way
I now know that I can put my trust in You.

Erin N. Brenize, Grade 12
Faith Tabernacle School

Little Girl

She rests her head on her hand
And stares out the window, her brown
Corkscrew curls falling over her cheek
And covering her green imaginative eyes.
Soon, the curtain of curls becomes a white satin
Veil of a princess' wedding gown as she
Marries her Prince Charming and is
Carried away to her castle where
A valiant silver-clad knight
Conquers dragons and rescues damsels.
The fairytale castle becomes a storybook
Cottage where carefree birds visit doorsteps
And butterflies and fairies dart and dash
Among the velvet cherry blossom orchards
Where the wind carries honeydew melodies
To the flowers in the meadow as they
Bow and curtsy to one another along
A small brook that meanders and glides
Into an ocean with no boundaries
Where a message in a bottle carries
Dreams and wishes to distant lands.

Emily Fogelsanger, Grade 11
Faith Tabernacle School

Ripples

The flying green frog
Soaring from small rocks to pads
Making small ripples

Daniel Kazmerski, Grade 11
Pittston Area High School

Snowflakes

Lie on my back and watch them soar above me.
And I wonder, do they see me?
Because I can't even see myself.

A few sometimes land on my eyelashes,
Give me butterfly kisses,
'Cause that's the only type of kiss I ever get.

The rest rush on past
And I wonder if they can tell
The difference
Between themselves

Or is it just the scientists?

Do they even know
Where they're going?

And as the snow numbs me
I feel everything fly away
With them.

Deanna Selioutski, Grade 12
Northwest PA Collegiate Academy

the Light!

A night sky
illuminated with the dreams
of millions of stars—People
rushing about, losing sight
Stars flicker, and dim
diversity, the night sky loses
the colors, and shades of a generation
Lost forever—Extinguished
lives, stars with potential—Wasted
opportunity…

Cultivate Your Color, tend—Your Star
is unique, special
With the capacity for an Impact
One candle lighting the other, one star igniting another
Saving it, then shepherding it
The night sky illuminated—Once Again
teeming with the hues of a generation…
On the horizon: the rising sun, threatening to
((band together, ignite each other: the Light!—must not))
extinguish.

Zonia Moore, Grade 12
Vincentian Academy

Beach

Let's go to the beach
Where the waves crash at your feet
Feel the sand and heat.

Jenna Galli, Grade 11
Pittston Area High School

Portrait of Reverie

If I could paint you a melody
A masterpiece of vibrancy
With every stroke a different string
Of harmonic enchantment softly sings

If I could paint you my love
A passionate dance of colors entwine around celestial doves
One for you, my dear and one for me
Nestling under that old magnolia tree

If I could paint you my favorite scene
It would be a silhouette of dancing figurines
Marble-soaked sky could not trace
Hand in hand, the warmth of your embrace

One last piece I wish to place
Alongside your loving embrace
That such an artist I would be
If I could paint you back to me

Hannah Graham, Grade 11
PA Cyber Charter School

Ballet

Begin at the bar in first position
Plies and tondues to start up the class
What comes next is the teacher's audition
Stretch like a band and jump high like a bass

Move to the center to learn a dance fast
Remember the steps to earn a big role
Show off your technique so you're not put last
Make sure to perform from the heart and soul

Rehearsals have passed to practice your part
Show time is here and butterflies arrive
Audience waiting for the show to start
Curtain opens your performance is live

Dozens of roses cover the stage
Another show next year at a new age

Jillian Starinsky, Grade 11
Pittston Area High School

The Taken Chosen One for Me

She is the successor of a brighter tomorrow,
the rose with infinite petals that can't wither,
the revolution that's around my head like stars when dazed,
the carol I can listen to all night,
the shine on the shoe that never fades,
the oranges and reds of the sunset,
the faith of which I restore every evening,
the bongo that beats like my heart does,
and her name is the rhythm,
my one and only for me…yet she's with him.

Andrew Russell, Grade 11
Carver High School

Fall

Piles of leaves all spread across the front lawn
Everywhere is painted yellow and brown
Day by day the wind blows from dusk to dawn
As the temperature drastically goes down

Putting on our scarves, mittens and our hats
As we sit, watch and feel the fireplace burn
We're all getting used to these habitats
Slowly waiting for summer to return

The best part is the big feast at the end
Giving thanks for what we have in our lives
All the food ends up a delicious blend
It's always a fun time when this arrives

If you haven't guessed this season is fall
My favorite season around of them all

Shannon Turner, Grade 11
Pittston Area High School

Sweet Surrender

Cotton strokes ivory like a whisper,
Caressing it like a cherished old friend,
Comfortably settled while eyes flutter,
At last, my dear has come tonight to spend!
Soon wrapped tightly in love's gentle embrace,
I bid thee, my beloved, make great haste
To follow me in spirits, so make chase!
For doth thou wish to catch my sweet lips' taste?
For now dearest, have no fear — I am here,
In thine arms, I seek solace from the day —
Night's reflection of day in a mirror.
Drifting in peaceful slumber, come what may;
As visions of night shall soon bid farewell,
For first blush brings a break to thy dream spell.

Marybeth Anna O'Connor, Grade 12
Norristown Area High School

Stars

Present are the angels watching from above.
Sparkling and shining with such brightness —
We are the stars, we watch over everything.

Present here throughout the galaxy.
Present here throughout the entire universe.

Sparkling and shining with such brightness.
Decades, millenniums,
and even farther back in time we have watched.
What place do we have?
What roles do we play?

We are the stars.
We watch over everything.

Brittany Knauss, Grade 10
Whitehall High School

Riding High

The morning sun
Peeks its blooming face
Above the horizon
Of splintered toothpick trees.
The moist, broken dirt
Fumbles and tumbles
Behind the plow,
The earthen aroma
Folds around the crisp, autumn air.

The roar of the tractor's motor
Thumps in the youngster's ears
As his father's strong arm
Cradles him tightly.
Riding high on the tractor,
Nestled against his father,
The young boy enthusiastically
Watches his father's swift maneuvers
From the cold, rubber knobs to the frosty metal of the brakes.
The youngster looks out over the acres of rolling land
Like a king over his domain.

Candace Y. Feaser, Grade 11
Faith Tabernacle School

A Never Ending Dream

Dreaming,
Never awake,
To sleep,
Awake with a start,
Never knowing where you'll find yourself.

Kissing the blackened night,
Staring in the darkness,
Finding a life that you never knew to be yours,
Leaving it behind,
The journey of a lifetime before you,
And you don't know where to begin.

Loving the filly that crosses your path deep in the night,
Leading you into eternal darkness,
Then finding the light.

The beauty of this scene,
I cannot say,
Just know,
You will find yourself one day.

Keeley Whitney, Grade 12
PA Cyber School

Snow

Boundless seas of white
Flurries falling endlessly
Cool air fills your lungs

Calvin O'Boyle, Grade 11
Pittston Area High School

Good Bye

It's been years since I've seen you, And all I know is I miss you,
So I think back to the past, And pray that my memories last,
You build your house, As I build mine,
A house of dominos, Memories in time,
Just like our houses, Never to last,
You had to leave…
And I'll miss you dearly,
And I hope you know,
Of all the memories that I chose,
I chose the one where I didn't know,
That sometimes grandpas have to go,
So suddenly…all I see…are the memories,
Where all the dominos are tumbling down,
And you're smiling, And I'm smiling,
And we watch as the dominos fall,
Without a care at all,
All the dominos are gone,
So of all the memories, The one I chose,
Is the one where I didn't know,
That sometimes grandpas have to go
Forever in my heart.

Elizabeth Anne McClelland, Grade 10
Trinity Sr High Schoolnc

The Muddled Puddle

As the flowers wither away,
I find a reason to stay and roam in this quaint, wholesome home
I call silence and despair.
Perhaps when it knocked, I never knew
What stood behind the opaque door
While I melted slowly to the floor.
Uneasiness fueled the flame.
Therefore, I have myself to blame.
Seconds turned to minutes and later to hours.
Only love waits for cowards!
However, wait too long and love shall sing its farewell song.
Then, only the puddle of fear remains,
Which shall leave a stain of regret, shock, and pain.
Only that single puddle shall recall
All the opportunities it let fall.
These little chances of bliss added up
Into a mess like a spilled cup.
Now the liquid must evaporate;
That's what happens on the other road of fate.
Everyone shall see the cloud,
But never the love of two; the perfect crowd.

Lauren Coggins, Grade 10
Abington Heights High School

Christmas Night

A sleigh bell ringing
Reindeer prancing through the night
Santa comes tonight

Kierstyn Satkowski, Grade 11
Pittston Area High School

Sneakers

Sitting upon a shelf, I am consistently displayed,
Until one day when I am suddenly taken off
And put into a dark room,
With someone who looks just like me,
I wait and I wait,
Developing a nervous feeling in my sole.
Then suddenly,
I see the light again,
And a giant white monster invites itself into me.
The monster shows its hands,
And ties my tongue in knots.
Life is different on the ground,
I happily sing, "Squeak, Squeak," slowly as we trot along.
I go for a treasure hunt,
Finding coins, wrappers, and the infamous gum
Which the monster carelessly gets stuck on me.
I hear talking, assuming it's about me,
And if I weren't a red pair of Nikes,
I would blush.
When we get home, the monster leaves,
And I sit, panting, with an empty feeling inside.

Dan Frasch, Grade 11
Quakertown Community Sr High School

Stranger

A stranger haunts these private caves
Running deep through my dark stained maze
I alone know what this man craves
For this man is me, who I once was
Words that came out twisted have undone,
Shades of day have melted, as waters run
And the process evoked long ago is almost done
For my roots have begun to wither and rot
He lives without lone reason or time
No walls or mountains stand near to climb
Shrouds and colors cover brown nylon lines
For help is more than a mere yell away
We both search for similar yet unsure goals
Mere strangers with views of new born fools
We know of the growing abyss of our wholes
For what am I to myself than a stranger
Lurking through the narrow halls of strife
Longing to reunite the dying, life to life
While a darkness gathers, taking our patient light
But tomorrow's just another stranger to greet
And another day of chances for us to meet again

Michael Weidman, Grade 12
Serra Catholic High School

Beach

The waves are crashing
My little toes in the sand
Summer has arrived!

Raeann Loftus, Grade 11
Pittston Area High School

The Sleeping Giant

There she is just sleeping,
Tree-covered, old, and still.
She wears a hat of ice and snow,
But little did we know
Here she was just lying
Waiting for a chance
To blow her top and deciminate
All living things around.
One serene day in the State Washington,
The mountain erupted, exploded, and corrupted
The brisk morning air.
The side of the mountain was
Blown to pieces
Dark clouds of ash
Spewed out.
Ashes of colors black and gray
Lay like snow on ground of clay
The forest burned, smothered, and killed
The scene is dead, dead and still.

Eric Shreiner, Grade 10
Faith Tabernacle School

The Men of Red and Black

First was king David of Judah.
He slayed the giant and composed his psalms,
And ruled over all of Israel.

Next there was Alexander the Great.
The strong, young conqueror came from Macedon
But died in Babylon at only the age of thirty and two.

Then the mighty Julius Caesar
Changed a republic to an empire,
But failed to take care of his Ides of March.

Last, king and emperor Charlemagne
Lived a long and very full life,
But his life ended — the same as all of ours will.

Can we say anything of these men of red and black
But that, like card houses in the wind, they are never coming back.

Alex Searer, Grade 11
Eastern York High School

Creativity

Poetry is not my strong point
But creativity is.
I'd rather write and draw and paint
Than be a science and math whiz.

Whether painting a picture with words,
Or writing a story through pencil strokes,
I find myself the happiest
When I let my mind just flow.

Nicole Piccoletti, Grade 11
Pittston Area High School

Birdie

Fly away birdie
Fly fly away
Your journey will be rough
But nothing you can't overcome
So sing your sweet song
And be on your way

Fly away birdie
Fly fly away
Your destination is far
But good times are near
So sing your sweet song
And be on your way

Fly away birdie
Fly fly away
Time isn't on your side
But the wind is at your back
So sing your sweet song
And be on your way

Lauren Villella, Grade 10
Bishop Canevin High School

What Has Happened

What has happened
   to your manners,
      mother, father, sister, brother?

What has happened
   to your virtues?
      Have they all been killed by vice?

What has happened
   to the good
      that always triumphs over evil?

It seems that all the good of day
has been sacrificed to night.

Margaret Russell, Grade 12
Bishop Shanahan High School

Stress

Stress.
Blood rushing; adrenaline pumping
Broken-down cars and missed flights
Deadlines and due dates pressing
Bosses fuming and customers cranky
The whirling, swirling of things to do
Countless sleepless nights, thinking
Tossing and turning in midnight beds
Worry lines, a pug-wrinkled forehead
Shoulders weighted down, drooping
A throbbing sledgehammer headache
Stress.

Karla Yeager, Grade 11
Faith Tabernacle School

Luxury

Eyes like a twinkle in the sky (oh-so-cliché)
Hazel gazing through my lifeless soul
Awakening every dull moment
Arising the fine hairs
 Behind my neck
 Beyond my body
Goosebumps spread
Popping out of my sensitive skin
 Higher and higher
My weariness trembles as I breathe in your saccharine scent
My heart beating at the pace of insanity; my palms sweating at the race of this "fantasy"
Your hair falls so flawlessly down your delicate spine
Brown waves; dark as bark
Blonde streaks; bright as light
A shy shade of red outlines your cherub face
An eccentric glow surrounds your hourglass figure
Blood rushes to my cheeks as you look at me with wonder
After silenced seconds of my speechless stare
A tingling in my tummy
Speaks those three simple words
Once again.

Ashlee Mankowski-Gilmore, Grade 10
Bishop Canevin High School

Realization

I loved your smile, your eyes, and the way you loved me.
We ended in pain and hatred.
I believed I missed you so much because I loved you,
and loved having someone there, always.
Watching the doves gracefully float into the distance, peacefully,
I realize I don't miss you, I miss the past.
I miss happiness.
I miss smiling.
I miss laughing.
I miss being carefree.
Then laying and reflecting on that moment,
I realize I miss it all so much because I may never get it all back.
Looking at the giant mob of blue and gold gowns,
I know I'll have to walk across that stage soon enough,
but I don't know who will accompany me. Will you be there?
Our realistic and optimistic plans created only a year ago now seem so far fetched.
Nothing is sacred anymore.
We can't count on tomorrow let alone 2013.
All I want is our graduation dream to come true.
All I want is to spend high school with my best friend like a normal teenager.
Is that really too much to ask?

Brittany Walls, Grade 11
Kennard Dale High School

The Valley

Deep in the recesses of the Appalachian Mountains
Surrounded by shadowy dense woodland,
I discovered a small unnoticed valley
That was surely molded by God's loving hand.

In the very heart of the forested little valley
Sleepily rests a small azure lagoon.
During the twilight hours, the lake reflects the serenity
Of that little valley, lit only by the glowing moon.

The massive forest enhances the valley's beauty.
The rustling trees' white blossoms explode in the spring.
They provide shade for me from the summer sun.
In autumn, the leaves provide a canvas for their King.

Gurgling down the gently-sloping mountainside
Is a brook, meandering past many a maple and oak
That slowly trickles over rock after smooth rock.
Discovering this jewel is like finding lost Roanoke.

Jeffrey A. Rosenblad, Grade 11
Faith Tabernacle School

Who's to Blame?

Who broke it,
my heart.

I feel very cold,
like the snow that falls,
from the wintry sky.

I think he was the reason for my broken heart.
He seized the beautiful sun away.

Instead of showing me a blue sky,
he turned it to gray,
and walked away.

A boy so careless, how could you do this?
I am now left with nothing, thanks to your selfish pride.

Siba Chekeif, Grade 10
Whitehall High School

Trunk of Secrets

Stowed away high in an attic so old
Is a trunk full of secrets
That will never be told.
Unseen by the world, your bond can't be severed
Safe in my trunk in the attic forever.

Locked and protected are things you so cherish
Concealed from those who don't understand,
Love can't simply perish.
No eyes see the trunk, the secret is thine.
No eyes will ever but yours, and but mine.

Hayley Morgans, Grade 10
Bloomsburg Area High School

Of Love

In the world above, what's left to love,
After disaster strikes in the hands of a glove.
Part broken, part unseen,
How fragile the world can be.

Leaving alone the ones who've shown,
Any compassion for the unknown.
Hearts on their sleeves, blowing with the breeze,
Showing how much they have grown.

Too much to tell so we try and repel,
Any hope of help we can get.
Not knowing we fell straight in to hell,
But it's too late so we start to regret.

And so he shines a light on me,
In hopes that one day we will both be free.
And we put up with everything,
In hopes of finding the one true meaning…of love.

Felicia Herder, Grade 12
Pennsylvania Leadership Charter School

Opened Eyes

By avoiding the truth, I became blind
I told myself "after the storm appeared the sunshine"
But for some reason, the rain never left my side
I never stopped giving you a reason to keep being mine

You deceived me by using your smile and laugh
And I never really bothered trying to look back
But then you left me with my heart in half
And I realized honesty is something you lack

While pacing my memories searching where I went wrong
I asked myself "could it be, was it me?"
I tortured myself bearing the sorrow tool long
But I did find someone who opened my eyes and let me see

Everything I did, you blew up in my face
But now for this next certain someone, nothing is going to waste.

Kevin Jimenez, Grade 12
Avon Grove High School

The Escape

Through the drizzling rain we saw the other side,
We saw the route to our freedom.
While sliding down the slippery rainbow of success,
The blue of lights, green of cash, and red of a Diablo
Had reflected in our eyes like diamonds.
Now clovers and fresh cut hay provide a sense of peace.
Then above the din, the summer sun emerged,
And beamed a magnificent yellow smile.
It beamed encouragement, a wink to go on,
Throughout the fight ahead.

Donovan J. Steele, Grade 10
Faith Tabernacle School

One Day

One day when the sun was up so high
In the white cloud-speckled sky,
I laughed and played through bright sun rays
Thinking, "I'll remember this day for always."

One day when the clouds hugged the darkened ground,
There were black pooling puddles all around.
I looked out the dewed window, sad and alone,
Until Mom walked in with an ice cream cone.

One day when the world was dressed in white,
Dad bundled me up all nice and tight.
I went outside and played in the snow,
'Til dad yelled that it was time to go.

One day when the birds chirped and the flowers bloomed,
I never realized that my life was doomed
To an endless wheel of seasonal turning.
The feeling to break free in my heart is yearning.

One day, I'll make my great escape
From these never-ending days I hate.
One day, I'll have my own way,
When I break free from this one day!

Courtney Hummel, Grade 12
Faith Tabernacle School

Beautiful Presents from Heaven

Two beautiful presents were sent to me;
I knew that only from God they could be.
Those perfect chubby cheeks and that dark, silky hair,
Sent to me were an answer to prayer.

The first I received on November the first.
That God took her back, I cried, was the worst.
After awhile, God comforted my soul;
But because of this loss, my heart will never be whole.

On October the eighth, the second one came;
Jennifer Tianna became her name.
My soul elated, a tear-filled smile on my face,
I lovingly took her into my gentle embrace.

Her big blue eyes stared up at me;
A smile spread on her face so beautifully.
Her tiny fingers then clasped around mine;
Her heart and my heart forever entwined.

God had taken my first niece away,
But He left my second niece with me here to stay.
Two beautiful presents were sent to me,
And some day in Heaven with both I will be.

Kayla Keeney, Grade 11
Faith Tabernacle School

All Through the Winter

All through the winter, all through the cold
Laughs were shared, stories were told
We needed no spark to start a flame
Friendship then was a simpler game

Our hearts were inspired, yet never grew tired
Of the winter's cold as we sat by the fire
We shot the breeze and were satisfied
Until the day our friendship died

We didn't ask questions, charged no fee
All we asked for was unity
And try we did to stay together
Our friendship now has gone forever

Not a thing has been gained, yet everything lost
When we took separate paths, I knew the cost
That we'd have to face the world alone
'Cuz we turned our backs on the place called home

Great is the pain and the sorrow I feel
And I hope to God that my wound will heal
But lost friendship is a terrible thing
And now I have no more bells to ring

Sam Bojarski, Grade 12
North Allegheny Sr High School

Losing Control

Her life, like a frame,
Was set in the boundaries of each edge.
The rules for her were laid down
Just like a harsh game.

The die was rolled;
The pawn was moved.
At last, the card was drawn,
And she did what she was told.

It was the point of no return,
No turning back.
She had to keep going;
She had a lesson to learn.

An eerie feeling came over her,
As she stumbled and lost control.
Like a rag-doll, she crumbled to the ground,
Surrounded on all sides by her foe.

The harsh reality stung her face.
She had crossed the forbidden line,
And now, she must pay
For her steps that she couldn't retrace.

Megan J. Funk, Grade 10
Faith Tabernacle School

It's Up to You

Why can't I stop this feeling?
The raw pain in my heart is unbearable,
All brought on by the thought of losing you.
I try not to make it obvious, try not to show my fear,
but there are a few who see, the crumbling mask I wear.
Do you see it? Perhaps you ignore it, I don't know.
Your parents are right you know, you deserve better than me,
Me a pathetic loner, of average looks and average intelligence.
I may act out, but it's all a cover a ploy to hide my pain.
Do you see behind the mask? God I wish I knew.
Do you see you see the broken girl who loves and cherishes you more than the world?
Or do you see the tomboy who hides behind a mask?
I know it's cruel, hiding my past and pain from you, but I feel like a burden.
Holding you back from success.
You could be so great, have an amazing future,
but is it right for me to love you when there are others more deserving than I?
I can't pretend like I'm not afraid anymore,
so read this over and treat this information with care,
because the ball's in your court now and it's your choice to make, whether to continue or turn back.

Olivia Szlasa, Grade 10
Lehigh Career & Technical Institute

Friends

Alyssa didn't have many friends; at least none that I could see. Once she told me, "I have many, but they only belong to me."
Thinking nothing of it, I simply let it go. As time ticked by I started to notice suspicious signs beginning to show.

She'd broken all her dollies; scattered remains all that lie. In her defense she'd always say, "It was my friends, not I."

At the time I figured it was just a children's game.
Imagining up invisible friends, so they could take all blame.

Alyssa grew up; all her childhood games played.
But one game refused to leave; Alyssa's "Friends"…they stayed.

Those friends guided Alyssa straight to drugs and alcohol.
Those friends advised Alyssa to shut down once and for all.

Alyssa knew her path was wrong, but one could not soil her name.
For everyone who knew her knew, "My friends are to blame."

Alyssa struggled day by day, Alyssa lost the war. Alyssa lived with her friends all her life, but Alyssa is no more.
So here I am, without Alyssa I am alone. Alyssa's friends, however, came to me and made themselves at home.

Blair London, Grade 12
Sharpsville Area Sr High School

Being Free

Freedom, what everyone wants and desires, why do I love thee?
So wondrous and powerful like waves rolling across the open sea.
We fight for it, write about it, and hear it in songs.
It may also be taken away and for it we will long.
Many have fought, many have died,
and the thought of it would make many young black slaves cry.
When you look at the flag, the great red, white, and blue.
I hope it is something you will think about to!

Cortney Vrabel, Grade 10
Whitehall High School

I Can Hear the Music

I can hear the music.
I can hear the loud, melodic trumpet surround me.
The brazen sound soars above all.
Glistening, you see the brass shine in the warm rays of the sun.
Overwhelmed by the sound, the people smile.
They can hear the music.

Reagan Miller, Grade 10
Whitehall High School

Savior

I cannot run,
I cannot hide.
Darkness is surrounding me,
Hopelessness is all I feel inside.

I try to sleep,
I close my eyes.
Dreams of all those broken butterflies,
That tore their wings against sharp thorns;
The pain and suffering they've endured.

I can see light,
I can feel the glow.
From fragile hearts wanting to know.
Looking deep into your crystal eyes.
A few tears fall, memories arise.
It is then I realize,
I see there what I feel inside.

Brooke Figdore, Grade 11
Eastern York High School

Thanksgiving

I gorged my face with cranberries,
And slurped my soup to chase it.
I gobbled up my baked potato,
So fast I didn't taste it.

I devoured all my salad,
And had seconds of the peas.
I guzzled down all my pumpkin pie;
Could you pass the breadsticks, please?

"It's a shame you bought a turkey;"
I unsnapped my pants and huffed,
"You could've stuck me in the oven,
'Cause I'm nicely dressed and *stuffed*!"

Jenny Kline, Grade 12
Mount Saint Joseph Academy

To Truly Know a Person

Go a mile in their shoes.
See things their way.
Walk around in their skin.
Be them for a day.

Imagine all the things
You may not even know
About this someone
And what they had to undergo.

The world could be a better place
If we talked to people face to face.
A simple "hello" and "hi"
May even save a person's life.

Kerrianna Wallace, Grade 10
North Pocono High School

Stars

They turn to us in the dark of the moon
they turn to us and they fold.
Hand under stomach and foot over neck they compress
into the smallness of their allotted compartments.

But the night did not begin this way.

Their faces were twisted over ours, not emerging
until the skies had purpled and the glow of the sun had all but disappeared.
They were only bright eyes
yet at the same time they did not see us in the way we saw them.

They are — always have been — objective.

Now that they have molded themselves into their iridescent glory
they rise and stretch — yawn as we yawn; wake as we wake,
and their spires crawl across the blue-canvas blankness,
illuminating our dirty knees, scraped hands and sweat-stained t-shirts.

They rise to glory in the pitch; in the tar,
and only small patches are left black above us,
making shadows over our curled-up forms.
Soon they will fall, and for a short time the sky will be empty
The stars will fade to blue, then gray;
shift as they must to become one with the swipes of colour in the dawn,
when the sun will rise back above us and again take over the skies.

Hannah Fouche, Grade 10
Palmyra Area Sr High School

The Crabapple Tree

Morning. Stretching my arms in sync with the sun as she spread her rays across the field.
Verdant blades of grass were slivers of gold in the light.
    Everything was waking.
Everyone was asleep.
Embers smoked in the fire pit, last night a memory.
Sneakers soaked with dew, but the silence of the morning was a deafening symphony
of nature;
    birds singing in the trees rustled by the breeze,
    playful leaves danced and spun on limbs.
Mist rising off the lake, reflecting the
pale blue sky,
the moon was fading, sun racing to see his face before he left.
(She tried every morning but never could, fate fell short.)

Transparent minnows basked in the shallow warming water.
I was engulfed in the transition from sleep to wake, night to day, dawn to morning.

My lungs could not get enough clear air,
my tongue could not taste enough of this day,
my eyes could not blink in fear of missing a moment,
my hands could not grasp the adventures ahead,
my heart could not be more full.

The crabapple tree was not holding its breath.

Morgan Costello, Grade 11
State College Area High School

Statue

mounted from grand-
stone

standing over all
things

in the central
square

night, day it
stands

waiting for the
day

it will be
admired

Mike Eible, Grade 10
Whitehall High School

White Lie

He asked me how he looked
Ridiculous, I thought
But to his face I smiled
And said, "You lookin' hot."
He grinned and flexed his muscles,
Miniscule at best
I looked down to hide the scream
Rolling through my chest
I patted his thin shoulder
In silent contemplation
And in my mind bloomed
A small realization:
The sweet candy of kindness
Is often wrapped in lies.

Shannon O'Leary, Grade 12
Mount Saint Joseph Academy

a single tear drop

a single tear
drop falls into a stream

though it flows
with the crisp waters around

it's salinity makes
it Stand Out among others

wanting to fit
in with the other droplets

but it was
made to be completely different

Alyssa Brooks-Wells, Grade 10
Whitehall High School

Grades 7-8-9
Top Ten Winners

List of Top Ten Winners for Grades 7-9; listed alphabetically

Leah Berry-Sandelin, Grade 8
Mahoney Middle School, ME

Naomi Davidson, Grade 8
Decorah Middle School, IA

Olivia Estes, Grade 9
University Hill Secondary School, BC

Faith Harron, Grade 7
Horizon Middle School, ND

Lily Lauben, Grade 9
University Preparatory School, CA

Alex LePeter, Grade 7
Oak Knoll Middle School, VA

Sarah Lynch, Grade 7
Holy Innocents School, NJ

Ally Merrill, Grade 9
Hamilton Freshman High School, OH

Shelby Senger, Grade 8
Emmanuel-St Michael Lutheran School, IN

Anna Sixsmith, Grade 7
St Thomas More School, PA

All Top Ten Poems can be read at www.poeticpower.com

Note: The Top Ten poems were finalized through an online voting system. Creative Communication's judges first picked out the top poems. These poems were then posted online. The final step involved thousands of students and teachers who registered as the online judges and voted for the Top Ten poems. We hope you enjoy these selections.

Family

Freshly cut grass beneath my feet
Feeling love and joy when I walk through the door
I bite into a juicy cheeseburger,
And hear speaker shaking rap music in the living room.
As the day goes on I play the Wii;
I might not always win,
But at least I am spending time
With the ones who love and care about me.
As the night slows down
We are all still wound up.
I smell a citronella candle, calling the family outside
Everyone gathers outside
Around the toasty campfire,
Sharing memories through the years
The feeling of love comes back to me
And I remember that feeling
As I walked through the door
Time sure does fly by
When you spend time with a loving family!

Megan Kudla, Grade 8
St. Anselm Elementary School

Without the Sun

There is no light in my eyes,
The colors died, no surprise.
There is no warmth upon my skin,
The darkness tears me, limb from limb.

Lightless, frozen, discolored, depressed,
Colorless, lonely, horror, and all the rest.
All I hear is crying and weeping.
The sadness inside me is slowly creeping.

The darkness is sucking the blue from my eyes,
There is nowhere to run and nowhere to hide.
My whole entire soul is growing weary,
My colorless eyes are becoming teary.

Darkness follows me everywhere, stalking my traces.
It's pulling the color right out of all of our faces.
Okay I give up! The darkness has won.
Life is simply horrible without the sun.

Erica Storey, Grade 7
J R Fugett Middle School

Trees

Trees
Being born with just one seed
Growing taller with water they need
When autumn comes, the leaves will change color
Great big trees provide a nice cover
Then when winter comes some trees will pass
Then yet another tree will grow in that grass
Trees

Peter Foggo, Grade 7
Strath Haven Middle School

My Colorful Socks

I love to collect colorful socks
I keep them in my secret box.

This box lies in my bottom left drawer,
I'm not sure I can fit any more.

They are rainbow and striped,
Bright green, purple and even white.

There are silly patterns and polka-dots,
I especially like the ones with the splattered spots.

My mother tells me to stop collecting,
Each pair she keeps rejecting.

She hides them from me,
But they're so bright,
I can always see,
Where they are hidden out of sight.

I place them back in my box,
She tells me to get rid of those awful socks,

I love my socks, that will never change
She will just have to accept I'm kinda strange.

Gabrielle Gevaudan, Grade 7
St James School

The Blizzard

The light,
Quietly sneaking through my window,
Awakens me.
I peer outside and see the snowflakes
Drifting down, so softly, calmly like a lullaby.

Do I dare go outside?
I prepare for the cold weather, and scamper outside
Where the wind calmly whips at my face
And the cold nips at my toes.

As dusk falls I trudge back inside, shivering, and frozen.
I hold a warm cup of cocoa in my aching hands.
Suddenly the lights flicker.
Then with a snap the electricity shuts off in unison.

What will we do now?
The house is lit by candlelight,
Like brilliantly, twinkling stars.
The family gathers by the glowing fire for heat.
Eyes sparkling with love,
As night arrives.
With snow still peacefully falling
I drift off to a much awaited sleep.

Allison Murmello, Grade 7
St Thomas More School

Fluorescent Love

When I look into the sky
And see a million stars
Not one of them can lie
His girl is more precious than his cars
She stares at the moon, each and every night
Just praying that soon
He will see his own fluorescent light
That makes jaws drop, and heartbeats pound
Her heart is what he stole
Which is nothing close to new
Because every girl is in love with his smile
No other guy can compare
To his laid-back style
And enchanted lasting flare
All eyes locked on him
People will shove
All throughout the nation
Just to see his talent and beauty
Like a glowing valiant
They're the best this world's got
And they don't even know it

Ashley Hade, Grade 8
Greencastle-Antrim Middle School

I Don't Like the Way You Treat Me

You rub right up against the page.
It fills me up with rage!
I'm sure the paper doesn't like it either.
Though I stain him with love and hate.

He doesn't argue, but I know he feels like me.
With my power, I can't tell you how much it hurts.
You don't care as you press me hard onto the page.
But with this, I tell you.

Please when you use me, be careful.
Think about my feelings.
What you do.
So that you don't hurt me too.

Courtney Jones, Grade 7
Landisville Middle School

A Day at the Beach

I get to the beach and all is well,
the sand was hot from the sun,
I didn't care because I am ready for some fun,
I walked around to spot some shells,
instead I tried to grab some crabs, not a good idea at all!
I decided to sit and take a rest,
the ocean was roaring and seagulls were soaring,
I grabbed my surfboard and hit the water,
it cooled me off so I could stay a little longer,
I love the beach because it's a good time,
until the sun sets and it's time to say goodbye.

Caleb Schaeffer, Grade 7
Greencastle-Antrim Middle School

Life or Death

Disease	The Cure
I am Disease	I am the Cure
I corrupt and disable	I protect and battle

We fight to the death

I spread as fast as light	I get your family through the night

I cause affliction and distress	I bring peace and joyfulness

We can change your life

I meander through your body and bring you billows of pain	I look for your problem as I slither through your veins

We go forth in our dangerous plight

So, here I am, your cause of death, your life I will diminish.	And here I go to save your life, to defeat this noisome menace.

I will win this fight

Noah Richardson, Grade 7
Interboro GATE Program

Quiet Summer Night

The pond was lit with a full moon
The summer night was silent, absolutely silent.
Not even the crickets were chirping
There was no owl hooting in the distance
There was no wolf howling at the moon
No; it was a quiet night
So quiet, that the dropping of a pin could be heard
The night was silent; calming actually
Where was the noise?
The usual noise of the night
There was no frog croaking
There was no cicada humming
No noise at all
There was only complete, peaceful silence

Hannah Johnson, Grade 7
Landisville Middle School

Happiest Time of the Year

As the glistening white snow falls,
I'm caroling, "Deck the Halls."
Families all around decorating green trees,
Children everywhere are filled with glee.
I'm feeling the Christmas spirit,
Can you hear it?
Colorful lights, they're so bright!
Children lying excitedly in their beds,
Christmas wishes filling their heads!
Stocking hung over the fireplace,
Could this beautiful memory ever be replaced?

Emily Evans, Grade 7
Armstrong Middle School

Yesterday

A mist hovers low to the ground close to the potatoes
With their withered leaves and stalks, crumbling, black as soot.
My feet are soaked and covered with cold mud from walking through the field after the recent rain.

Dull, muted clouds cover the sun,
The dark potatoes are like a sponge, soaking up sun rays until the scene is left grey.
If only I could be a sponge, eliminating the grey,
Bringing back the cheerful sunlight of yesterday.

As I walk, the water from the muggy ground squishes underfoot.
My dogs howl, disapprovingly, as they smell the stench of our rotting food.
I turn as the thick wooden door to my family's home opens with a low groan.
Looking at the soiled crop, the sound of gasps travel to where I am standing.
My wife starts to talk but I don't listen.
Listening won't make yesterday come back.

I stand there, feeling the cold air close in around me like an icy embrace.
Devastated, it seems to me that all the hope from yesterday has rotted with the potatoes.
The loss of our only food source has made my heart drop,
And thoughts about tomorrow make me feel worse.
Knowing what to do is something that feels impossible.
I want to survive, and I want my family to survive,
But that can't be guaranteed unless yesterday can come back.

Will yesterday ever come back?

Julia Lega, Grade 8
Saucon Valley Middle School

Beach Day

The ash-gray day lingered above the steady beach,
Like a chandelier over a table.
Everywhere middle school gym floor brown tinted sand.
We are isolated in deep, muggy humidity.
Translucent Jell-O jellyfish squish between my grimy toes, my expression twists and locks like an old pretzel.
Irritating seagulls plummet towards us to rapidly embezzle our delectable food.
I hear their insufferable, no stopping squawk,
Squawk, squawk, squawk!
In Ocean City the overwhelming salty reek and the stench of curly fries pestered my nose and me.
Lance buried in the sand
I hastily squashed my finger down on the play button recording him being attacked by the superior seagulls.

Lily Marigliano, Grade 7
Holicong Middle School

Death

"Everyone knows they're going to die, but nobody believes it." — Tuesdays with Morrie
Death is everywhere and all around,
It creeps up behind you tingling your spine causing goose bumps,
Death has many ways of showing itself to human beings,
Death will come for us when our hour glass is done or when the wick of the candle has come to a finish,
Death shall follow us forever and ever,
BOO!
Thump, THump, THUmp, THUMp, THUMP says the heart,
The heart has stopped and it goes silent, death has appeared and it was quiet,
Everyone shall experience it, but when?

Jordan Zaffrin, Grade 9
Holicong Middle School

Leaves

Leaves, leaves, so colorful and bright,
They make me wonder why birds take flight,
When you step on them they make a crunch,
But unlike food, they aren't lunch,
And you only find them in a bunch.

Leaves, leaves, all over the ground,
Lifeless, not making a sound,
Until the wind moves them around,
You always see them when you look down,
And somehow they never make you frown.

Leaves, leaves, get raked away,
Then made in a pile to let a kid play,
They scatter everywhere,
But no one seems to care,
Leaves, leaves, I hope they always stay.

Joseph O'Hara, Grade 7
J R Fugett Middle School

Memories of You

We used to have fun together
When will be the next time? Never!
Since you've been dead, nothing else goes through my head
Sometimes I want to ask God, Why?
But I don't dare to try
There's got to be a reason that we had to say goodbye
Why? Why do I want to die to be with you
You helped raise me, you're why I grew
We've sometimes had bad times
And yes, we've had our climbs
I remember when we pushed you outside and locked the door
But we just can't do that anymore
You probably miss us, but we miss you more
There are laughs and cries
Hellos and goodbyes in life,
But love doesn't die, people do
So we'll always have the memories of you...

Jhayda Edwards, Grade 7
Armstrong Middle School

Forgiveness

You say your sorry but you're not,
you say you love me but you don't,
Forgive and forgotten is what I do.
I trusted you I thought this was true,
We all make mistakes,
That's what they say,
but to forgive is not as strong as we think,
you break a heart and no you can't erase what you've done.
You say you're sorry but you're not,
you say you love me but you don't,
My heart was stolen by you and your looks,
you tricked me so no you won't be forgiven.

Lateeka Brown, Grade 9
Carrick High School

Wonderful Worlds

My library carries all sorts of worlds;
You get lost as soon as you walk in the door.
So many people and places to explore
There's Tolkien and Poe and so much more.

I can be spellbound for hours in mythology,
There are so many creatures that I'd like to see:
Pegasus, chimeras and dragons to meet—
You can do it all, sitting in your seat.

It's amazing how a book can take you so far,
To African jungles, Middle Earth, or Mars
Both real and pretend, different places you'll roam,
While all curled up in your armchair at home.

I check out ten books every library trip,
The newest book series I really can't miss,
Percy Jackson and Eragon are the latest attraction,
And reading them gives such great satisfaction.

Books are my favorite things, you see,
And that's why the library's the place for me.

Molly Harnish, Grade 7
The American Academy

Problematic Poems

Rhyming is hard; that's what I've been told.
Then I get an idea, and I'm told it's, "Too bold."

Some students have fun as they write about school,
That's about as much fun as saying, "Boys rule."

Others can rhyme just about anything;
I can't rhyme my name with even one thing.

I'm under pressure to complete this poem,
My mind, however, continues to roam.

So I will submit this poem I have written
Hoping the judges with this rhyme will be smitten.

Samantha Ludlum, Grade 8
The American Academy

The Polar Bear

The polar bear was as white as snow,
he traveled on the ice as the cold winds blow.
The polar bear traveled West to find some fish,
because everyone knows that's a polar bear's favorite dish.
Some would say he's a beast,
but for his cubs he provides a feast.
He pounces and bounces, and plays all day,
then curls up with his cubs and finds a place to lay.
Although the polar bear looks fluffy and nice,
it's better to leave this beast on the ice.

Taylor Siner, Grade 7
Greencastle-Antrim Middle School

Where I'm From

I am from Greece, Italy, Germany, Ireland,
all pieces of the puzzle that is me.

Halloween, Thanksgiving, and Christmas
Max (my dog) dressed up like a fire truck
41 cousins to celebrate with

I am from sports
watching the puck drop for the Pittsburgh Penguins
hearing the crack of the bat for the Pirates
waving my Terrible Towel for the Steelers
playing soccer and tennis

I'm from the ocean at Myrtle Beach or the lake at Lake Erie
(I can still remember
the waves hitting me
like they were my own)

American Girl dolls,
Bratz dolls, Play Mobil
playing with my friends
and my sister, my childhood

My heart is where I store my memories
memories from hanging out with friends and my large family
adding pieces to my puzzle.

Daniella Sandora, Grade 7
Jefferson Middle School

My Grandpa Erickson

My grandpa was one of the best in the world,
And it is hard to live without him.

My grandpa was as happy as a cheerful robin
And spread joy like sunshine on a dark, dreary day.

My grandpa always brightened my life
When I went to visit him.

He was the owner of Blocher's Meat Market
And a pastor of our church in Altoona.

He liked to sing and praise God
And was a great example for us all.

He showed great love to all in need
And helped all those he could.

He loved trains, and his entire family
And also loved to play the game Rook.

I would love to visit him for Christmas
Because he would correctly discern his shiny, brightly-colored gifts.

My grandpa was one of the best in the world,
And it is hard to live without him.

Sherry Goodyear, Grade 8
Faith Tabernacle School

The Preacher's Son

He's the one to stand up for what's right,
He's the one who keeps the Lord in his sight,
He's the one to get out of the way
When his friends devastate his day
(Like a politician can),
He's the preacher's son.

He's the one to pull his load
He's the one to give God his love that he owed,
He's the one to help around the farm
When his dad's down with his broken arm,
He's the preacher's son.

He's the one who prays at night
He's the one who knows what is right,
He's the one to come to in despair
When no one else seems to care,
He's the preacher's son.

He's the one who risks his life
Trying to help his family's strife,
He's the one who took a stand
When all others turned and ran,
He's the preacher's son.

Bruce A. Yeager Jr., Grade 9
Faith Tabernacle School

Oh Yeah!

In my life five major food groups you'll see,
That give me fuel to play ice hockey.
The first of the five is good pizza to eat,
The greasy goodness of the cheese just can't be beat.

The second major group has to be beef,
The enticing smell beats a lettuce leaf.
Beef can be prepared as a succulent fillet,
Or a cheeseburger I could eat almost every day.

Ambrosial ribeye makes my taste buds sing,
And New York strip makes me feel like a king.
Anything Italian makes up group three,
Tomato sauce and pasta fills me with glee.

Baked ravioli is delicious as can be,
And savory chicken parmesan's great, you'll agree.
The fourth group is certainly Mexican.
I can eat tacos or fajitas again and again.

And finally seafood for the fifth:
Calamari, crabs, or fresh lobster bisque.
These are the five food groups I abide by,
Oh wait, oh no, I forgot pie.

David Null, Grade 9
The American Academy

Afternoon at the Beach

I sit in the car for two hours in anticipation of a great beach day. As we sit through traffic, I think about how good it will feel when I pounce into the cold and clear waves. Minute after minute goes by — waiting — and waiting. Finally we arrive! I jump out of the car only to be greeted by tons of people and the burning hot sun. I grab my chair and towel and slug myself through the sand. I set my chair up. There are the sounds of loud chatter, music, sea gulls, and my favorite...the clashing waves. I feel the sand simmering between my toes. I am sitting at my chair and I start to feel the sun wrapping its harmful rays around me. I get so hot; I just have to go in!!! I pull myself out of my chair. I walk through the crowd trying to get to the waves without kicking sand on a sunbather. I dip my toes into the water. It's so COLD! I take a jump in. I AM SO COLD! I feel my legs tingle. I quickly dip my head under water. That enough for me, I get out. I retreat to my chair shaking. I sit, and I feel the sun start to warm me. I sit for what seems to be forever. I fall asleep. "Peyton, it's time to go," is what I hear. I stand up I feel so happy until I look down onto my RED sunburned body...Oops! I forgot the sunscreen.

Peyton Brownlee, Grade 7
Strath Haven Middle School

Middle School

First left...then right...then left again
I turn the small, round, black handle of my locker
"POP" the latch lifts, and I grab my pink Language Arts binder out of the messy, filled up, big,
Gray locker. I race down the big empty hallways, my feet slapping the ground with every step I
Take, it was minutes now seconds
3...2...1...BEEP I run into class seconds late.
I
Sit
Down
I have made it...late, but I am here.

Olivia Parente, Grade 7
Strath Haven Middle School

The Sport I Love

Lacrosse, one of the fastest sports on two feet
I love the adrenaline you get when you're speeding your way up field
It almost seems like you're traveling the speed of light when you get that big steal
The goal is directly in front of you now and just out of shot range, but then you see it
There's a breach in the defense and one of your teammates is running open
You remain calm though never losing focus
The ball rockets out of your stick directly in to your teammates and he stuffs it home
Pure joy is what you feel in the next moment; after all you just won the game in overtime with that astonishing assist
On this field is where you're truly happy, you can finally be yourself here
Most people think of lacrosse as just a game but I think it's deeper than that

Dylan Taylor, Grade 9
Conrad Weiser High School

A Leaf's Journey

Trees throw leaves down to the street, left only to shiver and shake in the cold. With clouds threatening the ground below with snow, leaves can only hope for a fast-coming spring. The snow arrives in sheets covering the leaves until light is faint. Days pass, then weeks. As the snow melts the leaves are resurfaced. Showing off their dark brown colors as they end their journey.

Ari Feldman, Grade 7
Strath Haven Middle School

Loving Ice-skating

Once there was a kid named Nick
He was never ever sick
He loved to skate on the ice
And he was very nice
He likes science, but English was not his pick.

Nick Peck, Grade 8
Chichester Middle School

Past, Present and Future

Sky is blue and the rhythm is too
games speed life what a wonderful sight no matter what you do
the timeline will always follow you until the book falls
and the paper and pages don't get old we are connected so
the reader places back the timeline and your soul.

Alannis Soto, Grade 8
Southern Lehigh Middle School

Earth…

I'm polluted, sick; help me please.
I can't stand it, you humans hate me.
Don't like me do you? UGH
You, all of you; mortals
Talk about the world ending.

Well soon, soon it shall end.
Unless….

You help clean me up.

I will stop destroying
Your continents.
Stop polluting me, and I will
Help you rebuild. Help me…
Please, I'm sick…polluted.
Kaitlyn Larkin, Grade 7
Armstrong Middle School

Flood's Destruction

Here it comes;
Run for your lives!
Floods a-comin',
It's on the rise!

Floods a-comin'!
Now he's here;
Get a runnin'
And take those dear.

That fast foamy water,
Cold to the touch,
Roars like a lion
Pungent with soggy debris.
The flood can be mightier
Than the sea.
Ryan M. Steele, Grade 9
Faith Tabernacle School

You Saved Me

You've saved me from myself,
You've helped me through it all,

You've stopped me from,
Thinking about anything,
Other than happy thoughts.

You've made me smile,
Through good and bad.
You've made me feel,
Wanted and loved.

I thank you for that.
That's how you've saved me!
Breanna O'Brien, Grade 7
Armstrong Middle School

Colors Describe Me!

Part of me is pretty pink,
nice, happy, and shy when
I meet new people.
Deep inside I'm a fiery red
violent, and dangerous, mean
and loud when you get on
my bad side.
These colors are quite common,
They both describe me!
Other days I'm an ocean blue,
calm relaxed, and chill, hanging
with my friends, playing
basketball.
Many days I'm a violet purple
helping people, making them
happy when they are sad
and doing my work to
get good grades.
Teresa Santos, Grade 8
Chichester Middle School

Hummingbird

Bursts of bright colors,
fluttering, flitting, flying.
Drops sweet like honey,
drip from a flower nearby.
Wings beat furiously,
but delicately all the same.
Flowing like a melody,
beautiful as a symphony.
My feathered friend flies by.
But just for a moment,
and then she is gone.
Flying away,
away to the sky above.
Just one moment,
just one image.
That's all you have to keep.
But it's just enough
as fireworks fly away.
Sarah Dunn, Grade 8
Springton Lake Middle School

A Lion

I'm like a king on a throne
Except on a rock.
All the animals obey me
Except hunters who hunt for me.
I like to hunt for predators
Who don't obey or I like to eat.
I like to eat meat.
Especially red, raw meat.
This is why I'm the king.
So that means you obey me.
Jacob Myers, Grade 7
Greencastle-Antrim Middle School

Sparkling

Sparkle, twinkle, shine
A jewel in the sky
With stars and a moon
In the distance you see
Birds fly, clouds swoop
Rain falls, hail shoots
The sky is a sparkling place

Sparkle, twinkle, shine
The sky is like the ocean
But, it is up above
The sunrise and sunset
Bright then dark
The sky is a sparkling place
A sparkling place
Ashley Lennick, Grade 7
Charles F Patton Middle School

What's More?

The world is big and bright,
Full of wonders and delights,
Color, shapes, sound, and more…
All different in their own way,
But the new things these days,
Phones, iPods, laptops, sports galore,
They seem so new, so special,
But oh-so grand!
Wrapped up, taken away,
Slowly lead you away…
From what was precious,
Dear to you so long ago,
So take a moment,
Just to think,
What is truly more?
Lianne Covington, Grade 8
Fred S Engle Middle School

Lemons

Looking around,
My table full of fire-red
Sour faces,
Surprised expressions,
Eyes bulging out.
"Oooo!"
"Ahh!"
I sigh
My first experience with sourness
In the crammed restaurant.
Though the bitterness
Creeps into my paper cut
Stinging it with the power of
Delicious lemon juice,
I lunge forward for more.
Stephanie Morley, Grade 7
Holicong Middle School

Art Room

The art room is so colorful,
and full of inspiration.
It's full of past memories
and memories in the making.
It's full of lost dreams,
and hope that has been shattered.
But anyone can start
on a clean page.
Marguerita M. Cruz-Urbanc, Grade 7
Strath Haven Middle School

The Beginning of Spring

The sun is greeted with a bird's song,
Flowers awaken beneath the snow
As a warm breeze fills the air,
The snow has left to give us rain
And help us enter a new season,
The trees have gotten new leaves,
Animals awaken from their slumber,
Winter has left and spring has entered.
Dylan Tyas, Grade 7
Armstrong Middle School

Pain

Pain is something that you can't hide
Pain is something that hurts so much
The more you hold it the more it hurts
That's why we have friends
Friends help you with the pain
Friends have your back
Friends ease the pain
Michael Vazquez, Grade 7
Armstrong Middle School

Hero/Villain

Hero
Philanthropist, brilliant
Preserve, rescue, safeguard
Champion, redeemer, reckless, scoundrel
Destroying, overthrowing, ruining
Evil, wicked
Villain
Madeleine O'Neil, Grade 8
Good Shepherd School

A Dusty Snow

Snow
Cold, wet
Rolls, falls, soaks
Ice, water, dust, dirt
Blows, covers, irritates
Dusty, dry
Sand
Alden Funston, Grade 8
Good Shepherd School

One Dreadful Hairdo

Staring in the mirror at my reflection,
Toward my hair I have no affection.
It poofs up in more than one place,
Overall it is really just a disgrace.
I went to a salon to get a new 'do,
Bursting with excitement, I shouted woohoo!
Joyfully, I pranced over to the mirror filled with glee,
Anticipating how pulchritudinous my new hair would be.
The mirror revealed a disastrous do, is this really what I see?
It is me back in time, before I was the queen bee.
Suddenly, I could see myself, young and dull,
I was on the beach looking at this laughing seagull.
I couldn't figure out why it was chuckling,
Then I knew it was because my hair made me look like the ugly duckling.
Tearfully, I left the salon to wander and roam,
Reluctantly, I ended up returning home.
My mom stood at the front door, she must have known.
With a brush in her hand she began to comb.
This made me feel so very blessed,
To have a family who cared, no matter how much my hair was distressed.
Tara Monaghan, Grade 8
Sandy Run Middle School

The Loose Tooth

It was a cold, December night on the first day of winter break
Family was gathered around the table, laughing and talking about life
I slipped away to play a tune on the piano
My fingers gliding across the keys, like waves in the ocean
Then pausing, I reached into my mouth and twisted
My tooth wouldn't budge, so I yanked
Returning the black and white keys, I play for about ten seconds
Pausing once more, I wiggled the tooth again, "Pop!"
It falls out onto my tiny, red hand

"I lost my tooth!"
Yelling, as I scampered into the kitchen
They completely ignored me
"I lost my tooth!"
I exclaimed once more
This time, heads turned and hands clapped
I was ecstatic to crawl into the covers that night,
With a happy grin on my face,
Hoping to get some cash, on that wonderful,
December night
Gabrielle Meme, Grade 7
Richboro Middle School

Fall Has Left

When I leave my home my shoes crunch the leaves upon the ground
Those colorful red, orange, and yellow beautiful bits of nature.
They're blowing away as that cold wind comes—winter is near.
Soon those nature bits will be under snow just waiting for the warm spring to come soon.
As I walk later small cold ice crystals fall from the sky sprinkling
the ground like the sprinkles covering a cupcake. Fall has left.
Hilal Ayarci, Grade 7
Armstrong Middle School

Scuba Diving

Morning.
The splash of the deep, sapphire blue water,
Bubbles surround me.
On descent, bright, rainbow colored fish,
Swimming through the rough coral,
Poking in the silky, snow white sand,
Scavenging for food.
The soothing, steady sound of bubbles,
They rise to the surface,
Where the sun reflects off the water like a mirror.
I feel the rubber on my gauges,
Realizing it is time to ascend,
Kick legs like scissors,
Fins fluttering like wings,
Cling onto the slimy, algae covered rope.
Glancing up, seeing the murky black boat bottom.
On the boat, the dive is done.

Spencer Sterner, Grade 7
Holicong Middle School

Take-Off

3:30 a.m., a dreadful time.
A time to be asleep and in peace — not a wake up time.
Bed hair and morning breath linger.
Chalkboard-black circles under my eyes.
Excitement.
The blazing circle of fire peeks up from a meadow.
Painting a scenic mixture of purple and orange.
Hauling luggage.
Shoulders contort to keep the wheels steady.
The automatic door yawns with exhaustion.
A melting pot of people snake through the accordion of ropes.
The cool air draws a chill down my spine.
Goosebumps wake me up.
Boarding the plane, leaving a trail of happiness.
Smacking on gum, preventing ear popping.
A color wheel of houses below.
I reach out and put a cloud in my pocket.

Katie Carr, Grade 7
Holicong Middle School

True Friendship

My faithful friend is always there.
When I am troubled, she always cares.
Our memories throughout the year
reflect moments of joy and even some tears.
Although I can't make sure she is always safe and sound.
I trust God's love will always be around.
We laugh and we cry
as each encounter goes by.
She's the kind of friend who shows compassion.
I also enjoy so much her sense of fashion.
We'll be together until we die.
We're best friends — that's why.

Brianna Lozada, Grade 8
St Peter School

The One Person Zoo

The sun slowly rising
The aroma of pancakes fills the air
I am about to take a delightful bite of pancakes
Baaw laa!!
The one person zoo has officially opened
The water of the shower halts to a stop
I hear 100 crazed animals
On a rampage going down the stairs
I brace myself to be trampled
Instead, I see,
Loud obnoxious noises are coming from
My Brother David
His silly face slowly comes down the staircase
His face exploding with a fiery orange glow
His hand ostrich is slowly sneaking up
Baam
An ostrich fight erupting in the kitchen
Even though a neuro-science student
A fun and silly older brother at heart

Rachel Eisenberg, Grade 7
Holicong Middle School

A Horse Love

My horse and I have this consistent bond,
Always together in each other's hearts,
No matter the time, place, or happening,
I am always thinking about him,

There have been times when it seemed rough,
But there are more times when we are having the time of our lives,
We leap over our fears,
We enjoy our time together,

We are a single team,
Just the two of us,
We pursue to set goals,
And conquer them,

Nevertheless, someday the time will come,
Where we will always win champion,
Where we are known as the best, but for now,
We must take a moment to enjoy our riding together.

Molly Hansbarger, Grade 9
Holicong Middle School

The Wonders Below

The unknown surrounds us everywhere we go
But nowhere is as full of it as the wonders below
Where blue meets blackness and strange creatures dwell
You shouldn't enter this scary big hell
Where cold water numbs and no light is given
Where the sea is not so forgiving
You should be careful of where you go
When you're down in the deep below

Catherine Coates, Grade 7
Boyertown Jr High School East

Opposite Students

School is everything.
I reject the idea that
I need sleep and social time
Rather,
I need straight A's
I don't believe that
Teachers assign too much homework
In fact,
There should be more projects and essays
Who thinks that
School is worthless
I agree that
Grades
Matter more than
Friends
Based on my own values,
School is the most important time in your life
How can anyone believe that
School isn't everything.

Now, read backwards for the opposite student.

Max Naar, Grade 9
Holicong Middle School

The Visionary

You see her, while no one else does
You see the talent, while no one else does
You see the change she could make, while no one else does

She is different, everyone sees
She isn't average, everyone sees
She's a loner, everyone sees

You try to reach out to her
While no one else does
You try to help her succeed
While no one else does
She asks you why you help her
While no one else does

You look into her eyes, her soul
That no one sees
You tell her what you see
That no one sees
You see a visionary
While no one else does

Jennifer Strine, Grade 9
Spring Grove Area Sr High School

The Passage

Always controlling us.
Always controlling all our thoughts and moves.
It is an invention of our own,
And a silly one at that.
It is the most controlling thing I know.
Always creating confusion and stress.
Determining when and where we go.
It drives me crazy.
It is like a schizophrenic and voices.
It is always there,
I know it is always happening.
No matter how hard I try.
I still can always tell,
That time is passing,
And bringing me along.

Joe Carter, Grade 8
Bellmar Middle School

The Last Leaves of Autumn

Leaves come in all sizes and shapes
Leaves embellish all landscapes
Leaves in the fall turn many colors
The fall foliage can be beautiful to some,
But to others it can be a mess of dreaded chores
When they finally plummet to the ground,
Where the base of the trunk meets the earth
They will create a strung out pile waiting to be raked
Each and every leaf has its own distinguishable features

As fall comes to an end and winter starts to take shape
You can be sure to look out your window and see,
A bare tree with only,
The last leaves of autumn still hanging on, because
Each and every leaf has its own distinguishable features

Alex Ayers, Grade 7
Landisville Middle School

The Foul Ball I Could've Had

Ryan Howard is up in the bottom of the 5th
In his cherry-red uniform
Instead of a home run, CLANCK
A line drive foul ball over my head, no chance
Awakened by the ringing of a rail
The ball started plummeting back down to earth
In a flash, a teenager with a broken arm
Pulled his arm out of a sling
And caught the ball with three fingers
It was the best catch ever, even if it wasn't by me

Thomas Meinert, Grade 7
Holicong Middle School

My Pap

Pap was what I called him,
While others called him Jim.
He had a whistle like a bird,
Probably the best I've ever heard.
Even toward the end he never lost his perk,
He even managed to continue his yard work.
Pap had a slew of things he loved to do;
Painting, sports, and building too.
But now that we are at the end,
There is an empty place in our hearts that even he cannot mend.

Lauren Ritz, Grade 8
Sewickley Academy

I'll Prove You Wrong

Don't tell me I'm not good enough,
Because I'll prove you wrong.
The more you say I'm a bad singer,
The louder I'll sing my song.

The more you say my hair isn't long enough,
The shorter I'll cut my hair.
The more you say you hate my style,
The crazier clothes I'll wear.

So yell at me, beat me up,
I'm used to it, immune.
Tell me I'll never achieve my dreams,
It means nothing coming from you.

Because the more you say I am a bad singer,
The louder I sing my song.
So don't tell me I'm not good enough,
Because I will prove you wrong.

Emma Kobb, Grade 8
Chichester Middle School

The Beach

A cool breeze sweeps by,
As the waves wash the sand
Under my toes.
Children laughing, sharing jokes on their towels.
Dogs run, fast and far, yipping at gulls.
Boats floating beyond reach on ocean waves,
In the endless water.
Shells and
Seaweed
Lay in the sand, as pretty as diamonds and gold.
Palm trees sway to the rhythm of the sea breeze.
The sun's rays lightly dance across the water,
Bright and graceful like dancers on water.
The salty smells fill the air,
Carried with the wind.
The cool waves hit my feet as I pass along the shoreline,
Reaching out,
And finding nothing but the sand.
Peaceful and soothing.

Megan Shea, Grade 7
St Thomas More School

The Shining Moon

The moon beaming in the night sky,
Draws attention to my eye.
Sometimes it looks as if it smiles down at me,
A million miles away.
The black sky provides the perfect scene.
Oh what a sight.
The moon beaming on a winter's night,
Shining bright throughout the night.

Ty Zborovancik, Grade 8
Bellmar Middle School

The World

Where is the place God put us to live?
It's a place where we sin, and learn to forgive.

It spins on its axis, all year round,
It doesn't stop rotating, around and around.

Whenever we look, our eyes catch a glance,
Of diverse countries, such as the USA, Italy, and France.

Some tourists travel it, all their lives,
They might've gone for a hike, a tour, or maybe even deep-sea-dives.

This world was a beautiful place, but what a shame,
That is have been ruined by popularity and fame.

I believe we need to go back to the original plan,
Where God envisioned us walking hand, in hand.

Emma Saftner, Grade 7
St James School

Without Light

Fear is a suffocated, rising scream,
Welling up inside of you, but no sound can escape,
It's the dropping, chilled feeling in your stomach
When you find the truth.
It's the whisperer with no form,
And the footsteps of your heartbeat.
Flames charring your memories,
And a last goodbye in sight…
Fear is being locked inside yourself,
Your own walls caving in.
It's the storm that roars endlessly,
And the waves of regret that could kill.
Fear is the thought that you could break, snap, at any moment.
It's wondering what lies where the street lamps don't reach
Because fear is not the days in the dark,
But what the light will reveal,
When it returns.

Kylie Brown, Grade 7
Schuylkill Valley Middle School

Raptor

Clink, clink, clink, the sound of the climbing neon-green Raptor.
Then screaming, screaming, screaming,
when the car starts falling, falling, falling.
Over,
under,
around,
across,
the path the deadly Raptor takes,
while weaving through the tracks.
Flung high, skimming the ground,
Twisting, turning, slowing down,
and suddenly midnight-black graveyard silence.

Garret Sutterlin, Grade 7
Holicong Middle School

The Poor

Walking down the street
I see the poor
I see where they sleep and eat
I have no more

For they're going down the slope
You may say
They're even losing hope
Each and every day

You may give them a gift
Like food and water they may pray
But they are still adrift
What they really want is a place to stay

A nice home
With a comfy bed
To call their own
So they may rest their head

Right next to a mother or father
With a nice big smile
That they know they're your son or daughter
That will last awhile

Dylan Houser, Grade 9
Armbrust Wesleyan Christian Academy

Life Is a Roller Coaster

Two kids are at the Rapid Rolling Roller Coaster Amusement Park
They are sitting on a bench, they are eating lunch
They are silent, they are happy, then one of them says:
What did we just ride? While the other ignores and says…

"What do you think of life?" I asked my friend
He answered, "I think life is…fun and happy,
Good and nice, scary and funny, a gift from God,
Entertaining and religious."

"What do you think of a roller coaster?" I asked my friend
"Exciting and wild, happy and cool, awesome and amazing,
Scary and funny, entertaining."
"What do you think?" My friend asked

"I feel like life is a roller coaster, It has ups and downs,
Twists and turns, highs and lows, awesomes and amazings
Joys and scares, but both are gifts form God."

He replied, "Why is that?"
I replied, "We were just on a roller coaster."
"It had ups and downs, highs and lows, it had joys and scares,
awesomes and amazings,
And it was a gift from God."

Sammy Porter, Grade 7
St Joseph School

The Waves

Every day I watch the waves
I see them drop and float away.
I see them dancing along the ocean beaches
Just to see them barely out of reach
Every night I hear the sounds,
Of every wave, crashing down.
It is delightful every dawn
Just as if it was created in human hands
But yet it wasn't,
It was created by God's bands.

Dylan Mulroney, Grade 7
Landisville Middle School

A Snowy Day

The air is chilled all around
As activity bustles through the town
Snow is gently falling flake by flake
Each one delicate and unique
As the ground is covered with a blanket of snow
The sun looks as though it glows
Branches slightly swaying in the breeze
As all the leaves have left their trees
The birds echo in the sky
As the clouds hover up above high

Brianna Byler, Grade 7
Landisville Middle School

Friends

What are friends?
Friends are people, who are supposed to care
Friends are people, who are always there
Friends can change just like the seasons
It hurts to lose a friend
Especially for a stupid reason
When you lose a friend,
Maybe you can gain one back
Because when you're not with them
It feels like you're under attack.

Valerie Fiorentino-Martin, Grade 7
Armstrong Middle School

Christmas Eve

The excitement flows through the air,
as children run through the snow without a care.
They know Santa will come soon,
So they look at the moon,
to see if the reindeer run by.
They go inside to have some pumpkin pie.
They laugh and have fun with their families,
And enjoy the Christmas spirit.
Christmas Eve,
A time to believe.

Lindsey Collins, Grade 7
J R Fugett Middle School

The Human in Me

It's humoring that they call us humans, because sometimes, I feel as if I have a piece of every animal inside.

Long, curly hair runs wild and free with the wind, like a horse's mane when it's galloping.
And, like a horse as well, I startle easily to sounds like thunder or the creaking of the black barn roof.

Looking deeper inside, my personality is like a young puppy. One moment I am peppy and hyper,
Playing games and goofing off with friends, the next moment, collapsing off into deep slumber from exhaustion.

Sometimes I feel like a fish swimming across the vast ocean, curiosity telling me to explore every nook, every cranny,
Every reef, every crack in the opaque, black rocks. But conscience shouts, "No! That's dangerous!"
I feel so confused, so lost, so aggravated, so torn.

At other times I am like a cheetah, strong, athletic, confident in myself. Bolting onto the field, the jungle I need to find rhythm in.
My position is half-back, a field hockey defender, protecting the goal so the ball won't race in, protecting the den so the ferocious
enemy won't invade, the rival cheetahs.

But still, digging farther and farther into my soul, I'm a moody, sneaky calico cat. Keeping secrets, slinking around,
Lashing out at anyone trying to comfort me. Later I am a quiet, understanding rabbit. I apologize by nuzzling them with my tiny,
wet nose. As consolation, I let them pet my fur, soft and spotted.

Then, I am a baby mouse, miniscule, helpless, that spots a giant, menacing cat, teeth thrashing, sharp nails flashing.
I scamper into my warm, inviting hole, quickly moving, so that I am huddled against my soothing mom for comfort.

Though all of these animals describe me, deep down inside, in the core of my soul, there's a part, a section of me,
That I'll never fully be able to describe in words…
The human in me.

Lydia Halkias, Grade 7
Mellon Middle School

The Life of a Child

Life was great as a child.
The mile long smile I had on my face when I got that huge pink and purple doll house for Christmas.
The fun I had when my brother and I would play Star Wars and fight with light savors.
My mom cheering for my brother as he dashed down the football field for a touchdown.

I remember getting older and life getting harder.
The heart breaking news I felt when my parents said that we were going to move to Kentucky.
The big loading trucks in front of my house to put our belongings in it.
The day I was lying on my bed crying because my mother wanted to divorce my father.
The excitement I felt when my father said we were going to move back to PA.

Getting older is not how I planned it would be when I was young.
There are no rocket ships in my back yard.
No super heroes with funny looking costumes.
No ugly, man eating monsters under the bed or in your closet.
And those imaginary friends seemed to have faded away.

Things do not always happen the way you think will happen.
I did not think we were ever going to move.
I did not expect a divorce.
Or my dad getting remarried in 2009. And gaining two step brothers.
But in the end being older is pretty good.
So now I guess I have to wait to see what will come of me in the future.
Hopefully there are more light savors!!!

Megan Stauffer, Grade 9
Conrad Weiser High School

They've Changed

I walk to the bus stop eager to speak
To my friend about the cartoon last week
But as I begin to unravel my thinking
He swiftly changes the subject, not even blinking

As I take my seat in science that day
Looking to my left my mind goes astray
Kids wearing Hollister I'm stuck with Gap
They're all the popular kids I feel like crap

As I walk pass by the lunch tables looking for mine
My friends aren't there, a chill down my spine
They sit with kids way out of my league
I sit by myself enclosed in fatigue

A girl who I like texts me that night
About homework, I reply, filled with delight
Until I ask her if she'd like to chat
And she says she has to go, and leaves it at that

I'm lying in bed and I think for a while
When had been the last time I truly gave a smile
My friends have changed in confusing schemes
Things don't make sense, but one question gleams

Why have they changed, and why haven't I?
Adam Prager, Grade 8
Saucon Valley Middle School

My Cat

She hits a toy with her paw,
Then stops and pretends no one saw,
Her ears seem tall for her,
Listen and you'll hear her purr.

There's one plant,
That she tries to resist but can't,
It's her catnip summer treat,
That she loves to eat.

She sleeps on anything in sight,
She sleeps all day and all night,
At night when she's in bed,
She puts her paw under her head.

She doesn't bother any other animals or pets,
She still has a ton to do yet,
She has to give herself a bath by tongue,
To make herself look pretty and young.

The thing she likes best,
Is when the family is up and not at rest,
When the family is here,
She always stays near.
Aislynn Lowery, Grade 7
Landisville Middle School

My Shoes

I have these wonderful pair of shoes
For one reason or another I always seem to lose.

They're a majestic purple with an enormous green dot,
They sound really weird, but I like them a lot.

I've hunted and searched almost everywhere,
I'm becoming quite frustrated, ready to pull out my hair.

My mom says stop looking and put on another funky pair,
But those are the only ones I want to wear.

If I have to look till dawn, I'll stay up all night,
If anyone tells me to stop I'll put up a fight.

It's getting late, where do I look now?
Wait, I hear something strangely familiar, meow.

Ugh that's just my fat stupid black cat,
He's a ball of fur just waiting to attack.

Wait there they are right under him,
I would have seen them if he were slim.

I am now so mad that they have been here all along,
Why didn't I look here before, I've been looking for so long!
Molly DeFilippo, Grade 7
St James School

Ode to Chocolate

Purely scrumptious,
that's what you are.
So creamy, so sweet.
You leave me begging for more.

You are the center of my happiness.
With your strong arms,
you lift me up and out
of the sad and depressing cave
I sometimes climb into.

Kids happily snatch you from the store counter,
their faces full of glee.
They await the dramatic moment
when they can finally unwrap
the gleaming silver wrapper
to uncover your velvety, smooth, rectangular body.

Because of your favorable flavor,
you could be wed with almost anything.
Peanut butter, cookies, strawberries, ice cream.
The list goes on and on.
Oh dearest chocolate,
thank you for being so delicious.
Courtney Byrne, Grade 7
Jefferson Middle School

Dance Like There's Nobody's Watching

Late afternoon
Several bodies swarm
All inside one single door
Lights hit the ground
All the different styles
Begin with a song
Long painful exercises
Quick thunderous claps
Never giving up
Remain
Slippery dead bars
Holding baby-pink point shoes
Perfect and precise
Sweat, tears, and groans
Grasping the stage one final time
Recital
Ruby-red curtains
Each dancer takes the place
Time goes by too quickly
No turning back
Dance like there's nobody watching
Sarah Burton, Grade 7
Holicong Middle School

Who Gives Smiles

Gabby,
Honest, funny, caring and helpful,
Sister of Crystal, Michael, Sam, Kim
And Abby.
Lover of poetry, happiness of people,
And the bright summer sun,
Who feels nervous in front of a
Crowd, happiness at the beach,
And sadness at the sight of people
In pain.
Who needs weekends, books, and
Friends.
Who gives smiles, support, and
Happiness.
Who fears pain, spiders and the end of a
Good book.
Who would like to see peace all
Over, more respect for others, and
Better housing or the poor.
Who lives in a small red house
on Chadwick Avenue.
Gabby Lanholm, Grade 8
Chichester Middle School

Mistakes

We all have made them
It's the nature of man…yet
They divide our souls
Andrew Choffo, Grade 7
Charles F Patton Middle School

Portfolios

I really have better things to do.
All these projects make me blue.
Math, programming, literature too,
Portfolios for all, the same day due.
Where should I start? How do I begin?
Disliking teachers and school, is that a sin?
Distractions and lack of motivation have I
Parental pressure causes me to cry.
Anxiety, anger, confusion I feel
Are these subjects all for real?
No fun, no enjoyment, no time
Must this poem always rhyme?
Will these portfolios ever away fade?
I wonder if I will still get a good grade.
Now that I have complained all day
What new portfolio will come my way?
Sarah Knuth, Grade 8
Commonwealth Connections Academy

Not Friends; Sisters

Not Friends; Sisters
Late morning
Bright and sunny
Big bustling moving van
Dirt-brown dog
Running oh so speedily
Dusty rusty car
Smell of chocolate chips trailing like smoke
Immediate eye contact
Laughter stinging the air
The hose blasts
Water sprays
The car sparkling
Not Friends; Sisters
Amanda Kilgore, Grade 7
Holicong Middle School

Cat vs Mouse

I quickly scurried along the wall
    to snatch away some cheese,
But then I heard the deadly call
    of the family's Siamese.

I shoved the cheese inside my cheek,
    and made a dash for my hole,
But around the corner did I peek
    to see eyes as black as coal.

I jerked away in the other direction
    with the eyes right on my tail,
But without my hole as my protection,
    there was no place to bail.
Megan R. Fogelsanger, Grade 8
Faith Tabernacle School

Sushi Is Awesome

starvation
sweat and
anticipation

that
chopstick-
licking good stuff

proper sitting
whispering and not
knowing why
peering through
open windows

"treat food"
bittersweet
frigid and juicy

creative
stylish
life
Elsa Rash, Grade 7
William M Meredith School

A Beautiful Day in Jamaica

The sun smiles at me
    brightly from above.
The waves welcome me
with their light and pulling tug.

The sand is as white as snow
as it falls lightly to the ground.
The sea is as blue as the sky
when it shimmers all around.

The streets are bustling,
filled with music and laughter.
The smells of different foods fill the air.
The street vendors catch my eye,
    "Oh! Look at that!"
What a beautiful day in Jamaica.

Friends unite to have a good time,
to dance and eat with each other.
The steel drums play while the sun sets
on a beautiful day in Jamaica.
Meghan Fleming, Grade 7
Richboro Middle School

The Pond

Sun and trees reflect
Water like glittering sparks
Pretty reflections
Gwendolyn Buckley, Grade 7
Charles F Patton Middle School

Teardrops

Teardrops glisten,
Precariously perched on the lashes,
Things of deceiving beauty,
Crystals forged from sorrow.
They decorate me,
Like dew decorates grass,
Gently rolling down my shuddering face,
A product of my sadness.
They are back again,
But different this time,
Still decorating a trembling face,
But trembling in relief, not sorrow.
Teardrops glisten,
Precariously perched on the lashes,
Things of honest beauty,
Crystals forged from joy.
Nicholas Wrigley, Grade 8
Sandy Run Middle School

Inferno

As the wind rolls by
I heave with a sigh
and breathe in the morning air
I know I shouldn't really care
but the fire is coming
and the bees are still humming
yet the land, hills, mountains, and valleys
will all be at earth's galleys
for the end of the season is near
and the dragons plundering will be here
I fear for the life of many
and the land that has brought them plenty
the inferno of its breath
means your certain death
for the dragon fire will come
and nothing can be done.
Luke Eberwein, Grade 7
St. Thomas More School

Christmas

It's almost here
This is a time to sing and cheer

This holiday's fun
It's a good time for everyone

If you've been bad
This holiday will be so sad

If you've been great
I bet you can't wait

Family and friends
I hope this holiday never ends
Shawn Yardley, Grade 7
Armstrong Middle School

Duel of the Fencers

Heavy blades screech by your head
taunting you to frustrate you
tricking you with feints and jabs.

Round 2 has just begun
you block and you dodge
but it keeps on coming
taunting, tricking, and devastating
as a jab of pain goes up your arm.

Your anger…spurs
you strengthen, and leap,
towards the enemy sword.

It screeches away with a cry of pain,
and you lunge forward.
your rival,
utterly defeated.
Roman Nikonov, Grade 7
Strath Haven Middle School

My Father

My father tells stories
From long ago
Before he knew of me
He was a child once
Although it's hard to believe
He was a troublemaker, too
He speaks of movies
Of teachers
Of schools
Of people
People who are long gone
He talks about his mother
And his father as well
Neither of which I have met
I see tears in his eyes
And suddenly I hope it's me someday
Telling those same stories
To my children
Liz Wetjen, Grade 8
Coventry Christian Schools

Long Live Freedom

They rushed by
Leaving me behind
To ponder on
What's going on
We are doing what is right
Taking back what is ours
The common man
The hard workers
The world is ours
That was when we ruled the world.
Dylan Hutchinson, Grade 8
Bangor Area Middle School

Ode to the Beach

Waiting and waiting to get to you.
Finally, I am here!
I step out and
The salty ocean and the cool breeze hits me.
I hear the beach calling me.
I run to the ocean and…
Crash!
A wave brakes before my eyes.
My hair blows back.
I sit down to take it all in.
I start to dig my feet into the sand but,
The sand crawls between my toes.
It is so exciting.
I hear a bell…then I hear,
Ice cream!
I run and get my favorite, a chipwhich.
As I sit and enjoy it I think,
This day could not get any better.
The perfect day comes to an end.
I say good-bye to my second home,
The beach.
Darby Borden, Grade 7
Richboro Middle School

The Storm

The wind whispers lies in my ear:
"Don't be afraid. I don't bite."
I hear her loud stomping,
While I see her flashlight shine over me,
Her next victim.
The trees grab at the power lines,
Attempting to break my connection to light.
The rain knocks impatiently on the door,
Wanting to come in.
She seems never ending.
Her determination showing
With every gust of wind.
Every crack of thunder.
Every bolt of lightning.
Every blowing tree.
Every drop of rain.
Until…
Everything ceases.
Silence. Stillness. Peacefulness.
She has moved on.
She has found a new victim.
Olivia Spring, Grade 7
Strath Haven Middle School

Tears

Water drips downward —
Bleeding the hue of sorrow.
Murdering my soul.
Nicholas Yang, Grade 7
Charles F Patton Middle School

Spring Is Right Around the Corner

Hop-hop goes the Easter bunny, as it visits family and friends.
Bees start their search for honey, In all of the flowers' curves and bends.
Spring is right around the corner.

Winter is coming to a close, and the snow finally is at a stop.
The green slowly shows, and the bunny's ears flop.
Spring is right around the corner.

Purple, pink, and yellow are the flowers, red and orange are very bold.
There are days of sun and days of showers, no more days of purely cold.
Spring is right around the corner.

Seeing people smile from ear to ear, laughing with happiness and joy.
We know it's that fun time of year, For the bunny to visit a girl and a boy.
Spring is right around the corner.

Feeling the breeze blow on your skin, and the sweet smelling scent in the air.
Spending the day with your kin, who not only love, but also care.
Spring is right around the corner.

Easter egg hunts are open to beginners. Easter eggs are all different colors and shapes.
Hurry and hunt quickly to be the winners, for they may even be hidden in the drapes.
Spring is right around the corner.

Blue skies are a pleasure, they brighten up my life.
Each day is like opening a new treasure, like spring weddings, when two people become husband and wife.
Spring is my best friend.

Tessie Kalathas, Grade 7
St Joseph School

Nature's Gift

I look outside to see a crowd of happy children playing in the crisp, fresh leaves.
The wind is light, yet it blows the fragile leaves around in the air like graceful, splendid blimps.
I tighten my coat as I start to walk, and to my surprise my eyes are filled
With a firework display of orange, red, brown, and light green leaves.
Every step creates a short "boom" of a crunch.
The sun's rays filter through spreading warmth around my body.
The air is brisk and cool as it complements the lush trees and grass.
The leaves sway back and forth as if involved in a joyous jig.
Flowers of maroon, magenta, yellow, red, and rose-pink are scattered in the tan mulch.
Bees buzz around to collect the last of their pollen.
All is well as the atmosphere is calm and relaxed.
The sun races in the sky as sparks of red and pink highlight the soon-to-be-evening sky.
Temperature dips and the leaves become stiff as if preparing for the night's sleep.
The sun lowers into the horizon as the blue sky pigments into a dark navy-blue.
The breeze once again blows slightly lulling the town to sleep.
The sun has set and the children retire into their homes.
I look around and go to my own cabin.
What is this? I ask myself.
And I say to myself it is nature's gift
The season of fall.

Lasya Rangavajjula, Grade 8
Arcola Intermediate School

What Is the Meaning of Life

A gentleman asked me "What is the meaning of life?"
The words immediately struck me like a knife
I thought it over, night and day
And finally, I called the gentleman to say,
The meaning of life is being kind and happy
Laughing, singing, and writing stories that are sappy
Treat others the way you want to be treated
Have fun and live life to the fullest
Call your loved ones to say
"I love you dearest"
Cry, let your miseries out and share your experiences
Years from now when they ask you "What's life's true meaning?"
You tell them "I am life's true meaning, end, and its beginning"

Sophia Soleta, Grade 8
St Thomas More School

Cheese Steak Calzone

8 p.m. after a Friday night football game
Hear the sizzle and frying of my fresh-cut onions
Melted cheese drips out of the loaf
Green and red peppers scattered throughout the sandwich
Succulent slabs of steak
Slightly hardened bread, gold as a dollar sign necklace
Insides soft and mushy. That's the good part, but not the best
Salt and pepper slightly added
Heavy loaves of bread
My stomach growling, hungry and appetized
Ketchup added to every bite
Plate clean, stomach quiet and full, all drooling has stopped
Stuffed for the night, I can only think of what I'll get next time.

Michael A. Gresko IV, Grade 7
Holicong Middle School

Ice Cream

I love this word.
C ertainly on a hot summer day.
E specially when going for a long walk in the

C ity.
R eally hot and tired, but,
E ating ice cream.
A re there more pleasurable,
M oments than this one?!

Valya Nazarenko, Grade 8
Chichester Middle School

December Love

December
Cold, snowy
Snowing, freezing, celebrating
December gets dark earlier, but light shines at Christmas.
Gift-giving, Christmas caroling, sledding
Fun, happy
December

Joseph Viggiano, Grade 7
Holy Child Academy

A Sweet Slumber

Drifting away quickly too quickly for my liking.
My breathing is scarce and s l o w,
but steady in its solemn beat.
Tonight, will fear slip into my mind like a sly silent cat?
Or will a ray of shining hope come beaming in as my hero?
Maybe I will stay,
In my peaceful serenity and forget what happens tonight.

But my eyelids are heavy weights
too hard to bear.
Pulling
dragging
slowly
d
o
w
n.
While my reality seems to die
till night subsides.

Isabelle Stringer, Grade 8
St Thomas More School

Austrian Exploits

My parents' trip to Austria
Had many wonders in store.
When they went to check the Salzberg Cathedral
A towering dome they found in its core.

Mozart's residence held many surprises,
Destroyed in World War II.
Yet there stood the piano, not harpsichord,
Looking as good as if it were new.

Vienna was the next stop on their trip
Where they saw Hofburg Palace,
Which boasted many ornate fountains,
With silver settings, including a chalice.

Austria overall's a great place to go;
There are so many sites to see.
So when my parents return I'll ask,
Why in the world they didn't take me.

Nathan Master, Grade 8
The American Academy

My Best Season

Fall is the best season of all
Some call it autumn, but fall is my call
In the year, it's our third season
The leaves, the chill, are two of my reasons
It is not too hot nor too cold.
If fall was for sale, in a minute it would be sold.
So, ask me again what my best season is of them all
Now you know that I would pick fall!

Adam Berry, Grade 8
Chichester Middle School

Real Friends

Real friends cry with you
They don't watch you cry
Real friends stick with you
They don't leave you
Real friends make you happy
They don't make you sad
Real friends tell the truth
They wouldn't tell a lie
Real friends give you good advice
They don't' watch you do something bad
When you have a real friend
They stick with you 'til the end
That is what real friends are!

Katie Knight, Grade 7
Armstrong Middle School

Crocodile

It's hungry
Slightly submerged underwater
It finds its prey.
Wait for it, wait for it now, POW!
He launches himself into his prey
While all the other ones run away.
Dragging his prey deeper into the water
He drowns it
It's time for a feast!
Crunching, chomping, devouring
It's gone, all that's left are the bones
All you animals out there watch out
Because this reptile will be waiting for you!

Savion Grazette, Grade 7
Greencastle-Antrim Middle School

Life Is a Roller Coaster

Life is a roller coaster,
Full of thrills and chills,
Ups and downs,
Positives and negatives,
From start to finish.
With not one track but two,
Good and bad,
Smart and dumb,
Easy and hard.
But in the end everyone is happy,
With no regrets,
Knowing they had fun.
Even though no one asks.

Garrett Wholf, Grade 7
Holicong Middle School

Morning

Mist filling the air.
Birds chirping and trees swaying
Early in the day.

Casey Shaw, Grade 7
Trinity Middle School

Meant to Be

Some people are meant to be together,
Yet no one realizes,
Except for one.
As I walk past,
I can see the eagerness in his eyes,
Yet his face remains expressionless.
I can sense his impatience,
As he waits for her.
I can feel my heart shatter.
It feels as if my heart is made of glass,
And it has been dropped onto a cold, colorless concrete floor.
The tiny shards glint in the overwhelming light.
It seems useless to try and piece it back together,
I feel that I should just sweep up my heart's remains and throw them away.
But instead I put an impenetrable case around the small fragments.
I promise myself to leave the case there,
Leave it there until I can piece my broken heart back together.
It may take centuries,
But I know I must move on,
Even if,
It was meant to be…

Lauren Guthre, Grade 7
Indian Valley Middle School

Good vs Evil

What is evil? Evil is pain, the Devil gripping your flesh with excruciating pain, nails gripping into your skin dragging you down into the depths of hell. Evil is a knife slicing in the darkness, breaking your skin in pain.

Good comes in and stops the blood loss flying up into the cloud, filling you with happiness realizing that you've seen the light and seeing your dog once lost.

But what's in the middle of good and evil? Is it melancholy? It's not quite good and not quite sad. Will the world come to an end? Evil is silence filling a room full of mourning people. Good is everything you'd ever imagine.

So please break my confusion cruel world. Is this what we are living in?

Julia Murphy, Grade 7
William M Meredith School

Archery

It's 1:00 in the afternoon
The sunlight makes my arrows shimmer silver
I hear the snap of the arrow notching onto the bowstring
Through the sight I can see the goldfinch-yellow of the bull's-eye
The aroma of the outdoors fills my nose
I can feel the pressure of the bowstring against my hand
The camp archery range disappears as I get ready to let loose my final arrow
Whoosh, the arrow flies through the air
Thock, the arrow sinks into the bull's-eye
The whistle blows
I feel the dirt underfoot
The match is over and I am the victor

Tristan Marshall, Grade 7
Holicong Middle School

True Self

It's not meant to be hidden
Not supposed to be a lie.
But instead to be shown,
To be seen.
To be appreciated.
Don't try to run from it,
Embrace it.
Be proud of it.
It's you.
Not anybody else.
It's you.
It's the real you.
Who you are,
Who you should want to be.
It's not anybody else,
Not anyone else.
Just your true self.

Paige Parshall, Grade 8
Bellmar Middle School

The Beginning of School

School has now begun.
Summer was just short-lived fun.

I wish I could be in the pool,
But now I'm stuck in school.

Waiting for time to pass,
While in second period math class.

When trying to divide a fraction,
The window is a big distraction.

I can't wait until the final bell,
To tell my teacher farewell.

Longing for the end of the year,
Can't wait for summer to be here.

Alexis Griesacker, Grade 7
St James School

The Mirror Friend

The friend I see every day
Never runs astray
The friend I see in the store window
I can tell her everything
Whether a cry or yell
She won't laugh or judge
If I do something wrong she's still there
At night she tends to go away
But at the break of sunlight
I see her again
She is The Mirror Friend
Who's just like me

Josie Clymer, Grade 7
Armstrong Middle School

My Inspiration

You who inspire me
Without any strife
You help me
You love me
You're always a part of my life

When I was young
I sat on your lap
You are my partner
The one I call "Pap"

From music to softball
You are always on my side
Cheering and coaching
You are a perfect guide

You're my inspiration
You push me to do more
I love you with all my heart
You're the one I will always adore

My Father

Olivia Jenkins, Grade 7
Armstrong Middle School

Snow Boarding

Swwwwwisshhh!
As I furnish a sharp curve
Snow springing into
The air, I straighten up with the ramp
I bend my knees 90 degrees
Attempting to gain speed, I hit the slope
Twisting my body 180 degrees before I soar
Into the air I feel like I'm flying
I retrieve back down to the ground
And nailed the landing
I climb back up the hill to go
For the next jump

Kalil Poe, Grade 7
William M Meredith School

Cats

I hear the soft
Sound of little feet
Coming this way
Then she leaps onto my lap

She sits and stares
Soft, shiny, black fur. I hear the
Soft faint sound of purring.

My cat Bella, small, cute, soft, and black
Gets up and jumps down and all I can
Hear is little feet walking away

Melanie Gonzalez, Grade 7
William M Meredith School

Amidst the Blizzard

In winter
above the earth,
you will find me.

Atop the hill,
among the snow,
Amidst the blizzard
I feel brave.

Despite the cold.
On top of my sled,
throughout my body,
chills race.

Alongside my friends,
during the snowfall.
We challenge and joke,
against the wind.

Above the world,
without a fear.
I descend.

Galen Sunseri, Grade 7
Jefferson Middle School

A Man

There once was a man
He changed his life
Because he accepted Christ
The god he knew he had to please or die
But the real God gave him grace
And loved him unconditionally
His life was hard
His faith was in God
So God got him through
God loves him and you
How about your "God?"

Sierra Watts, Grade 7
Blue Ridge Middle School

Dream Place

There it is
The most beautiful
Place on earth
Where everything is
About the beauty of nature
Blossom flowers
Magnificent trees
The place where
I'm liked for just being me
Everything so great
Nonviolence place
Where killing is impossible
The sweetest place on Earth.

Fatu Kanu, Grade 8
Henry C. Lea School

The One Who Was Waited For

He is such a sweet child,
Oh so nice and mild.
The boy loves and cares,
His spirit is in the air.
It is all around us,
Feels right and just.
The feeling of love
Is like a beautiful dove
Soaring through the air,
He is everywhere.
He watches you even though you don't know it,
His presence makes your hopes lift.
He sits up in heaven,
Now an adult.
You should praise and adore Him.
He is the one who saved us,
The one who was waited for.

Caitlin Hoeing, Grade 7
St Thomas More School

Bible

The Bible is a special book,
So open it up; take a look.

There are so many people, such as Adam and Eve,
Many sinned, but all believed.

Bibles are found almost anywhere,
You can also call it the Book of Common Prayer.

The Bible contains stories of women and men,
Who we can copy, now and then.

If we all read this amazing book,
We all would have a better outlook.

So read this book from cover to cover,
And you'll be amazed at what you can discover.

Dylan Osheka, Grade 7
St James School

Imagine

Imagine
A world with no hate
Imagine
A world where race doesn't matter
Imagine
A world with no lies
Imagine
A world where what gender you are doesn't matter
Imagine
A world with no crime
Imagine
A world where you can love who you want
Imagine
A world with no death
Imagine
A world where we are all treated equally
Just Imagine

Maya Brown-Hunt, Grade 7
Holy Child Academy

The Forest

The forest is a wonderful place,
It is full of danger and grace.

The animals roam wild and untamed,
None of the creatures are quite the same.

Some are big and some are small,
Some are short and some are tall.

The trees of the forest twist and turn,
Growing through the ground great and firm.

The forest provides protection from critters,
Just as a mother protects her own litter.

The forest is alive during any time of year,
It truly is a wonderful frontier.

Stephen Jancart, Grade 8
St James School

My Home Sweet Home

What   is
home?   Home is
not a physical location.
Home is a place where you
are not afraid to show and
express yourself. Home is a place
where you   can share joy
and love   with your
friends and   family. A
home is a   place where
you feel safe   and secure.
It is where   you belong.

Shanelle Ileto, Grade 7
Good Shepherd School

The Candy Bag

The candy seems to jump at me whenever I walk by
And when I take a peek at them they seem to smile at the light
They like it when I reach in the bag and take a piece out
They like all the attention they receive
They like all the smiles they put on my face
The chocolate kind is my favorite
Their taste is so great
It seems they were made special for me with all the attention I get
They dance right on top of my tongue
Tingling my taste buds with every second
When I swallow the candy they seem to cha cha slide in my stomach
And sing until they can't anymore

Jesse Jacobsen, Grade 7
Strath Haven Middle School

The Show Stopper
Today is the day, I will strut in my first show,
Styled in luscious clothing from head to toe.
With curls billowing down my back and the perfect smoky eye,
I look across the room and see my dream guy.

The music is blaring as it begins to play,
Slow and steady I strut onto the runway.
Then I saw the guy again, he looked like he had been sent from heaven,
With his beauteous high bone structure and eyes as blue as an ocean, out of ten he was an eleven.

Slowly, and surely, I turned around,
I felt my dress tickling the ground.
Elegantly, I walked in my glitzy, heart-covered dress,
When I saw him again my smile was like a light bulb, it was him I had to impress.

Now, it was time for my final look,
I saw my dream guy and my breath he took.
When the show was over I found out his name,
Now that Joe is in my life, it will never be the same.

Lindsey Schlackman and Lauren Kintzley, Grade 8
Sandy Run Middle School

Playtime
WOOF! WOOF! It's 6:00 A.M., my usual wake up time.
My alarm clock jumps on my tired, smooth face.
His strong, hard head smacks against my head as I drift back asleep.
His long, soft, golden tail brushes against my puny toes, as they wiggle from the ticklish feeling of his tail.
I'm laughing with little to no energy, as my eyes as half open, begging me to close them.
His wet, slimy, cold tongue brushes against my smooth, small face, as he is begging me to get out of bed.
It's time to play.
I throw his old, dirty tennis ball down the steep hill.
I play tug-of-war with him, and he always beats me, earning every victory every time.
We lay together on the soft, green grass, taking a very short break.
A couple minutes later, it's play time again.
But now, I have nobody to throw balls to.
Not anybody to play tug-of-war with.
Not one person to lay on the grass with me,
And nobody to wake me up for "playtime."
I cry and cry as I think of all our good memories together.
Will I ever see you again?

R.I.P Quincy
Nov. 24, 2002-Oct 27, 2010

Brynna Haupt, Grade 7
Schuylkill Valley Middle School

A Change Has Come
A beautiful, colorful fall morning, with the trees smelling wet and new.
The unusual days when the warm sun's rays have gone away and drift away to someplace new.
My taste buds go wild with the taste of minty hot chocolate in the chilly fall breeze,
as I am watching the leaves fall to the ground, creating a wet red and gold blanket across my field.
Unified colored leaves fall wet with tears as they leave their homes and fall between my fingers.
From a distance you can hear the crackling of leaves from squirrels collecting food for their winter hibernation.
A nice fall breeze sweeps through my hair, causing it to fly with the wind.
I am nice, calm and relaxed drinking my hot chocolate from the balcony and watching the blanket of fall run over my backyard.

Dominique Edwards-Lofland, Grade 8
J R Fugett Middle School

Hallway

RING
Out we go
People, people everywhere
Push one way shoved the other
Finally the sea breaks
I breathe
RING
Oh no
My footsteps echo
Alone…Accompanied by no one

Isabel Cardi, Grade 7
Strath Haven Middle School

Heroes

Men and women working together
Fighting side by side, eliminating crime.
Loyalty and bravery,
Fighting for their country,
Protecting who they love.
Air or sea or even land.
Officers and soldiers all working together,
Risking their lives for our freedom.
Military soldiers are the
Heroes in our hearts.

Allyson Berstler, Grade 7
Armstrong Middle School

Spunky Pink, Lazy Blue

Part of me is spunky pink –
adventurous and hilarious
Full of energy and sweetness,
Hanging with my friends,
But on some days I feel lazy blue.
Relaxed and clumsy,
Soothing and restless,
This happens on rainy days
They are both sides of me
And they are both very true.

Brianna Hastings, Grade 8
Chichester Middle School

Dandelion Yellow

Some days I'm dandelion yellow –
always smiling and full of laughs,
like my 1 year old nephew when
he sees a car!
Another color I can be is pale
grey, moody, depressed, sad
and self-conscious, tired, frustrated,
and feeling useless,
Don't worry cause today's the day
where I'm dandelion yellow!

Grissel Castillo, Grade 8
Chichester Middle School

Swimming

When I'm up on the block I feel like I'm about to
SWIM   FOR   MY   LIFE
All I see is the length of the pool like there's a barrier only around
MY
Lane
Before I clear my head the last thing I hear is my mom screaming over
EVERYONE
Saying
"YOU CAN DO IT"
All I can
SMELL
Is the chlorine in the water like if it was still dry and I was in the plant it's made at
The only tastes in my mouth is revenge to win over my arch rival
The feel of my calluses against the block hurts
My final goal for this race is to have
MY
Name up on that record board for everyone to see

Mikala Persky, Grade 7
Schuylkill Valley Middle School

A Day of Infamy

Ten short years ago,
Four planes flew into buildings high and low.

In those four planes these terrorists did try,
To take away our country's pride.

They did what they did out of anger, it was not right,
We must learn to forgive, not to fight.

But those who risked their lives for others did not regret,
What they did for their country, we will never forget.

We must stand strong and wave our flags high,
For together, united our country will never die.

The souls of the heroes that gave their life for others now rest in heaven,
We will always remember that day…*9/11.*

Marin Auth, Grade 7
St James School

Sunset Beach

It's 5 p.m. at night,
The gum-pink and fire-orange setting sun is shedding its sparkly glow across the ocean
Gentle soaking sand is spreading across my feet
Peaceful, happy, family relaxing
Itchy sand fills our swim suits
Around us sneaky birds luring to steal our meal
Our deep tans glowing in the small light poking out from behind a cloud
We are the last ones on the beach and it's peaceful
The only sounds are the small sighs of relaxation
Smiles creeping onto our glowing faces

Emma Prajzner, Grade 7
Holicong Middle School

My Grandmother

I remember her sparkling eyes
the way they looked when she was happy
like the ocean — deep and blue
endless mysteries that lay within

I remember her eccentric stories
those in which she escaped the vicious war
fleeing from Hungary for a better life
the remarkable courage — just a little girl

I remember her cooking
always delicious, always ample
the everlasting grease scent
perpetual — she loved it so

I remember her garden
spending the days just watching
fresh grown vegetables, vivid flowers
obtaining all kinds of life

I remember her hug
filled with warmth and love
like a fire on a winter day
always there no matter what

I remember my grandmother
Rachel Szabo, Grade 9
Fox Chapel Area Sr High School

Hockey

Buzz goes the horn
Glean of fresh ice
Rumble of the Zamboni
Whistle of the referee

The crowd is singing
Tapping of the stick
Aroma from locker room
The sweaty gloves

The puck goes down
Crowd roared like lions
Whoosh goes the skates
The booming announcer's voice

Bang goes the checking
Boom of the boards
Clickety, clack, clickety, clack
Referee wears white and black

Snap of the blade
Slide like a penguin
Flick of the blade
Our opponent is slayed
Ryan Lindsay, Grade 7
Arcola Intermediate School

It Rises

Slowly, but steadily,
It starts to creep.
Taking steps, deadly.
It's coming.

Taking its time,
It builds slowly, inside.
It starts to mime,
Previous perils.

It knows what it wants,
Control it desires.
Carefully, it taunts,
The unsuspecting victim.

It's rising,
Breaking all boundaries.
All spirits and hopes, dying,
Finally, it's free.

Raging like fire,
It has come, furious.
The situation is dire,
For Emotion, has broken lose.
Katherine Xu, Grade 8
Holicong Middle School

About Me

Jazz –
Nice, honest, calm and funny
Sister of Zappa and Debra
Lover of hanging out with
    Friends, watching TV and
    being with the people I
    love
Who feels calm in school,
    hyper when I'm outside
    and happy with my friends
Who needs weekends,
    friends and phones
Who gives advice, smiles
    and support
Who fears palamedo bugs,
    alligators and giving
    presentations
Who would like to see
    respect for others, good
    grades and Canada
Who lives in a small green
    house on Cherry St.
– Dougherty
Jazzlynn Dougherty, Grade 8
Chichester Middle School

Silence

I sit in silence
Just sitting, letting my mind wander
But this is far from silent
Birds chirping
Cheep Cheep Chiiirrrrppppppp
Cooooooo
This is far from silent
Leaves on the ground, in the trees
Rattle and rustle in the wind
This is far from silent
Squirrels scuttle around me
Scratch, scratch
They find a nut at the same time
Squeaks pierce the air
This is far from silent
Wind whistles
It screams its eagerness
Knowing winter is soon to come
This is far from silent
I listen, letting the symphony of silence
envelop me
Sarah Myers, Grade 7
Strath Haven Middle School

Not My Real Self

I wake up in the morning
Wearing my true face
When I get to school,
It disappears without a trace.
I see my friends and say,
"Hi!" and "How are you?"
When I really want to say,
"Please leave me alone!"
When I walk into the classroom,
All my peers are smiling
So I do too.
But underneath that smile,
Is a sad, childish expression.
I act like a "goody two shoes"
And join every club.
But in reality, I'm sick of it all!
I can't take it anymore!
Let me out of this cage!!!
No I will not do this and that
For other people!!!
Now, I'm doing something for ME!
Ryan Bain, Grade 7
Armstrong Middle School

Fashion Designer

Sequence, sparkles and
fabric galore are stuffed in
my sewing machine.
Nicole Sternberg, Grade 7
Richboro Middle School

Family

Family so loving and caring
Family always daring
Family love never dies
Family always there for your cries
Family giving and getting
Family always betting
Family love is the best gift you'll get
Family love is best even against your best bet
Family is your own personal sun
Family love is never done
Family love is never breakable
Family love is never interchangeable
Family love is like dancing
Family hearts are always prancing
Family is always together
Family love will never weather
Family love is like a cupcake always sweet
Family love is like a treat
Family love always lasts
Family love is always a blast
Family so loving and caring

Caitlyn Umek, Grade 7
Armstrong Middle School

Summer Silhouettes of Her

When the horizon is right
for the vanishing light,
the silhouette in the trees
leaves feel a slight breeze.

From the window,
I shall watch,
the great macaw linger
straight to my finger.

I trace that dear face,
over and over
through the dark days
without her.

Morgan Carney, Madison Carney and Megan Carney, Grade 7
North Pocono Middle School

My Winter Wonderland

Cold, freezing, need to be covered
When the sun shines on the untouched icy snow
It's almost blinding
Up to my upper shin thick cold and fluffy
The sun is out and slowly, slowly melting
My winter wonderland away, away
In the next year I'll be waiting for my gracious winter wonderland
To come back and fill my eyes with joy
And happiness and fear of losing it again
Although it will always be in my heart
I hate to see it go.

Corey Higgins, Grade 7
Strath Haven Middle School

Soccer

Getting to the field confidently,
When I get out of the car the cold crisp air smacks me in the face,
Chocolate-brown mud everywhere,
Sprint over to my team in excitement,
We practice before the game nervously,
Cherry-red noses everywhere written cold all over them,
The stomach dropping whistle blows in my frostbite-covered ear,
The ball goes every which way,
I have the ball,
I go to net bursting with fear,
Will I make it?
I shoot upper right corner,
Goalie dives,
GOAL!
I score to win the game,
Neon orange jerseys now cover the field screaming,
WE WON!!!!!!!

Hannah Zach, Grade 7
Holicong Middle School

A New Beach Day

Morning:
Marigold-yellow sun peeks over the sleepy blue sky.
Salty-sea-smell whiffs its way around me.
I hear
Planes overhead advertising activities
Smell
Sunscreen, strong, and mighty
See
Children making sandcastles.
I soak in the loud, curious seagulls
Screeching for attention and leftover food.
The warm, grainy sand beneath my toes.
Rough, lively, and bright,
The waves pull me out to sea.
I look above my perch and see multicolored kites
In the hands of the sky.
A new beach day has begun.

Brooke Swales, Grade 7
Holicong Middle School

Solitary Victim

Wasn't it you I saw at the station?
Wasn't it you on that uncertain day?
Isn't it cold outside when you're dying?
Isn't life always a little too late?
Wasn't it youth that built you together?
Wasn't it time that tore you apart?
Isn't it hard to have to remember?
Isn't it sad when there's nothing to say?
Wasn't it you who played your smile loosely?
Wasn't it you who dared to be shown?
Isn't it true that your courage has died?
Isn't your new life like an unopened window?

Russell Little, Grade 7
Pittsburgh CAPA 6-12 School

Highlighted Beauty

An ocean to a mouse,
but a spilled cup to an elephant,
Always flowing,
never any time to rest.
The river holds many wonders and secrets.
As the sun's glare's glittering path
of crystals guide my eyes to its source,
so does the canal,
its surface rippling and wrinkled like an old lady's skin.
It leads all who enter its watery depths
on a journey downstream.

The sea of life,
the riverbanks splashed with green,
as if the water itself took a pen
and highlighted its banks to pronounce its beauty.
The river feeds the plants, which feeds the wildlife.
It pays close attention to muffle
the infinite train of cars and trucks.
So, as the crickets chirp, and the ducks bob on the water,
as I look upon this waterway,
It calms me.

Jacob Richards, Grade 8
Pittsburgh CAPA 6-12 School

My Grandfather*

A quiet guy, but filled with laughs, fun, care and love…
Bravery, strength, honesty and wisdom…
He didn't take no for an answer,
He stood up for what he believed in,
He risked his life fighting for our country,
And didn't live with stuff he didn't like, he told me,
"Never wait for something to happen, make it happen."
He told me to
"Stay strong and don't give up hope."
He treated people with respect and tried to keep others happy,
He thought of others first,
And taught us to do the same,
He grew up losing his older sister, but made the best out of it,
He raised an amazing and loving family,
But one day,
My grandfather was diagnosed with lung cancer.
He fought it on strong, but it was his time,
My grandfather left us…
With his small words of advice, and my family uses them every day
To help make ourselves,
Better people

Valerie Henderson, Grade 7
Strath Haven Middle School
*Dedicated to my grandfather

Popularity

Popularity is something that is big in school
All the kids calling you a fool because you are not cool
But maybe they should get to know you
If they did, they would see how cool you really are

Popularity is something that is not always good
All the kids who lie about what they did or have
But maybe they should think about their futures
And realize where their friends are really taking them

Popularity is something that you can never control
All the kids forcing you to be something you are not
But maybe they should get to know you
They should go on with their lives and leave you to live yours

Franklin Venegas, Grade 7
Armstrong Middle School

Rain Drops Falling

Raindrop fell last night soft, gentle rain
It slid down my roof and banged on my window pane
Woke me up out of a scared sleep
Fixed my heart, too glad to weep
I believe it was too good to be real
All my sorrow was then healed
Shh!!! Listen hear that sound?
That's the soft rain hitting the ground
I hear your voice so loud and clear
Looking around you seem so near
So I opened my window so big and wide
To let the rain all come inside
It kissed my lips and my hair
And that's when I knew you were there

Marpue Gittens, Grade 7
Armstrong Middle School

Wake Me Up

Wake me up wake me up
from this nightmare
why can't anyone hear me scream
it's like I wake up in another dream
each time it's worse and worse
why won't someone just wake me up from this nightmare
WHY CAN'T ANYONE HEAR ME SCREAM
just wake me up

maybe I'm not asleep maybe it's all real

Nick Wolf, Grade 7
Greencastle-Antrim Middle School

Cupcakes

C akes so sweet petite.
U sed for weddings, birthdays and more.
P ink, purple, and blue are some of the icings you can use.
C hocolate or vanilla are the flavors I choose.
A pple cupcakes are what my mom likes.
K angaroo sprinkles are yucky, but cows taste good.
E ggs and flour are what you need, it's a very simple recipe.
S ummer, spring, winter, or fall cupcakes are a hit with all
It's simple you see cupcakes are the thing to eat.
No matter how infamous they are I think cupcakes are a star.

Jennifer Knode, Grade 7
Greencastle-Antrim Middle School

The Steel Family

Our family is a suit of steel armor. Mom, the helmet, protects our heads, our brains, and our minds.
Without her, our family would corrupt abruptly. She serves faithfully, and is trusted to ward off the
dangers of the battlefield.

Stephen is the broadsword, sharpened on a gritty whetstone, and essential in the event of an emergency.
Great for both defensive, and offensive acts, both kind and spiteful, he works best when unsheathed,
ready, and focused. He slices through predicaments with ease, as if he were a knife cutting through a stick of
freshly churned butter.

Anthony is the cuirass, crafted by a very gifted blacksmith, made as a bulwark for the chest, and the heart
full of love. He is the body of the family, and a quality aegis, made tough and dependable, yet still
penetrable, although he serves as a second skin most of the time.

Dad is the pair of greaves, designed painstakingly for more comfort, and maximum mobility, especially if
there's a problem. His purpose is to absorb damage, so it is not felt. He puts up a defense which is the
opposite of paltry, and still maintains balance.

Jenna is the pair of vambraces, which guard our human arms, so we will always possess the ability to
reach out, and heartily greet her, by rubbing her tabby pelt. She is two separate pieces of the set, one
which spends time playing with us, and another serious and hungry.

Jack is the pair of gauntlets, of course, which strengthen his paws, so he can sprint out the door swiftly,
even when he's not allowed to. He favors a good meal, to promote well stamina and endurance, and helps
to grasp and control Stephen, guiding and thrusting him through the opposite warriors.

And I am the armor straps that hold us all together with my love, assuring that everything stays in place,
and nothing is jostled around.

James McCarthy, Grade 7
Strath Haven Middle School

What Life Is Made Of...

All those first of life, make life.
Their first breath. First sound. First laugh. First tears. First steps.
All the first make life, life is fast, quick, sly, generous, noisy, loud, and magical. Look for the firsts in life.
Because that's want makes life, shapes its ever flowing body.
Her first hug, kiss on the check, or giggle, her first song, high five, 'I love you' or first friend to cry and laugh with.
I'm telling you love is hidden in every corner of the world,
waiting for someone to walk forward, not away and lend a hand to help spread its greatness.
The first fight, scream or time they came running for your help, your guide.
The first time they catch a ball or hug you in public or kiss you on the cheek.
First time they run for the bus 'til the first they beg not to go.
The first time they have a crush to when they date.
Life is made of all emotions not just the ones you like.
They were made for a reason so respect them they're not bad, they're just emotions.
Life is so lovely; you should love it with your heart.
The first time their friendships are tested to their limits,
Or they show a sharp tongue to sobbing or stand up for a friend or stranger.
It's doesn't make you a man to hide your feelings it makes you one to show those tears.
Life is made out of the first times like when the wind is in their hair,
When they dance in the rain, laugh when soaked, feel the sun on their back, stare at it setting up in a tree.
These are signs of grace in the world.
Just wait and be positive and you will find the simple riches in the ever flowing life in this world.

Grace Harris, Grade 7
Richboro Middle School

My Room
Me looking into the stars
On the ceiling

Jumping up and down
Winding up on my butt

My haven where there is
Nothing there but me and peace

Me getting away from the traffic
The car to car highway the beeping
To get out of the way

No one screaming
No one
Crying

It's just me and my room
Isaiah Jones, Grade 7
William M Meredith School

Fishin' Is the Life
Every summer, I always
    Go down to Big Spring Creek
    With my fishin' rod,
    And there in the water I once
    Saw a big brook trout.
I set my fishin' rod, lay
    Back, and thought about
    The salty taste of cooked fish.
Suddenly, I felt an unexpected
    Tug,
And, boy, did that trout
    Give a fight!
The struggle lasted hours, and
    Finally, that trout just died!
I took it home for supper.
Boy, was it good, good, good!
So fishin' is amazing and the
    Life!
Andrew F. Fogelsanger Jr., Grade 7
Faith Tabernacle School

The Deer
You see it bouncing up and down.
Its white tail straight up.
You know you want to shoot it.
But you know it is wrong to.
So just pull the trigger.
But it is so cold.
Bang that's not good.
I pulled the trigger.
I saw the feet go up.
I went down to see and there it lay.
Tyler Hapgood, Grade 7
Greencastle Antrim Middle School

I Am
I am creative and kind
I wonder why we laugh and why we cry
I hear people laugh
I see people cry
I want to be happy all the time
I am creative and kind
I pretend to be famous
I feel happy when I feel important
I worry that I'm less than perfect
I cry when I feel worthless
I am creative and kind
I understand that there is sorrow
I say that there is always tomorrow
I dream about what's said and done
I try just to have some fun
I wish for a happy life
I am creative and kind
Shawn Fisher, Grade 7
Strath Haven Middle School

Long Beach Island
Hot August breeze
Pushing people to the shore
Where emerald-green ocean water is found
Dropping clear-as-glass jellyfish
Here and there
Waves crashing every minute
Asking me to come closer
Telling me where I am
Long Beach Island
The wind whispers repeatedly in my ear
I hear people laughing in the village
As I smell the salty ocean air
Beneath my feet
Is the delicate
Boiling
Sand
Sadie Shaw, Grade 7
Holicong Middle School

Mailbox
It sits outside your house
And waits for news to come
A man walks down the street
A blue suit behind the trees
Dogs bark in anger and rage
But it beats them to the bite
Bones hidden in its chest
It even stalks in the night
But if you go to check on it
Hidden it will stay
For if you were not there
Its meals would go away
Ethan Van Metre, Grade 7
Strath Haven Middle School

Hiding
Living behind a lie.
A lie is my smile.
I don't know why I'm hiding it,
Probably because everyone believes it.

Living behind a lie.
A lie is the way I laugh.
I don't know why I hide it,
Probably because it makes everyone happy.

The way I smile.
Is so hard to do.
Because no matter how much I try,
I just can't think of living without you two.

The way I laugh.
It sounds so real.
But no matter how much I try,
I can't let you know how I feel.

I need both of you in my life.
Please don't leave.
I need both of you in my life,
I'm tired of wearing my heart on my sleeve.

Please Mommy and Daddy, stop fighting.
Jenna Smith, Grade 8
Paxon Hollow Middle School

Winter Hemlock
The cold, brisk air and
The nights, silent flare,
Tells that the Winter Hemlock is
Close at hand, close at hand

When the shadows fall,
And the trees begin to call
You know the Winter Hemlock is
Close at hand, close at hand

When you start to get near,
You are overwhelmed with fear,
You know that the Winter Hemlock is
Close at hand, close at hand

You continue to worry on,
For they will never be all gone,
Because you know the Winter Hemlock is
Close at hand, close at hand

When you reach the nearby clearing,
You feel yourself cheering
Because the Winter Hemlock is
In your hand, in your hand
Zac Glinsky, Grade 7
Landisville Middle School

Halloween

Treats of all kinds
Little ones
Big ones
All kinds
And all yummy.

Costumes galore
Scary
Cute
Funny
And colorful
All unique
And all wonderful

Decorations everywhere
Pumpkins
Lights
Vampires
Witches
And Ghosts
Scary, yet very cool

Matt McAndrews, Grade 7
Strath Haven Middle School

Death of a Sister

I see her lying there,
lifeless as can be.
I wait, for something to happen,
but I don't know what.
Then disaster struck.
Fate has fallen,
Call it what you will, but I call it Death.
Yup, you guessed it, she is dead.
I run out of the room as fast as lightning.
You'd think I was on hot coals.
I find a stretcher and jump on it.
I pull the covers over me.
I cry my heart out until
my dad and his friend
come over to comfort and calm me.
I calm down and stop crying.
I try to gather up all of my thoughts.
I go to my mom and hug her.
We go outside with a balloon
and let it go into the air,
in remembrance of my sister, Abigail

Christopher Hollhumer, Grade 7
Richboro Middle School

Distance

Fog is rolling in
Standing on a forlorn hill
Will you come save me?

Hannah S., Grade 7
Charles F Patton Middle School

Me Myself and I

Amanda
nice, quite, funny
Sister of Brittany, Michael, Sophia
Lover of art, basketball, friends
Who feels happy with family,
Sad at graveyards and nervous
at the doctor's office.
Who needs weekend, happiness,
laughter.
Who gives advice, support and love.
Who fears bugs, ghosts and death.
Who would like to see Taylor
Swift in concert again.
Who lives in a big white house.
Wagner.

Amanda Wagner, Grade 8
Chichester Middle School

Where Do I Fit in the World?

Where do I fit in?
As a girly girl or a tomboy
As someone quiet or loud
Or maybe a teacher's pet

Do I even fit in?
Am I what everyone wants me to be
I don't fit in, people push me around
And call me names

Now I fit in as me, the person I picked to be
I'm someone I picked to be
I'm someone loud
Someone I want to be
That's where I fit in

Tamyia Tolbert, Grade 7
Armstrong Middle School

Block

An empty paper just sitting there
Waiting for inspiration to strike
It's waiting for you to make a masterpiece
But you can't
You're stuck
You can't think of anything
You've already written so many before
But nothing clicks
You're done
You feel defeated
Then it hits you
Defeat
One word starts you off
The block is over
The one word starts a masterpiece

Matt Benicky, Grade 8
Bellmar Middle School

F-250

The F-250 is a sign,
Of a truck with a perfect design.

With a V-8 and 300+ horses,
It can be used in many different courses.

When you hear the engine roar,
It sounds like a raging war.

It has a soft glossy interior
That make other trucks inferior.

This truck is a steel wall
That stands six and a half feet tall.

This truck is fitting and fine,
And someday, I hope it can be mine.

Darren Feaser, Grade 8
Faith Tabernacle School

The Many Phases of Love

Love is like a red rose;
Every relationship has its thorn.

Love is like air;
It lifts you off the ground.

Love is someone's trust in you;
It's never ending.

Love is hope;
You should never give up on it.

Love is like a gentle, flowing stream;
It will always flow through your heart.

Love is like rain;
It showers down upon you.

Hailey N. Peffley, Grade 8
Faith Tabernacle School

Pens

A pen
Pen, pastel, crayon, quill, marker,
Writing utensil
A simple idea
An incredible object
It's astounding, the significance it reflects
I use a pen just about every day
I feel that there is no way to repay
The use it gives in every way
So the next time you want to express
How, why, or when
Write it down and thank a pen

Lincoln Mimidis, Grade 8
Bellmar Middle School

Blue

Blue is the color of the skies
The color of jackets and shirts
Blue is the color of sadness and cries
Of pretty violets that grow outside
Blue is all over my English notebook
My lead pencil, folder and cap eraser
The color blue is seen all over the place
From across the world
To the ocean blue
Josie Palamattam, Grade 7
Armstrong Middle School

Math

Fractions, decimals, and much more
Oh what fun!
I just adore.
Addition, subtraction
I felt the attraction.
Without my teacher,
Who is such a preacher,
Math would be a chore,
And such a bore.
Kate Matyas, Grade 7
Landisville Middle School

Blanket

So soft,
So fuzzy,
It lies so still
From a sheep's wool
To my head
It keeps me cozy
Its colors kind and mellow
Seem to rock me to sleep until my eyes shut
Enveloping me in a cocoon of comfort
Ryan Tucker, Grade 8
St Thomas More School

Clirty

Clean
Shiny, polished
Brushing, sweeping, sparkling
Wash, purity, bacteria, mud
Growing, soil, blemish
Disgusting, moldy
Dirty
Caroline Swade, Grade 8
Good Shepherd School

Whiteout

Covering the ground
Trees drooping with all the weight
Yet it keeps falling.
Cameron White, Grade 7
Trinity Middle School

Frustration

Frustration is a terrible feeling
You feel like you will never get over it
It starts over one small thing that grows into something huge like the sky
Usually you can't seem to control it
Your body just knows you're frustrated
Then you just blow
Sometimes you even cry in frustration
The tears just pour down like rain
Then people start yelling at you for crying
And that just makes matters worse
But you can't stop crying,
because there is nothing else you know how to do to show this feeling except to cry…
You finally start to calm down, taking deep breaths, drying your tears
It's finished…
The storm has gone away
That is how I explain frustration
Georgia Naples, Grade 7
J R Fugett Middle School

Mr. November

Tragedy ended, the healing has begun.
Two months passed, the city comes back to life, and cheering for my team.
It's one of the biggest games ever played.
The pitcher is looking down and discouraged, still rattled from his blown save.
Then I step into the box, full count, bases empty, bottom of the tenth.
The clock strikes midnight, it's the first World Series game ever in cold November.
As the pitcher sets, the crippled nation's eyes turn to me.
The pitch, a fast ball in the zone.
I swing.
My bat makes contact, the ball sails over the right field fence.
I run past first with my fist in the air and turn to see the pitcher
with tears streaking down his cheeks.
I sprint to home plate, my teammates embracing me, hugging and screaming
because we have just tied the World Series!
With a comeback today as a baseball team,
we will continue to rebuild tomorrow with a new energy inside of us all.
AJ Abate, Grade 7
St Thomas More School

The Fields of Amber

The wind lifts our heads now heavy with plump kernels,
We look up to the sky the color of blue opals.
The harvest now drawing nearer,
Now what must happen is clearer.

A man came the other day and broke a head off the stalk next to me,
He observed the kernels and nodded his head with glee.
All of us held on until the dreaded day
When they plucked us from the ground and took us away.

I remember the days of swaying in the prairie breezes
When life was the way it was supposed to be.
No longer do I soak up the sun
But instead I sit on a shelf as a whole wheat bun.
Amanda Grube, Grade 7
Landisville Middle School

Winter

Young children here and there
Young children everywhere

Is like a falling snowflake
Cold as a milkshake

I'm laughing loudly
And smiling proudly

I'm feeling bold
And brutally cold

I sled down a hill
Passing my friend Jill

Stepping in some smushy slush
Man, this is such a rush

Winter, winter you're so much fun
I just can't wait for you to come

Erin Triebl, Grade 7
St Anselm Elementary School

Cheerleading Competition

Competition season is almost near
We tumble, jump, dance, and cheer

Now that our routine is complete
I pray the bases will hold my feet

Practicing the routine one more time
Trying hard to stay in line

I know tomorrow my body will ache
But, for what I love it's what I will take

Remember the smiles, forget the tears
We are one big family for the past 2 years

With big smiles, on the floor we go
With sparkly clothes, and our big bows

You're proud of yourself, you did your best
You know you're as good as the rest.

Amber Harris, Grade 7
Armstrong Middle School

Winter

W hite snow.
I ce cold.
N ight before Christmas.
T reacherous snow storm.
E very day is cold.
R ipping winds.

Austin Wilson, Grade 8
Chichester Middle School

Afternoon on Chincoteague Island

On Chincoteague Island, you can see the ocean reflecting the blueness of the sky.
You hear the seagulls' cries as they circle . . . circle . . . circle . . . seeking leftover food.
The saline scent being blown in from the sea.
You feel the warm sand under your feet before you pluuuuunge into the cooooool ocean.
A stealthy wave knocks you over and you are completely submerged.
Then, you come up from beneath the waves coughing.
Salt in your mouth.
It stings your eyes.
No matter, you dive in again, and again, and again.
Until, it's time to return to the beach house and catch some crabs.

Joshua Luo, Grade 7
Strath Haven Middle School

A Rose

A rose is worth one thousand years of love and joy without horrid fears.
The fear is crucial to the mind as it helps create to get inside.
Inside to everything we learn and know, all the way, from head to toe.
The toes that help us walk the Earth, to support, discover, and know what is worth.
Life is worth way more than things, money, gold, and even diamond rings.
The rings we hold, the rings we keep, the many memories we all hold deep.
Deep, deep inside the ocean blue, hold secrets man may never do.
Actions we do, we give and take, assist us as we decide to destroy or make.
But we must make our futures shine bright, to avoid the dark and follow the light.
And the light we follow, the light that knows, all is explained through a single rose.

Joseph Dantes, Grade 8
St Anselm Elementary School

Hope

There's a ray of hope around you, and a ray of hope around me
I know that we're lost, but we'll make it somehow
Together we walk side by side, wondering where we are and how we got here
People laughing, kids pointing, and grown-ups pushing their children faster
Not many clothes to put on, never taking a shower, our feet are as black as coal.
Always wondering, "What if we were rich?" or "Do we even have a family?"
Remembering the day my brothers and sisters were playing hide-and-go-seek,
Me watching, sipping on lemonade.
There's a ray of hope around you, and a ray of hope around me.
There it is.

Shayna Hallman, Grade 8
Southern Lehigh Middle School

Imagine

Imagine if the world were flat,
Imagine if the trees were blue and the sky was green,
Imagine what would happen if the earth had no gravity,
We would float through the air like birds soaring through the sky,
Imagine what would have happened if dinosaurs hadn't gone extinct,
Imagine what would happen if we didn't have thumbs,
Imagine how life would be without food and water,
Our lives would be different and so would we,
Imagine if we didn't need to sleep,
Imagine what life would be like without any diversity.

Paul Browne, Grade 7
Holy Child Academy

My Wish

To all I preach
I wish I could spend all my time at the beach
Nowhere else in the world
So I could I watch the waves go by, like a ribbon being curled

If no teachers could teach
I wish I could spend all my time at the beach
I would be reminiscing on the better days
As I wave hello to the passing-by summer haze

Thinking about the seagulls that screech
I wish I could spend all my time at the beach
I'd listen to not only the seagulls, but everything on the beach talk
With my toes digging in the sand as I would walk

If I were to be able to put my greatest joy in my reach
I wish I could spend all my time at the beach
Sun shining down on me
A farfetched dream I wish to see

Emily Ross, Grade 7
Holicong Middle School

Youth

Youth is thought to be amazing,
Thought to make your heart ablazing,
While others think it a burden,
And think youth should be hurtin',
Few think youth, is a great stress,
Having to learn to clean their own mess,

What do you think, A, B, or C,
Are you an adult who begs to say B,
Or perhaps you're a Child, who despairs in C,
Me, I chose D
The answer for A, B, and C

Youth is filled with happiness,
Fatalities and loneliness,
Even with the ups and downs,
(Sometimes there is a turn around),
Youth is always the greatest pro,
For youth is the one which lets you grow

Jonathan Kenney, Grade 7
Greencastle-Antrim Middle School

A Snowflake's Journey

As I get stuffed and puffed
And cleaned until shiny, white, sparkling and bright
I shape myself in a very unique way
So everyone can see that it's me
I get ready to jump down
Hoping to land on the ground
To meet the rest of my friends
As I fall
The wind starts to blow me away
I flow in the wind's direction
And finally land on the ground
I lay on the soil for the rest of the day
Letting everyone stack upon me
Until the sun comes up in the spring
And melts me away
There, I start my new life over, up in the sky
When winter's arrival comes
I jump off the clouds
And land onto the ground once again

Priscilla Tran, Grade 7
Landisville Middle School

Confusion

She never realized she was lost inside
Until her nightmares came true.
Now she has nothing left to hide
And no idea what to do.

Her nightmares bid her left, then right,
Twisting her mind, thoughts, and peace,
Ensnaring her in the devilish night
With naught a bitter hope of release.

She walks with darkness, her only friend,
Uncared for, unexplained, and unfound,
Watching the shadows slope around the bend
And her silent feet shuffling on the ground.

Her name? None other, but Confusion.
Her mind is one full frightening illusion,
In which far she wanders, and fast she roams,
Waiting for someone to come lead her home.

Rebecca E. Feaser, Grade 9
Faith Tabernacle School

Today Is

Today is summer slowly fading away into the distance.
Today is a leaf waiting anxiously to change from green to gold.
Today is shades of gray and green and blue.
Today is wet and wild, yet soft and sweet.
Today is the wind singing a dreary melody.
Today is a rain cloud drifting through a muted purple sky.
Today is an orchestra tuning their instruments.
Today is a beautiful painting.

Hannah McGrath, Grade 7
Holy Child Academy

My #1 Dream

Flashing lights on my helmet,
Crowds screaming my name,
Teammates have my back,
Coach's screaming at me what to do,
Jumping into the crowd after a winning game TD,
Practicing hard,
Winning games every Sunday,
That's my #1 dream.

Arren Pulinario, Grade 7
Armstrong Middle School

Basketball

My team trembles on the court as the ref blows the loud whistle
The ref tosses the bumpy textured ball in the air
Who will obtain the ball?
"Yes."
My team receives the ball
Sweat swivels down my forehead as I hustle towards the net
I attempt to make a shot but the mystery is,
was the shot countable
It was good the ball slips through the pure white net
My team glides into defensive position
They miss the shot
Buzz
That's the game
We win
1, 2, 3
Teamwork

Taylor Young, Grade 7
William M Meredith School

The Beach

The beach of
Golden sand blankets the shore.
The violent, turquoise ocean waves,
Crash noisily on the powdery sand.
The waves wash up a myriad of shimmering, shining, seashells,
On the shore.
The fish slice through the ocean,
Like zigzagging bullets.
Seagulls gracefully plunge down hoping to
Find a salty snack in the lustrous, sapphire sea.
Families sit on white lounge chairs,
While the radiant sun slowly slides across the conspicuous sky,
Your day at the beach
Reflects the portrait of God's great Earth,
Like the sun shining, glimmering on the ocean.

Jordan DeMatteo, Grade 7
St Thomas More School

The Orchard

The smell wafts into my nose.
I scan the trees searching for the right one.
In a sea of green, a ray of sun shines like a halo upon it.
Crunch!
Flesh bursts, filling my mouth with a wave of sweet juice.
White insides keep my jaw busy,
as my taste buds relax and relish in the journey.
As my first bite comes to an end, the taste lingers on my tongue.
I swallow the mashed pulp,
as I take another bite my senses explode!
I can't stop.
Crunch!
Crunch!
Again and again until the once plump globe,
diminishes into the funnel of a crested wave.

Sophia Detweiler, Grade 7
Charles F Patton Middle School

Fear

"The only thing to fear is fear itself" I once heard from a teacher.
She said that a very famous person named Roosevelt said it.
My question is what is fear?
What makes people be fearful?
After pondering that for a while I found that it is ourselves.
Ourselves that make us fearful
We let ourselves be afraid
My grandmother always says "if you are afraid…
Face your fear"
Don't let yourself fear it
Then why don't we ever face our fears
We let them take over our life
We spend so much time being fearful that sometimes…
We miss out on something great
We over think things and end up regretting it
It is a quality that humans posses
It can be good
Or sometimes bad
But we have to remember
That if we face them we will no longer posses them.

Alexandra Shatzer, Grade 8
Connections Academy

Forever

she felt as if she didn't matter
she wanted to matter to you
but you let her leave
and you didn't give her a reason to turn back
you should have held her close and never let her go
you could have made her stay
but because you didn't wrap your arms around her
then tell her how much you loved her
she had to go away
it didn't have to end that way
because of you, she is now gone
her life has ended tragically
it has been taken away from her
but what you didn't know…
was she took it from herself
in no less than a few short seconds
all because you were too selfish to realize how much you cared
and to see how much you needed and loved her
but now she is gone…forever

Olivia Osman, Grade 8
Penn Cambria Middle School

Out There

Looking up just seeing darkness and stars
Look harder to see so much more
You'll see amazing things like shooting stars
Amazingly different planets than ours
But if you look as hard as you can
You'll find something past the planets and the stars
But you'll never know unless you look

Hope Lubbert, Grade 7
Beaver Area Middle School

The Best Game Ever

The pitcher winds up.
The batter gets ready to hit.
The runner prepares to dash off.
The ball is coming.
The bases are loaded.
Here comes the ball.
CRACK!!!
The game winning grand slam.
That's the best game ever.
Thomas J. Oates, Grade 7
Armstrong Middle School

Friends

I'm sky blue sometimes
    calm and cool
    collective and shy
being the quiet one in school but out
of school there's another side bright
yellow, like the afternoon sun
    loud and funny
    bouncy and buoyant
having fun with my friends
Zack Romano, Grade 8
Chichester Middle School

Yellow

Bright and smart
Alive and moving
Helping friends is the life
Happy when I am excited
But on some days I am gray
Useless, grumpy, careless, sleepy,
and stressed
Like when I did not get enough sleep
But usually I am Yellow
Ricardo Quiambao, Grade 8
Chichester Middle School

Cell Phone

It sings with glee
As a message for me
Comes through the black
And turns into white
The sound flashes around the room
A shake then...
OFF
Travis DeBruyn, Grade 7
Strath Haven Middle School

Snow

Winter's snowflakes fall,
Leaving bare trees a bright white.
Footprints in the snow.
Michelle Biksey, Grade 7
Trinity Middle School

Almost a Dream Come True

I am backstage and everything goes dark.
I see the orchestra lift their instruments and the stage lights shine bright.
The other performers begin to dance across the stage.
I look down to the ground and, to my surprise, I see two silky pink pointe shoes on my feet.

Backstage it is dark and I can barely see my own quivering hands.
As I step onto the stage, I am blinded by the bright spotlight.
The lights begin to settle and dim to a blue color.
Oh no, what is happening?

I hear the orchestra begin to play a soft song, and I feel that this is my cue.
As I begin to dance across the stage I hear the soft sound of my feet brushing off the floor.
I can hear the "oo's" and "ah's" of the crowd as I gracefully waltz across the stage.

I feel the fear slowly draining out of me.
I am gaining confidence as I swiftly dance across the stage.
I feel thousands of eyes on me; they are watching my every move.

Will I mess up?
What will the audience think of me?
Am I doing my best?
Will I ever get another opportunity as good as this one?

Too bad it's just a dream.
Too bad it's just a dream.
Too bad it's just a dream.
Lauren Skillinge, Grade 8
Saucon Valley Middle School

Ode to My Contact Lenses

O contact lenses, you bring sight to my eyes,
Even though to put you in it takes a lot of tries.
Your bubbly, cool texture has a silky kind of feel,
Without you I can't see, oh how I need you my dear!

Blue, green, hazel, brown. In all colors you come.
Clear, so I can see my eyes, is my favorite one.
You twinkle in the sun, but you dry out in the breeze.
On a cozy day, I can read a book with ease.

I could just wear my glasses, but it's just not as good.
If I could wear you day and night, you know of course I would.
And even if I'm mad at you because you won't go in,
I think of what a team we are. Together we will win!

You're wet, you're dry. You're in, you're out. You do as I command,
Only someone with contacts too could really understand.
I dot my i's and cross my t's with 20-20 vision,
In class at school, I read out loud. There is no indecision.

It's half past ten (near time for bed!) I'd better take you out.
My eyes say "Ahhh" and breathe fresh air as they dart and peek about.
I've laughed and cried. I've done it all, and with me you have been.
Tomorrow morning I will wake and do it all again.
Kristen Loughlin, Grade 7
St Joseph Catholic School

Soaring

Eyes flash open.
White with a tint of orange fills my vision.
Snowy hills,
Everywhere is white.
Then with headphones on,
Music blasting in my ears,
The goggles tinted orange
Are put into place.
Gripping my boots
To the board,
Legs struggle to pull me up
Preparing
To soar down the hill.

CJ Angelella, Grade 8
St Thomas More School

The Shot

I awoke from my sleep
There was a loud knocking sound
Like something was urgent
Then a police man came in
he told a horrible tale
My father had been shot twice
"He is in intensive care," said the cop
My grandma was coming to watch us
My mom was going to Temple Hospital
I cried for an hour or so
When I went to school, I cried at recess
I cried but then…
After two months, he was going to be okay

Kevin Walker, Grade 7
Armstrong Middle School

The Hurricane

A hurricane hit here
Here on the east coast of the U.S.
It became very strong then weak
Lots of damage caused by Irene
From Jersey to Pennsylvania
Houses flipped over
Buildings destroyed
Tons of flooding
Some families were lost in the flood
Children died, too
Huge sinkholes
No one can forget
Irene

Dominic Schoettle, Grade 7
Armstrong Middle School

Black Care

blackness engulfs me
slowly dying in my thoughts
darkness all around

Delaney Elling, Grade 8
Trinity Middle School

Stupefying

Whooooosh!
Wind whirls around me,
nipping playfully at my rosy red ears.
Shivery chills travel like sneaky spiders up and down my back.
Leaves seem to defy gravity as they slowly float up, up and away,
creating what appears to be a mini leaf tornado;
Stupefying.
Trickle, trickle…
Flowing, rolling; breathtaking beauty.
Time freezes as the mesmerizing rhythm captures my heart.
The creek trickles, drips.
Never ending in both directions;
Stupefying.
Ahhh,
A small, content sigh escapes as I admire the wonders of fall at work.
Though dark and cold, a shy little patch of sunlight
peaks through the tall towering branches of the mighty pine.
Simply, stupefying.

Claire Van Duyne, Grade 7
Strath Haven Middle School

Daydreaming

During class as the teacher is explaining how to answer a problem
My foolish mind starts to wander as I gradually lose focus of all around me
All with the exception of my own mind
Daydreaming is such fun
I can leap unimaginable heights, soar from galaxy to galaxy, or sprint a thousand miles
Anything that I want…desire…daydream…
I can be thinking about anything
Food, sports, school
And the best part is…
No one can stop my mind
No one except me…
Actually…there's one exception and that's when suddenly —
"Jifu, do you know how to answer this problem? Jifu? Hello?"
"Oh uh…um wait what?"
That embarrassing moment when my teacher calls me back into reality
And the whole class is there to laugh at me but hey
I deserved it
I wasn't listening because I was just too busy…daydreaming…

Jifu Li, Grade 7
Strath Haven Middle School

Dancing

Twist, Turn
5 days until the show, 16 moves to learn!
Fall
4 days until the 30 foot stage, 10 moves to learn.
3 jumps
3 days until my bare feet go crazy, 7 moves to learn.
1 split
Today everyone looks at me and my classmates
On the 30 foot stage. And in 5 minutes all you hear is, "Give it up for…"
All I can think is there's no turning back!

Taylor Arbitman, Grade 7
William M Meredith School

The Last Bell

Forty minutes sounds like a pest
but just forty minutes left—
information left and right
but the last minute is in sight—
5
  4
    3
      2
        1
          RING!
It's like a herd of wild animals
trying to be the first on the bus
and to think…
Just forty minutes left!
McKenzie Haller, Grade 7
St Thomas More School

Lucky

The affection he shows when
He notices you
The way he greets me and
Gives me a big hug

When I stroll into the house
I listen to his paws
Pattering on the ground next to me

And when it's time to go,
He craves to go too

Lucky
Alexis Ngo, Grade 7
William M Meredith School

The Candle

Darkness surrounding the flame.
Nothing but the sound of the crackle.
Through the frosty bitter window, you
can see the dancing orange and yellow
light. Eager to spread its warmth, but it is to
remain in one spot. The sullen night
powers over the flame, but yet the
glow still leaps around.
Coral Gincley-Tillman, Grade 7
J R Fugett Middle School

Smoke

White
Clean, soft
Soaring, billowing, flying
Doves, clouds, ravens, ink
Distorting, creeping, falling
Dark, shady
Black
Pia Alderman, Grade 8
Good Shepherd School

Me!

This is me.
Dark, shoulder-length hair
with Shirley Temple curls falling down in soft ringlets,
then hastily pulled back with the hair doodle at my wrist.
Hazel eyes that are a portal into my soul.
When I dance, I dance for the beauty of the movement,
up on stage as though I was born there.
My flute sings like a bird
trilling and slipping through the song as though flying through the air.
When I sing, I can almost see the notes sailing in the air,
like colorful ships on a sea, their destination the ears of my audience,
striking gold in their eardrums.
When I write, the story or poem creates itself from a seed of thought,
into a tree of words.
My smiles and laughter are as precious as slices of silver-studded starlight.
My friends are as rich as kings from my smiles they receive every day.
But, my sister is richer still, with years of my smiles locked away.
My Olive Garden is filled with fettuccine alfredo trees and tortellini bushes,
and it's always populated by herds of Italian food lovers.
Blossoming into an adult, my spirit runs wild,
Forever and always, free.
Jennifer Bell, Grade 7
James Buchanan Middle School

A Whole Other World

The beautiful, blue sea looks as though it has been painted
Along with the sky,
That has puffs of pure, white clouds
The air being as refreshing as an ice cold cup of water
The distant mountains with hints of green,
The mountains call you over,
Daring you to make the long, hard journey across the sea
You don't know what awaits you
But far away, you can hear
The sounds of people talking and enjoying the beautiful sight
On the other side of our world
They whisper to you, calling you, telling you what a wonderful life you could have
Sanjana Shah, Grade 7
Holicong Middle School

Worrying

Worrying is … as harmful as a disease.
Worrying is … like a superstitious man crossing paths with a black cat.
Worrying is … like a powerful spell that puts you in a trance.
Worrying is … like being given thousand pound weights to carry all day.
Worrying is … a million butterflies swarming in your stomach.
Worrying is … like punching a wall when you're mad. Does it solve anything?
Worrying is … like sitting in a rocking chair. It gives you something to do,
but gets you nowhere.
Worrying is … pointless.
Worrying is … stupid.
Worrying is … not to be worried about.
Don't worry … be thankful.
Emily Kalman, Grade 8
St Thomas More School

Nature

I like trees, I like bees
I like grass, I like sea bass
The world is a rainbow

I like butterflies, I like fireflies
I like tasty tangerines, I like sardines
The world is a rainbow

I like dogs, I like frogs
I like birds, I like herds
The world is a rainbow

I like tomatoes, I like potatoes
I like the day, I like hay
The world is a rainbow

I like bears, I like pears
I like bear claws, I like waterfalls
The world is a rainbow

I like fawns, I like ponds
I like an owl, I like water fowl
The world is a rainbow

I like mountains, I like water fountains
I like ice, I like rice
The world is a rainbow
Grant Mizak, Grade 7
St Joseph School

The Cycle

The cry of new life
A small shadow emerges
Waiting to be seen

The symbol of hope
She timidly steps forward
And tumbles back down

Tears stream down her cheeks
The door slams on the way out
This is but a phase

The ring shimmers bright
The love is white and pure
Soft and sweet kisses

Wrinkles on her face
Little ones sit in her lap
But her grip is weak

The sun is shining
The stone is weathered and old
A rose on the ground
Kirena Manivannan, Grade 9
Holicong Middle School

Eternity

In eternity we share a flower,
In forever we share a shower.
In the past we share a tear,
In the future we share a fear.
In the now we share it all,
In the now we share the fall.

In the flower we have a love,
And in the love we have a closeness.
In our tears we have our laughs,
And in our laughs are our fears.
And in it all we have the world,
And in the world,
We have eternity.
Savannah Butcher, Grade 8
Arcola Intermediate School

The Shiver

First comes the shiver,
the scare of haunting eyes.
Next comes the fear,
from that unknown surprise.

Next it's the thoughts,
that creep into your mind.
Then it's the dark,
for in it you are blind.

Are you afraid now,
of this dark and gloomy night?
It will all come to pass…
For it's Halloween night!
Haley Grimm, Grade 9
Frazier High School

Whale Watching

Sun high in the sky
Clouds hung from above
Birds squawk as they circle
The boat towers over us
Sapphire-blue sea
Water swirls as we board
Slapping against the ship
We set out for whales
Excitement fills the air
The smell of salt engulfs us
Clinging to the rail
Sea boils and turns seaweed-green
Water erupts from the surface
Whale flies high in the sky
Victoria Veltri, Grade 7
Holicong Middle School

Perfectly Imperfect

Perfectly imperfect
Is what she is.

Her nose
Is too
Small.

Her feet
Are too
Big.

She walks
With a
Limp.

She eats
Like a
Pig.

Perfectly imperfect
May be what
She is,

But being perfectly imperfect,
Is what a wordsmith is.
Anastasia McClendon, Grade 8
Abington Heights Middle School

Normal

I am a normal person,
With a normal name,
With a normal family,
And with a normal house.

Everybody imagines that they're
special,
But I'm normal.

People imagine that imagination is
weird,
But it's not weird,
Imagination is fun to me.

Everybody's got friends that are cool,
But my friends are not cool,
They're normal.

People in this world imagine that you
have to be cool or special.
But you don't have to be cool or
special,
you can be normal
like me.
Jalen Reid, Grade 7
William M Meredith School

Seasons

Winter comes in with cold days.
The days become shorter and nights become longer.
In the morning frost covers the frozen grass, snow falls from the sky onto the cold ground.
The brisk wind sends chills up your spine, winter leaves with new plants.

Spring comes in with cool days.
The sun begins to shine and the snow begins to melt.
The nice morning dew covers the cool ground, rain begins to fall to make small pools on the sidewalks.
The leaves dance in the wind, spring leaves with sunshine.

Summer comes in with hot days.
The sun beats on the warm ground.
The rain puddles from the spring evaporate, flowers grow with the sunlight.
The sun awakens in the morning and melts in the moonlight at night, summer leaves with brisk weather.

Autumn comes in with cool days.
The leaves turn into beautiful shades of orange.
Windy days blow them away, leaves fly through the air.
The many shades of autumn disappear, autumn leaves with white snow.

Devon Koehler, Grade 8
Holy Child Academy

Ocean Waves

The ocean waves are happiness, read a book with lemonade is perfect bliss
They crash among the shore, the children will never bore
Seagulls stealing Sally's sandy sandwiches, the waves rise, the sand ditches
Fish, whale, dolphin, and shark, the waves keep going even when it's dark
Sandcastles crush, while palm trees sway, it's so hot even though it's May
Jellyfish sting but the sun will burn, put on sunscreen, didn't you learn?
Let's head over to the hot-dog stand, in between the sandcastles is no-man's-land
While we play in our fantasy land, the adults won't get it they'll misunderstand
Swimming in the water makes me cold, the good thing is you're never too old
Seashells glistening by the sea, ouch! A crab just pinched me
Buying sweatshirts on the boardwalk, all I can hear on the boardwalk is talk
Over the sand dune is a sand dollar, I pulled the dog away by the collar
On my foot there is a starfish, there is sand in my ice-cream dish
There goes the ice-cream man, look! I am so tan!
For dinner tonight we're having seafood, some people get sick but I'm always in the mood
Tonight we're going to see a show, a good way to end; it's time to go
So to the beach: I love you, I will always miss you too
Finally it's time to pack: toothbrush, toothpaste, and comb, I'll miss the beach but it's good to be home

Abby Williams, Grade 7
St Joseph School

Firefighter

As I run down the street, I suddenly stop and think what could it be? Could it be a car into a tree, could it be a house on fire, or a C02 alarm with a bad wire? As I get ready, I stand unsteady with the thoughts and fears of what I might hear. As I arrive I see the fire's alive. As I move through the first floor breaking down a few doors. As I break down the door I hear a loud roar. It's collapsing like a deck of cards. I run so very fast and hard, I think of what might happen I stop in a sudden reaction. I hear a faint voice of a child I turn around without a smile. I look; I search, so very hard with nothing else to be heard. There it was again, so I gave a big grin. I see the child all buried in a pile. She's okay so I cleared the way. I make it to a door with an unsteady floor. There's help for the girl so I turn back to do more. As I put out the fire I grow very tired. As the fire goes out I hear a loud shout. It's the chief to all of our relief. I walk out with my dignity and pride with a fellow firefighter by my side. As I leave the scene, I bow my head and pray, thank you God for the help you gave us today.

Karingtin Sklodowski, Grade 8
Penn Cambria Middle School

I Am

I am sharp and focused
I wonder what the camera really sees
I hear the buzzing bee
I see the river in the early morning light
I want to freeze time
I am sharp and focused

I pretend I am a chef when I'm cooking
I feel the breeze brushing my face
I touch the smooth button
I worry about the test result
I cry when I say goodbye to my family in Mexico
I am sharp and focused

I understand moments in life
I say let's freeze them for life
I dream I will be a great chef one day
I try do my best work and effort in anything I do
I hope to be successful in life
I am sharp and focused

Alex Leon, Grade 7
Charles F Patton Middle School

Do You Remember

Do you remember
When there was no drama
Nothing to fight about
When we were all friends

Do you remember
How much fun we had
Together as a group
Never wanting it to end

Do you remember
How much different it was from now
We all grew apart
Everyone changed

Do you remember
How we thought we were going to be friends forever
I do and I miss it
Those days where we all loved each other
And we were all friends

Caitlyn Degner, Grade 9
Neshaminy High School

Eagles

Eagles run Eagles dive
If they get a better coach they will surely strive
Vick will pass Vick will play
Cheer for them and say hurray
Here goes Jackson down the line
There's the touchdown I'm sure they'll be fine

Christopher Shaw, Grade 7
Charles F Patton Middle School

The End of the World

As I trudge my feet out the door,
My brain flashes to terror and nothing more.
The sound of scissors rings through my head,
Oh, how I wish I were at home instead.
Inevitably, they call my name as I glance at the wall,
Then I stare at the culprit, a man named Paul.
It's hard to act naturally on account of how much I want to ditch,
Yet Mom says if I stay we'll go to Abercrombie and Fitch.
As I step on the chair and slowly rise up,
My stomach feels queasy and I shake like a pup.
As the ice-cold water hits my shiny hair,
My eyes glisten in anger and despair.
Within the first snip,
My war was a sunken ship.
It felt like Paul was pulling and scratching my scalp for days,
Dreadfully, it hurt awfully in so many ways.
With the last agonizing cut, I grimaced with pain,
And I had so much more personal power to regain.
As I creaked open the front door to my house and began to roam,
My eyes envisioned the words "home sweet home."

Shira Freiman and Brianna Smith, Grade 8
Sandy Run Middle School

Somewhere Tonight

A hurried siren splits the darkened night.
The streets come alive with the frenzied light.
And as the wail carries faintly on the breeze,
There is no telling how many lives it will seize.
The pagers crack as they beg for assistance;
Prayers are forgotten as volunteers travel the distance.

A mangled car and a dying man,
The screams and shouts and helping hands;
The scene comes together on the street below.
Death is nigh, and the people all know.
They are running a long race against time,
And the clock is ticking as the hours it chimes.

But just two blocks away the siren enters the windows,
Of a little girl as she lies awake in the shadows.
She closes her eyes and lays her head on her pillows.
She drifts back to sleep as she softly whispers,
"God, whatever you do to set things right,
Please, don't let anyone die tonight!"

Kimberly J. Funk, Grade 9
Faith Tabernacle School

Bubbly

Bubble is as bright as the sun in a deep dark sky,
It tastes like a ripe mango in the July sun,
It smells like a fragrant rose standing in a vase of faith,
And it reminds me of the warm silky smooth sky in June,
It sounds like a leaky sink that will never stop splashing
Bubbly makes me feel like a tender rainbow after an April showers.

Kaitlin Moyer, Grade 7
Schuylkill Valley Middle School

Life

Life is full of many things,
A lot of memories are made.
Either good or bad,
Or in-between.
Some things you'll regret,
Some will make you proud.
Some will make you sad,
Some will make you laugh.
You sometimes wish you could fast forward time,
Or even go back to the old times,
And pause at the good times.
People will change,
Some will stay the same.
You'll feel differently towards things,
Or maybe stay the same.
But that's it,
It's life.

Sarah Tilakdharry, Grade 7
Armstrong Middle School

Danger Zone

Gracefully skipping outside in the snow,
Some ice waits ahead but I did not know.

The ice slopes downhill and off the cliff,
I tumbled down, cold and stiff.

Holding onto a tree I shout out for help,
My grip starts to loosen and I let out a great yelp.

Twisted trees and jagged rocks lie beneath the snow,
Just what would happen if I let go?

Someone is coming; I shout out and yell,
Be careful there's ice for I slipped and fell.

They reached down and locked her hand in mine,
She asked me if I was ok, I answered fine.

Makena Szejko, Grade 7
Schuylkill Valley Middle School

Bryonna

Bryonna
Caring, loving, helpful, honest
Sister of Brandon and Bryen
Lover of movies, funny people, and puppies
Who feels happy when with family, nervousness
in front of people, and angry when not understood
Who needs friends, family, and cell phone
Who gives hugs, support, and love
Who fears big dogs, the zoo, and mice
Who would like to see war end, poor people get
better lives, and the Eiffel Tower
Who lives in a brick house on Market Street

Bryonna Hamm, Grade 8
Chichester Middle School

My Grandmother*

When I close my eyes,
The one person I see is,
My Grandmother.
She stares at me,
Her eyes twinkle.
I try to speak,
But my mouth is silent.
I give her my hand,
She refuses it.
My heart shatters.
She begins to disappear,
And her eyes fill with tears.
October 23, 2010
Is when breast cancer took my grandmother.
And we will never see each other again,
Until our souls meet in heaven.

Casey Blum, Grade 7
Strath Haven Middle School
*Dedicated to my grandmother

Magnificent Maggie

I wake up to another lazy summer day,
But today is totally different.
If we are lucky, we will have a new addition to our family,
And our dog Max will have a new playmate.

Max is restless when we arrive at the rescue.
Tails are wagging from
East to west and north to south
With fur floating all around.

Then we meet her. Maggie. A four year old pup.
She's as rambunctious as a bull in a china shop,
Yet as sweet as marshmallow fluff,
With a golden silk blanket of fur.

I will never forget that fateful day
August 1st in 2011

Daniel Behler, Grade 7
Schuylkill Valley Middle School

Family

In a family you have a mom and a dad.
If your parents are divorced it can be really sad
Going back and forth I just want to stay in one place
Always moving it's like a big race.
With my dad always moving I don't have a place to call home.
The places I lived keeps piling up like foam.
Brothers, sisters, and nephews can get on your nerves.
Having a big family can have so many twists and turns!
With your family you can have so much fun.
Your family's love is brighter than the sun.
Family doesn't just give hugs and kisses.
Family makes your happiest wishes.

Tawni Feeney, Grade 7
Bellmar Middle School

A Friend

A friend is someone you can trust,
Laugh with, and be yourself around.
Someone you love and can't live without.
A good person you look up to
And admire.
A friend is someone you know won't hurt you,
Or make you feel down.
A friend is a person you can always count on
Through the good and bad.
A friend, a great person, never lets you down.

Ashley Staltmayer, Grade 7
Armstrong Middle School

Baseball Is My Drug

Baseball is my drug
And without it I cannot live
It's my passion
It's my one true love
Just like it was to all the
Players who played in the old days
And just like it is to all players who play today
And just like it is for all the fans
Without baseball
We cannot live

Nicholas Stanley, Grade 7
Armstrong Middle School

Music

What flows around us like water,
Smooth and cool like glass,
It is the wonderful flow of music.
Music, what a beautiful word
Whether rock, pop, country, or just your ringtone.
Music is in our daily lives,
Whether a good day or bad,
Music has the sweetest taste,
Music has the wonderful sound of pure joy.

Mackenzie Stewart, Grade 7
Armstrong Middle School

The Souls of America

A splash of color rises in the night
Souls of soldiers lay to give us light
Music plays as we watch the display
Only few thinking what really is that day

Men shed blood to keep ours safe
They hold our home for little waifs
America is one by these brave souls
So stand and represent what flies on our poles

Cierra Gross, Grade 9
Sunbury Christian Academy

Seashell

As I gaze into a pink conch shell
First it is cotton candy pink
And then it is the smooth surface of glass
And then it is like the ocean roaring as I hold it to my ear
And then it is like a lost jewel, absolutely magnificent
And then it becomes the ultimate prize
And now it is my treasure
And now it is mine
And now I am found

Jo Tebay, Grade 7
Charles F Patton Middle School

Bunnies

Bunnies are gentle and neat,
after every long day they clean their feet.
They rest during the day and are awake during the night;
I guess it doesn't bother them to sleep when there's light.
Each bunny is quiet and would never hurt a soul or start a riot.
They harm no one, but just hang around and lay
all through the evening, night, and day.
Bunnies love to explore, so be careful if you get them out to play,
that they don't have an opportunity to hop away.

Cassidy Fritz, Grade 7
Greencastle-Antrim Middle School

Seashell

As I gaze into the hole in the light orange seashell
First it is a dark hole of emptiness with nothing in it
And then it is a scary storm covering the sky
And then it is like a twisting and turning road that never ends
And then it is like a ripe peach ready to be eaten
And then it becomes an instrument playing a soft tune
And now it is a smooth black car driving in the rain
And now it is a cheetah with orange stripes racing through the fields
And now I am a crab lying in the sand

Abhay Malik, Grade 7
Charles F Patton Middle School

Caught

My head drowns with the thoughts
Of what they would think
If I would sail in the ocean and suddenly sink
My body shivers with the wondering thought
and I'm desperately hoping I wasn't caught
Caught in the action of hoping and dreaming
of what could be
But the world comes
and smashes them in three

Annabella Kolasa, Grade 7
Schuylkill Valley Middle School

December

Flurries fall from a sky
As black as a raven
Or as white as the oncoming snow
As the Arctic air surges
Blowing the warm air away
Everything falls silent
Then as the first snowflake falls
Always landing on the tip of your nose
And December finally begins
Snow falls and covers the ground
Covers the ground like a carpet
Snowmen appear out of nowhere
The wind howls
The snow falls
The world turns a glittering white
But inside fires burn bright
Gillian Chestnut, Grade 7
Holy Child Academy

The Beetle

It scurries past
Not too fast
Hardly shoddy
Is its armored body
A foot stomps
And yet it tromps
It has six feet
But it's not so neat
It's plain
And it hides in the grain
By its maw
Are two sharp jaws
Used to eat
Any bug it meets
The beetle, not too modest
Hurries on to get its harvest
Cory Kendall, Grade 8
Punxsutawney Christian School

My Goal

As I dribbled down the field
Everybody froze.
Sweat trickling down my face,
My feet pounding against the ground.
I arrive at the goal.
I shoot.
The ball skids off the side of my foot
As grass soars into the air.
The goalie dives,
Lunging for the ball
But it slipped through her arms.
The ball now flawlessly placed,
Bounces into the corner.
I score!
Ali Hankee, Grade 7
St Thomas More School

The Ocean

Tumbling and crashing
Forever across the
Smooth, ocean rocks

Stirring and shifting
The sandy floor
In its salty blue sea

Foamy water clouds
Break apart as
Glistening fish
Burst through the surface

This beast roars and
Has the strength
To build sandy dunes
Of once smooth land

When the power is spent,
This beautiful entity
Shimmers in the sun
Like it's made of scales
Drew Adamczak, Grade 7
St Thomas More School

Neon Pink

Part of me is neon pink
Nice and pretty,
Fun and loving,
Helping kids and enjoying the spotlight
But, deep inside
There is another part
Dark purple, like a secret agent –
Shy and violent
Bossy yet self-conscious
Scared when someone wants to fight me.
Yet both colors in me are equal and real.
Mariah Law, Grade 8
Chichester Middle School

Family

Laughing, screaming, hugging
Smiles from ear to ear
Clinking of glasses
Telling of stories
"I love you"
The smell of sweets
Lime-green grass feet
The pounding of feet
Running towards you
Tackled with love
Happy heartwarming cheers
Joined together as one
"Family first"
Emily Lunny, Grade 7
Holicong Middle School

The Foul Shot

Going to the line,
Nervous energy fuels him
To launch the biggest shot ever.
Two deep breaths,
Squares up his feet.
The audience, off their seats,
Roaring with excitement.
Referee tosses him the ball.
One more deep breath,
Then his routine —
Dribble, dribble, dribble, spin,
Dribble, dribble, spin.
Perfect situation:
Elbow in,
Knees bent.
He's ready to go,
No sound from the crowd.
He flings the ball
And it soars through the air
Rolling like a vortex —
And goes in!
Jake McLinden, Grade 7
St Thomas More School

Talent Show Grandma

9:30 PM
I was a star
As a grandma
Grandma
Seaweed-green clothing
Looking like Ugly Betty
Talking like a dying cat
Around 100 people watching just me
Laughter drowning the room
But it wasn't a flood
It was an erupting hurricane
The only other sound was me
Me
Croaking humorous things such as
"Pens are dangerous"
Or "That doll's shoes are too pointy"
Not only was I the star
I was the shooting sun-bright star
Shooting for the moon
10:00 PM
1st Place
Sara Kimball, Grade 7
Holicong Middle School

Over You

This doesn't seem to be getting better,
It might be getting worse.
I don't know what to do,
I've tried everything to get over you.
Gabrielle Zerbe, Grade 9
Mechanicsburg Area High School

A Life in Heaven

September 24, 2009, at 6:00 a.m.
I went to school that day
When I came home
My dad told my sisters and me our grandma had died
I know she went right to heaven
I ran over to my best friend to tell her
I cried and cried
The next day I hoped not to go to school
My little sister was going so she wanted me to go
So I did
I just cried and cried there
When I went home I cried some more
When I hear the word heaven
What comes to mind is…
Grandma is not sick anymore and a baby once again
She lives her life all over again
She is playing with everybody in heaven
I hope she is playing with my dog, Champs, too.

Hannah Swanson, Grade 7
Armstrong Middle School

My Name

My name is the air around you
So plentiful and always there
My name is the grass in a field
So numerous you can't count
My name is the first flurries of winter
So expected
My name is like the rustling of trees in a light breeze
So quiet nobody takes notice
My name is so easy to slip off your tongue
So it's natural to say
My name means introspective
So you always have to think about it
My name is common
So that means there are many people behind the name
My name is perfect
My name is me
My name is
Alex

Alex Brown, Grade 8
Strath Haven Middle School

Sadness

Sadness, black as a moonless, starless night,
    And about as majestic
It tastes like a bitter lemon, makes you want to
    Spit it out and throw it away
It smells like a hospital, clean and unforgiving
It reminds me of lost ones, forever looking
    Over us in the heavens
It sounds like the heavy, raspy breathing
    Of a very sick person
Sadness makes me feel like there's nothing left

Kale Graybill, Grade 7
Schuylkill Valley Middle School

Sixteen Hearts

Sixteen hearts enter a single room,
    as eighty-eight keys begin to play,
and one thousand and two worries begin to melt away.
Thirty-two satin-bound feet
    rise to their three hundred and twenty toes,
while fifteen mirrors surround us
    on one glistening floor.
Ten lights shine down on us now,
    as we dance for just three more hours.
5 pirouettes,
3 jumps,
6 steps,
1 pique.

But the music doesn't last.
The mirrors are tucked away,
    and as the lights are shut,
and the hard little shoes saved for another day,
    nothing is left but us few,
sixteen hearts sharing sixteen dreams,
    of dancing for one million people.

Anna Morreale, Grade 7
Strath Haven Middle School

Leah

Leah,
Funny, loud, happy
Sister of, Danielle, Amber and Sharron
Lover of blue skies, animals, and babies
Who feels happy when with friends.
Sadness when someone passes,
nervous around heights
Who needs, friends, family and weekends,
Who gives, helps, laughs and smiles.
Who fears bears, darkness and scary movies.
Who would like to see respect for
teachers, clean streets, and more friends
Who lives in a big blueish-white
house on Mulberry Street.
– Wright

Leah Wright, Grade 8
Chichester Middle School

Fear

Fear is when you're sitting there
    Up in the air
    As the ferris wheel goes round,
    Wishing you were on the ground.
You can feel the movement of your adrenaline
    Hoping the seat does not tip again.
There is no way you're making it home,
    When you're in the dark, all alone.
You know you're not going to make it out alive,
    You can see it in your fearful eyes.

Gracey Butsack, Grade 7
Schuylkill Valley Middle School

What Am I

It came from within
when I was forgiven for all of my sins.
Invisible as it may be
the closeness to God envelops me.
It's greater than you could ever know
and in every day action is when it shows.
Even if it is put to the test
praying and believing will always be best.
When you hear His voice
you will know that you've made the right choice.
For it is a sign of courage
that will lead you on a lifetime voyage.
To share with others and experience that love
is evident in the peace that can only come from up above.
If you're asking yourself, "What could this be?"
It is the faith that you are given freely.

Venus Cabrera, Grade 8
St Peter School

The Rising Sun

When the sun rises,
Like a fiery hot snail sliding around,
Everything rises with it,
But does the sun make a single sound,
Like the incessant rambling of the world below,
It stays in the sky like a silent guardian,
Rising from the abyss with a warming glow,
Like a lone candle unfazed by the wind,
It floats solitary and proud,
Like the Earth's shining medal of glory,
And maybe people can learn from it,
How to respect the golden warmth of silence,
How not to rush to the top like an effervescent soda pop,
To be patient but proud,
And work your way up slowly,
Like the rising sun.

Noah D'Souza, Grade 7
Holicong Middle School

Winter Morning

I question as I walk through the snow on a frigid winter morning
Should I have heeded the weatherman's warning?
There is no one around
And the sun is nowhere to be found
Which brings thoughts of coldness and temptation into my head
To run back home to my warm, cozy bed
Then the wind whispered into my ear
In tongues that didn't make my temptation disappear
As in the distance, a little sliver of brightness appears
Like a spark of a fire abruptly igniting
The sun lighting the sky with its luminescence
This is God in his true essence
The way the coruscating sun shines away my solemnity on this
Cold winter morning

Casey Laudadio, Grade 7
St Thomas More School

Snow

While I lay in bed last night
The stars flurried down and assembled in our yard
Those gentle little creatures so quietly lay on the ground
Seeking warmth from the frosty air.
They stacked and stacked without a complaint
Producing the most beautiful sight all year.

They hide the Earth's faults and cracks and blunders,
Hugging each and every one until
Their new soft dusty layer is done.

The new stars in the sky shine brighter than the last,
Than those that lay before me,
But these twinkle as if golden dust was sprinkled on the ground
Reflecting their enemy's light into the curiosity of our eyes.

The serene seldom scene sparks joy into children
Their ultimate instinct to run and throw and dirty it
However they leave a number of lingering patches
Of perfect stars that remain untouched,
Thus a few still remain another silenced night.

Kacy Hafertepe, Grade 7
Strath Haven Middle School

Stone Grey

Most of me is stone grey
spotted with purple.
Lazy and absent.
Noticed but left alone.
Listening but paying no attention.
But while my body is slacking
my mind is racing.
A mix of napalm red and tiger orange.
Thinking and daydreaming.
Imagining scenarios never to happen.
Explosions of creativity and imagination.
Thoughts running through my mind like my brain
is a marathon.
Waiting to be finished.
But impossible to complete.

Ethan Hammelbacher, Grade 8
Chichester Middle School

All About Me

Ryan –
Baseball
Brother of Michael
Lover of pets, sports
Who feels happiness, sadness, pain
Who needs music, sports, friends
Who gives respect, friendships, presents
Who fears heights, bridges, ghosts
Who would like to see the president, Titanic, moon
Who lives in Upper Chichester in a townhouse

Ryan Janvier, Grade 8
Chichester Middle School

Blooming Flowers

Spring is here
Flowers are blooming
All their bright colors are booming.
One by one
Each flower pops out of a bud.
I really hope they don't end up in mud.
Now that would be awful
I want my flowers bright, bright as the sun.
Lucky for me they are bright and fun.
Just like a firework show
Bursting with color and spark.
They light up the park.
They dance in the breeze
Just like a ballerina.
Or the boats floating in the marina.
These are my flowers
I don't ever want them to hide.
Because they make me happy inside.

Kira Thomas, Grade 7
Landisville Middle School

Gazing at the Stars

When I gaze at the stars
I know you're up there
But I just can't find you
Please, please show me where you are
Are you the brightest star?
Sure you are, you were always a star
In my mind you shine
Your spotlight will never die
We all feel your spirit
Wherever we go
I just hope you know
That you were wonderful
RIP in loving memory
When I gaze at the stars
I gaze at you
When I miss you
I look at the stars
To find you my shooting star

Kaitlyn Porter, Grade 7
Armstrong Middle School

Apple

Your first when you were five
Cider, sauce, pie
An orphanage for homeless worms
Crisp, juicy, flavorful
As indecisive as a child taking a test
Tart, sour, sweet
Sticky on a child's hands in the fall
Red, green, yellow
A treasure of nature that all enjoy
Mutsu, Fuji, Gala

Claudia Sacks, Grade 8
St Thomas More School

Celeste

Celeste
Funny, smart, cool, and an A+ student,
Sister of Randi, Jacque, Brian, and Joey.
Lover of winter, the beach, and games.
Who feels excited when getting new
    clothes, going to the movies, and
    hanging out with friends.
Who needs my family, food, and
    the beach.
Who gives kindness, appreciation, and
    love.
Who fears ghosts, homework, and
    roller coasters.
Who would like to see California,
    my dead pop-pop Bill, and Emma
    Stone.
Who lives in a big white house on
Patriot Ct.
–Sloss

Celeste Sloss, Grade 8
Chichester Middle School

The Perfect Game

He is standing on the mound
Not making a sound
He looks at the crowd
But they are loud
Because he has a perfect game
And he is one "out" away
He waits and waits
For the batter to stroll to the plate
He thinks about the end of the game
And all about his future fame
So he throws the ball
But then…
The batter hits it over the wall
He leaves the field in tears
Although the crowd is in cheers
And to his dismay
this game is just…
Another day.

Kris Mazur, Grade 7
St Thomas More School

School

In school you
Learn and have knowledge,
Through the years
You will get better
And have courage,
Day by day you
Learn something new,
Go to school to
Become a better you.

Sarah Griscavage, Grade 7
Armstrong Middle School

Just a Rainy Day

Plip…plop…
The rain falls,
Splashing against my window.
I open my blinds;
I peek outside.
Darkness is what I see;
Wind whistling is what I hear.
Shimmering droplets,
Like tears
Racing down my face when I cry,
Splattering on the sidewalks,
Forming tiny pools.
I close my blinds,
Hop into my cozy bed,
Seal my eyes 'til morning,
And hope that sun will soon shine
At the break of dawn.

C.J. Lynch, Grade 8
St Thomas More School

My Cow

Hello cow how are you today?
swinging your tail loosely I might say,

with your black and white spots,
and your huge body that can't fit in a cot,

with your black and wet nose,
and no toes,

with your oversized pink ears,
never shedding any tears,

unlike my comic books you never
    jump around and say POW!

but, I love you because you are my
    cow.

Courtney Norris, Grade 7
Greencastle-Antrim Middle School

My Dearest Butterfly

My dearest butterfly
I love the way you fly
The color of your wings
Makes me want to sing
You always fly
So high in the sky
It makes me wonder why
You never drop by
My dearest butterfly
I thought you may have died
Then I realized
You were in my heart the whole time

Alyssa Rice, Grade 9
Westmoreland Christian Academy

Sky/Ground

Sky
Blue, gray
Storming, flying, clouded
Clouds, sun, grass, tree
Stepping, covered, lying
Grassy, muddy
Ground
Rebecca Reese, Grade 7
Richboro Middle School

Animals

Monkeys tigers and more
Roaming on the jungle floor
Slithering swinging flying too
The inner animal
This is you
Madisson Bear, Grade 7
Greencastle-Antrim Middle School

My Dog Leroy

I have a brown dog named Leroy,
He loves to play with his red toy,
When I throw it on the ground,
He jumps up and down,
Oh that toy brings him joy.
Matthew Robinson, Grade 8
Chichester Middle School

The Packers

The Packers are the best
In the NFC West
Aaron Rogers is a champ
He sends teams to training camp
He is constantly followed by the press.
Andrew Harron, Grade 8
Chichester Middle School

Music

M usic from old to new, fast to slow
U nique beat that gets stuck in your head
S ound we enjoy at all ages
I ncredible rhythm that makes you move
C atching tune that goes with any mood
Hallie Faries, Grade 8
Chichester Middle School

Two Simple Friends

There once was a ferret
Who was friends with a parrot
They once had a fight
During the night
Over a small, simple carrot.
Johnny Green, Grade 8
Chichester Middle School

My Sunshine Beauty

A summer's eve as beautiful as ever
The sun reaching out to touch the sky with its finger tips
Stretched wide trying to cease the night from claiming the day
A man sits on the porch with a baby in his arms
The slight breeze teases the baby's auburn hair.
Then he speaks, his voice softer than a whisper
You are my sunshine, beauty my love from above, and I love you.
Summer turns to autumn; autumn turns to winter; and winter turns to spring
This cycle continues for twenty years then stops on a beautiful day
Just like the beautiful auburn-haired child.
She has grown up and is about to wed her other half, her love
She sits upon the patio that her father sat on twenty years before
Her father wanders out, holds her close, and barely whispers
You are my sunshine, beauty
My love from above, and now I am losing you forever
Dawn breaks, and she holds his arm tight
She whispers I am your sunshine, beauty your love from above,
And I love you
And I will be gone, but never from your heart.
For I am your sunshine, beauty forevermore
Forevermore
Meg Cramer, Grade 7
Dallastown Area Middle School

Lullaby

Sand squeezes between my toes with every mesmerizing step I take,
while the sunflower-yellow sun beats down on me
with its fiery stare.
The salty breeze blows through my hair
as I gaze at the cotton balls in the sky
making a masterpiece.
Colorful kites meet my eyes in the sapphire-blue sky.
The smell of sun screen fills my nose,
while I dip my toes in the freezing water, white with foam.
I look out at the horizon to see ships sailing along in hope to reach their destination.
The crashing of waves and squawking of seagulls soothe me to sleep,
like a baby listening to a lullaby.
Brooke Grant, Grade 7
Holicong Middle School

The Leather Couch

The leather couch in my house has gone through years of wear.
It has fared through its long life without even a tear.
Oh how I love its warm embrace,
All comfortable and cozy by the fireplace.
I can sit to homework; lay down for a nap,
Play a game with my sister, or just have a snack.
Sometimes my siblings fight for the space,
It takes all I can muster to find my own place.
On the couch, we map out our territory so the situation isn't quite as inflammatory.
Peaceful in our spots, we regret that we fought;
We seem to be feeling this a lot.
Although this couch has survived with flair,
I think I actually prefer the reclining leather chair.
Serena Johnson, Grade 7
St Thomas More School

All That's Left

Azure sky
conceals broken promises,
You never did come back.

Slowly, apathy spreads
through newly found time,
writhing in the darkness,

as single spotlight
projected from the undying moon
highlights imperfections in the house.

The broken soldiers, the marks of red,
have a certain heart
wrenching feeling like
something gone terribly wrong.

That worn crate restrains
the unforgettable memories.

Salvaged by sporadic
hideaways and coverings,

is a suffocating of what really maters
to those who leave without goodbyes,
is all that's left.

Leah DeFlitch, Grade 7
Pittsburgh CAPA 6-12 School

Clouds in the Sky

Clouds in the sky
as they gently glide by
take form in my eyes;
I see a cow or a butterfly.

I can lay there for hours
spotting buildings and towers
grasses and flowers
just one more hour…

My mind just falls away
my thoughts astray
oblivious of what others say
as I stare upward all day.

I might be the odd one out
but I don't pout
because there's no doubt
it's the clouds I can't live without.

Clouds in the sky
and the shapes that I spy
it's a joy you can't buy
a sight you can't pass by.

Annika Sundlof, Grade 8
Saucon Valley Middle School

Phillies in the Clutch

3 pm, the clock ticking down
Game is almost over
Clinching the playoffs
Towels spinning rapidly
Waves of die-hard "Phanatics"
Planes zooming above
Ketchup-red seats being seen
Everyone is standing on their feet
To catch a final glimpse
At the last pitch, sailing to the catcher
Strike 3, Game over
A deafening roar of the crowd
As players celebrate
The electric vibe strengthens
To the playoffs, we march

Colin Marhefka, Grade 7
Holicong Middle School

Rainy Day

Woooooooosh
Go the cars,
Zooming down the wet slippery road.
Plop
Goes a raindrop,
Landing in a puddle.
Chirp chirp
Go the birds,
Sitting in the tress.
Rumble
Goes a jetliner,
Thousands of feet above me.
Wirrrrshhhhhh
Goes the wind,
Blowing the leaves in the trees.

Max Memeger, Grade 7
Strath Haven Middle School

Autumn

The cool, dark air floats overhead;
Thick enough to cut.
And the whip of the autumn wind.
A night stroll down a trail;
Distant rumblings; a train.
The scornful cry of a crow;
They combine.
A strangely melodious tune.

Old Man Winter; he swipes,
Claws his way forward;
But why be worried?
No, rather, at ease.
For the soft crinkling of leaves;
It testifies.

Dan Joyce, Grade 7
St. James School

Things Aren't What They Seem

The happiest person alive
Can be the saddest inside
Bottling their emotions
Making them hide
Their plan to keep others
Cheerful in motion
So look around
Try to see
The happiest person
You know to be
Then think
Do I really know them?
Do they really know me?
Things really aren't what they seem.

Dymond Cummings, Grade 7
Armstrong Middle School

Cupcakes

My
Favorite
Thing
To eat is
Small but very sweet.
It's really fun to make. Oh!
I love my cupcake. The icing is
So smooth, it makes me want to
Move. People scream for ice-cream.
I want you to listen to find out what
You're missin'. Cupcakes are so fun,
They make me want to run! I love
To eat that fluffy cake. Oh! I can't
Wait for my next cupcake break!!!

Molly McCormack, Grade 7
Good Shepherd School

PopPop

It has been three years now
Since you left us alone
It has been hard
But we try to cope

Father's Day and Christmas Eve
Are the hardest for our family
We think of all the fun times
And gather on your birthday

We miss you very dearly
You will never know
But we always try to remember
God only takes the best

Nicole Bowker, Grade 7
Armstrong Middle School

Stink Berries + Purrell + Spiders = A Terrible Morning

I stroll outside and feel the morning chill
In my stomach is my sinus-infection pill
Unfortunately I hear a big KIRPLUNK!
I look down and my heart sunk

My shoe is covered in a brown mush
I try to wipe the shoe on a bush
Now my hand is covered in stink berries
I find Purrell, no more worries

On the bus a humongous spider jumps on me like Spiderman
I crush my shoulder on a seat BAM!
I look down; my arm smells like spoiled food
There are stink berries on me, now I'm in a horrendous mood

Finally, I wash off my arm like a doctor with no harm
The morning bell tells me to go to class like an alarm
What worries me waits on my flesh
A nasty Purrell smell which is a mess

Brian Hampton, Grade 8
Sandy Run Middle School

Bees

Playing basketball
On a calm
Twilight
And found a gaping hole
Full of bees hovering, and buzzing
Flying
In and out
Bringing glowing, amber, orange honey
To their big fat queen
I hate bees
They scare me
Their loud buzzing
And sharp stingers
The bumblebee-black-and-white striped bees
Scary
When they sting me
I feel a pinch of terror
I want to kill them
So I do

Jacob Berger, Grade 7
Holicong Middle School

Haunting

H ouses decorated with scary things
A wesome ghosts lingering in the dark
U nder the bed hides the monster
N o one can hide from the spirits
T rick or treaters running through the neighborhood
I solated and frightened
N ow you want to leave
G one like the wind — never to enter there again

Ryan Stipe, Grade 8
Chichester Middle School

Orange Leaves

Katie –
Timid, smart, loving, and overprotective,
Sister of Eddie,
Lover of the cold silence of night, the
     crisp chills of autumn breezes, the darkened
     sky on a cold winter day,
Who feels joy at the sight of orange leaves, sorrow
     at the sound of a child's whine, calm
     at the sound of rustling leaves,
Who needs comfort when burdened by the cold,
     friendship at the end of a dreadful day,
     serenity when willfully alone,
Who gives an ear when anyone's down, a smile
     when someone's feeling sad, happiness in
     the midst of tension,
Who fears falling downwards through endless black,
     growing up too fast, a friend's tears,
Who would like to see everyone happy, my brother
     teaching me guitar, no more wars that
     destroy any peace,
Who lives in a house on Clayton St.

Katie McClure, Grade 8
Chichester Middle School

The Storm

Outside it was getting very, very dark.
The night was as windy as a hurricane;
The rain was falling hard.

Lightning flashed,
Trees fell,
And dirt flew.
After it was over,
There was a peace that only lasted for a short time.

After the peace, all night you heard
Elephant-roaring chain saws burning,
Wet clumps of sawdust blowing.
The noise went on for days until finally,
There was peace again.

Our trees lay on the ground for days.
They still sit there cold and dead.
It's been several months now,
And I hope to see the rest of our yard soon.

Jason McGuire, Grade 8
Faith Tabernacle School

How to Stand Out

Being a follower is like being a wannabe
after you have no leader you're just a Barbie
Never let someone tell you who and where you belong in this world
it's your choice
either it's good or bad it's your decision

Izhane Crockett, Grade 7
Ridley Middle School

December Snow

The snow glistens under the moonlight,
Snowflakes fall, big and white.

Every one is a different shape,
It creates a cover, much like a cape.

It falls here and there,
Covering every inch of air.

The children cry in joy and glee,
While mothers stand inside with hot tea.

The snow falls once in a while,
Creating big and little piles.

Seeing it brings much joy,
More than a brand new toy.

It snows for days and never ceases,
The snow never gives or releases.

The snow glistens under the moonlight,
Snow is still falling, it's a beautiful sight.

Natalie Ciepiela, Grade 7
Landisville Middle School

Broken Hope

Broken hope is a gruesome figure.
It is like the broken light bulb,
Forever shattered.
It is a childhood hero,
Crushed by the villain.
But like all hope,
It can be reassembled.
The bulb, replaced.
The hero, risen from the grave.
It shows that however hard,
Or shattered hope is,
It can be revived.

Brendan Marani, Grade 8
Fred S Engle Middle School

My Brain Is Rotten

My brain is rotten.
I've forgotten,
everything I have to know.
For poetry is not my strength,
I am struggling to a great length.
My brain is rotten.
There is no cure,
I have to say I am sure.
But what I'm dealing with right now,
will not take forever because I know how,
to fix my brain that's rotten.

Boni Trinter, Grade 8
Fred S Engle Middle School

Life

Life is just a game where you can play and play until you don't have any more lives left
Life is nothing to me because I don't think we've reached it yet
All we have here is disaster
Crime in every corner
Every block and every hood
Shots rang out and no one knows who shot who
They keep secrets because they think they're going to get shot too
But all you have to do is tell so the day can end how it should
Taxes go up each and every day
You can't even park on the streets because it's too high to pay
Food is so high you might as well starve
Light, gas, and water went up so you might as well say bye to that lovely house of yours
Election day is here so choose wisely
But how can you do that because you don't know who's lying
They can be lying in your face thinking it's funny
Take all the money we've got and make this a poor country
We've got the first black president saying we are going to make a change
But all I see is change going the wrong way
I wish there was a button that can undo all of this pain
But right now that doesn't exist
Because life remains the same, as a disaster, that we created but it can also be changed.

Erica Greer, Grade 9
City Charter High School

My Bad Francesca

Francesca, I'm sorry for running up your electric bill.
Sorry I took your hamster to clean myself.
Sorry I slapped you because I was having a nightmare.

Sorry I broke and can't replace your blow drier.
Sorry I talked during the movie.
Sorry I told my other friends about your rash.

Sorry I set your fireproof curtains on fire and nearly burned down your house.
I'm sorry I used all of your toilet paper.
But we're cool, no hard feelings, right?

Bryce McManus, Grade 7
Charles F Patton Middle School

Autumn

Trees tell the leaves, "Change color for your final days."
Flowers reluctantly give up their petals and leaves.
Trees bare, they prepare for the fate winter has given them.
From their vantage point, the withered flowers see all the changes.
Trees dance in the wind, sheltering animals from the blustery conditions.
As the winds prepare for winter storms, some go on joy rides.
The squirrels chatter amongst themselves in apprehension for students to rush through a portal to the outside world.
The world seems to be in hyper drive.
Cars are zooming, speeding, and honking their horns.
The metal monsters have taken over.
No more bike wheels spinning or strolls through the park.
Maybe you can get a brief moment to enjoy yourself or you may not.
But that is expected during the time when the leaves fall and the wind starts to blow.

Brinn Campbell-Olson, Grade 7
Strath Haven Middle School

Famous

Cameras flashing everywhere,
Everyone look at what I wear.

All eyes on me,
Need to get in a limo ASAP.

Where do I go next?
I never knew being famous could be so complex.

Singing, dancing, concerts every night,
All I can think of is, "Don't get stage fright."

Everywhere I look, everywhere I stare,
Cameras, cameras are everywhere.

Screaming fans want my autograph,
I think we need a bigger security staff.

Posters, hats, T-shirts and more,
Bearing my name they truly adore.

Anna Wieneke, Grade 7
St James School

Speed

Speed is like a super car racing down the road.
It is like a prancing horse kicking up some stones.
Like a raging bull throwing off its rider.
It looks like Cole Hamels pitching a slider.
It smells like burning rubber on the Top Gear test track.
It is like heat melting an ice cream cone in the scorching hot sun.
It is like a crazy monster on a rampage down the street.
Speed is like being burnt by a flame.
Speed is like a slap across the face.
Speed is like winning a Formula One race.
Speed is like getting an 'A' on a test.
Speed is like surfing on the beach.
Speed is like a splash of ice cold water.
Speed is like an intense game of football in the rain.

Benjamin Stephens, Grade 7
St. Anselm Elementary School

Loving Family

She was always there to dry my eyes whenever I cried
whenever I sighed you always had me speak my mind.
You helped me find my way
you're that glowing spark that speaks to me and says, "Hey!"
My loving brave family who is my wall that seems to never fall.
Even when it feels like I lost it all.
The wall has still not fallen.
but how can I lose it all with a loving family like you all.
You are there through thick and thin
that's why we'll always win in the end.
Blood is thicker than water, love is the definition of my family,
caring is the definition of me.

Shamia Washington, Grade 7
Armstrong Middle School

Sister's P.O.V.

Did you know
that life was no piece of paper
that you can fill with simple words
so when you mess up,
you can just erase and start over?
You need to realize that some people
are like pieces of glass.
Cold, fragile and leave you with more
of a mess than when you started.
And I want to let you know
that having to be told what to do
or having to share with others are not
the hard decisions of life.
Maybe at your age, when boys have cooties,
you make wishes on shooting stars
and pinky promises are important, you may think that.
But when you grow up, things change.
My little sister will learn
the truth soon.

Emily Schwager, Grade 8
Pittsburgh CAPA 6-12 School

Friends

Always there for you
Through thick and thin
They will stay true to you
No matter what happens

Some are close
Practically family
The ones that are there for you most
And can get a smile out of you on your worst days

Some are not as close
Nowhere near family
However, they are there for you
And you love them anyway

You have many friends
During the fun times
Yet, when the rough times roll around
Is when you discover who your true friends are

Caitlyn Degner, Grade 8
Maple Point Middle School

My Life

A peaceful place where I like to be
No trouble in the world that can bother me
Cool friends, loving parents and a quiet neighborhood
But where I live there's a scent, a smell that is not good
The smell from the drugs that some people smoke
If I stay away I can have a good life
I will get a good job and finally get away
From that bad scented smell in my life.

David Wilson, Grade 7
Armstrong Middle School

Ocean

Deep, dark, and dangerous
That's how I would describe
The ocean.

There are so many creatures
In the deep blue.
Dolphins, sharks, jellyfish
Seahorses, and clownfish
Those are just a few.

All the fish are
So beautiful with all their colors.
They are like an enormous rainbow
In the middle of the sea.

The ocean is such
A mysterious place
To live in.
It's so deep, dark,
And dangerous.

Kylie Blaettler, Grade 7
Landisville Middle School

Him

His laugh,
His smile,
His hugs,
Worthwhile
His eyes,
His voice,
My heart,
his choice
Our jokes,
Our laughs,
Our love,
Will last
He is wonderful
In every way
I think of him,
Every day
Accepting imperfections
Is easy to do
When you know someone
Feels the way you do too.

Julia Holland, Grade 7
Armstrong Middle School

Waiting

When waiting,
Time slows down
As in boredom you drown
While time goes half as fast
Then finally the moment comes at last.
Was what you were waiting for worth it?

Dominic Walker, Grade 7
St Joseph School

Can You Hear Them Now?

The language of the deaf
The one I want to speak
I can hear them, but they can't hear me.
So how do we communicate?
The hand spelling
It looks like nothing to you,
But means everything to me
Giving them the tool to talk
Without this,
They are not heard
This is the language that sets them free!
The language that lets them be heard
Without them hearing at all
Sign language means nothing to you
But means everything to me.
So,
Can you hear them now?

Julia Balchak, Grade 8
Bellmar Middle School

Grandmother

To my loving grandmother,
Who's been there through thick and thin.
I've always loved you dearly,
Especially your caring grin.

But on the Fourteenth of November,
You left this world for someplace better.
Because of the shocking heart attack,
You let God take you in.
You had to leave your children,
Grandchildren and rest of kin.

Yet so soon you would meet your mother.
Some friends and more ancestors,
Whom loved you dearly also.
Your smile laugh and gestures,
So rest in peace my mommom.

Alyssa Clausen, Grade 8
Chichester Middle School

Peter John Keller

Peter
Gone from the world
Never gave up
But he was subdued
John
He was a good man
He was loving and loved
Cancer took him hostage
He fought a losing fight
Father of one, Nick
Keller
His love will never be forgotten

Nicholas Keller, Grade 7
Armstrong Middle School

Just Me

It's just me sitting here
looking around, not knowing what to do.
Who am I, where am I, and why?
I'm the different girl; the odd one out.
The one in the back of the room.
Not being seen or making a sound.
On the boys' basketball team.
Just one of the guys.
The horseback rider:
trotting faster and faster.
Said to be so weird.
Well that's just me.
I know the strangest facts.
I laugh at everything.
I happen to be different.
And that is fine with me.
Not like anyone else.
Different is different
and different is me.
I won't change for anyone.
I am me and it's the best I can be.

Anna Lutz, Grade 7
St Vitus School

Christmas

Christmas is about Christ,
Christmas is amazing,
Christmas is about His birth,
But I think most of us have forgotten.

I think Santa has stolen Christmas,
I wish I saw more nativities,
Sitting cozily out front,
Or placed under a tree,

We all need a reminder,
Of how it all began,
Children and adults both,
All across our country,
and the world.

It's not about the presents,
It's not about the stockings,
It's not about leaving cookies for Santa,
It's not about the lights on your house, no.
It's about the Lord, our Savior's birth.

Ryan Gettis, Grade 7
Armstrong Middle School

Spring

Vegetables grow.
Potatoes start to be picked.
Carrots end up in soup.

Jacob Richmond, Grade 7
Trinity Middle School

The Wind

The wind was blowing gently
across the lush green grass
swaying in the wind a small tree
just barely has leaves
one by one the leaves fall off
a red one, a yellow one
a green one, a brown one
Many different colors
raking up the leaves
many different colors
children play
parents watch in amusement
as the children jump into the piles
of many colors
the children look like trees
with leaves stuck to them
parents brush their children off
the children play some more
but the little tree just sits and listens
to the amusement of children in lush fall air.

Emily Saylor, Grade 7
Landisville Middle School

Softball

I can feel my heart in my head, beating hard.
I feel eyes watching me as I go in the batter's box,
Just hoping the pitcher will give me something to hit.
She starts her wind up.
The bat heavy in my hands.
She releases the ball.
"Strike one," the ump says.
Another ball comes flying my way.
"Strike two"
My heart is in my stomach!
Now waiting to see what will happen.
The ball comes too fast to see.
But as I swing,
I see the ball hit the bat and go flying to the outfield.
Please don't catch it. Please don't catch it.
As I run to second base.
The ball goes over the left fielder's head as I run to third.
I brought in two runs as I ran.
An inside the park home run!
This day couldn't get any better!

Lana Duda, Grade 7
Strath Haven Middle School

Baseball

Baseball is the game I play
Late in the crisp October day
I love playing with my friends
My team fights, fights, fights, until the very end
But, sadly, the season ends today

Bobby Jones, Grade 8
Chichester Middle School

Figment

You were there.
And then suddenly,
you weren't.
A blessing in a way.

You were the fog that clouded up my view.
You were the thing always standing in my way.
You were a down looker,
someone whose standards I could never meet.
I'm supposed to say I'm happy you're gone.

Without you here, my vision is 20/20
I never want to look back at the clouded memories of you and me.
You seem merely a figment of my demented imagination now.
Without you, life is perfect.
Perfect.

But maybe what we had was the perfect balance.
Maybe I don't like my vision so clear,
my memories gone,
and my life so perfect.
Maybe we can coexist, without ever having existed at all.
Maybe we can create our own perfection.
Imperfectly perfect.

Jeremy Barson, Grade 7
Richboro Middle School

Ode to the Young Days

Oh how I wish I still had the days
When I was young, and small, and crazed,
With love and beauty
And only great sights
And had fresh new cookies every three nights

Oh how I wish I was small and frail
Yet careless and free of our times despair
Please give me a moment
To feel this way again,
To be happy and silly
With no weight on my shoulders,
To live free and to just live life

Give me the giggles
And splashes, and thumps
Of just everyday playing,
And falling on my rump

Give me the times
When small shadows ran beside me
And I didn't have to know too much,
Or too little,
To have anyone guide me

Allison Dubinsky, Grade 7
Richboro Middle School

Alcohol

When you have a problem, don't for a second think,
That all your problems can be solved with an alcoholic drink.

Once you drink, your brain cells will begin to rapidly decrease,
And soon after that, your right of judgment will begin to cease.

Your problems may subside and even go away,
That's because you begin to drink more day by day.

After a long day of drinking at your local bar,
You fumble with your keys, and then get in your car.

You can't seem to focus your eyes on the road,
You never knew to stop at the crossroad.

In front of you, your life had flashed,
Right before you deathly crashed.

This could be you! So do yourself a favor and think,
Of what could possibly happen from a simple drink.

Riley Horvath, Grade 8
St James School

Autumn

F alling leaves
A ll colors and sizes
L ying gracefully on the ground
L ike snow in winter
I step and they crunch
N ow and then they make tornadoes
G oing 'round and 'round

L eaving other leaves behind
E ach leaf cares only for itself
A ll are special and
V ery colorful
E ach day the
S outhern winds beckon, wanting company as they move on

Mikala Hardie, Grade 7
J R Fugett Middle School

Carmel

The best birthday gift I ever received was a small fury orange pet.
Carmel is the cutest guinea pig you have ever met.
When he runs and hops, he's full of joy.
Carmel is better than any other birthday toy.
He requires a lot of love and care.
When he wants attention he will stop and stare
He stands on his hind legs for a lettuce meal.
When the refrigerator opens you can hear him squeal.
It is funny to watch him run and dart.
I love my guinea pig with all my heart.
I wonder if he knows how I feel.
This love I Have for him is very real.

Colin Heckmanski, Grade 7
St Anselm Elementary School

Good versus Evil

The story of good versus evil,
An age old tale,
Throughout history, it has gone on.
From ancient times to the modern day,
The heroism of one man against the savage beast,
To the thousands of souls engaged in combat.
Our world revolves around the immortal battle,
Our actions, our thoughts, our beliefs,
Reflect the engagement between the two.
At times, though, good prevails, others the evil.
If one would cease to exist, society would fall,
Succumbing to the pressure to do good or evil.
Our way of life would forever change,
Gone mad, rundown, obsolete, and miserable.
Without each other there would be no good or evil.
The destruction of those obsessed with power,
To those who wish to save it all.
What would our world become...?

Brandon George, Grade 8
St James School

Walking in Snowfall

On a frigid winter morning,
I trekked out into the dawn,
While brilliant snowflakes, frozen crystals
Floated down from the clouds above.
The rising sun could not yet be seen,
Its warmth barely touching the surface.
A sheet of pure white clouds obliterates the heavens.
The trees, cold and leafless, beg for spring;
Their bare silhouettes reach for the sky.
Still the snow falls,
Silencing all but the whistling wind
Which slices the air on its icy path.
The flakes continue their descent,
Finding refuge in shadows cast by darkened trees.
They pile on the ground,
Inching forward until they dominate the landscape.
As I watched, the forest grew sleek in a frozen dream,
Coated in dunes of snow and sheets of ice.

Nicholas Carolan, Grade 8
St Thomas More School

Imagine

Imagine lying on the beach, with the ocean nice and calm,
Imagine the cool summer breeze, skimming on your palm.
Imagine the sand all soft and hot,
Imagine playing like an energetic tot.
Imagine getting up and going for a swim,
Imagine being by yourself when the afternoon is dim.
Imagine riding the waves like a blue dolphin dashing,
Imagine diving into the waves when the waves are crashing.
Imagine going home now, which is such a bummer,
Imagine waiting a year and going back next summer.

Christopher Hibbs, Grade 7
Holy Child Academy

If I Had a Horse

I wish I had a horse.
If I did, I'd brush it, of course.

If I had a horse, I'd let it eat grass.
And no more my mother would I sass.

I wouldn't mind cleaning out its stall.
I'd rather do that than go to the mall.

If I had a horse, I'd hope it to be white.
I'd ride it fast like a bird in flight.

My horse would be a beautiful light,
Shining bright in the dark, dark night.
Rachel Peterson, Grade 7
Greencastle-Antrim Middle School

Monkey

Very hairy
Also can be very scary

Loves bananas
And loves trees

A monkey can be
Just like you and me!

Sometimes they jump, sometimes they fly
I once saw one touch THE SKY!

Monkeys hurt and monkeys save,
But they will always be my fave!
Tyra Rowland, Grade 7
Greencastle-Antrim Middle School

Cats

He pounces on a ball of yarn
and sometimes lives in a barn

He thinks he's the king of the house
But all he does is chase the lonely mouse

He is sly as a fox
and likes to sleep in the box

His favorite drink is milk
And sometimes likes to lay on silk

When his day comes to an end
He goes to sleep with his best friend
Kara Wright, Grade 7
Greencastle-Antrim Middle School

A Working Progress of Aspirations

Falling backward
I can't compete
Sighing hopelessly
Should I claim defeat?

It sings to me like a morning dove
Calling to me
Like a longing love
Slipping away from me
Tasting like a fading dream

Slipping forward
There's a sound of drums
Realizing efforts
This is not a dream anymore!
This is worth fighting for!
JanaBeth Dellamedaglia, Grade 8
Wattsburg Area Middle School

My Best Friend

We do everything together
Share secrets, laugh,
And do crazy things.

When there is a time I
Need her
She's there

When I am crying she
Cheers me up.
She is there for me
I am there for her.

I will never regret
The day
I met her.
Teresa Yeager, Grade 7
Armstrong Middle School

Life Is

Life is a rocky mountain road.
Life is the door not opened.
Life is an imaginary wall.
Life is never knowing what's ahead.
Life is every opportunity possible.
Life is the steepest hill.

Life is short lived.
Life is long felt.
Life is never winning.
Life is your best efforts.
Life is your only try.
Life is the work of one will.
Life is the impact you make on others.
Tyler Harris, Grade 8
Chichester Middle School

The Wolf

The paw prints in the dirt
As distinct as footprints are on fresh snow
Deserted, alone
She walked
Till she found the lake
A lake that in the moonlight
Was a flickering candle
About to go out
Like she was…
If she didn't make it
Running, running, running
People spend their whole life running
But from what?
The wolf turned around
And found what she was looking for
All along.
Ana Paula Martinez, Grade 7
St. Thomas More School

Who Would Like to See Happiness

Emily
Honest, nice, careful, helpful,
Sister of Heather,
Lover of sports, drawing, coloring,
Who feels excited when traveling,
Scared in the dark,
Frightened in the dentist's office,
Who needs friends, family, and weekends,
Who gives support, encouragement,
Happiness,
Who fears snakes, sickness, and
Cancer,
Who would like to see family and
Friends filled with happiness,
Who lives in a small white house
On Church Street.
Emily Hogan, Grade 8
Chichester Middle School

Invisible

She wasn't knocked down
She was walked through
She was alone
She had no one to talk to
She watches as the world moves around her
She waits for some hope to surround her
She cries out for help
But no one hears her
She asks for a band-aid
But no one heals her
She begs for a safe haven
But in the end she only finds heaven
A heart breaking
A life being lost in the making
Hannah Mogaka, Grade 8
Fred S Engle Middle School

Snow

Snow is falling, falling down
It doesn't even make a sound
We play around in the snow
I hate to see it go
I know it will come back next year
Even if I shed a tear
Snow is falling, falling down
Oh I hate to see it go.
Colby Smith, Grade 7
Landisville Middle School

Nature

I see leaves falling,
And hitting the ground
I hear the birds go tweet,
In the trees way up high
I feel the cool air,
As the wind smacks my face
I smell my neighbor's dinner cooking,
I taste the fresh air of the outdoors
Kali Wright, Grade 7
Strath Haven Middle School

Dance

Sliding feet across the floor
Crowds clapping and cheering for more
The music beats through my chest
Wanting a solo so dancing your best
Muscles hurt when we stay in a pose
Sweat building as we leap in our clothes
Now our muscles are in a bend
Waiting backstage for the recital to end
Victoria Silva, Grade 7
Armstrong Middle School

My Boyfriend

T alented
E nergetic
R adiant
R espectful
A mazing
N ice
C ourage
E xciting
Shelby Himes, Grade 8
Chichester Middle School

The Uses of a Chair

Relaxing and reading a book,
Studying before a final,
Sleeping when you won't walk upstairs,
Eating dinner at night,
Watching TV on a cold day.
Max O'Brien, Grade 7
St Joseph School

Transitions to a Dream

Blue, green, gold,
To blue, red, white,
A flight across the plains,
Could change one's life.

The family left behind,
Caught in the weeping rains,
But a new life flourishing,
Could take away the pain.

A life in this new land extended new decisions,
Out of other countries America was a striking vision.

Mom came from way down south,
My dad's clan did too.
Both came from other worlds,
America the beautiful brand new.

From Portuguese to English,
Rio to New York,
Surely then this person changed,
Now accustomed to this newfangled and delightful life.

She never let go of her roots,
And always stays close,
My mother was very strong, and leaving her home to her was never wrong.
Ana-Sofia Puig, Grade 7
Holicong Middle School

Life

Life
It can be short or long.
It can be happy or sad.

Life
It can be a box of pictures filled with great memories.
It can be an empty box filled with nothing but bad memories and loneliness.

Life
Is like a crazy rollercoaster; it has its ups and downs.
Or it can be like a calm ocean in the soft cool breeze.

Life
Can be filled with family and friends
Or it can be standing alone.

Life
Should be filled with love
If it is not
Then what is life?

Life
Is what you make it.
Strive to make it right.
Lily Mello, Grade 8
St Thomas More School

Life

Life is black and white
But has colors everywhere
Life brings anguish and happiness
Like when the leaves turn orange and brown

Life is spoken in millions of tongues
But only yours is clear
Life has two roads
But a third is always there
Like a mother's love
Or a father's well-earned care.

Life is wealthy and penniless
What we are determines its worth
We are life
Life is us
Life is eternal and everlasting
Like the songbird in the spring
Life is a gift
A gift to all.

Liam Clark, Grade 9
East High School

The Tall Oak Tree

Whirrrr
As the brief wind flies throughout the trees
Making the thin branches brush each other
In the tall oak tree.
Riiiinnngg
The wind chimes clash against one another
As the loud hummingbirds peck the trees
Near the tall oak tree.
Whisssttllliiing
The soft birds chirp throughout the day
Before they fly through the clear blue sky
Above the tall oak tree.
Shaaake
Squirrels running through branches
While I watch while they gather nuts
Inside the tall oak tree.
Swisshhh
I look to see the leaves dancing on their branches
Before they fall onto the green grass
Under the tall oak tree.

Christie Shaughnessy, Grade 7
Strath Haven Middle School

My Gift and My Curse

Today I died and I'm up in Heaven,
Looking down on the world archangel number seven,
I was sent to Earth with a mission to complete,
My memories remain bittersweet,
Messenger with a double duty burst,
It's my legacy my gift and my curse.

Kelley Love, Grade 8
Chichester Middle School

The World

How is this world still sane?
Nothing is just plain.
There's less love than war.
Which is worth more?
Gas pollutes the air.
So do chemicals. I swear.
Not many people are happy.
Some so mad or sad they're snappy.
There are so many crimes committed.
So many punishments are not omitted.
Some are homeless, starving, or needy.
While others are greedy.
Some economics are horrible.
The rate of getting better is probable.
History is fading away.
The future lights the way.
Technology is believed to make things better.
What happened to writing a letter?
I don't see how we enjoy technology.
When there are other things like biology and zoology.

Ashley Warner, Grade 7
Landisville Middle School

Memories

Long hair, brown eyes, and a smile so free,
Looking down at the picture, it's all that I see.
Pink dress, tiara, and a wand in hand,
She's ready to go to her imaginary dreamland.
Innocent as can be, worry free,
Oh, I remember those days so clearly.

I remember being a curious thing back then,
Always blabbing again and again.
Running around playing hide and seek,
When "IT" would find me, I would laugh and shriek.
Everything was so exciting back then, so free,
But the years have gone by a little too quickly.

So as I look back at the picture in front of me,
I remember that day so perfectly.
The day I dressed up as a princess,
A moment that was just so priceless.
And the years, they went by way too fast,
But the happy memories will always last.

Jona Mojados, Grade 8
Chichester Middle School

Best Friend

My best friend is someone who is home, every single day.
He eats, sleeps, and he also loves to play.
When I come home, he is waiting,
And when he sees me his tail starts to sway.
When I see him, and he sees me,
I know it's him, my dog, Shawnty.

Alex Hiller, Grade 7
Landisville Middle School

The Storm

The lights flicker off…
The dark gray clouds start pouring onto the Earth…
Huge waves begin to form in the water…
A storm has arrived…
"Whoosh!" cries the howling wind…
"Splash! Splash!" exclaim the waves crashing across the rocky shore…
"Ruff!!!" Rosie and Pepsi yell at a squirrel attempting to find shelter…
"Pitter patter…pitter patter…pitter patter…" sings the rain while pounding down on the roof…
"Thump…thump…thump…" says the tree knocking its branches against the window…
All…of…a…sudden…
The lights flicker on…
The wind stops howling…
The sun moves in front of the gray clouds…
The singing on the roof stops.
All of the animals seeking shelter enjoy the newfound sun
"Chirp! Chirp! Chirp!"
Announce the birds telling everybody
The storm is over!

Zoe McElroy, Grade 7
Strath Haven Middle School

Hungry as a Horse

The smell of the ocean was in the air, food in buckets everywhere
Ice cream, doughnuts, brownies galore, an eating contest down at the shore

My stomach growled before the start, I was full of adrenaline and a pounding heart
The owner shouted, "Go" as I dug in, gobbling down this much must be a sin

I started off strong and on a great pace, soon to be sick and want out of the race
I was halfway done when my body screamed, "Full," I had to keep eating, be as tough as a bull

Coming down the home stretch, almost all the way through, the ice cream started to look like stew
Finally, I finished my task was complete, I then passed out landing right in my seat

I woke with water being splashed in my face, I staggered over to get the trophy out of the case
The colossal-sized trophy now all mine, I'm the next Fat Albert, this is a sign

Unexpectedly, I'm as skinny as can be, but I prevailed as far as anyone can see
I was a bear, I won this fair and square

Benjamin Stern and Dan Warszawski, Grade 8
Sandy Run Middle School

What One Person Can Do

Here I am, spending yet another day in this same dismal atmosphere,
laying low under a blanket of regrets that I've been weaving for so many years.
I don't think I can last too much longer, hiding in this shadow containing the fears of my past,
the worries of my present, and the possibilities in my future.
No matter how pushy the 'populars' get, no matter the quantity of my complaints,
no matter how drastic the problems actually are,
there's always this one person who's always here to listen. This person talks to me on my weak days,
but keeps away on my weakest to make me feel a little bit stronger…a little bit tougher.
This individual is like the sun poking out from seeming miles of stormy skies; like a flower growing out of a patch of weeds. The
tears that continuously flowed are now not worth crying. The silence I once held within is now a voice, loud and clear. I find it
true: The lonely are the strongest.

Brittany Coulter, Grade 7
Moon Middle School

Flowers

Millions of shapes make flowers form.
They are red as a heart, yellow as corn.
Flowers are so pretty and they dazzle me.
Attracting lots of bugs, even a bumblebee.
Flowers dance together, in the fall breeze,
As the autumn trees let go of the leaves.
The petals fall as winter comes.

Sophia Russo, Grade 7
Landisville Middle School

Lovate

Love
smitten, tender
revere, endear, hypnotize
immortal, congenial, pique, spite
abominate, loathe, abhor
hostile, bitter
Hate

Tori Fanucci, Grade 8
Good Shepherd School

Popcorn

P oppable,
O ften delicious,
P ortable,
C armel can be added,
O ily and buttery,
R emember a napkin!
N ever get sick of it.

Madison McHugh, Grade 7
Landisville Middle School

Desert

Desert
hot, dry
running, hoping, walking
cactus, sandstorm, bones
shifting, changing, moving
soft, firm
Lake

Eddie Rice, Grade 7
Greencastle-Antrim Middle School

Winter/Summer

Winter
Cold, white
Snowing, freezing, skiing
Ice, snowboard, cocktail, swimsuit
Playing, swimming, loving
Hot, red
Summer

Maike Hueckelheim, Grade 7
Richboro Middle School

Me, Myself and I

I say to myself every day, I love the way you look today.

But then other times, I look in the mirror,
And hate what I see, Sometimes I just hate being me!

I wear a fake smile everywhere, so people won't stop and stare.
There is so much in my mind that I wish I could leave it all behind.

When I see the other girls pass me in the halls, I wish I could be like them.
Rich, popular, and always taken.

Sometimes I forget who I really am, but then I see my best friend,
And I remember why I'm here, to make her happy year after year.

So me, myself, and I agree, no one could be exactly like me!
I am special in my own way no matter what other people think or say.

So watch out for me I am on a roll
I love who I am and I love my heart and soul.

So no matter what you say I will never change
Because, me, myself and I like being this way.

Sabrina Young, Grade 7
Landisville Middle School

The Woman in the Window

The crystal chandelier shines like a thousand stars on the people below.
Whose faces are not only hidden by lavish masks but by lavish lies,
Adorned with priceless gold silk and the faint stench of sour poison.
She didn't deserve it,
No one did.
Though what happened that night,
That cold winter night,
Was between the two of them.
For I,
For anyone in that elaborate ballroom would give a thousand faces of silver to know,
What she knew.
What he knew.
What the woman in the window knew.

Maeve O'Brien, Grade 8
Arcola Intermediate School

Civil War Reaches Home

I'm angry.
Not frothing-at-the-mouth angry, not about-to-spontaneously-combust angry,
Not angry like a psychopath killer,
Just simmering, slow, hiding anger, careful not to overflow.
I'm angry that the soldiers take whatever they want,
Angry that my farm has become a sea of death,
Angry that there's no resolution in sight.
I remain quiet, cautious, patient,
Willing to help and willing to give.
I let my anger hide and bide,
But I'm really still angry, deep down inside.

Kathleen Bracken, Grade 8
Mother of Sorrows School

Fall and Winter

Snow and leaves
Leaves and snow
I know one must go

Snow in winter
Leaves in fall

In each one I have a ball
In the snow I make a lump
In the fall I jump

At the beginning of fall you close the pool
Compared to winter which is so cool

In fall it's all yellow and red
In winter you wear a hat on your head

In the fall with the leaves you rake
In the winter it's fun to bake
Mary Thomas, Grade 7
Landisville Middle School

Snowflake

Forming in the clouds
intricate in shape and size
he is so happy and delicate
and will never tell a lie

His friends and family gather around
ready for the descent
jumping into the starry sky
a life he will never forget

Falling slowly past the moon
looking all around
for friends and family that left before him
spread across the ground

His flight is almost ending
tiny as a grain of sand
untouched, unharmed
into a winter wonderland
Abby Ciach, Grade 7
Charles F Patton Middle School

My Brother

What can I say about my brother?
Second offspring of my father and mother.
He is ten years old,
And very bold.
He loves to sing in the shower,
And is gifted with athletic power.
Similar to me in many ways,
Yet separated by two years and two days.
Megan Zimmerman, Grade 7
Holy Child Academy

Life

Silence
It can often be louder than any words spoken aloud
It can have more meaning than words or even strife
Some may think you're just hiding, alone, in the crowd
When maybe you're just thinking, thinking about life.
Noise
It can be annoying, comforting, stressful, or nice
It can be the calming sound of a mother's coos, blaring music, maybe someone in strife
Some may think you're loud so you entice
When maybe you're just talking, talking about life.
Helen Haile, Grade 8
Fred S Engle Middle School

Fear

Fear is a man lurking in the dark
Fear is a vicious dog's horrifying bark
Fear is Chucky, chasing you with a knife
Fear is running for your life
Fear is a zombie's moan, breaking the silence of the night
Fear is the pain, of a vampire's bite
Fear is trying to scream, but unable to make a sound
Fear is seeing your life flash before your eyes, as you plummet to the ground
Fear happens in the absence of light
Fear is knowing…not everything will be …all right
Olivia Roth, Grade 7
Schuylkill Valley Middle School

I See

Beautiful
Ocean as clear as drinking water
The sand whiter than paint
The calm ocean splashing into the sand
People saying "Let's stay longer!"
The salt water all night smells like sea salt
The beautiful air like a candle that you just opened
The salt water in my mouth when a wave comes and pushes me into in the water
The very popular dish, jerk chicken
Very relaxed as if I was in a spa
Allecia Stiles, Grade 9
Conrad Weiser High School

Baseball

Baseball, baseball, it is…
Amazing, exciting, and maybe sometimes boring
It can be tough but you will get through it
It can be hot, warm, cold, or even rain but you still play
You can get mad, or happy whatever it is
There are nine or more innings
You work with your team as a team and you will succeed
There is running, catching, sliding and even throwing so don't worry
Baseball, baseball it is an amazing game to play
Jordan Brown, Grade 7
William M Meredith School

My Cat

All afternoon, a dark and dreary day
The elephant-gray drowsiness of my home
Meow, meow, she cries for help
Petrified when I see her losing control
The voices in and out of my head
Crying
Petting the soft, gray and black hair
Softness, gentleness
Hoping for better
Feeling furry hair
Calmness
Hanging on to the sight I will never forget
Lindsey Ahearn, Grade 7
Holicong Middle School

I Am Three Shades

Part of me is neon orange
Lively and crazy
Funny and weird

Other days I'm pale purple
Sleepy and all worn out
Careless and useless

Sometimes I'm a fiery red
Angry and ready to explode
Want to be alone
Wanting to go home
Natalie Coates, Grade 8
Chichester Middle School

Regrets

If I was perfect,
I would have
Not a single regret.

If I was perfect,
When I look back,
There would be no mistakes.

If I was perfect,
Then I would not
Be writing these words.

Emilie Masterson, Grade 9
Holicong Middle School

Eagles

E nergetic
A ggressive
G reat
L oved
E ntertaining
S uper Bowl bound
Andrew Galazeski, Grade 8
Chichester Middle School

The Petrifying Cut

Terrified one morning, I saw my reflection
My hair style needed a whole new direction
Quickly, I hopped in the car and set the GPS
Dreading the hairdresser seeing my horrifying mess

Desperately, I pleaded for the trendiest cut
My mom deflected my plead, "no ifs, ands, or buts"
The dresser thrusts my neck back
from across the country you could hear the crack

Her long with like nails clawed into my head
thinking to myself, I will soon be dead
A river of shampoo slid into my eyes
Everyone in the salon laughed as I cried

Dye after dye oozed into my hair
My hair was rainbow ashes but at this point I didn't care
her sharp, shiny, sheers attacked my locks
The horror brought me back to when I had the chicken pox

My mom said I looked breathtaking so I checked her nose
she sounds like Pinocchio; her dishonesty shows
As my mom paid the check I was one infuriated girl
two hundred dollars for this cut? I felt like I was going to hurl
Laura Marmion, Danielle Sternberg, and Hannah Lamberg, Grade 8
Sandy Run Middle School

The Miracle at the Meadowlands

We talked about this game all week.
For a win we did not seek.
We were losing by twenty one.
Loudly, Giants fans were laughing and having so much fun.

But then Jeremy Maclin secured a touchdown pass.
The Giants' lead was now easier to surpass.
The Eagles' defense came onto the field.
The Giants thought they had the game sealed.

Then suddenly the amazing Asante Samuel got an interception
And speedy Desean Jackson caught a forty yard reception.
There were four minutes left in the game.
If we lose the momentum now, that would be a shame.

When Trent Cole, like a crazy man, forced a fumble
The Giants stadium started to grumble.
Then David Akers kicked a quick field goal
And that pulled the Eagles out of the hole.

The Eagles stopped the Giants with sixteen seconds to go.
Tom Coughlin said to punt it out of bounds and Matt Dodge said, "No."
Quickly, Desean Jackson caught the ball, started running and could not stop.
The Eagles just made a comeback and now they are on top!
Joseph Siwinski, Grade 8
Sandy Run Middle School

Blue Chevy

I remember your blue Chevy the one with the silver stripe and the splotches of rust.

I remember when you used to take me out to the field of yellow and red poppies.
And as we rode through the hazy brown morning I was your flower child, forever yours.

I can still feel the wind in my hair, blonde spikes whipping at my cheeks.
I remember the day we rode around the city three times just to get away from it all.

I can still hear your soothing laugh — like the sweet pluck of a guitar string.
I remember when you called me honey, when I was anything but.
No, we were just two crazy kids in a rusty old Chevy.

It was that color the sky turns after an evening of dancing in the rain — barefoot.
I remember the sound, the rumbling and growling of the car.
Warning us to get home before our parents awoke.

That car was more than just a hunk of metal. It holds all my memories of you and I together.
Our Chevy was a part of us. But like that old car, our bond got old — and rusty. Until it broke down for good.

Sometime back then I could've sworn that Chevy would be together forever.
Raising kids in it, taking family drives to the meadow.

Looking back now, I cry. We've moved on like everyone else in this dump of a town.
But those days will forever stain my memories. So now it's certain —

We're no longer two crazy kids in an old rusty Chevy, the color of my tears.

Curran O'Neill, Grade 8
Pittsburgh CAPA 6-12 School

All for the Love of the Game

Two teams step onto the gridiron, snarling and seething,
With a feeling like no other,
One of energy, of single-minded focus, of purpose, of the unstoppable will to win,
And the feeling that no one can, or will stop them.

But alas, only one team can walk off of this field a winner,
As the champion, the conqueror, and the victor,
And neither team will accept anything but victory,
And still one team must be chosen the winner.

At the first blow of the whistle, they come upon each other in a storm of rage,
With boundless amounts of energy, they batter each other to and fro,
Each trying to outdo the other,
Refusing to accept defeat.

But soon, adrenaline wears off, and the contest becomes a fierce battle of wills,
Exhaustion threatening to overcome them,
Despair clutches at their hearts as momentum swings back and forth,
But still they refuse to accept defeat.

But finally, one team emerges victorious, as everyone knew they must,
Heads held high, feeling pride for themselves,
Knowing that they have given everything they have, their hearts, their time, their minds, their bodies,
All for the love of the game.

Will Baumgardner, Grade 7
Landisville Middle School

Peace Is…

Peace is the rising sun
Peeking over the mountains;
It is the sun-sparkled water
Drifting over huge fountains.

Peace is the quiet
After a thunderous, cracking storm;
It's the glimpse of a vibrant rainbow
After it has fully formed.

Peace is the shining dewdrops
On a blade of sharp, needled grass;
It is the sun's glow pouring
Through a piece of stained glass.

Peace is a single candle
That is brightly lit;
Peace is wherever you go,
You just have to find it.

Karen R. Witherow, Grade 8
Faith Tabernacle School

Rain

Clouds are rolling in,
not a single sign of white in them.
My disbelief is bigger than myself.
Slowly a droplet falls from the sky,
slowly more follow.
Water dripping off the leaves,
water falling from the sky.
So long ago you disappeared,
so long ago you said "Goodbye."
Too long you have been away,
too long have I waited.
Silver droplets signing,
silver droplets soon disappearing.
They hug my body,
soaking me and quenching my thirst.
But soon it ends,
leaving and saying "Goodbye" once again.
I know not when I will see you again,
but hopefully soon.

Shania Soler, Grade 7
Landisville Middle School

Fall

The leaves change color,
And they fall off the tree,
They scatter on the ground,
As many colors as can be,
Green, orange, red, yellow, and brown.
The grass is dying,
As are the flowers.
Snow will be falling soon.

Brock McCulloch, Grade 7
Bellmar Middle School

The Day

Many bad things have happened to my family,
The day my dog never woke up,
The day we went into debt,
But nothing will hurt as much as,
The day,
The day that was all normal,
The day I went to school and had a good day,
The day I came home to a warm and cozy house,
The day I said hi to my mom, she spoke, oddly. Like a foreign language,
Sadly, the day she collapsed,
The next day, still not as well,
The day after the day,
Sad to say, the last word I ever spoke to her on the day,
Was, I love you.

Alex Castellano, Grade 7
Schuylkill Valley Middle School

Life Is a Dream

My Dream is life.
Magical creatures and mystical places.
Mysteries of life soaring.
When bad things occur, nightmares erupt, destroying the calm.
The sound of war and murder,
The feel of suicide and cries in the night,
The voice of pain and suffering.
The curse of sadness is finally cured.
When the gracious Dream continues, happiness overflows your life once again.
Death is close and memories fill your head as you near the end of the Dream.
Awakening into a new life as the Dreamer's eyes open.
Somewhere better.
Somewhere new.
Somewhere real.

Madison Pierson, Grade 8
St. Anselm Elementary School

What Is Love?

Love is as innocent as two little children holding hands walking down a path
The love they feel, at such a young age, though they might not understand it, so pure
Love is like the twinkling eyes of a loving married pair
The love they have for one another is so rare
Love is like the nurture of your mother
Her comforting touch comes from no other
Love acts like a playful child
Never stopping to rest, and wild
Love acts like a newborn baby
So naive, so oblivious to bad wrath
I feel love all around my life and maybe
One day I'll feel true love for another
Love feels like an opening door
Each day there's a chance to discover even more

Cara DiMarcantonio, Grade 7
St Anselm Elementary School

Snow White

Mirror, Mirror on the wall
Show me
The apple of poison that has
A small bite taken out of the side.

Show me
The girl at the table
Who lies asleep
From a deadly bite.

Mirror, Mirror on the wall
Show me
The seven who loved her and
The Charming Prince who failed to wake her.

Oh Mirror, oh Mirror
On the wall
Reflect my lonely and twisted heart.

In the end
Everything under that snow-white skin will be revealed.

Mirror, Mirror on the wall
Reflect my heart that is
Withering.

Jill Tebay, Grade 7
Charles F Patton Middle School

Black Friday Shopping

The clock sounds the time — ding! — Midnight
I'm still not in bed;
Not 'til later tomorrow — tonight
So elated am I.

Now at Sheetz we sit
Buying a midnight snack
Of donuts and cappuccinos
So hungry are we.

Five a.m. strikes the clock
Ready to push and shove
For the best deals
So equipped are we.

Now in a long line we stand
The lady behind me
continuously ramming her cart into my leg
anger etched on my face,
So peeved am I.

Six p.m. strikes the clock
One more store
To explore
The walking dead are we.

Krista M. Feaser, Grade 9
Faith Tabernacle School

Loose Tooth

The last kid in first grade to lose his first tooth.
That was me.
Then, at last,
One single tooth
Started to come loose.
I pulled and pushed and pushed and pulled it,
But it was no use.

When I got home from school that day,
My parents said that eventually,
My tooth would come out naturally.
But I was eager,
Like a little kid on Christmas,
So I kept on pulling.

And finally, right before bedtime:
"Pop!" Out came my very first tooth!
I was very proud of myself,
And I showed my little, white tooth
To the whole world!
And all the next day, I was smiling away!

Evan Kutney, Grade 7
Richboro Middle School

Halloween

One silent night,
While I was alone in my house,
I hear you from the trees,
Saying your head would be in my soup.

I got scared and began running.
I heard frogs, owls, bats, and other animal sounds.
"Ha, ha, ha, you are in Death Valley," I screamed.
Then my friend jumped out of hiding and said, "It's Halloween."

I wore the Halloween suit,
And celebrated Halloween with them,
In my new country,
The USA!

Mohammed N. Jarbie, Grade 8
Chichester Middle School

A One-of-a-Kind Mother

I have a one-of-a-kind mother —
I know no other like my mother.
You know, to me, she's like a clown
Because she makes me smile when I'm down,
And when she starts making jokes, she goes to town.

I looked the whole world over;
I searched over the rough and stormy seas
In search of someone like my mother,
But in the end, I had found
There is no other like my mother.

Kara E. Steele, Grade 7
Faith Tabernacle School

Loud and Opinionated

Danielle –
Loud, caring, smart, and opinionated.
Daughter of Karen and Brian.
Lover of winter, laughter, and family.
Who feels nervous at the doctor's
    Office, loved when around family,
    And joy around kids.
Who need friends, softball, and racing.
Who gives advice, kindness, and support.
Who fears needles, small spaces, and
    The Easter Bunny.
Who would like to see kids respect
    Their elders, the war end, and
    Global Warming end.
Who lives in a small white house
    On Central Avenue.
            Danielle Sharp, Grade 8
            Chichester Middle School

Power

Power is like control
It's like a drug, it's addictive
The power pushes and persuades
The never-ending drive
To the deepest depths of the earth
Innocent from afar
But with claws up close
Just like a wild bear
As dangerous as the truth
And just as appealing
You seek it out
Determination unfazed
It's gripping
Like a vise
Intoxicating and beautiful,
But sinister all the same.
Isaac Beachy and Amanda Page, Grade 9
        Cocalico Sr High School

She's My Best Friend

We met years ago.
Before the winter snow.
She was a friend and a fellow Girl Scout.
Then we lost it out.
She found me again,
Best friends like ink and pen.
Preparing me for school,
She was so cool.
Showing me every turn,
I really had much to learn.
We talk like sisters,
Putting friends before any mister.
Like we are never apart,
True sisters at heart.
    Amanda Worthington, Grade 7
        Armstrong Middle School

Nighttime Skies

As
darkness
falls upon
the earth, I
look at the
nighttime sky,
seeing the bright
stars that seem to
dance. I stare into
the face of the
moon, while it
sends out such
a brilliant glow
to light up the
earth below.
The night-
time sky
is what
a sight
!!!!!!
    Megan Sajer, Grade 7
    Good Shepherd School

Hockey

As I dribble back and forth
My stick cradling the ball
I must get past the defense
Into defeat I shall not fall.
I pass it to my teammate
He passes it to me
And now as I approach the goal
An opportunity I see.

I am running at my full speed now
Opponents not far behind
I draw nearer to the goal
With the goalie tucked inside.

I prepare to take a shot
In the corner is the aim
I shoot
The ball goes in
I score!
With that I end the game.
    Anthony Veschi, Grade 7
    St Thomas More School

My Room

My fortress
my place to celebrate or mourn
my place designed by me
my place to clean up or make messy again
my place of peace and comfort
My room
    Owen Salsbury, Grade 7
    Strath Haven Middle School

War Is a Contagious Disease

War is a contagious disease
That swells across the land.
It starts out small and unnoticeable
But can quickly grow out of hand.
It may start between two countries,
A private struggle of their own.
But the disease speedily spreads,
And other countries are overcome.

War is like a horde of locusts
Seeking to be fully filled.
Unfortunately, this will not come about
Until many others are killed.
War marches on and on and on,
Being neither merciful nor kind
With peace and prosperity before it,
And destruction and ruin behind.

War does not last forever.
It slowly fades away.
But in many hearts it will never go,
But will be there to stay.
        Caleb E. Foster, Grade 9
        Faith Tabernacle School

Colorful Me

On the outside I am deep plum purple
Shy and quiet
Caring and fair
Letting people in too easily
But on the inside I am bright canary
Yellow
Bubbly and friendly
Silly and loud
Letting a joke out at any time
If you're lucky enough to see my yellow
Don't let that go.
        Emily Ewing, Grade 8
        Chichester Middle School

Griffon

The terrifying screams
Very horrible drop
Nerve-wrecking anxiety
While climbing up
Extremely high up
Turning the corner
I sit staring at the drop
The coaster stops
Down we drop
Straight down
97 degree angle
Then we go up and down
On the steel sky-blue tracks
        Anna Rosenquist, Grade 7
        Holicong Middle School

Why?

Can you tell me why?
Why parents do it,
They make their kids cry,
Because they have been hit.
Why do they do this?
They hurt their kids
Instead of giving them a kiss
When they know God forbids
They should be ashamed
What they do is wrong
Having their kids maimed
And hitting them with prongs
Why do they hurt their son?
Why do they hurt their daughter?
They would want to run
But their parents just come down harder
I am not one
My parents do not abuse
Life can be fun
Why do it if we'll all lose?

Emily Killinger, Grade 7
J R Fugett Middle School

Tinaysha

Tinaysha,
Athletic, funny, hyper, and smart,
Sister of Daniyan,
Lover of my family,
Who feels excited when your
birthday is near, scared when
you're alone, and nervous in
a doctor's room,
Who needs friends, food, and
happiness,
Who gives hugs, kisses, and
love,
Who fears bugs, the dark,
and weapons,
Who would like to see
people recycling, people caring,
and smiles on everyone's face,
Who lives in Willowbrook
Apartments,
Thorpe.

Tinaysha Thorpe, Grade 8
Chichester Middle School

Spring

S unny days to be outside.
P erfect weather to play with my friends.
R ainy days I just relax.
I s the best season of the year.
N ice cool nights to enjoy.
G lorious sunshine, I love it!

Vinnie Petrucelli, Grade 8
Chichester Middle School

I Am From

I am from a daycare center where doodles drawn on construction paper
hang form the walls and the smell of crayons and Cheerios fill the air.
I am from a summer day camp with warm peanut butter sandwiches
stuffed into brown paper lunch bags, coconut-scented sunscreen and creek walks.
I am from a bedroom decorated with giant green and yellow polka dots,
photographs of friends, and stuffed animals.
I am from a house that I walk to and from school each day
lugging a backpack that weighs more than me.
I am from a family with a younger brother who desperately wants a new puppy dog,
a full drum set, and a tree house.
I am from a family with an older sister that likes to swim, text, and shop.
I am from a family where I am right in the middle.
I am from Arcola Intermediate School where I've learned
that I am a good student, athlete, violinist, and friend.
I am from a place where I am happy and surrounded by people that care about me.

Laura Furtek, Grade 8
Arcola Intermediate School

Jesus

A perfect person is Jesus.
He is, was, and always will be
The person who gives me light so I can see.
Jesus Christ was sacrificed just so that we could be saved.

He performed miracles
Including rising from the dead,
He also fed 5,000 people from just one loaf of bread.
Born by a virgin and an ordinary man though there was none like Him in all the land.

He's the mighty God
And in control of everything.
He's the Lord of Lords and the King of Kings,
He's the beginning and end but also our Savior, Messiah, Redeemer, and friend.

Ashleigh Hartz, Grade 8
Coventry Christian Schools

A Sweet Sunday Morning

A sweet Sunday morning.
Bright and jubilant, but early enough that the sun has just risen,
And the birds have just begun to hum their melody.
The billowing trees keep me company.
The calm, trickling water of the nearby stream speaks to me.
The air surrounding me listens, and a light breeze passes through me in response.
Whisper
Whisper
A sweet Sunday morning.
I tiptoe through the moist, dewy grass, careful not to disturb the life around me.
It is not exactly noticeable — I feel its presence but still feel like I'm alone at the same time.
Yet they're all around me, signs of living plants and animals;
Joining me in the meadow like old friends.
On a sweet Sunday morning.

Katie Gergel, Grade 8
E N Peirce Middle School

Her

Waves of chocolate brown
Curling at the ends
Gracefully swaying with each step
Green gems, flashing with happiness
A strong shell, protecting a soft
Joyful soul inside
Conversation seems to come easily
For what we have in common is limitless
So beautiful, so serene
Almost what seems to be
Too good to be true

Jared Chick, Grade 8
Holicong Middle School

When the Sun Sets on the Deep Sea

Some days I'm sunset orange –
   outgoing and fun
   active and a great friend,
   enjoying every beautiful moment in life.
Other days I feel totally opposite,
   I feel deep sea blue –
   tired and grumpy,
   lazy and being a couch potato,
   avoiding everybody.
Probably seven days in a year I'm blue,
   but mostly I'm orange, like today.

Jasmin Singh, Grade 8
Chichester Middle School

The Night

As the shadows dance
The creatures lurk in the night
Hiding from mankind.

Never sway too far
From the safety of the light
Or they will find you.

The fiends of the night
They hide in the shadows still
Waiting for their chance.

Joe Duckwall, Grade 8
Southern Lehigh Middle School

Halloween

H orrifying chills
A utumn leaves falling around
L ights all around houses
L overs of candy
O ut till late
W indy nights of Halloween
E ating till they feel like they're hyper
E verything gets spooky when it's dark
N o one sharing their candy

Alexis Hoffman, Grade 8
Chichester Middle School

Where I'm From

I am from the puck and the net in my basement.
In which I would spend hours down there. From the rainy days in Seattle
(the gloomy days always bored me).
I'm from the city west of Wales just west of Europe.

I'm from the zebra scooter
that I would ride every day as I would push across
the hardwood floors making that rolling noise.

I'm from the BZZ!! of the buzzer and
the shaving of the ice.

I remember the thunderstorms calling me
and the rain calling me as if
they were my friends.

I remember the black cat's purr
and the meow that always soothed me as I
was petting her softly and gently.

The box in my closet with my memories stuffed
in that one box all with the different stories
behind them.
I will always be the apple that never falls far from the
tree.

Will Eson, Grade 7
Jefferson Middle School

Where I'm From

I'm from the high hills and steely gray winters of Pittsburgh.
   I'm from the Nob Hill apartments, where my first steps were taken.
     I remember the pool there, and all the great times.
      Although I have not lived there in a decade,
      I remember that pool as my own.

I'm from the little red wagon and the Mt. Lebanon Park.
   I rode on that wagon all day combing the park for tennis balls,
     which I would do anything to dig up.
      I am from the second generation of hanging out at the pool

I am from the crack of the bat, and the kick of the ball towards the goalie.
   My sports heroes Jeter, and Pedroia, make me strive to do my hardest against all odds.

I'm from any body of water, which perfect blue color beckons me to dive in
   (I can still sense that feeling on terrible winter days).

I'm from 60's rock-n-roll bands, like the Doors,
   to today's bands like Eminem and the Black Eyed Peas.

I come from "There's always something to do so you should never be bored,"
   and the Deger and Lebon branch.

I am from deep roots of a huge family tree, which will grow stronger and steadier over time.
   I am the first of many roots and I will grow strong with that tree.

Teddy Lebon, Grade 7
Jefferson Middle School

The Revolution

In the 1770's the colonists longed to be free,
So they chose to take action against the English tax on tea.

They held the Boston Tea Party; they were very clever,
And their ties to Britain they vowed they would sever.

A force to America was sent by George III,
This silly rebellion he thought was absurd.

On the nineteenth of April the fight began,
The colonists beat the redcoats, back to Boston they ran.

Sadly, things didn't keep going so well,
At Long Island and Bunker Hill the Americans fell,

The English began to win fight after fight,
It seemed the rebels had at last lost their spite.

But after Saratoga, the British had cause for concern,
For after this fateful battle, the tide began to turn.

With renewed faith, the Americans fought on —
Soon the British hopes for the War were gone.

The British finally surrendered at Yorktown,
The world truly had been turned upside-down.

At last America was free,
And to think it all began over a tax on tea!
Ryan McNelis, Grade 7
St. James School

Ode to a Pencil

Oh pencil,
you are a needed utensil.
My hand guides you across the page.

I am the director and you are the star,
shining in your own special way.

When I want a new style I feel like
I'm picking out an ice cream cone
with so many options to choose from like the
mechanical, colorful, rubber, or even just plain old #2.

Since 1564, you
have written down stories, pictures, and poems.

You, and your eraser sidekick,
have competed against
pens, markers, crayons, and more.
You aren't just the #2 pencil
everyone knows. You are #1
plus pencils numbers 3, 4 and 5.
Rebecca Labovitz, Grade 7
Jefferson Middle School

Ode to the Oceans

Throughout the day, you shine.
Toward the shores, you walk gingerly.

Inside of your transparent skin,
you hide many secrets, that the world is dying to hear.

Underneath your ample amount of waves,
we study you, with great care, looking at your beauty.

In your waves, animals can breathe
and they can drink your fine and refreshing water

Your water and grace perplexes us
in so many different ways.

Without you, we could not live.
Within your water, though, we wouldn't survive.

Outside of your beautiful waves, we live, and breathe,
but, we are dying to go back into your fine water.

On top of your waves, we float,
inside of you, we fly.

Through your beautiful waves, we prevail
and embark on our own journeys.

Upon your water, the sun glistens past your beautiful waves
until you reach the shores again.
Sara Galley, Grade 7
Jefferson Middle School

Fearing Life

Fear is living for the same nightmare
You call life
Fear is being spit upon for
Not being good enough
Fear is to love and to have lost
To walk away eating your bitter, sad tears
With your rotting, broken heart
Fear is creepy porcelain dolls moving all around your room
Looking at every little thing you own
With their creepy little stares
Laying on your bed motionless
Until you go to bed.
Fear is being held against your will
And you do what they ask
For fear of your life
Fear is heart-racing
Palm-sweating
Spine-tingling
Hair-raising
Madness
Fear
Allison Kutzler, Grade 7
Schuylkill Valley Middle School

A Dark Whirling Broom
The blue sky
Turns black as coal
Like a woman's cry,
A sudden crack of thunder

The funnel reaches down from the clouds
Full of gloom
Looking like a never-ending tunnel
Leading to a certain doom

The winds swirl
With fury,
Trees and limbs hurtled across the fields
Oh, we must hurry

This monster,
This massive Cyclops
Leaves nothing behind but fear
And one blade of grass
Matthew Hidalgo, Grade 7
St Thomas More School

A Little Flower
On a dark day,
During the war,

Beyond the dark gates,
of an abandoned zoo,

Inside an aviary,
Under the roof,

Below the birds,
Within the trees,

On a grassy sidewalk,
Between two rocks,

Near a pond,
Upon a tiny flower

The sun shines bright.
Sarah Long, Grade 7
Selinsgrove Area Middle School

Sounds of Sports
Thousands of screaming fans
Tons of lights flashing
The growling of the linemen
The smack of the bat
The swoosh of a basket
The sound of sports
All around me every day
Wish it could last forever
Thomas Reilly, Grade 7
Armstrong Middle School

Fear
Fear is as dark as the midnight sky, like a world with no light.
It tastes as acid in your throat does, burning.
It smells like a tree burnt from lightning.
It sounds like a monster feeding on your soul till there's no joy left in the world anymore.
Fear makes me feel like hiding when there's nowhere to go, it eats at you from the inside out.
Nicole Frank, Grade 7
Schuylkill Valley Middle School

Middle School
Middle school is a place where you feel like you don't fit in.
Middle school is a place where you laugh and have a ball.
Middle school is a place where your brain is thinking nonstop.
Middle school is a place where you feel like you're always a competitor.
What is middle school?
Kayla Battista, Grade 7
Strath Haven Middle School

How the Game Goes
Bounce! The ball becomes the other team's possession.
Bounce! Bounce! The point guard is walking up the court, deciding what play to call.
Bounce! Bounce! Bounce! He/she decides to take it themselves, shooting a three-pointer.
Swish! A new basket increases their score.
Bounce! The ball becomes the other teams possession.
Sam Kelly, Grade 7
St Joseph School

Just Me
Brianna –
Funny, tall, loud, and honest
Sister of Makayla and Madison
Lover of her best friend, funny
    movies, and taking pictures
Who feels happiness when she
    gets her report cards, tall
    when she stands by her mom,
    and funny when she makes
    others laugh.
Who needs friends, jokes, and support.
Who gives smiles, jokes, and hugs.
Who fears death, spiders, and
    being alone.
Who would like to see everyone
    happy, young girls respect
    themselves, and myself
    with blonde hair.
Who lives down Fronefield Avenue.
Brianna Byard, Grade 8
Chichester Middle School

Earthquake
Earth shakes under foot
City trembles, buildings crack
So much progress is at stake.
Toby Cullings, Grade 8
Trinity Middle School

The Clutch Player
I get the ball.
Everyone's depending on me.
The crowd's wondering
What they're gonna see.

Dribble, dribble
Ten seconds on the clock.
Dribble, dribble
No time to talk.

Attack my defender.
Juke him out of his shoes.
When the shot goes up
He knows he's gonna lose.

Post game interview,
I've never been a talker
But the crowd still screams
Kemba Walker!
Alex Sabram, Grade 8
Southern Lehigh Middle School

Tsunami
A phenomenon —
tides of water towering,
obliterating.
Ben Hill, Grade 7
Trinity Middle School

Horseback Riding

Carriage wheels,
Horses whining,
And the clip clop sound
Of them walking on the pavement
Up
Down
Up
Down
As I trot back and forth
But he slows up
I made the wrong move
Moving into a walk
Hands
Down
Hands down
The trainer is yelling
I struggle but eventually get it
Katelynn Spyker, Grade 7
Schuylkill Valley Middle School

Peaceful Place

A place with colorful leaves,
Oh, feel the refreshing breeze!
Lo the beautiful wood!
Its syrup is so good.

Excitement is hard to contain!
Maple syrup in vats we gain.
Ere bed we play laser tag,
And droll jokes make us gag.

Forever we endeavor,
To stay there forever and ever!
The thing I like the best:
There's nothing there to test.

We always have plenty of bounty,
That peaceful place: Potter County!
Molly Wells, Grade 7
The American Academy

Dancer

She glides so swiftly
Across the stage
The bright lights
Beaming on her
This is her time to shine
She will show the world
She jumps, she spins
She sees the people
They are smiling
Then she smiles
She showed the world
She can do it
Christina Brambilla, Grade 7
Armstrong Middle School

Frosty Night

Looking through an icy window
Out into the night
You see a face staring back,
Telling you to come
A thief
Beckoning you to the unknown
So, you walk out into the frosty night,
Against your better judgment
Confusion crosses your expression
A gleam of metal by his hand,
Catches your attention
You turn to go,
You fight to leave,
But are frozen there, in place
And that's the last you know
Because that thief only took one thing
And that would be your life.
Beth Celona, Grade 8
Fred S Engle Middle School

Ballet

On the top of my tippy toes,
My hair covered in frilly bows

My big tutu twirls and ripples,
As I do an amazing triple.

I can't help it, I just love to dance
I always feel as if I'm in a trance.

Finally all my work has paid off
In a few more years my career will take-off.

Then I will soar across the big old stage,
I feel free, not as if I'm in a cage.

It will be true, someday you'll see
I will make this dream a reality.
Hannah Feldhues, Grade 7
St James School

Midnight Stare

As I catch a glance of the midnight
I focus my eyes on the
Sky above everything else
Yet in the distance it looks like it merges
With everything and yet
As I stare I am attracted in to the blackness
As if it were pulling me awaaaay
From reality
And I drift to sleep
Unwilling to let my eyes
Close and yet
Slowly they fall and I drift away
John Coppick, Grade 7
Strath Haven Middle School

Rain

One by one they come,
Staccatoed in a majestic rhythm.
Heavier and faster they fall
Like arrows shot by gods in war.
Catapulted from heaven.
Wrung from the steel gray blanket above
To the soaking grass below
Sounds muted together
Like static from a radio.
Rumbles in the distance
Are like gunshots on the moon.
As Nature's tears trickled to the Earth
A wind blows
Ruffling the willows,
Soaking them to the bone,
The tears tiptoeing across every surface.
Listen closely,
Hear them whispering,
Their soft voices like a lullaby
To the sleeping satin earth.
Anna Sixsmith, Grade 7
St Thomas More School

What Bugs Me

When he says goodbye.
When he says whatever.
When he becomes shy.
When he says it won't last forever.
When we're not together.
When life's not the same.
When my heart drops.
When I was lonely.
When he told me.
When my heart was about to crumble.
When I felt like nothing.
When I couldn't find someone.
When I never knew hearts could crush.
When I never blushed.
When life put me down.
When it made me sink to the ground.
When my heart would pound.
When I could feel it in my head.
When I felt like there was a problem.
When I felt like my heart bled.
Hope Solosky, Grade 8
Saucon Valley Middle School

Soccer

S unny days
O pportunity to score
C oach is directing
C orner kicks
E xciting
R unning down the sidelines
Conner Popo, Grade 8
Chichester Middle School

Dancing

Spinning, twirling, leaping, jumping,
that's the best to me.

Spinning, twirling, leaping, jumping,
makes me feel so free.

Modern, jazz, pointe, ballet,
dance comes from the heart.

Modern, jazz, pointe, ballet,
is my gift to impart.
Bethany Joyce, Grade 7
Landisville Middle School

The Night's Light

The moonlight glows,
The river flows,
The top of the water glistens
All is silent,
All is still,
All you have to do is listen

At the bottom of the river,
The stones will begin to light
The stones will shine, and what's to thank?
The brightness of the night.
Bridgette Olavage, Grade 8
Maple Point Middle School

Tucker

I love his special look
He licks my face
his thunderous bark
His speckled muzzle
Always below my feet
Snoring under my bed
Playing ball in the yard
He loves me, I love him
I miss him when he's gone
Please, never leave
Tucker, my friend, my dog
Kayla Boltersdorf, Grade 7
Armstrong Middle School

Goal

I dribble down the field
The mud slopping under my feet
Passing a player on the way to the goal.
I'm getting closer, closer still

I reach the goal with time to spare,
I take a breath or two
Staring at the goalie, ready to shoot,
Bam! A goal I hear.
Elana Lindner, Grade 7
Charles F Patton Middle School

The Second Spring

The world is a flower garden, even in fall.
"Simply a second spring where every leaf is a flower."*

The world hums gently, with the sound of autumn.
Leaves slowly dance and hit the ground with a soft "bruph."
A leaf crumples out of my hand, the edges sharp.
It shatters as if it were made of glass.
That a careless mother left out and was quickly spotted by her 3-year-old.
But as a slight breeze pushes my hair out of my face…
And blows the shattered leaf off my lap…
I realize, it was never broken. Just…waiting.
Yes, it was waiting.

The smell of autumn blows into my nose.
The smell of nature, pine, love…and loss.
The smell was cold and dry, and burned my nose.
Yet I thrived, hoped and longed for it more than ever.

The world is a flower garden, even in fall.
"Simply a second spring, where every leaf is a flower."

*Quote by Albert Camus
Sabine Hoermann, Grade 7
Indian Valley Middle School

Fall Showers

I shiver as the cool autumn breeze pierces through my jacket.
Thoughts are whirring through my brain as I try to find which street is mine.
Leaves are crackling loudly under my feet,
As soon as I get to the stop sign I feel the first drop.
The rain is beating down on my jacket as I hurry home.
Once inside I sit and listen to the wonderful humming of the rain.
The splatter of water as it rushes out of the gutter.
As the rain quietly slows down to just a faint whisper
I realize that the storm is passing,
And a rainbow is shining through the clouds.
The worst is over, and I set out to investigate.
The trees are dripping, and deep puddles antagonize me.
The beautiful rain has ceased, and autumn has begun.
Jacob Knauer, Grade 7
Strath Haven Middle School

I Am Me

Sabrina
Free spirited, loving, loud and stubborn.
Sister of Billy
Lover of scary movies in fall, newborns, and long car rides
Who feels secure in a hug, alone in silence and calm on rainy days
Who needs a good song, a good laugh and her mom
Who gives love, a smile, and a listening ear
Who fears roller coasters, bears and strangers
Who would like to see respect for the autistic, kindness to everyone and
less harsh judgments
Who lives in a cute gray and blue house with pumpkins on the porch.
Sabrina Bethard, Grade 8
Chichester Middle School

Parents

Parents can do anything
They work hard every day
They clean their houses
They teach their children
They build things for other people
They bake food for other family members
They cook food for parties
They drive people places
They can be funny people
They influence me every day
They are my heroes
Nathan Schipilow, Grade 7
Armstrong Middle School

Lover of Family and Sports

Athletic, cool, funny, generous
Brother of Jarrod
Lover of sports, family, and friends
Who feels happy, cheerful, and energetic
Who needs shoes, clothes, and money
Who gives money, food, and advice
Who fears spiders, snakes, and deer
Who would like to see Lil Wayne, Eminem,
and Meek Millz
Who lives on Anderson St.
Jimmy –

James Lavery, Grade 8
Chichester Middle School

The Willow Weeps

As the wispy willow cried
in the misty air
it did not cry for help
but for love.
And the willow wept.

It lived one hundred years old
A life which is very bold.
And it cried out
But spring will come in time
And the willow wept. And the willow smiled.
Ryan Hunt, Grade 7
Arcola Intermediate School

Inseparable

We are inseparable
Our hearts are always together
Inseparable, against all odds
We long to embrace again
To see each other again
Our wishes will be granted
When we meet again in Heaven
We are inseparable
Our hearts will always be together
Anmarie Misterkiewicz, Grade 9
Schuylkill Valley High School

The Cold Nights

It is so cold at night and the grass is covered in dew,
The stars are so bright and the sun is becoming anew.

The birds are singing their quiet song and the air is so crisp,
I am sitting here far too long it's like the rest of the world doesn't exist.

The trees are going bare and it is now morning,
But I am not completely aware that the chill gives out a silent warning.

I am very cold now but so long I sit,
I shall sit here as long as my body will allow but the flame in me is no longer lit.

My eyes start to drift my vision is getting blurry,
My life is starting to shift as I loose all feeling in a hurry.

I feel the life pulling out of me in the distance there's an unfamiliar land,
Its the sky that's all I see now next to God that's where I stand.
Mason Grimes, Grade 8
St James School

Fall

The crimson color of leaves and clean crisp air,
I'd know that season anywhere!

It's fall, when the leaves drift to the ground,
And you can feel the excitement all around.

It's so much fun to jump up and down,
And land in the leaves in a pile on the ground.

The things I like most about fall,
Is my birthday, and fuzzy sweaters, but to tell you the truth I love it all!

I look in vain at the last leaf falling,
The sight seemed to me very appalling.

Thankfully all seasons come once a year,
And my favorite season will soon appear.
Clotilde Cirilano, Grade 7
St James School

Dark versus Light, "Wrong" versus "Right"

I am the darkness	I am the light
People meander out of my way	A profusion of characters come to stay
Emptiness is all I have.	It's hard to get others to go away.
It is pointless	
I am like a bug, unwanted by all	I am the hero
I'm void of color	I have copious varieties
You have it easy	
People are stricken with fear once they see me	Love is all I see.
I am "evil"	I am "good"
I am always so misunderstood.	

Lily Martin, Grade 7
Interboro GATE Program

A Match

As I walk down the hall, I hear people gawking in awe, "Look at her, she's so tall!" Those words spoken as if I weren't there at all.
Sometimes I feel alone, as if there is nobody in this world, in which I can condone.
I try to blend in, I really, really do, but my head peaks above the rest like Mount Everest, analyzed by a height review.
All the teachers regard me with sympathy, while I look away from the rest timidly.
But there's one, different from the rest, I may do, things good, but he does them the best.
His name is not known to me, but I'm sure we'll get along together, like mating bumble bees.
He's in all my classes and smart as calculator, his voice as firm as a commentator's.
I'm not the girly type, but his voice is as melodious as a reed pipe.
They say there is a time in a girl's life where love comes to the line, he opened my heart like a love vine.
I don't know if he knows me, but I hope he does, because there are a million things in this world that will go abuzz.
He's my age, my height, and in my grade and I hope he sees my love is conveyed.
He's popular, handsome, and I think he's cool, doesn't look twelve, he looks as if he belongs in high school.
He's athletic and he gets good grades, his presence strikes my heart like a grenade.
It's astonishing that I've found my love on only the first day of school, I fell for this boy and now I won't come through.
You may say I've been struck by cupid's arrow, yes it's true, and I have in my life found my golden sparrow.

Nathaniel Tadesse, Grade 7
Landisville Middle School

The Big Autumn Day

In the evening the crisp wind welcomes me to the outside world.
I hear the musical sound of my neighbor raking his leaves.
As I go to the car that sound disappears into the evening
as the sun sets I reach my grandmother's house
then I start to think back to 3 years ago to the sound of the football game on the old TV.
The smell of the sweet savory turkey as it enters my mouth
oh boy I could never forget that moment.
As I walk in I can see the apple orchard in the distance.
The smell of burning wood and pumpkin pie bring me back to a night like this when I was five.
As I sit down I see the blue pot filled to perfection with the hot and salty mashed potatoes
and the turkey as the juices glisten in the light.
Then we begin!
But after 1 hour all the good eating ends as we get up to leave with stomachs happy and full.
But we shall return next Thanksgiving Day.
But now we must rest and we can't wait to see my grandmother once again in May

Nathan Yarnall, Grade 8
J R Fugett Middle School

Young Love

Girl   Boy

He struts into class 5 minutes late,   There's this girl who sits right behind me,
my friends think he's going to ask me on a date.   she's the closest thing to perfect I see.

Too bad he doesn't notice me,   I'm so nervous to ask her out,
to him I'm just a mystery.   part of me just has a doubt.

October 9th he asked to borrow my pen,   She does everything with a smile,
we've been talking a lot ever since then.   which makes me happy for a while.

He gave me a hug at the end of the day,   So I wrote her a note, "Will you be mine?"
I'd do anything for him not to go away.   she wrote me back, "It's about time."

Lauren Binn, Grade 8
Saucon Valley Middle School

A Home

I know that you can't talk,
But it's a wonder you can walk,
I can see your pain,
And that's a shame,

Person by person they walk by the bars,
The more people that walk the more nervous you are,
The more you bark the more you play,
Just makes the people wanna walk away,

But if they knew your story,
I think they would worry,
And help you find a home in a hurry,

If they don't you'll be laid to rest,
With all the other animals that weren't treated the best...

Megan Lewis, Grade 7
Liberty Jr/Sr High School

Keep Help in Helpful

Many people are described as kind and helpful,
Yet how many people meet those standards?
To be kind and helpful is to be compassionate and understanding.
To always be ready to help others in need.
Like getting the newspaper for the old lady down the street.
Or to offer to do the wash without being asked.
Saying, "Watch your step," or holding the door for a disabled person.
Showing your neighbor how to work their new iPad.
Pushing a resident in a wheelchair in the nursing home.
To run an errand down the hall for your teacher,
Making a card from scratch for your friend on their birthday.
Donating clothes to charity when they don't fit anymore.
Making your mom breakfast in bed when she's sick.
Being a volunteer to the community you live in.
Doing whatever you can to make the world a better place.
This is keeping help in helpful, try doing this today!!!

Ricky Benevento, Grade 7
Landisville Middle School

Sister of Nikky

— Sam
Funny, careful, trustworthy and nice
Sister of Nikky
Lover of cheerleading, her friends, her family, and Taylor Lautner
Who feels happy when she makes people laugh, sadness
when people are hurt, and loneliness when watching sad
movies.
Who needs her parents, her little sister, and music
Who gives advice, encouragement, and laughter
Who fears death, the dark, and scary movies
Who would like to see people become happy, world
peace, and better care for animals
Who lives in a tan and brick house on Susan Lane.
— Klatchko

Sam Klatchko, Grade 8
Chichester Middle School

The Giraffe

Giraffe, giraffe
Friendly and fun. With
Its
L
o
n
g
Neck, living under the sun. A brown-
white animal, peaceful and nice. If
I could I   one, no matter
   w   t
   o   h
   u   e
   l   p
   d   r
   b   i
   u   c
   y   e.

Christian Kilroy, Grade 7
Good Shepherd School

In Loving Memory

My grandma
My friend
My family
Till the end

I loved her
And she loved me
We were as happy,
Happy as can be

Even though you're not here,
The eight months that passed seems like years

Your smile and laughter made my days.
I will never forget you not for one minute of my day.

My heart aches for you because you're not here,
But I know you walk beside me every day of the year.

Leann Potts, Grade 7
Armstrong Middle School

Sunny Yellow*

Part of me is a sunny yellow
Funny and creative
Boring and lazy
Having fun in the sun
Another part of me is grass green
Full of life and buoyant
Courageous and fearless
Yet they're both very real
And they're both me!

Sean Lucci, Grade 8
Chichester Middle School
*Patterned after "Myself" by Kayla Joanna Woods

Honey Cobra

Honey badger
Rough, bulky
Ferocious, cunning, strong
Healthy, savage, strong, powerful
Slithers, hisses, bites
Slippery, long
Cobras
Mitch Wolfe, Grade 8
Good Shepherd School

Fall

The leaves danced down the hall.
As the wind whispered in my ear.
Rrrooommmm yells the car as it races by.
The pencil danced across the table.
The rain kissed my cheek.
Time flew by.
Trees shaking with fear.
Gracein Hoyle, Grade 7
Strath Haven Middle School

Floweeds

Flowers
Romantic, elegant
Dreaming, revering, brightening
Tulips, roses, crabgrass, dandelions,
Destroying, hating, despising
Constricting, ugly
Weeds
Hope Joyce, Grade 8
Good Shepherd School

Sunny Night, Dark Day

Day
Bright, sunny
Walking, working, playing
Sunshine, light, stars, moonlight
Sleeping, snoring, dreaming
Dark, gloomy
Night
Christian Tegene, Grade 8
Good Shepherd School

Holidays

Christmas
Freezing, joyful,
Giving, receiving, loving.
Presents, Santa, monsters, candy,
Scaring, creeping, hiding.
Spooky, dark,
Halloween.
Emily Brown, Grade 8
Chichester Middle School

The Ocean

The cold air runs through my hair, like Medusa
As my bare foot steps, into the sizzling, hot, sand
I hear screams of children, and rings of ice cream carts passing
When I walk closer, to the rushing water
I pass the lifeguards, almost like statues,
So focused on one thing
About a foot in the water, I see waves break before me
As if they were overcome by something greater.
Hurt so much they were forced to crash into the mushy, wet, sand below
Some boys nearby found a crab and are chasing it around
Obsessed with what will happen after they catch it,
The "Ooo"s and "Aah"s following what they thought was a magnificent prize.
By then, I was waist deep in the trembling, cold, water
Jumping below the surface to avoid colliding with a wave.
Almost as if I was a little girl
Scared of a pretend monster, that lay underneath my bed
After endless hours, I must leave my favorite place
Where I always feel safe, by the ocean I want to stay.
August Hughes, Grade 7
J R Fugett Middle School

The Bus

I walk to the corner.
I wait.
The chilly early morning air nips at my fingers and nose.
Cars roar as they zoom past.
Their cruel, gleaming eyes scowl at me with an icy cold glare.
I shiver and wait, impatient.
Will it ever come?
I hopefully glance down the street. No luck.
I sigh and wait, the cars' merciless, malicious stares piercing the dull, dreary fog.
I turn to look down the lane again.
And there — Can it be?
The warm, friendly, yellow snout of the bus pokes out from behind the bushes.
And the whole beast turns,
Cheerful, frisky, playful, and grinning,
As it jogs, panting, toward me.
I can almost see its wagging tail
As it stops at the corner
And opens its welcoming doors wide.

Katie Wenger, Grade 7
Strath Haven Middle School

Walking Through the Woods

As I walk through the woods, I see leaves fall like snowflakes.
When I walk I hear the crunch of dead leaves beneath my feet.
I see different shades of red, orange, and green changing as fall is coming.
The wind blows the soft leaves in the sky; they are small airplanes soaring in the wind.
As I walk I can hear leaves whistle in the wind.
I start to hear a frequent "pitter-patter" as I watch the ground soak.
I can feel the branches brushing against my sides.
The stench of wet, dirty, soggy leaves reaches my nose as I continue to walk.
I look to my right and see a damp sassafras tree standing motionless; as I stare,
I can almost taste the soggy sassafras leaves dancing on my tongue.
Molly McCarthy, Grade 7
Indian Valley Middle School

Friendship

Friendship is
Laughter and smiles
Love and hugs and trust
Even if it feels like fights spread you apart by miles
Not all friends are going to be true
It takes some time to find someone who's there for you
But when they are there
They stay to the end
They'll make memories and inside jokes
Even if there's that someone
Who's jealous and figures they must
Tear the friends apart
Those true friends will stay strong 'til the end

Michela Rehfuss, Grade 7
St Anselm Elementary School

Joey

Joey;
Nice, fast, helpful, friendly,
Brother of Amber, Bella, and Morgan,
Lover of the sunshine of summer, the crisp autumn
days, and the excitement of a new baby,
Who feels happy when fishing, loneliness at night,
And mad when yelled at,
Who needs happiness, friends, family, and adventure,
Who gives support, help with homework, and cheerfulness,
Who fears big shots, missing animals, and death,
Who would like to see a scorpion and tarantula fight,
Someone come back from the dead, and the Amazon Rainforest,
Who lives in a big yellow house down on Ridge Road.

Joseph McVaugh, Grade 8
Chichester Middle School

It's Time

Tick, tock goes the clock,
As time drifts by,
1:00, 2:00, 3:00…
Tick, tock, tick, tock,
When will it ring?
Whispering is all I hear around me,
It's time! I know it is!
When?! When will it…
RRRIIINNNGGG!!
Stampedes of children run as fast as they can,
You know the day culminates now,
As I run out the door you hear my teacher say,
"Have a great summer!"

Megan Christner, Grade 7
Bellmar Middle School

Trees

Standing big and tall
Limbs that swing to nature's sound
Trees are full of life

Aaron Bellgren, Grade 8
Chichester Middle School

Never Changing

A part of me is vibrant sunburst orange,
Nice and helpful, always lending an ear,
Caring mind, gracious and always loving,
Every morning, never changing,
But on the inside, I'm underwater blue splats,
Hurt and angry, living in darkness,
Yet fighting for what I believe in,
All day, wallowing in self despair,
My life is a mixture, of darkness and light.

Jake Marvain, Grade 8
Chichester Middle School

Football

Football is a game I like to play
All the time…night and day
The tackling is so much fun
But not when you have to run
Covered with bruises from head to toe
Sometimes it feels like I'm getting hit by a pro
The mud makes my uniform look brown
From all the hard work it took to score…
The game winning touchdown!

Edward Manzella, Grade 7
St Thomas More School

A World Without the Sun

Life without the sun wouldn't be fun.
Life would be drab, I would be sad, on a world
without the sun.
Sunny afternoons would be no more.
Life would be a bore. On a world without the sun.
Rain would be everlasting, never passing by.
Why, a world without the sun, should have no one on
its wet surface, because there's no purpose for a world
without the sun.

Victoria Bell, Grade 7
J R Fugett Middle School

The School Bus

Dragons are not mythical but real,
I saw one just this morning,
A yellow dragon came slithering down my street,
It stopped at a red sign, still huffing and puffing,
It opened its mouth and children dashed in,
The dragon then closed its mouth,
The yellow creature then continued on its journey,
Stopping to eat children once in a while.

Sofia Sheehan, Grade 7
Strath Haven Middle School

The Parthenon

The Parthenon is
In Athens, a place of old
Where the olives grow

Ryley Flanagan, Grade 8
Chichester Middle School

They

It was chilly out,
But they didn't care.
All they wanted was
Love's warmth to share.

Together they sat,
Watching leaves fall.
The feeling they got,
Made their skin crawl.

He looked at her through closed eyes,
And wished he wasn't so shy.
For if he wasn't, he'd take her by the hand,
He'd ask her to dance, and they'd stand.

A smile would cross her face,
They'd keep swaying at a slow pace.
The dancing would come to an end,
And forever, they would be, just friends.

Marissa DiSilvestro, Grade 8
Chichester Middle School

Lies

His beautiful eyes shine,
Like all the stars in the sky.
Little did I know,
He was living a lie.

He seemed so sweet,
So genuine.
But the way he lied,
Was like a kick in the shin.

It truly hurt, I can't deny.
But he seemed so adorable and shy,
He caught my attention,
And I started to believe.

That I was the one
For him,
And he was the one
For me.

Michaela Nicole O'Brien, Grade 8
Chichester Middle School

Snow

Snow is just a blanket of delight;
that shines in the white moonlight
With every snowflake;
there are chances of joyfulness to take
Once the snow melts;
the joy is gone,
but once the spring light shines,
happiness is dealt

Brandon Barnhart, Grade 7
Greencastle-Antrim Middle School

The Nerd Herd

Lunchtime comes and there is an abnormal smell in the air,
As if we were outside on a fresh summer day.
The smell of cedar in the air combined with graphite.
It was twelve o'clock and we were not focused on food.

As the pencil flows off of your ear,
Your mind is overflowed with information.
Line after line your hand is unstoppable until,
The point on your pencil dulls.

Your proof is no longer neat,
You must do something quickly or it will slip out of your mind.
You quickly reach into your backup supply of well-protected pencils,
The pencil, all neat and sharp, is ready to go.

You complete the last line of your proof and are stunned at your accomplishment.
Taking time to check your success,
You scan and scan and come up with no mistakes.
Your proof is done and you are ecstatic.

The smell of burnt cedar fills the air from your speedy success,
With your proof done you relax with a sense of gratitude.
With a feeling of satisfaction you take a time to reflect,
Next problem.

Jack Sheehan, Grade 9
Holicong Middle School

These Roots

I am made where not even a single beam of light breaks through
Eagles nest. And every little snapping twig or "Oh my God, what was that?"
makes you timid.

I am safe where the ocean's curling waves feel everlasting.
Where I dive deep to the sandy bottom and feel the ocean's heartbeat.
Steady and strong.

I still live in a rain-swept land where I mounted my first horse
Alone.
With only my courage to lead me.

I am from Callie's pig farm where I feed newly born pigs and pet them
as if they were puppies sleeping gleefully.

I belong to the dirt underneath horses' hooves.
Where Cappi sleeps undisturbed.
(Whose sleeping habits I feel have come from me.)

I am from a lengthy line of family
Whose roots seem to spread from our house
all the way down to California.
Sending outstretched limbs that grow their roots in every heart.

Montana Elder, Grade 7
Jefferson Middle School

Invincible

We stroll through the golden forest
invincible under the autumn leaves,
weaving about the stiff ferns.
We stop by the icy lake
and sigh into the water.
Hooves merging into the liquid ice,
we bend our necks down to the lake's surface,
a submission to the greater vastness
of nature that surrounds us.
Muzzles dipped delicately into the fluid,
crystal water slides down our throats
but we pause

turn heads
gaze amber eyes into amber eyes
love flows from a doe
to her beloved fawn

Karolin Velliste, Grade 7
Pittsburgh CAPA 6-12 School

Winter

Wintertime is the best,
It brings snow and Christmas,
Unlike the rest.
It's the coldest time of the year,
But we don't mind, we just cheer.
In November we turn back our clocks,
Back one hour until it locks.
When we miss school because of the snow,
We don't mind, we go play in the snow.
Wintertime means longer nights,
This means we must use more lights.
Winter is the season of Christmas,
When all the little kids are making their wish lists.
Hoping Santa comes that night,
On December twenty-fifth he just might.
So we are sad when winter ends,
Until it comes next year again.

Joey Setlock, Grade 7
Landisville Middle School

Friends

Always there for you
No matter what you do
Cheer you up when you feel blue
No matter what you're going through
It's like you were never apart
They'll always be in your heart
Even if they are near or far
Even if they are here or there
You know they have always cared
You will never forget the times you've shared
They might act a little strange
But that is how you know that they are there

Frankie Nugent, Grade 7
Armstrong Middle School

Time Goes By

From the day we are born to the day we are in a retirement home.
Time moves fast, from our first steps, to first words
We all have to grow, whether we want to or not
Growing is a big part of life, we grow from kids to adults
We are all childish at some point
But we all have to grow up and be mature
Before we know it we will be going off to college
If we want to, that is
Jobs will be the next thing we go for
Getting married, having a few kids too
We all have to get old whether we want to or not
When the time comes and you're sitting in an old rocking chair
Thinking about the life you once had as a child running in the park
And getting your diploma, walking down the aisle
Or even naming your firstborn child
You sit and remember all of the good memories
You sit and think about what a wonderful life you had.

Zaria Livingston, Grade 7
Armstrong Middle School

Fishing Trip

Go get your rod
We're gonna go fish for some cod

We'll make a short stop for the fish's meal
While we're at it let's get a new line for the reel

Let's get in our boat
And hope that we float

We'll bait the hook
To make sure they look

So let's eat our macaroni salad
We'll resume our zip, splash, zip ballad

Let's leave the fish alone
Because now it's time to go home

Jacob Hockman, Grade 7
Greencastle-Antrim Middle School

Buddy

I miss Buddy oh yes I do
He was my kitty, a loving companion so true
I look at your picture and I start to cry
When I look at your picture I want to die
I only want to die, because I miss you
You're my little kitty and I love you
If you miss me, which I hope you do
I'm just letting you know I miss you too
Don't worry, my kitty we will meet again, someday
I so loved you more than words could say
You were my best friend and always will be
Until we meet again one day, my precious kitty

Jordan Ruiz, Grade 7
Armstrong Middle School

Penalty

A crowd gathers on the cool grass beneath the hot sun,
One girl stands alone in the center of all these people,
Behind her stands a line of girls, waiting in anticipation,
As she draws a breath and raises herself onto her toes,
She jogs toward the difference between a win or a loss,
She leaves her mind behind her and lets her body take control,
All of the people lean forward in anticipation,
Will she do it, or will she choke?
As her laces strike the ball it soars into the left side of the net,
The keeper never even saw it coming,
The crowd cheers as a smile spreads across her face,
She is lifted on the shoulders of her teammates,
She has saved what could have been lost forever.

Megan Engeland, Grade 9
Pennsbury High School

Kids Bring

Kids bring all kinds of
Stuff home from school
Including pink eye,
The recipe for building a strong family,
Now, another great way to fight poison plant itch,
Start,
Follow us the Paper Patrol,
Sort your traveling words,
Power of breakfast,
They'll vanish faster than you can
Say new Marshmallow Pebbles,
Wonder milk
Will make a memory that sticks.

Cory Kirstein, Grade 8
Unami Middle School

Love, Hope

L aughing every time I am with you.
O h how happy you make me!
V ibrate is what you are.
E motional is how I get when I am not with you.

H eart is what I gave you.
O h how much I love you!
P ier is where I go to cry when I miss you.
E yes are what I love most about you.

Randy Soley, Grade 8
Chichester Middle School

My Heart Holds a Lot of Love

My hair is wild as a lion.
My eyes shine like stars in the night sky.
My lips are soft as a newborn's skin.
My personality is as nutty as a fruitcake.
My heart holds a lot of love that is red as a rose.

I live in the future and eat up the past.

Jailene Hernandez, Grade 7
Schuylkill Valley Middle School

What My Gram Did for Me

I remember when I'd spend every day with you.
We'd walk and talk as I learned and grew.
You made me the person I am today.
And you've changed me in each and every possible way.
You introduced me to everything new.
You did everything a grandma could do.

Thanks to you I know right from wrong.
And you introduced me to the miracle of song.
You raised me to try and be smart,
And showed me the beauty in art.
You were beautiful, strong, and incredibly brave.
On one day of each month I visit your grave.
I lay your flowers down and they fall with the tears.
The pain just gets worse with the growing years.
And even though I know that you've been gone,
I'll never be able to forget or move on...

Dylan Sullenberger, Grade 9
Westmoreland Christian Academy

Virginia

I grabbed my camera, and the picture began,
Visiting the caverns,
Stalagmites and stalactites blanketing the cave.
Condensation,
Sky-blue water dripping on my face.
Finishing the caverns,
On our way for horseback riding.
Horses up and down hills,
Stomping their feet,
Going whatever which way controlled.
Starved like we haven't eaten for days,
Stopping at a gas station with chicken,
Not normal.
After enjoying our food, eating like pigs
We got ice cream from a shed.
Loads of excitement,
But we decided it was time for bed.

Melissa Andris, Grade 7
Holicong Middle School

Victory at Last

Smoke-dark, cold fall night
The soft coffee-brown couch
The grass-green turf
Delicious chips and dip, tingling with taste
Losing to the Colts, all seems meaningless
Dead graveyard-silent room, all eyes on the TV
All of a sudden...throw...pass...INTERCEPTION!
Running like a cheetah through defense
To the 10...the 5...TOUCHDOWN SAINTS!
Delighted crowd on their feet
Confetti everywhere, cheers fill the room
VICTORY AT LAST!!!

Griffin Henjes, Grade 7
Holicong Middle School

No Brokenhearted Girl

No brokenhearted girl
Not gonna be like that anymore
Try to tear me down

Try to yell,
You can scream
We always end up in the same fight
But still, no brokenhearted girl

You can always say you don't love me
While you say you don't want me
I see you run me down
Why do you have to chase me down
You're trying to break me down

I sing songs of broken hearts
But now I know that it's not right
I'm done running in circles
I've had enough
See — look at me now
That's right, you see no brokenhearted girl
Alesha Cooley, Grade 9
Waynesburg Central High School

The Race

The whistle blows
   she silently climbs onto the block.
As the starter hollers
   she quickly bends over.
A buzzer sounds,
   she flies into the pool
     soaring like a bird.
Slicing through the shimmering water
   she glides on.
Aching to let up,
   she pushes on.
Then hearing the low ding of a bell,
   she kicks harder.
Rushing for the wall,
   slamming her hand into the touch pad.
Nervously,
   she glances up at the board.
Snap! Her eyes open.
   It was only a dream.
But she wakes up with hope
   for today was race day.
Colleen Daday, Grade 8
St Thomas More School

The Hidden Pain

The world is a rose,
The pain of the thorns,
Is hidden by the beauty,
Of the flower.
Tim Morrison, Grade 8
Chichester Middle School

Savior

I miss you
I'm not sure
That you miss me.

What If you do miss me?

What if It all comes down
To a sunrise,
Or a sunset?

Whichever one is longer
so I
Can have more
Time with you.

Will you be my Savior?

If you be
My savior
I will try to
Be yours

You have already
Saved me now
Let me save you
From yourself
Madalyn Westfall, Grade 8
Valley Middle School

Icarus

soaring
we hit the skies
our wings catching the breeze
free

flying
we rode the wind
I sailed the sky; no, I ruled the sky as a god

forgetting my father's warning
I climbed the sky
eager to see the sun chariot
myself

melting
wax and strings and feathers and things
cast themselves off
as I plummeted

would that I had listened to my father
would that I had not played the bird
but now I reside solely in Hades' realm

and I can never fly again.
Allison Sclar, Grade 7
Charles F Patton Middle School

My Eternal Heroes

Flipping crisp pages
New story unfolds,
Irresistible to me
Pulling me in
Wonderstruck by things before me
Discovering intriguing characters
Mesmerizing magical lands
Firecracker images popping
Into my head
Labyrinths and enemies,
Oceans raging wild
My heart pounding,
Heroes fight on
Thunder escapes silence
Lightning shatters darkness
My champions prevail…
Inspiring my chase
Because, I remember,
Heroes are forever
They will always
Be with me
Maggie Moyer, Grade 7
Holicong Middle School

Is the World…

Is the world…real?
Is the world…fake?
Is the world…one big earthquake?
No, there is no possible way!!!
But the world obviously has deeper truths
Is the world…dark?
Is the world…light?
What could happen to human fright?
People think of aliens
People think of ghosts
But people don't think it is actually real
Is the world…protected by a magic seal?
But is that possible? Who knows!
For what is real could also be fake
But how is that thought of?
It is not
It could just be our thoughts, imagination
Is the world…real?
Or is the world fake?
Who knows?
Darn!!! Back to point A
Shomari Holmes, Grade 8
Chichester Middle School

Hawaii

Beautiful calm days.
All day with the sun on me.
Love those kinds of days.
Mackenzie Miller, Grade 8
Chichester Middle School

Reliable and Active

Brianna –
Reliable, active, honest, and funny
Sister of Savannah
Lover of the snow of winter, the Black Eyed Peas
And my family
Who feels nervousness at the doctor's office
Fear crossing the road, and
Happiness hanging with my best friend.
Who needs friends, music, and happiness
Who gives support, laughter, and food
Who fears spiders, snakes, and humiliation
Who would like to see a 'Lil Wayne concert
More food for the needy, and
more shelters
Who lives in a white stucco house,
In Marcus Hook

Brianna Taylor, Grade 8
Chichester Middle School

Humiliation

With all the worries and butterflies in my stomach,
I can't concentrate,
Friends telling me it'll be okay,
But it doesn't make me feel any better,
Wishing this performance will just get done with already,
The beginning goes all fine,
Until,
I trip,
The biggest embarrassment ever,
I feel disappointment in myself,
Felt like I let the whole cast down,
Tears shedding,
Mind shut down like a bunch of computers being turned off,
Want a place to hide,
Then I realize I'm overreacting,
I just got to learn from my mistakes

Brandon Cruz, Grade 9
Conrad Weiser High School

Sadness

Sadness sounds like a crying baby.
Sadness can come when someone is lying.
Sadness feels like a rainy day.
Sadness looks like an overflowing bay.
Sadness is when someone dies.
Sadness makes tears fill my eyes.
Sadness feels like losing a championship game.
Sadness feels like someone calling you lame.
Sadness is serious as a fire in your house.
Sadness is when you bury your pet mouse.
Sadness is when you have school.
Sadness is when someone acts like a fool.
Sadness is when you can't go out and play.
Sadness is like having a bad day.

William Palmer, Grade 7
St Anselm Elementary School

Great Grandmothers

Great grandmothers are more than the eye can see,
They bring great joy to both you and me.
The memories we had were very fond,
Because we shared a special bond.
She told me of a time that I did not know,
I'm certain in an effort to help me grow.
I remember fondly the stories we shared,
I knew this was the way she showed me she cared.
Remarkable, tough and special, too,
Unique and caring to me and you.
Amazing, caring, loving, and kind,
Keeping all of her special family in mind.
Somebody this special is never really gone,
Her memories last our lifetimes living on and on and on!
Since she had to go, her spirit has flown away,
We will certainly have the privilege to see her one day.

Ian Brumbaugh, Grade 8
Penn Cambria Middle School

Theodore

Rarely awake,
Seeming so weary.
Yet so full of energy,
Conserving it,
For the perfect time.
Lying so very still.
Then at the right moment,
He pulls himself up.
So very slowly,
Until finally he hears it.
"Clank, clank"
Then he dashes so very fast,
Darting down the stairs,
Sounds of paws smack against the wood.
Finally he reaches his journey's end.
Coming to a stop and begging to feast on his food.

Mario DeRosa, Grade 8
Bellmar Middle School

Honest and Friendly

'Keirah –
Honest, intelligent, confident, and friendly
Sister of Zhané and Keith Jr.,
Lover of the freshness of summer, singing
and hot pink.
Who feels joy when texting my best friend, winning,
and being with my family.
Who needs sunshine, summers, and to smile.
Who gives smiles, support, and encouragement,
Who fears bugs, pain, and death.
Who would like to become famous, have peace,
and have friends.
Who lives in a white 3-story house on,
Summit Avenue.

Zha'Keirah Robinson, Grade 8
Chichester Middle School

The Bird

Flying through the sky,
Graceful and free.
The bird lands on a tree.
Singing its beautiful, sweet song,
Bringing happiness to everyone.
Kaitlyn Schiffer, Grade 7
St Joseph School

Silly Billy

There is a young boy named Billy
He is very funny and silly
Mrs. Bottomley had it and kicked him out
He got very angry and began to pout
This all happened in Philly.
Billy Whelan, Grade 8
Chichester Middle School

9/11

Debris was in the air.
Sobs were everywhere.
Osama didn't care.
Our country in denial,
and in despair.
TJ Biondolillo, Grade 7
Landisville Middle School

Billy

I really like a boy named Billy
He is cute and very silly
He makes me feel warm inside
And I get emotions I just can't hide
We like to cuddle when it gets chilly
Kaeley Tellier, Grade 8
Chichester Middle School

Fast

A quick windy breeze.
A silent flicker of light.
Vroom! There he goes now.
Brian Deiss, Grade 7
Richboro Middle School

Water

Water gurgling
flowing softly over rocks —
the creek-bed whispers.
Ben Artuso, Grade 7
Trinity Middle School

Fire

Burning sensation
souls singing around a flame
heart to heart speaking.
Cole Filer, Grade 7
Trinity Middle School

The Girl

The girl who looks in the mirror wondering about the future.
Who can't wait to find out who she will be.
The girl who doesn't know her dad but wonders what it would be like if she did.
Who loves eating ice cream cones and swinging on the swing.
The girl who loves building snowmen.
Just so she can watch them melt away.
The girl who wants to travel the world taking pictures of everything.
The girl who has never been in love and doesn't really want to be.
Who can't wait to do the next big thing.
Who loves jumping into the air and seeing how high she can go.
The girl with the opera singer for a twin and a duck for her best friend.
Who can't wait to see her grandparents again.
The girl who loves to fall asleep cradled in her mother's arms,
Until she is woken up and told to go to bed.
Who likes lying on her back at night watching the stars twinkling in the sky.
The girl who wants to be everything she can be.
Just to make her mother proud.
Who loves chasing her dreams into the unknown.
The girl who can't wait to do a cannonball next spring.
That girl is all me.
Brilliant and extraordinary me.
Renata Weir, Grade 9
City Charter High School

The Car Crash

Space-black dusk is poking out over the eclipse-black horizon,
A sudden movement,
Flash, a car is abruptly in your lane,
Swiveling, avoiding an unexpected vehicle in your lane,
Smash!
Crash!
There, now staring at me dead in the eyes, a chocolate-brown telephone pole.
Police rapidly arriving to the scene of the accident,
Maple Lane, Newtown, PA
Worried shouting screeching from countless civilians,
Smelling the helium rising, like a bird, from the now-depleted air bags,
A glistening new car approaches from thin air.
Samuel Cooperman, Grade 7
Holicong Middle School

Chevelle

Chevelle —
Organized, honest, loyal, and generous
Sister of Brittany, Joranna, Dezara, and Donte
Lover of weekends, school breaks and
Hanging out with friends
Who feels nervous at volleyball games, happy when I passed a test
And disappointed when something doesn't go right
Who needs sleep, friends, and summer
Who gives advice, support, and comfort
Who fears spiders, insects, and rodents
Who would like to see a better economy, more people getting
Involved in the community, and people out of work back on their feet
Who lives in a town home in a complex on Chichester Avenue
Chevelle Thomas, Grade 8
Chichester Middle School

Cool as Ice, Calm and Nice

Part of me is light pink
Fun and nice
Funny and smart
Always on task and athletic
Sometimes there is another part
Blueberry blue, like a fresh blueberry
Cool and calm
Not hyper or crazy
They are both a big part of me
Today I was both

Michael Spurio, Grade 8
Chichester Middle School

How Wonderful

I see what you call a rainbow
It's an arch in the sky
There are so many bright colors
Some rainbows are enormous
While others are not
I love when they last awhile
But they will eventually fade
I don't call this just a rainbow
It deserves a much better name
More like a beautiful splash of life

Ciara Pretcher, Grade 7
Armstrong Middle School

The Sun and the Moon

The sun is like a blanket
Comforting and warm
The moon is a pearl
Alone in the night sky
Both are leaders
The sun sharing its brilliance
The moon shunning the darkness
Teaching to pass your light to others
And giving friendship so you're not alone

Bridget Stein, Grade 8
St Thomas More School

Gram

You were nice
You were fun
You made me laugh
But now you are up there
You are in my heart
Never to forget
You are watching over me
Making sure I do well
Now I miss you

Madison Roney, Grade 7
Armstrong Middle School

The Wonders of the Waves

I sit on my lily pad-green and bijou-blue striped beach chair
Each new wave reaching for my toes.
The sun kisses my back, and I can feel its heat
The only cure is the cool, blue water.
I stand up, gazing into the sea
Deep and dark and hiding so many secrets.
My feet lead the way up to the water's edge, my boogie board in one hand
This time, the water catches me, and I can feel its icy coolness.
The soothing and silky sand sinks under my weight
Every step I take, the water rises.
My body shivers; how I long to go back to my beach chair and warm up.
But the water is so persuading;
I duck my head under and feel a quick shock as the icy venom spreads throughout my body
But suddenly it feels refreshing, as though I just took a long drink of water after a run.
I wait in just the right depth of water for a moving mountain
And finally it comes; clear as glass and as menacing as a shark.
The war has started as I kick off the sand and start to paddle as the wave curls over
It smiles at me, like the curve of a razor-sharp knife.
It throws its best at me, but I triumph over it at the water blasts me towards the shore
I smile; a beam flashes in my face as my mom takes an everlasting memory
A memory of me becoming part of the ocean.

Micaela Kitchen, Grade 7
Holicong Middle School

A Mother and Daughter's Hated Love

"I'm sorry! Can't you forgive me?" asked Mother.
   "No!" yells Daughter. "Life is hard enough."
The two women fight as love cowers in a corner.
   Covered by a blanket, its warm heat and soft light are no more.
It crawls out, with light dim,
   Struggling to go over to the two women,
As it tries to bring the love back into their lives;
   But it's too late. The dreaded words are screamed:
"I hate you!" cries Daughter.
   An explosion echoes through the room.
Love's lifeless body lays on the floor as the women, still blind with rage, leave.
   Love lies there for many years.
   Cold, lifeless, dead!

Courtney Dohner, Grade 8
Faith Tabernacle School

Books

The cover, smooth and worn, holding its pages in place,
Words and meanings, always lessons to be learned,
Sizes, varying big and small, thick and thin,
Themes from nonfiction to fantasy,
Always holding my interest, keeping me glued to my seat,
Never stopping until I reach the end, never disappointed,
My favorite pastime, keeping me busy when needed,
My favorite hobby, never finding one fast enough,
Never one in my hand quick enough or long enough to keep me satisfied,
My passion, everything I love inside them,
The one thing that I enjoy the most, books.

Lauren Pankiewicz, Grade 8
Bellmar Middle School

Gridiron Forever

Tension and anxiety fill the air,
so much at risk with no time to spare.
The aroma of fresh cut grass is so present,
when we score the touchdown we feel so pleasant.
The speech of the quarterback fills us with excitement and zeal.
We are motivated to win — this we can feel.
Each game we play, we put forth our best skill
and we pray that victory will be God's will.

Edwin Cordero, Grade 8
St Peter School

The Way He...

The way his blond hair flies in the wind,
The way he moves when you need to laugh,
The way he hugs you when you're feeling down,
The way he kisses you when there's no one around,
The way he comforts you when you get hurt,
The way he watches the stars with you,
The way he looks at you when you're really mad,
The way he smiles when you tell him that you love him.

Sydney Kemble, Grade 8
Chichester Middle School

Mary

The mother of Him who has never sinned,
who was pure until the end of a spiritual wind.
To be sent to Her the gift of grace,
to the flowered lady, sheltered with lace.
It is She who has made the man of the land,
and it is He who calms the storm with his hand.
The beautiful lady covered with roses,
but had no choice but to walk with Moses.

Elizabeth Ruth, Grade 9
Southern Lehigh High School

My Family

My family is a swim club
My mom is the manager
Keeping the schedule straight
My dad is a diver performing at his best
JD is a swimmer taking many laps
Jack is a crazy kid going off the diving board
I am a lifeguard
Watching over the day's events closely.

Maggie Fleming, Grade 7
Strath Haven Middle School

My World

A place where hurt and pain doesn't exist,
You'll fall in love you can't resist,
The excess drama won't be missed,
All crying and tears will soon desist,
And every person could coexist.
I Wish, I Wish there was a place like this.

Jayana Raison, Grade 8
Pequea Valley Intermediate School

Pine Tree

The green pine tree was covered with snow
White as a fawn's speckled spots
A home for the tiniest bugs all cozy in their winter home
Pointy as a porcupine's quills
Roasted pine nuts fresh out of the oven
Food for the birds in winter
The pine nuts are as delicious as a pumpkin pie

Charles Misback, Grade 7
Pine-Richland Middle School

Dripping Fireworks

Someone splatters
paint across the
charcoal black sky.

The colorful ink scrapes
across, scooping out the stars.

Slowly, their colors
fade into a smoky gray
color as they string
towards the horizon.

Fireworks drip through
the blackout, streaking
down the sky over and over,
creating layers of smoke.

I look up at the misty vapor
and imagine the inky fireworks
smearing across the sky.

Nothing is there.

The dome of night above
my head is blank, and unwritten
on, like everything has been
erased.

Clare McGowan, Grade 7
Pittsburgh CAPA 6-12 School

Color Guard

Spin, twirl, toss and fly,
It takes time for the routine to beautify.
Rifles, flags, sabers and batons,
Make you look as pretty as swans.
I really like to compete,
My team is one that can't be beat.
Twirl a rifle, spin a flag,
Color guard is never a drag.
A smile is needed to perform a lot,
Although the flag may sometimes drop,
Just pick it up like you can't be stopped.
Color guard performers are always on top.

Jonni Brockway, Grade 8
Chichester Middle School

Jingle Bells

The cookie's aroma steals the oxygen of the room,
competing with the thick, spruce air from fallen needles.
They prick and prod as the light's weight causes branches to shift.
Mistletoes and the distinct red socks are hung.
Couples induce the cliché grasp of hands,
the intimacy demonstrated by a simple stroll.
Laughter followed by the first prick upon the tongue,
stifled play initiates from the shock of first snow.
Quaint jingle of bells and the warm laughter of an elder man.
The eyes of children simply swim with happiness and joy,
the season brings a capacious smile,
capable of holding the many gifts that rest beneath a tree.
The wind pelts each face like nips of ice,
rosy, swollen cheeks shine as if they're battle scars.
Melting mallows and a crackling cackling fire.
'Tis the season all remember, happy holidays.

Caitlin Shewbrooks, Grade 9
Holicong Middle School

Just Me

Vladimir –
Funny, carefree, nice, and content,
Brother of Hope and Ruthann,
Lover of the freshness of spring, the excitement
Of snow, and the suspense of fly fishing,
Who feels joy when traveling, nervousness in
A doctor's waiting room, and fright in the darkness,
Who needs a good fishing stream, easy Fridays, and
Funny friends,
Who gives smiles, support, and encouragement,
Who fears bugs, arachnids, and snakes,
Who would like to see conservation in the environment,
Respect for fisherman and hunters, and cheaper
Hunting stuff,
Who lives in a twin house on Market Street,
– Kravchuk.

Vladimir Kravchuk, Grade 8
Chichester Middle School

Darkness

Moments bleed together, no span to time
Fate decides until challenged by the fated
Desperate, relentless, condemned, empowered
Open your eyes and see you're not the only one falling
Illuminate the darkness
Illuminate the darkness
There's a girl within the darkness
Her fate has been decided
She's strong
But not strong enough
She knows she's going to die
In the darkness
But the darkness
Will go on

Shelby Snyder, Grade 7
Schuylkill Valley Middle School

Snow Day

The snow is gently falling outside my window, as I lay down in bed
The thoughts of a day off from school enter my head
I can hardly get to sleep I think the snow will be rather deep
School cancelations and closings galore
Are what all kids are hoping for!
Hours of sledding and outdoor fun
Make for a full day in the warm winter sun
I'll build a snowman for all to see
It'll be so big, even bigger than me
Snowball fights and tunneling in the snow
Will make for a really good winter show
Icicles glisten from rooftops above
Where are my ski pants, hats, scarves, and gloves
Warm hot chocolate and fresh baked treats
Along with snowplows that come and clean our streets
Another day off from school would be so sweet!

Brad Kreider, Grade 8
St Thomas More School

Sleeping

Sleeping, and sleeping,
All day long.
But something fuzzy lying over my face,
Its fur is as soft as a teddy bear.
Its little heart is beating so fast,
And when I pick it up it whines.
But then it licks and licks me.
It is about the size of a small paper plate,
Its little eyes have not even opened yet.
And it just sniffs everything and anything,
It has a little tail that wags at everything.
When I lay on the ground it comes up to me,
It lies right under my shoulder,
Then falls fast asleep.
It sleeps and sleeps,
For hours at a time.

Paige Robinson, Grade 7
Richboro Middle School

Sunrise

As the moon falls ever so slightly
We wait for the sun to shine so brightly

The glowing white moon sinks into the ground
The hearts of all people begin to pound

As the first pillar of light shoots into the sky
The sky gets bright as the day conquers with night

An aura if warmth surrounds a single spot
It comes without notice not even a shock

As a bright, yellow flash rises into the sky
The sun sits in the air for the day to go by

Robert Haigney, Grade 7
St Thomas More School

4 Wheeled Madness

The bushes whizzing past
The speedometer reaching 30 mph

The engine roaring as I need to shift gears
The cracking of the twigs from underneath me through my helmet

The fresh pine mountain air
The wetness from the dewy grass

The mud getting kicked up and thrown across the trail
The little twigs from the bushes hitting my legs

Like a bear in a corn field
With no accordance on where he is going

The only destination is back to camp
Just in time to go right back out

That is the 4 Wheeled Madness

Trent Good, Grade 9
Conrad Weiser High School

Danger Sailing

Wind curling through my hair,
The oriole-orange sun reflects off the sapphire-blue water,
Suddenly I feel a bump that rattles the boat,
I stand up,
As soon as I do so though, the water rushes to meet me,
SPLASH!
Instantly my body tenses in the freezing water,
I see the body of my captain,
Still clutching the deck,
The boat going quick,
The mast almost in the mud,
Then it would be stuck like super glue,
I reacted quickly,
Jumping on the rudder,
Flipping the boat right-side up again,
I saw the crayon-orange life jacket safely in the boat,
I dragged myself in,
And piloted us to safety.

Parker Hill, Grade 7
Holicong Middle School

The Seashell of the Dark

As I gaze into the dark void of the elaborate shell
First it is a black hole waiting to suck in everything without mercy
And then it is the starry night sky on a perfect summer night
And then it is like the cold merciless eyes of a tiger on a hunt
And then it is like a black panther on the hunt stalking its prey
And then it becomes a sweet clarinet playing out a soft, calm melody
And now it is a dark night with gentle tones of moonlight
And now it is a ominous room only to be brightened by a candle
And now I am a streak of light brightening the darkness

Jason Zhang, Grade 7
Charles F Patton Middle School

I Am a Parachuter in the War

I am a parachuter in the war
I wonder if I will ever get onto the battlefield
I hear stories from the other soldiers
I see the wounded in the hospitals

I am a parachuter in the war
I pretend not to notice what is going on
I feel sick, and want to quit
I touch my gun, and feel its cold metal
I worry I won't return to my family
I cry when I think of my family

I am a parachuter in the war
I understand the consequences
I say I can't wait to see my children
I dream about me hugging my youngest little girl
I try my best, and work my hardest
I hope I will see the day when this dreadful war is over

I am a parachuter in the war

Wyatt Siddoway, Grade 7
Saucon Valley Middle School

A Promise of Power

Time, pain, sweat, blood, and patience
Are all keys to vict'ry.
Through time we learn patience,
Through patience we learn strength,
Through pain we learn blood,
Through blood we earn fame.

Weary and worn,
Our body is devastatingly torn;
Through years of training,
The knowledge worth gaining
Is forever stuck in our mind and body
As we hope our work is no longer shoddy.

Fighting to protect our loved ones and family,
We're never worried 'bout words tossed at us too freely.
Even though we're provoked to attack
We must learn to walk away with pride that is sacked.
Within our hearts we know,
We could win anyway; there's no need to show.

Brady Chubb, Grade 9
Faith Tabernacle School

Ice Cream Sundae

My family is an ice cream sundae
My dad is the cone that holds everything up
My brother is ice cream that is the messiest person in the house
My mom is the sprinkles that help us stick together as a family
My sister is the chocolate sauce that spreads joy around us
I'm the cherry at the top that holds our family in one piece.

Ana O'Connor, Grade 7
Strath Haven Middle School

Dreams Come True

I dream of floating on a cloud
I dream of a bed of roses
I dream of pink grass
I dream of catching a falling star
I dream of my prince charming
I dream of visiting mars
I dream of love
I dream of life
And I dream, sweet dreams
Goodnight

Sammie Shuster, Grade 7
Armstrong Middle School

Heaven

What is heaven really like?
'Cause many would like to know
Can you do as you please?
And does it rain or snow?
Will your pets be up there, too?
In heaven do you start a new?
Is there really a pearly gate?
And do the angels and saints await?
As for now, I will never know.
I'll just leave it up to God to tell me so.

Isabelle Colaiezzi, Grade 7
St Thomas More School

Mom

Mom,
A beautiful loving person,
Always there for me,
Independent
Super intelligent
Very generous,
Hardworking woman,
The one and only
Lucy Damacela,
My mom

Jade Damacela, Grade 7
Armstrong Middle School

This Is Me

Some days I am lemon yellow
Lively and always happy
Bouncy and full of energy
Always laughing with friends
While another part of me is purple
Quiet and shy
Fearful and self-conscious
Don't like meeting new people
These are my colors and
This is me

Jacklyn Walker, Grade 8
Chichester Middle School

When I Was Young

When I was young, you were young
At daycare the sweet-hearted lady had sung
A lullaby that kissed a baby
Good night mommy, good night daddy
When I was young, our imaginations were wild
We were thinking of dinosaurs because all I was, was a innocent child
Ideas soared in a big blob of mess
We didn't care for anything except recess
When I was young nobody cared
All they wanted was for you to learn how to share
The scissors, the markers, or the crayons
Nobody cared about what clothes or what brands
When I was young it was a different way of life
That way got stabbed by the future with a knife
The future came crawling so quick, too soon
When all I wanted was to eat my PB and J at noon
When I was young we had pure bliss
We got some hugs, high fives, and maybe a kiss
My life couldn't be better than this
Forever young I will always be
I want to go back to the actual me

Aaron Laskowitz, Grade 8
Wissahickon Middle School

The Picasso of Your Life

Do you sketch delicate designs in the corners of your life?

When you feel something's boring and bland like a black and white photo,
Do you paint colors in places that are
Unimaginable?

Are you the holder of the pencil,
That etches in your life's details?

Be that person.
Add the swirls and waves of adventure.
Change the monotonous grey to a color the fits your feelings.

Don't be just the holder,
Be the owner.
Don't only etch,
Darken.

Be the artist of your life, the Picasso,
And add things that you think are beautiful.

Ashley B. Carpenter, Grade 9
Faith Tabernacle School

Autumn

Colors illuminate on the trees as the sun's rays shines on them.
Wind gently whispers in my ear.
The sweet smell of apple pie leaks into the air.
The smooth feel of leaves gliding off my skin.
Soon I'm sitting looking at the last light of sun before it disappears behind the hill.

Olivia Serafini, Grade 7
Strath Haven Middle School

Something Terrible Happened

One June 28th
It was right after my birthday,
That something terrible happened.
Someone is in heaven now.
I was terrified at first,
But now I am doing okay.
He should have never gone
On that motorcycle ride,
Then this would not have happened.
Imagine if this had happened ON my birthday.

Then I would never be able
To celebrate it again.
But never mind that,
Because he is gone.
But one day
I will meet him again.

Mercedes Batista, Grade 7
Armstrong Middle School

Living for Christ

L ove all people in the spirit of holiness
I dolize the name of God
V ery sacred, but oh glory confess
I t's north, east, south, and west
N eed for faith
G et up and get busy with the word of God, I pick the way that's best

F aithful unto thee
O h, how excellent, thy name
R ise up early in the morning to praise his name

C atch the word of God each day in your life
H ere for all people
R ighteous availeth much
I nside of us is our Heavenly Father
S ound of the trumpets is the day he cometh
T aketh not thou weary, but taketh the truth

Anthony Morgan, Grade 8
Chichester Middle School

Unique Work of Art

Dab the paintbrush on the palette
Waiting for inspiration
I mix blue and green on a huge brush
And draw a thick line across
Now I see the many different options I have
The canvas explodes with all the colors you can imagine
All the images flash through my mind
I don't know what I'm painting — but it looks good.
Each stroke of the brush brings me closer and closer to finishing
It's all come together, the image
Finally, the finished painting
I step back and admire the work of art

Helen Urffer, Grade 7
St James School

Fall

The trees have turned a fierce crimson, orange, and gold,
And the weather has turned from summer's warmth to ice cold.

The leaves have fallen, blanketing the ground,
As now wind blows, making a ghoulish sound.

The sky has turned gray and dreary,
When the fog settles in it becomes quite eerie.

The squirrel stores nuts in a field,
He stores them in the ground so they're totally concealed.

At night the silvery moon shines through the leafless trees,
Reflect off a silky pond that's beginning to freeze.

In the distance a gray wolf howls,
The leaves crunch under his pays as he begins to prowl.

John Peilert, Grade 7
St James School

Goodbye

I saw you soar across the floor,
Reaching for that magic door.

You asked me to come with you and play,
On that unforgettable day in May.

I just watched as you soared by,
You said to be happy, all I wanted to do was cry.

I know now that I can't come too,
For I still have things here on earth to do.

The time is coming soon for you to depart,
Please know that you will always be in my heart.

I see you now, soar across the floor,
Now entering through that magic door.

Juanita Bell, Grade 7
St James School

Colors of Me*

Part of me is a blue green —
    calm and chill
    quite and listens
    nice and takes a lot of things well
But inside there's another part.
    red, full of energy and smart
    remarks, funny and friendly, always
    looking for something to do and
    not sitting still.
They're both very real,
    and they're both me!

Dallas Leisey, Grade 8
Chichester Middle School
Patterned after "Myself" by Kayla Joanna Woods

Winter

Floating above my head,
Amassing down below,
Here, there, and everywhere,
Are myriad flakes of snow.

My skin starts to tingle,
As a chill cools me inside,
Cold weather forms around,
And leaves fall side by side.

Evolving around my feet,
Is a dusting of white snow,
Shimmering in the sun's rays,
Sparkles begin to show.

Soon that time will come,
When the leaves, again, grow new,
Petals form on blooming flowers,
And the new spring sky turns blue.

Ally Bish, Grade 7
Landisville Middle School

Rose

Life is all about
Learning to bloom
To spread your petals
There's not enough room.

When you do something good
They shine and extend
But when you fall downwards
Some breaks off one end.

You aspire to grow
In the sunlight or rain
It's all up to you
And your imaginative brain.

But in the end it depends
On your kind of pose
Twisty or turny
Just like a rose.

Abby Bittner, Grade 7
Landisville Middle School

True Friend

I want a friend that…
Picks me up when I fall,
that picks up my calls
over and over.
That never lies,
even to save me from tears.
And is always there
through the years.

Leila Katz Boyd, Grade 7
J R Fugett Middle School

Stress

Stress is a dark blanket, ready to encase you in its wrath
Stress creeps up on you like a tiger sneaking up on its prey
Stress overpowers you and controls you, like black controls white
Stress takes you to a dark forest, with poisonous snakes and high cliffs
Stress wears you down like sandpaper to wood
Stress is screaming in a tight box, when no one can hear you
Stress stares in your soul and starts to separate you from yourself
Stress will sink its sharp claws deep into you, until you give in
Stress will always be ready to pounce on you, so deal with it, and it will give up and go away.

Hannah Short, Grade 8
Fred S Engle Middle School

The Seashell

As I gaze into the swirling eye of a tornado, swirling, forming into a cloudy sky
First it is bright, drawing you into its deep gaze
And then it is spinning through a storm that will never end
And then it is like a magic gate leading you out of its changing world
And then it is like freedom, able to catch a tide and move, wherever it may take it
And then it becomes a passage, for the next to find it
And now it is a home for a roaming shellfish
And now it is a shell lying on the beach, waiting to start over again
And now I am back where I began

David Taylor, Grade 7
Charles F Patton Middle School

The Ocean

As the waves crash
a gorgeous melody comes into my head
of a symphony that is so peaceful
so lovely, as it stops ominous clouds come and destroyed my peace
as if they were an ensemble
the undead came to haunt me but wait I see out of the corner of my eye
the powerful beauty of the light in the ominous sky
brings joy to my heart
and the undead can no longer seize my peace and my happiness.

Peter Wagner, Grade 8
J R Fugett Middle School

By the Sea

Morning brings the sound of seagulls flying in the air.
The calm ocean waves seem to breeze through your hair.
Children running about in the sand, some holding hands.
The sun is hot, like it or not.
Beneath the waves is a world of creatures with many different features.
The day is night, the waves come near.
Listen, and you will hear the sounds without light.
Many agree it is a peaceful place by the sea.

Brandon Winn, Grade 9
Pittston Area High School

Autumn Leaves

Sand between my toes
Little grains are miracles
All along the beach

Hannah Keglovits, Grade 7
Charles F Patton Middle School

Dancing Cows

cows in the moonlight
waltzing their little hooves off
shufflin' all night long.

Eva Gnegy, Grade 8
Trinity Middle School

Seasons

In every season I play a sport,
My favorite is the one I play on the basketball court.

Winter is the time for lay-ups and rebounds,
While inside playing, the snow outside covers the ground.

Spring is the time that I join my softball team,
It is nice to be outside when everything begins to turn green.

You hit the ball and run the bases,
Always competing against teams from different places.

Summer is when the sport of swimming begins,
You get prepared before you begin your swim.

You dive off the block and go in the pool,
Then you get a rush because the water is cool.

Soccer starts in the season fall,
And to play you have to be able to kick a ball.

You must practice real hard on where to take aim,
The team with the most goals wins the game.

Season bring fun sports to play,
Go out and join, have fun today!

Julianna Skowron, Grade 7
St James School

Monsters

The dragon spews forth flames upon me,
I say nothing; it's too risky.
I'm afraid of what she'll do,
If I say something to urge her to.

The devil huntress scours my mind,
Leaving all my will left behind.
"You're pathetic," she taunts through my ears,
"You speak your mind but no one hears."

In rage, I try to break her hold,
But her talons are sharp; her heart is cold.
I resist her, but to no avail,
On my own, I can only fail.

Finally, the smoke clears out,
Flames and roars cease from her snout.
My heart is singed, but I'm okay,
I'm glad I've lasted another day.

You see, my life is in constant peril,
My life is shared with one quite feral,
I try to trudge on and persevere,
But the monster's presence only makes me fear.

Ashley Carpenter, Grade 8
Chichester Middle School

All Along

Forever afraid to be alone,
Not going to say a single word.

Never looked after us,
Left us here on our own.

Now there's only pain,
Behind the shades.

We gave you many chances,
But you couldn't chase them.

You pushed your baby girls out of your world,
You only brought pain to our world.

There's a hole in our hearts,
And they will not be healed until you make it all right.

Now there's only pain,
Like walls are closing down in our brains.

I can't forgive you,
Because I've waited for an apology all along.

But you never came back to find us,
Because you did forget you had us all along.

Josselyn Duarte, Grade 7
Armstrong Middle School

Autumnal Breeze, Beautiful Trees

Stepping outside, I feel a breeze,
As I gaze at the bright colors of the trees.
Orange, yellow, red and pink;
Fall is my favorite season — I think.

I feel the wind and hear a cricket,
Whose voice is chirping in a thicket.
It soothes the soul and calms the mind.
I look at God's nature and a treasure I find.

The flowers are gone, I'm sorry to say.
But never mind. It's a beautiful day.
The bears are hibernating; the birds are flying south,
The squirrel is storing acorns in his mouth.

The days are getting shorter,
The weather's getting colder.
Oh, how I love the season of fall.
I love to look at the trees so tall.

Summer's gone, winter's coming
Soon Christmas carols I will be humming.
Fall is beautiful, wonderful and bright,
It is sad to see the day turn so quickly to night.

Sarah Null, Grade 7
The American Academy

Water

Water is
Refreshing
Soothing
Peaceful
Water is life

Water is
Destruction
Poison
Slick
Water is death
Owen Swartz, Grade 7
Charles F Patton Middle School

Forgive and Forget

Look at yourself in the mirror
Things will get clearer
Don't listen to what people say
There will be that one day
That one day when they regret
They regret everything they said
One thing you can do
Forgive and forget
People will come and go
But you should know I'll be here
I'll remind you that joy is near
Clarice Manglicmot, Grade 7
Armstrong Middle School

Monkeys

Monkeys are really crazy!
They are never lazy.
They're always running around,
until they fall on the ground.
They get back up and eat a banana.
They get so hot, they need a fanna.
I love monkeys a lot.
Until they knocked over my flower pot!
I go to the zoo and feed them.
Then I realize I don't really need them…
Hannah Flook, Grade 7
Greencastle-Antrim Middle School

It Is Done

It is over
I'm leaving now
what I've said is done
the sun will not rise
the moon will never show
the stars will forever be gone
the love that I seek
the pain that I speak,
will be there forever in my
heart
Amanda Riley, Grade 7
Greencastle-Antrim Middle School

Ode to Zombies

Your rotten limbs stretch out in search
for living flesh.
Strong arms tearing through whatever comes within reach.
Mindless feeding, horrible screams, and warped flesh
bombard the senses
with a flood of awful sights and sounds.

You shamble, run, crawl, hobble,
and stagger towards your next victim.
Like a cirque du freak sideshow,
your twisted features show
what true horror is as your grotesque body slinks through the
mud and filth in which hundreds of gnarled bodies lie.

Born from the ashes of nuclear war,
you tear apart anything that isn't a baseball bat, chain saw, shotgun, or pickaxe.

You are the living nightmare that haunts the minds of millions.
You think (not really) that humans are
nothing but a source of food.

Crushing jaws rip meat from bones and your insatiable
need to feed drives you sheer numbers onto the delicious humanity.

You are the army of children, and strong men, and women, and animals
that will not, cannot, stop.
Eoin Wilson-Manion, Grade 7
Jefferson Middle School

I'm My Own

The world is a cruel place sometimes,
If the earth was your face, then the nose would be the problems on it
With the snot dripping down in lines because it's running.
Get it? Because the world's cold.

I get so irate when they dictate and degrade me,
Like they just played me and made me.
No wonder why I can't think straight
They laid out a trap and I took their bait.

They try to make me into something I'm not, knock me down while I'm hot.
Yeah, that's their motto, but I just hit the lotto.
Now I'm on top and you can bow down and I'll stop,
Drop and roll because I'm on fire as the stakes are getting higher,
I'll keep battling my way through a wave of critics.

I'm not anybody's Play-doh, I'm my own soul!
No one can mold me and fold me into their own.
Sculpt me into a culprit,
Carve me into a darling,
Mash me into trash,
Mix me in a flask.
But I'll thrash and kick to get out of their grip.
I'm not a puppet because I covet to be my own person.
Kendra Fang, Grade 8
Arcola Intermediate School

Summer

Summer is my favorite season.
The temperature is nice and warm.
There is no school and no homework.
You can stay up late with friends.
I like to go swimming.
My family and I go on trips.
I like to go to the beach.
Summer is fun while it lasts.
I have a better summer each year.
Mikayla Russell, Grade 7
Bellmar Middle School

A Poem

A poem needs to come from your mind.
Not your pencil or a word that just rhymed.
A poem needs to come from your heart,
Every word, every sentence, and every part.
A poem needs to have imagination.
If it does it will be a big sensation.
A poem needs to be very unique.
A poem that's good will never be weak.
Brandi Propes, Grade 7
Bellmar Middle School

Day-Night

Day
Bright, sunny
Laughing, playing, enjoying
From the beautiful sun to a shining bright
Moon
Resting, sleeping, dimming
Dark, calm
Night
Kaeley Pinkerton, Grade 8
St Anselm Elementary School

My Special Sister

I have a special needs sister
She's my older sister who acts younger
So I am her younger older brother
She learns a little slower
But loves to go on the bus and to school
She drives me crazy sometimes
But she can be very loving at times
She is my sister and I love her
Jared Cosier, Grade 8
J R Fugett Middle School

The Pig

Pig
Pink animal
Eating, snorting, sleeping
Always rolling in mud
Hog
Luke Ritz and Laurel Merriman, Grade 7
Greencastle-Antrim Middle School

Photographic Memory

I am from two young kids that met each other and never even thought that later,
love awaited their hearts.
Youngest of three I add to our wonderful family tree, a specific piece.

I see the many thick coloring books in my messy little room,
from the pedals of my bike, pumping for the first time ever.

I remember my Italian heritage, always.
Though they have gone through many kitchens, I remember the pizza and pasta
as if they were my own.
Germany, though far away, too far to travel still lives within me.

I'm all the way from a small couch with a big bologna sandwich, Tom and Jerry,
and the busy streets of Pittsburgh.
(The sleek vehicles speed past as the air stinks with exhaust.
I smile with the familiarity.)

I'm the softball, mitt, and the crack of the bat,
the unique feel of the balance beam beneath my sore feet.

Growing up, I am a girl of my parents' hopes
from the Vernacchio and Page limbs, extremely massive in size.

Memories from multiple places, mind, soul, heart.
They remind me of who I am and what I am made of.
A tree, much larger than my small section of branches, meek in comparison.
Roots that are sturdy, I'll continue to grow up, just like the family tree.
Ali Vernacchio, Grade 7
Jefferson Middle School

I'll Meet You There

There is a place,
Outside,
I'll meet you there,
We can run straight through the autumn air,
We can fly,
And dance across the clouds,
Living on nothing but the fact that we are we,
And they are they

There is a place,
Outside,
Where boundaries disappear,
The sun, the moon, and the rain can race around but all that matters is
That moment,
Outside,
Where we meet

When others just don't get it,
When others just can't get it,
We'll see what they won't see,
In a place,
Outside,
I'll meet you there.

Summer Martin, Grade 7
Strath Haven Middle School

The Red Flower

You could see that red flower,
The bright cherry red.
I could see that red flower,
All lonely in the wind.

You could hear the red flower,
Trying to speak in your mind.
I could hear the red flower,
"Look at me! I'm aglow in the light!"

You could feel that red flower,
All silky and smooth,
Like a well-worn quilt warming a small, sleeping girl.

I could feel that red flower,
Touching all her little leaves,
That look at her in awe as the wind sighs and breaths.

We could sense that red flower,
In our beating hearts,
Feeling the simple peacefulness blooming in our souls.

Kai McGinn, Grade 7
Richboro Middle School

My Feelings for You

When you look into my eyes
I can't stop staring into yours
You're so sweet
I can't even explain it
Every time you say hello my heart skips a beat
When you say goodbye my heart stops beating
When we kiss I fall for you even more
When you wrap your warm arms
Around me I get a warm sensation through my body
But when you let go I start to cry on the inside
My love for you is more than anything
I just hope you feel the same
Now you know how I feel
Now are we meant to be?
I love you!

Nicole DeFilippis, Grade 7
Armstrong Middle School

Archery

Any time any day
Eyes lock on the bull's-eye
As the tip of my arrow is lined up
The frog-green trees all around me full of birds
"Fwapp!" The arrow soars through the air
It hits the target setup in my backyard
"Thud!" I land another arrow on the target
I draw another arrow; smell the leather of my quiver
Feel the string on the tip of my fingers
As I draw another arrow

Luke Hamada, Grade 7
Holicong Middle School

Gray

Gray is the storm cloud
Gray is the smoke shroud
Gray is the day that goes by in a blur
Gray is the clock that seems to whirr

Gray is the shipwreck
Gray is the bird that gives you a peck
Gray is the eye that sees nothing
Gray is when you sit huffing

Gray is the day no one wants to play
Gray is the day no one says hey
Gray is the dying flower
Gray is when you want to cower

Gray is when you lose the game
Gray is when you're filled with shame
Gray is the day all you do is frown
Gray is when Cinderella refuses to wear her gown

Can you tell I feel gray today?

Stephen Ruf, Grade 8
Fred S Engle Middle School

Baseball Running Through My Mind

I walk onto the diamond bat in hand.
Bases loaded anything could happen
Here comes the wind up "cock, lock and fire"
There it goes out to center field
He drops it I put my head down and run
Rounding first lots of speed,
The coach tells me to come to third
Not stopping full power
He yells "Go to home"
Running fast here comes the ball
I slide, the dust settles
The umpire calls safe
We won!
Cheering and screaming all around me
Was that just me?

Brandon Linebaugh, Grade 7
Armstrong Middle School

Encounter with Death

Silent, bat-black night
Only my gasping for air making noise
Face color of blueberries ready to harvest
Hospital beds are all I can see, one after another
House or hospital, still unable to inhale
Nebulizer making a loud hummm
Needle in my arm, writhing and squirming
Death's bony white hands gripping me,
Ready to pull me in
Darkness no more feeling…then light

Justin Geiss, Grade 7
Holicong Middle School

On the Cliffs

Come back Come back
Come back my darling
These cliffs are too high for you to stay sane

Come close Come close
Come close my darling
That world's not for you, you're not one of the waves

Wake up Wake up
Wake up my darling
You're dreaming again, of magical things

Is this not enough to sustain your yearning,
Are the trade winds whispering to come, come away

Look down Look down
Look down my darling
You're wavering, hovering close to the edge

Enough Enough
Enough my darling
If your love for me is not strong enough, return to the sea.

Juliana Schnerr, Grade 9
East High School

The Family

It's time to get ready,
Ready for the family,
The old and the new,
Are coming this year,
More and more family every time,
We are happy to see them all,
Big ones, little ones, young ones and old ones,
We play games and share stories,
When the cold rolls in,
All of us go out to play,
In the snow,
The snow goes flying everywhere,
So that is how the family is,
And I love them so.

Jozlynn McCloskey, Grade 7
Armstrong Middle School

Hurricane

Rainy mid-afternoon,
Pouring rain beating a cadence against the windows,
Whipping trees shake,
Blustering heavy winds,
Dark elephant-gray ominous skies,
Static from the radio rings in my ears,
In my house shivering,
Coyote howling winds,
A dense wind sends litter flying,
Anxiously waiting for the storm to end

Sydney Somers, Grade 7
Holicong Middle School

The Winning Goal

His concentration is like an eagle
Swooping down on his prey,
So he cannot hear the roaring crowd
Like ocean waves
Crashing on the shore.
Down the sideline he scrambles,
Resembling a graceful dancer
As his feet glide across the damp, freshly cut grass.
Slicing, cutting, darting past defenders
Sweat drips into his eyes with a burning sensation.
One mistake, one misstep
Will cost his team a championship.
The fans and his teammates bellow his name
As his keen eagle eyes are glued to the spinning ball.
He knows he must score the goal.
With one last breath, with one last step,
He shoots —
Then he sees it —
The ball soars into the net —
Goal!

Michael Schnabel, Grade 7
St. Thomas More School

Caramel Snow

Middle of winter.
Nothing but notebook-white
Snow.
Midday.
Sunny, but no heat.
Inside, standing over a pot
Of golden. Bubbling. Sunray-gold.
Caramel.
Steam and a warm aroma,
Of delight.
First footsteps in the
Newly laid. Bunny-white.
Snow.
Crunch. Crunch.
Fresh snow, nothing but.
Humid breath, frigid air.
Sizzling, steaming, dripping, sunflower-gold.
Caramel.
A delectable treat,
Waiting to happen.

Liam Creedon, Grade 7
Holicong Middle School

Snowflakes

Snowflakes drift through the winter breeze,
Like a paper airplane.
They cover the world,
Like a big, giant blanket.
Snow flakes are like people,
Not one is the same and not one ever will be.

Caroline Wend, Grade 7
Holicong Middle School

Nahzja

Nahzja
Intelligent, caring, helpful, and energetic,
Sister of Chase, and Kennedy
Lover of the summertime, laughter of my
    Siblings and excitement of food,
Who feels nervous in the doctor's office,
    Scared of horror movies, and lonely by myself,
Who need Fridays, candy, and fun,
Who gives hugs, effort, and support,
Who fears heights, rats, and slimy things,
Who would like to see peace in the
    world, respect, and better homes for
    the poor,
Who lives in a medium size green
    house on Douglas Ave.

Nahzja Knight, Grade 8
Chichester Middle School

Baseball

I am up to bat, waiting to receive the first pitch
    Should I swing at it? Or take it for a ball?
I swung and connected with nothing but air
I just gotta stay calm, and just make contact
    The next pitch comes
    I took a big swing and fouled it off
    The count is now 0-2
I now have to protect the plate
I receive the next pitch
It comes straight down the middle
I took a nice, clean swing
Bang!!!
The ball goes flying, dead center field!
Outfield…warning track…fence…
    Gone!!! It's a home run!

Robert DuBois, Grade 7
Strath Haven Middle School

Fast and Cool

Keith
Funny, fast, cool, loud
Brother of Robert and Michael
Lover of sports, video games, movies
Who feels happy when with friends,
Creeped out in the dark, nervous when in
the dentist chair
Who needs weekends, friends, and video games
Who gives support, help, happiness
Who fears death, being alone in the dark
and something bad happening
Who would like to see sports games more often
money, friends
Who lives in a big house down on Mulberry Street.

Keith Kozak, Grade 8
Chichester Middle School

A Life Without Peanuts

I see Snickers Bars, Peanut M&M's, and Mr. Goodbar wrappers
Littered throughout a park
The last vestiges of a winning team's celebration.

I see empty peanut shells
Scattered up and down the rows of an empty baseball stadium
A crestfallen fan's way of consoling himself.

I see ice cream cones, chock full of nuts
Clutched in sticky hands and dripping onto a scorching sidewalk
A sweet way to quench the summer sun's swelter.

I see peanut butter and jelly sandwiches
Being gobbled amidst chatter in a school cafeteria
An easy lunch for a harried morning.

Sometimes I feel like I'm all alone,
Until I remember that there are other kids out there
Nearly six million, in fact.

Feeling the same loneliness
And often sadness
Every day.

Alexandra Curtis, Grade 7
Southern Lehigh Middle School

Daydream Adventures

Would you enjoy
A ride on a golden star,
Soaring through the cosmos
While the solar wind blows
Through your heart and soul?

Would you like
To dive to the depths of the sea,
On a scaly sea dragon's back,
Watching the fish scurry past
And feeling yourself become part of the ocean?

Would you take well
To a trip on a yeti,
To the snowiest peaks,
Climbing the tip of the grandest mount
So you can gaze from the top of the world?

Would you feel good,
To lie warm in your bed
Enjoying a moment of peace,
And as Dragon and Stars and Yetis fly past
Just lean back and dream for a while?

Nate Stockmal, Grade 7
Richboro Middle School

I Am

I am kind and helpful
I wonder what I will be when I graduate high school
I hear the screech of my sneakers when I play tennis
I see a full day to do whatever I want
I want to go visit a different continent
I am kind and helpful
I pretend to be a fashion model
I feel giddy when I play with my friends
I touch cold snow in winter
I worry about bad weather
I cry when I am worried about someone I care for
I am kind and helpful
I understand good days and bad days
I say there is an afterlife
I dream that I will have a great life
I try to work hard in school
I hope for a great future
I am kind and helpful

Holli Farrow, Grade 7
C.F. Patton Middle School

Why

Why do people embarrass the weak?
Have they not cried in shame before?

Why do people crush others' dreams?
Have they had their own taken away?

Why do people bring others to tears?
Does it make them stronger?
Is it a personal gain?

Why do people allow others to push them around?
Are they afraid of what others may say?

Why do people run away and hide?
Can they not see who the weaker ones really are?

Why can't people realize the truth?
That those who hurt are not worth the tears.

Emma Cullo, Grade 7
St James School

The Burden I Bear

My diabetes is like spending every day in a dark, lonely corner
full of pain…
My days are like blank pieces of paper waiting…
for the sorrowful words
My eyes are full of the love I haven't felt
My suffering is something that I hide well but not for long
My heart holds broken memories
That are as painful as eating shattered glass
I live in a dark corner,
And eat my pain.

Lydia Forsythe, Grade 7
Schuylkill Valley Middle School

Believe

Believe, the first word that comes to mind
I was once told things will change in time
I'm not going to lie I saved my life
Dream got me running around like it made my life
First I look down, but it's reflecting the sky
Take a look at my hood then I wonder why
why they look like this
Why my best friends' birthday is something that he missed
Why is there a home without water
Why they stand on people so they can be taller
You think we're dying inside, look at my heart, I feel alive
We can see the light in dark times
Now we spread out wings to meet on our flight
You ask if things will ever change
It's hard seeing dark clouds with no rain
Can we live in a world with no pain
Then you think about the future to think if it's the same.
I think I got a message through a dream
It didn't show how the future's meant to be
It didn't show if we will ever be at peace
It shared a man in the mirror and to always Believe.

Nahsir Bowser, Grade 8
AMY at James Martin School

Puzzling Pieces

There is no doubt about it, puzzle pieces will be lost.
They don't want to be together, they'd rather be apart.
After you place them together all the chaos starts.

It will seem the pieces just disappear.
Some will stay and some go.
Where they have gone, nobody knows.

You will look everywhere, yet never find them.
You will search the entire house,
Even the hole, which is occupied by the mouse.

Your kitchen table is where it will sit,
Haunting you every time you see.
You'll wish that unfinished puzzle would let you be.

Lex Weidner, Grade 7
Landisville Middle School

Bright Red and Dark Blue

Part of me is glowing red
Exuberant and lively
Talkative and friendly
Having fun with my friends and embellishing it.

But mostly, I am mellow blue
Shy and fearful
Self-conscious and tired
Shaking around new people
Yes, they are both the same person.

Chris Kozak, Grade 8
Chichester Middle School

Autumn

Here comes that cold breeze
knocking the colored leaves off the trees
the bare branches shiver from the cold
the tree has lost his leafy robe

Inside their dens animals get ready to sleep
we do too underneath our sheets
the jack-o-lanterns fill the streets
waiting for kids to take a treat

Tomorrow kids will knock on doors
with buckets of treats waiting for more
their costumes are cool but have to be warm
because gusts of wind blow like a storm

Children walk home ready to eat
all of their bags filled with sweets
their smiles wide as they take a bite
of the candy given to them on this special night

Dixon Damico, Grade 7
Strath Haven Middle School

With One Touch...

You make me feel like nothing is impossible,
But when the day came to say goodbye,

At graduation,
I couldn't help think of who else could cure me,
Like you did.

When it was time to say our last goodbye,
When the final hat hit the ground,
That's when you kneeled on the ground.
And took my hand and said,
Marry me.

From that day on I will not forget,
With only one touch of your hand,
Did I know I had found,
Not only my best friend,
But my...
Soul mate.

Liz Hawrylack, Grade 8
Fred S Engle Middle School

A World Without the Sun

In a world without the sun,
The world would be no fun,
It would be so dark,
With no sun to provide a spark,
We couldn't go outside,
So inside is where we'd reside,
If the sun were to burn out,
Astronomers would have nothing else to learn about

John Daly, Grade 7
J R Fugett Middle School

The Leaf

My color changes from green to red,
Soon I will blow off the tree, dead,
I hope that soon I will be whisked away,
When this tree I'm on starts to sway.

Here comes a gust, big and strong,
I jump off the tree as the city clock gongs,
I begin my journey all the way down,
But soon I'm taken back up and I can't see the ground.

Now my stem hovers above,
The ground awaits my landing, calm as a dove,
I finally touch down, light and small,
The tree is above me, mighty and tall.

My journey is finished; it's come to an end,
I landed on the ground; my color completes a fiery blend,
Now I sit, awaiting being raked up,
And slowly die, no longer going up.

Zack Walter, Grade 7
Landisville Middle School

Poetic Puzzlement

I cannot think of a poem to write,
Although I'm trying with all my might.
Rhymes, and words, and meters, oh my!
They stump me so; and yet I must try.

Creating a title is not so bad,
But what must go with it is yet to be had.
What I am writing I hardly know,
But the words on my paper continue to grow.

My mind is blank, oh woe is me!
Yet I must finish so I'll be free.
Time stretches by and moves so slowly
But if I don't finish I'll feel quite lowly.

I simply can't think of a thing to write,
Oh, someone, please help me in my sad plight!
But wait! Just look what I have done.
I have written a poem, and it was fun!

Nathania Hofstetter, Grade 9
The American Academy

Me

My personality is bright like the sun on a hot summer day
With eyes as green as a pond deep with secrets
With a mind as strong as my heart
Filled with love, inspiration, motivation
With hair as curly as waves crashing on the beach
With a life filled with memories
I love my friends and family
And eat up negative words and fill them with positive ones.

Megan Lynam, Grade 7
Schuylkill Valley Middle School

Goalie

Field hockey field hockey
It's what I like to do
I get to kick in the game
I can't resist the play
If we work together
We'll surely win the game
I yell, "SPREAD OUT!" so we can get the ball
But do they listen? NO!
I play in the game, I'm the goalie
I'm an important part of the team
They should listen to me!

Shaniya Moore, Grade 7
Armstrong Middle School

What's in Your Room?

A big, soft bed, where you rest your head
Slippery sheets are where you sleep
Millions of posters on the floor in a big heap
A mirror so you can see yourself clearer
Giant books in which you read and look
Big fun chairs with friends you share
In the closet my clothes I deposit
A door that drags on the floor
A carpet that gets very wet
My desk if it was neat would be picturesque
Windows where you look at crows

Jessica Yonney, Grade 8
Saucon Valley Middle School

High School Football

The banging brass band has begun.
The crowd is roaring wildly.
As we step out onto the turf,
Our uniforms flash in the stadium lights;

Our shiny helmets are dark, red and white.
Cheerleaders are chanting, coaches prepping.
The salty, smell of roasted peanuts
Mingles with the cool, crisp autumn air.
These are the memories we will not forget
Of the days gone by without a regret.

Tyler J. Yeager, Grade 7
Faith Tabernacle School

Dancing

I love dancing
Dancing loves me
God sent the talent to me from above
Dancing is a joyful sport
I love dancing
Dancing keeps me healthy
I love dancing
Dancing takes me away from everything else
I love dancing

Katrina Haer, Grade 7
Armstrong Middle School

Loved Ones

You have many loved ones,
People you care for and cherish.
You have many that will do
Anything for you.

They will give you anything,
And take you anywhere.
They are the shine of your life,

There are many loved-ones
You may not have met,
But you know they would love you.

Three people I have cherished the most
Have been taken from me.
I will always remember those special people,
My aunt, my grandmother, and grandfather.

I will love them
Until one day, I will meet them in heaven,
Where we will live happily forever.

I'yannah McCoullum, Grade 8
Chichester Middle School

The Sounds of Music

That wonderful sound, ringing sweetly in my ears
That wonderful sound, listen closely, can't you hear?

It pours onto the street, funky, fresh, fun!
It flows through the night and the daylight sun

This sound I speak of is music my friend
And the sound of music should have no end

The sound of music, it's heart-pounding beat
Its amazing rhythm has me tapping my feet!

Its lyrics send me into a thoughtful daze
A beautiful symphony to my amaze…

Ally Batot, Grade 7
Armstrong Middle School

A Happy Veteran's Day

Veterans are like Jesus
Who sacrifice all they have for the love of their people
A veteran is a boxer
Who never backs down to help his country
And fights even if the odds are against him
Veterans are like super heroes
Who protect their people when they are in danger
A veteran is a president
Who helps lead a country to victory
And takes on the toughest of challenges
Veterans…are our heroes!

Thomas Minutella, Grade 7
St Thomas More School

Safe

The sun is just starting to set
A strawberry-pink sky illuminates rolling green hills
A sea of horses washes over the pastures

I close my eyes and hear
Rhythmic hoof beats
Snorts and whinnies

I can smell
Sharp, cool air
Fresh, emerald grass

Nothing will touch me
Nothing will harm me
I am safe

I wish I could stay
Never leaving
Becoming one with the sea

My peace, shattered by a revving engine
Dragged back to reality once more
Time to leave pony paradise

Meghan Poirier, Grade 7
Holicong Middle School

Arctic

Far away on a polar ice cap,
A tiny penguin is taking a long winter nap.

A mere dot in the freezing snow from far away,
This little penguin may sleep the whole day.

The bright sun's reflection is blinding; intensified,
This penguin is not so difficult to find.

Yet he peacefully snoozed on,
Innocently; thinking nothing is wrong.

He doesn't see the shining surface of the water ripple.
Or the cloudy image of the seal starts to triple.

The penguin lifts its head and opens his big bright eyes,
What he sees really takes him by surprise.

His instinct tells him to swim quickly away,
Well, of course, he wasn't going to stay!

He plummets into the glistening sea,
Knowing that from here he must flee.

Julianna Nicolaus, Grade 7
St James School

The Beach

After a long stroll across the scorching sand,
I was finally able to let go of everything in my hand.

Then I heard the magnificent sound,
Of the waves coming in and crashing all around.

I quickly grabbed my boogie board,
And waited for the perfect wave to climb aboard.

Then I noticed that the wind was just right,
I ran out of the water and snatched my favorite kite.

I got it up much too high,
Then all of a sudden it went bye-bye.

So then I began to dig in the sand,
Hoping to find a gorgeous seashell in my hand.

The sand has finally cooled down,
And there are not many people around.

On my way I shall go,
Since I am now tan from head to toe.

Jessica Kerecman, Grade 7
St James School

A Prison Cell or a Heavenly Gate?

School is like a prison;
Books are like brick walls
With pens and pencils as iron bars.
Sometimes I feel like a convict there forever,
With unceasing, unending work.

Why have I been accused of this lifetime punishment?
What have I done to deserve this lifetime punishment?

But school has its purposes
And unending reasons to be there.
I know that school is one of the best parts of my life;
No school, no special friends, no heartwarming memories.

School can be like heaven;
Books are solid gold gates
That God opens with knowledge to let you in.
Pens and pencils are God's helping hand
That He lends you so that you can express feelings.

I realize twelve years isn't long at all.
It's just a time of life taken to help me
Become a stronger person

Dakota Vogel, Grade 8
Faith Tabernacle School

Jason

Jason
Careful, silent, thirsty, and funny.
Brother of Justin and Sue.
Lover of the trash men, the smell of coal burning,
And the sight of mountain woods.
Who feels happy when in a tree,
Sad when alone, and mad when ignored.
Who needs summer vacation, a cat, and a new Ipod.
Who loans pencils, paper, and crayons.
Who fears rats, horror films, and seizures.
Who would like to see Puss in Boots; Cumberland, Maryland;
And Middletown, Pennsylvania.
Who lives in a big white house on Flora Lane.

Jason Reel, Grade 8
Chichester Middle School

The Pack

A howl pierces the air once the moon comes in to view
Wolfs are coming hungry, looking for meat to chew
They spot a sleeping deer nearby, and facing them was its back.
The wolves are sneaking quietly, preparing to attack
Before the deer even knew it, its life was instantly ceased
And all the wolves began to feast.

Once finished they go back to their den
And then the next night they do it again
Hunting moose, caribou, and also deer
Whatever they hunt the wolves persevere.
Every night they would hunt down prey
And then go back home to sleep through the day.

Garrison Piel, Grade 7
Southern Lehigh Middle School

All That's Left

All that's left is the pain inside
All that's left the things we cannot hide.

All that's left we cannot let go
All that's left we already know

All that's left we don't' have no more
All that's left we are forced to ignore

All that's left lies on the floor
All that's left is like an open book, an open door.

All that's left

Amanda Morris, Grade 7
Schuylkill Valley Middle School

Fall

As fall approaches
leaves change color and fall down
to melt into ground

Joshua Coatsworth, Grade 8
Trinity Middle School

Opening Night

The fast pitter-patter of my crazed heart
The excited chatter floating aimlessly in the air,
I take a quick look at the chart
My time to go on—I wouldn't miss it—oh I wouldn't dare
The nervous expression plastered on my face
The shaking of my hands
My dream, so close, yet so far to chase,
It couldn't snap anytime, like a rubber band
Taking a deep breath, I know it's my time to go
I step behind the enclosed curtain—it's time for the show
Booming music fills my ears, applause then to—still silence,
I smile broadly and forget the fright
Of my unforgettable opening night.

Erin Neupauer, Grade 8
St Thomas More School

Autumn

In the season of Autumn, outside it's so breezy.
I just stay inside and have it made easy.
All the leaves are damp.
They're wet from the rain.
When it hits the leaves, you hear them in pain.
You hear kids screaming on Halloween night.
It gives them a big, big fright.
When they go home they feel very weary.
They look at the moon very, very clearly.
At the end of the day we are so exited.
But the day is ending and we just can't fight it.
Even though I know tomorrow will be awesome.
This is how it feels in the season of Autumn.

Jake Marcozzi, Grade 8
J R Fugett Middle School

Saturdays

Krista –
Caring, spontaneous, thoughtful and carefree
Sister of Connor
Lover of animals, roller coasters and science
Who feels spontaneous on roller coasters, caring
when around family and loving when with
animals
Who needs Saturdays, Science Olympiad and
VEX Robotics
Who fears bugs, haunted houses and dying
Who would like to see the Grand Canyon,
Sea World and no more hunger
Who lives in a big gray house on Larkin Road

Krista Mullin, Grade 8
Chichester Middle School

Springtime

The plants are blooming.
The colors are coming back.
Life is returning.

Santana Bulgarelli, Grade 7
Trinity Middle School

Trust Not Trusted

I give you back the trust
that you promised
I could rely on.
I couldn't.
I'm returning the trust
that you placed in my heart with a firm hand.

Your hand isn't firm any more.

I give you back your trust.
It'll be coming tomorrow
in a sloppily wrapped
brown package.

I didn't give it a second thought.

I'm returning OUR trust.
It evaporated with the rain
that refused to fall.

It's all your fault.

I release my grip
on the strand that holds you down,
and let you float away.

I give you back the trust
that I can't trust anymore.

Ruthanne Pilarski, Grade 7
Pittsburgh CAPA 6-12 School

I Give You Love

I give you love,
on those winter days when I hug you for warmth.
I give you love,
when you grab my hand and tell me that you love me.

You are in my thoughts,
when I sit at home waiting for the phone to ring.
You are in my thoughts,
as I walk and see happy couples everywhere.
You are in my thoughts,
always. You never leave my mind.

You love me,
as I sing you that lullaby.
You love me,
as I rock you to sleep.

I love you,
as you kiss my earlobe gently.
I love you,
And I will never stop doing so.
Don't you forget it.

Taylor Szczepaniuk, Grade 7
Pittsburgh CAPA 6-12 School

Your Imagination

It was a rainy day in a far off town,
The type that makes you wake up with a frown.

School starts at eight so you better hurry,
You sit on your chair and eat in a flurry.

You finish your cereal in a lethargic daze,
Suddenly into your mind comes a phrase:

If there comes a time when you are bored,
Pretend you're on a ship just climbing aboard.

The boat takes off and your adventures begin,
You travel great places that make your head spin.

Thick jungles with animals of the rarest kinds,
With wild natives that tie you with binds.

Undiscovered island with buried pirate gold,
That you find with a map unbelievably old.

You are the hero of your imagination,
The founder of this great creation.

You explore rare lands, amazed by everything you see,
Battling monsters, helping people, and saving cities.

Suddenly, you're back home again,
You check your watch, and its 8:10.

Charlie Veeck, Grade 8
St James School

Where I'm From

I'm from the paper dragon
and Lego fort I made
from when I was little,
and my cats who always forgave.

I'm from an igloo called Mellon
in the land of black and gold
(which I remember as if it were my own).
I'm from the street where I played hockey,
with the funniest bruise from my big brother
on the hot summer days.

I'm from Zinkhan's Beer or selling produce
in the strip district,
and even from the farms.
I'm from the 503rd Parachute Battalion
falling into the Philippines
From Ireland,
France and
Germany too.
The roots are almost endless.

Will Maniet, Grade 7
Jefferson Middle School

Waiting

We spend all our life waiting,
Just waiting.
Waiting for the leaves to fall, or the birds to sing.
We wait for the flowers to bloom, or the trees to grow.
But we spend the time waiting,
Just waiting.

We spend all our time waiting,
Just waiting.
We sit on the beach and stare at the sun, waiting for it to set.
We lay on a blanket under the stars, waiting for them to shine.
But all of this time we're just sitting and waiting,
Just waiting.

We spend all our life waiting,
Just waiting.
Waiting for the world to change, to work it out on its own.
We let it be, just sit and wait, we don't want to waste our time.
But if we want to change the world, we must first change our mind.

We spend all our life waiting…just waiting.
Amanda Espin, Grade 8
Walnut Creek Middle School

My Playful Puppy

I got a brand new puppy, her fur was fluffy white.
The first night we brought her home, she didn't sleep all night.

The next day we went outside, to run, fetch, and play.
I taught her how to sit and lay, and also how to stay.

My puppy did so very well, I gave her some new treats.
She loved the crunchy ones the best, but wouldn't eat the meats.

My puppy was very dirty, from running down the path.
I drew some real warm water, and she got her first full bath.

Tired, wet, and shivering, my puppy began to weep.
I wrapped her up and cuddled her, and she quickly fell asleep.
Jenna Carty, Grade 7
Greencastle-Antrim Middle School

Just Me

Alyssa —
Dependable, kind, funny, weird
Sister of Mark, Brittany, Amber
Lover of cats, summer, music,
Who feels scared in the dark,
Lonely without a good friend, and comfy in sweatpants,
Who needs braces, clothes, and shoes,
Who gives joy, smiles, and friendship,
Who fear pain, dying, sharks, and losing my family,
Who would like to see happiness, no fights, and peace,
Who lives in a small apartment in Pennsylvania.
Alyssa Stafford, Grade 8
Chichester Middle School

The Night Circus

It arrives without warning
And leaves just the same
At twilight it opens and at dawn the circus disappears

The acrobats flying and the concession stand mouthwatering
The bright lights that light up the acts
The clowns and elephants
The contortionist and magician
Everyone has a favorite

Dawn threatens the end of the glorious performances
All try to capture the lingering moments
As the sun creeps into the sky and no one wishes to leave

The gates close and the people have gone
The acts relax
And the people still dream of the acts

Night doesn't return quickly enough and people swarm the circus
Buying cotton candy and being mesmerized by the acts
And once again it all ends too quickly
Myra Brown, Grade 8
Holy Child Academy

What Is Love?

Love is a feeling
that is signaled by a dove.
It often brings healing
as it is a gift from above.
Love can close an open wound
that is brought upon by hate.
In the strangest of places it can be found,
even here upon this date.
Sometimes love can make us blind
and in others we become aware
of ways in which people are so kind,
but in others we refuse to care.
Love is an emotion which requires devotion,
for it is what sets our world in motion.
Michael Hilzendeger, Grade 9
Trinity Sr High School

Friends

Friends are always there for you,
No matter what you do.
A good friend is someone you look up to.
Trust a good friend too.
While you grow people will come and go,
But friends will always be there though.
Just because there are fights,
You'll always forgive, for as long as you live.
Friends will always have your back,
Even if someone tries to beat you up after class.
Friends are always there for you.
Katelyn Monillas, Grade 7
Armstrong Middle School

Cheetah's Life
A cheetah is wild and free
no limits, no restrictions
A cheetah is a tornado
speeding along chasing after animals
A cheetah is a fighter
bold and fierce not going to back down
A cheetah is like a Dalmatian
spotted and swift
A cheetah's family is a mother and her young
snuggled together under the cold moon
A cheetah's home is the vast grasslands of Africa
dry and barren
A cheetah's life is dangerous and unpredictable

Anna Younger, Grade 8
St Thomas More School

Christmas
Seven o'clock in the morning,
Kids are running down the stairs,
Pushing and shoving,
Can't wait to see what Santa brought them,
Smiles are on their faces
When they start to open their first present,
One they have been waiting twelve months for,
Waiting for this moment to come
Hoping to get what they asked for
Learning how to give
Not to be so selfish or ungrateful,
Christmas is a time to spend time with family
To thank them for being in your life.

Emoni Watts-Tramel, Grade 7
Armstrong Middle School

Freedom Is Not Free
In the United States we have it
Sometimes we take it for granted
We are like a rich family that has tons of food
And does not share with the poor and hungry families
Many people don't know what the price for freedom is
The price is countless lives taken from innocent soldiers
Nothing can replace a living person
Freedom is not
Free

Gabriel Walters, Grade 7
St Thomas More School

Blank Paper
As I stare at the paper,
Mocking me with no clever wordplay,
I know I will never find a topic,
A topic for my blank paper,
As the paper scowls and claims blind foolishness,
I know I will never find a topic,
A topic for my blank paper.

Lucas Myers, Grade 7
William M Meredith School

Goodbye Summer, Hello Fall
Goodbye summer, hello fall
Goodbye watermelons, hello corns
Goodbye fun, hello school
Goodbye swimsuits, hello costumes
Goodbye summer music, hello Christmas carols
Goodbye nature's flowers, hello Vera Bradley
Goodbye shorts, hello yoga pants
Goodbye brown bags, hello Abercrombie textbook covers
Goodbye blue and lime green, hello orange and yellow and red
Goodbye tan, hello snow-white skin
Goodbye softball, hello cheerleading
Goodbye short sleeves, hello North Face jackets
Goodbye flip-flops, hello Uggs
Goodbye all-nighters, hello school nights
Goodbye pool parties, hello bonfires
Goodbye ice tea, hello hot cocoa
Goodbye fall, hello winter

Denisha Williams, Grade 8
Pennwood Middle School

Watery Eyes
The ocean, the air, the beautiful sea,
I run in to the water and it starts to surround me,
My feet start to sink into the sands,
As I look at my beating red feet and my cold, pale hands,
The waves badger at me.

The gods churn and stir the big sandy pot,
Trying to heat the feet to make them hot,
It happens on hot sunny days,
When the heat is so hot it creates a haze,
The sun badgers at me.

Your feet feel like they are on fire,
Big watery tears form in your eyes,
The ocean's power I now admire,
My eyes are all watery and my mouth like salt,
I swim back to the beach which is nearby.

Bradley Tollen, Grade 7
Charles F Patton Middle School

Christmas
Lights lit!
Stockings filled to the brim!
Children waking the minute the sun rises,
yelling and running through the house,
making sure everyone knows it's Christmas.
Little children looking for the proof,
that Santa has come and left presents or coal
excitement runs through their bodies
seeing only crumbs of cookies and a drip of milk.
Lighting up when they find the big box is for them.
Christmas is like a fairy tale you have to believe.
Christmas is a memory, it's never forgotten!

Allison Lamb, Grade 8
St Thomas More School

The Snow

Falling softly on the ground,
Like little flakes of cheer,
Reminding you of the golden days,
Friends, family, snow

Making snow angels,
Having a snowball fight,
Putting the eyes on a snowman,
Family, snow, friends

From California,
To New Jersey,
Snow reminds us all of,
Family, friends, and good times

Brenna Fiore, Grade 8
Holy Child Academy

Gone

It's a normal day I jump out of bed
and then I remember she's dead,
No one left to lick my face
when I'm late to get out of bed,
No one left to bark when I'm doing
my homework till I play with her,
She's gone and no one can take her place,
No one to left to make me
happy when I'm sad,
No one left to make those stuffy
Christmas parties worth going to,
She's gone and no one can take her place,
I go back to bed weeping till my mom
comes to pull me out of bed

Lindsey Zimmerman, Grade 7
Schuylkill Valley Middle School

Fireflies

Tiny golden specks of light
Ascend towards the sky,
Little sparks within the night
Kiss the ground goodbye.

Count the fragments of our hopes
Rising to the stars,
Escalating on gentle slopes
To the world afar.

Each lightning bug is a messenger
In a glowing golden hue
Every one of them eager
To make our dreams come true.

Mindy Wen, Grade 7
Southern Lehigh Middle School

New Things

Rashawn –
funny, caring, curious, generous
Brother of Yasmin and Rasheed
Lover of girls when their hair
is wet and let down,
Who feels joy going to new places
and eating their dessert,
Who needs Fridays, pizza, and girls,
Who gives money, loyalty, and respect,
Who fears snakes, bugs, and
hobos,
Who would like to see Christ
Air in Rio, everyone having fun,
and clean streets,
Who lives in a big brown
house with a yellow top peak
at the end of the road on
Douglas Street.

Rashawn Ivery, Grade 8
Chichester Middle School

47 Minutes

"Arden wake up"
Startled, my eyes open to my mom
Staring, panicking
It's the first day of school
The chalkboard-black clock reads 6:05!
I'm 15 minutes late
47 minutes to get ready
Bounce out of bed
Snag clothes off polar bear-white hangers
I'm dressed finally
Plop, plop, plop
My feet pounding down the steps
Snatch the Cheerios
Got milk
Shove food down
Brush my teeth
There's the bus…
Made it!

Arden Hudson, Grade 7
Holicong Middle School

Cheetahs

Cheetahs are very fast
they never come in last
Cheetahs have spots
they kind of look like dots
Cheetahs need to eat
they really love their meat
Cheetahs are very vicious
they know their prey will be delicious
Cheetahs like the hot
Hope you have really learned a lot!

Morgan Clopper, Grade 7
Greencastle-Antrim Middle School

Writer's Block

I was trying to find something to write,
But I couldn't write anything right.
I was thinking of a daredevil's fear,
Or a mother's trembling tear.
There's oranges, grapes, and strawberries
And red-painted river boat ferries,
But all of these seem too nonchalant
To occupy my busy thoughts.

There's planets and oceans
And energy in motion,
Unending love,
Blue jays, and doves.
There's trucks and cars
And moons and stars,
But through all of this time
I can't get one to rhyme.

So I'm going to close
Without an idea that flows.
I'm sorry I couldn't surprise you,
But that's what writer's block does to you.

Shawnee Deimler, Grade 8
Faith Tabernacle School

There Was a Kid Named Phil

Phil —
Honest, successful, generous,
and kind
Brother of Austin and a sister
named Dallas
Lover of family, freshness, and
spring
Who feels happy, excited, and
joy
Who needs Saturdays, friends, and
vacations
Who gives support, smiles, and
happiness
Who fears mean dogs, dentists,
and doctors
Who would like to see respect, for
animals, environment, and for my family
to stop fighting
Who lives in a white house down
on West Main Street,
— Strantzalis

Phillip Strantzalis, Grade 8
Chichester Middle School

Fall

Trees wave back and forth
coarse wind calling out my name
cold rain comes and goes

Elizabeth King, Grade 8
North Star East Middle School

My Shoes

On the sidewalk, in the school hallways, everywhere I go I see shoes
Big shoes, small shoes, black shoes, and gray shoes
They're dirty and weak, I hate shoes
I run, I walk, I stand but I still see shoes
Ugly and miserable
On concrete, marble, carpet, grass…
I whisper, I hear, I listen and still, I see shoes, just shoes
These lonely and miserable shoes I see
I am weak, I am ugly
I am miserable, I am lonely and shy
I am scared, worried, and embarrassed to lift my head
But now I am sick of shoes
I finally gather courage to lift my head
I see the sky, the stars, and the trees
Bright and happy… not weak, not ugly, not miserable or lonely
I laugh, I giggle, I yell
And now, on the sidewalk, in the school hallways
Everywhere I go I see faces, not shoes
Those ugly and miserable shoes

Faith Kim, Grade 9
Fox Chapel Area Sr High School

Christmas Season

Christmas is a wonderful
Thing
Trees covered in
Bling
Candle lights flickering
Children snickering
Opening seasonal gifts
Pieces of ice that drift
Down roves slanted like cliffs
The crispy sweet smell of pine
People all dressed up in their skirts and their ties
Wonderful winter storms of snow
The freezing chilling winter blow
Mini homes of gingerbread
Christmas tales grandparents have read
Imperfect tall towering snowmen
Christmas lists written in gold pen
Especially all of the mounds of toys
And no one can resist all of these Christmas joys!

Taylor Bowman, Grade 7
Holicong Middle School

Timmy

You lay there in your death bed.
I see tears drown everybody.
I cry little 'cause I know what you are thinking.
I can see you standing there yelling.
You yell what is going on !
I want to answer but I can't.
I stop crying because I realize you are up there.
And your mom is waiting to greet you for a second time.

Tyara Snyder, Grade 7
Schuylkill Valley Middle School

Me

Nunshel –
   Honest, helpful, generous, respectful,
   Brother of Stherlie,
   Lover of the humidity of summer, the
     smell of delicious food and the
     sound of kids having fun.
   Who feels excited when getting a surprise,
     happy when playing with friends, and
     sad when you see somebody get hurt.
   Who needs money, siblings and happiness,
   Who gives love, friendship and care,
   Who fears the dark, spiders, and monsters,
   Who would like to see gifts for the
     little ones, peace in the world, and doctors
     for people who need help,
   Who lives in a big brown house on
     Winding Way.
     – Thys

Nunshel Thys, Grade 8
Chichester Middle School

Life

Life is like a giant roller coaster.
The ride ends when you get older.
In life you might need to lean on someone's shoulder.

In life your job can be a mail sender.
Maybe you can get lucky and be a trendsetter.
If you drive you can get into a fender bender.

You can lose your home and be poor.
Or you could play some sport's
And get paid to score.

You could get a job and become rich.
Or someday you could fall on the ground and get a stitch.
Your plans could end with a glitch.

You could have a big family.
Life gives you plenty of chances to be happy.

James Russo, Grade 7
St Anselm Elementary School

Love

The relationship was so undesirable
It was affectionate as could be
Something so unique turned into something so dysfunctional
That dysfunctional relationship became a poison to everybody
If you got caught in it you would be intoxicated
The relationship was supposed to have loyalty, trust, and happiness
I became too foolish to realize what I had
When I realized what I had lost it was too late
Only if I could have one last wish I would do it all over again
I will never take love for granted again

Mary Miller, Grade 7
Schuylkill Valley Middle School

The Essence of Time

Time is a beach;
Sometimes the water is calm,
But sometimes the waves are raging.
Each second is as tiny and insignificant
As a grain of sand,
Slipping and sliding right through our fingers…
And when they fall
We can never get them back.
So,
For as long as we possibly can,
We merely walk along the shore.
We collect our seashells
And memories.
But after we've been walking
For awhile,
The waves become dangerous
And take us
Away.

Erin Skibbens, Grade 7
St Thomas More School

The City of Wonders

Paris
See the lights
Hear the sounds
And smell the scent of French cuisine lingering in the air.
The lights
Are like dancing fireflies against the dark sky.
Paris
The city of love,
Where two people go to meet their special someone.
The Eiffel Tower,
Eminent over the city
With lights that shine for miles.
So many beautiful things
So little time.
It's time to explore
Paris
The city of wonders.

Aubrey Cintron, Grade 8
Bellmar Middle School

The Woods

Late afternoon on a bright sunny day
Birds swarm all around me,
The dull gray rocks,
The rushing Cookie Monster-blue water.
Touching the water sends a bone shattering chill down my spine,
The birds chirp.
The tree branches sway in the wind,
I realize where I am,
The woods.
The last thing I remember before I wake up,
Was the feel of the plants brushing against my leg.

Cameron Komonchak, Grade 7
Holicong Middle School

A Gift

Ballet is not just a sport
It is a miraculous gift that presents gracefulness
Like a swift angel
Flying in the sky

Ballet is not just a sport
It is a gift that makes my arms and feet
Act as machines that automatically turn on
When they hear the fluidity of the music

Ballet is not just a sport
It is a gift that makes my saut de chats higher
My toes point farther
And my arms stronger

Ballet is not just a sport
It is a gift that puts my radiant costume into the light
And my sweat and tears fall
The speed of my pirouette is the Tilt-A-Whirl
spinning me into a majestic, parallel universe

Ballet is not just a sport
It is a talent that God gave to me to cherish
And to be thankful for

It is a gift that I adore

Samantha Murmello, Grade 7
St Thomas More School

Ode to Passion Iced Tea

Your fruity taste makes my lips smack.
You are the highlight of my day.

Your foam
is like a
puffy
white
cloud.

The chill of your cool ice blocks
is the winter time.
Your sweetening crystal pellets
make you complete.

Even though your liquid is a deep red,
you shine as bright as the sun.
Your liquid dances on my taste buds.
You can be purchased in any size.
Your liquid is cradled in a transparent cup.

Sucking your sweetness is the pollen from a flower.

You truly
live up to your name.

Natalie Shaw, Grade 7
Jefferson Middle School

Sticks and Stones

"Sticks and stones may break my bones, but words will never hurt me."
I have never fully understood that classic saying.
Sticks and stones leave cuts and bruises, but they heal with time.
Words cut so much deeper; they lash at the heart, and make the soul bleed.
They fade into painful scars that never go away. They're always there, constant reminders of the past.
The pain starts as sharp and unbearable, then slowly, oh so slowly, fades into a dull, incessant ache.
Throughout a lifetime the scars grow in number, and the heart breaks a little more with every shallow beat.
Colder, and colder the soul becomes, until it turns to ice.
The heart mutates into something bitter.
Persistent verbal beatings will change people into something evil, sinister.
Sticks and stones may break bones, but words hurt so much more.

Abigail Moyer, Grade 8
Saucon Valley Middle School

Swim Meet

Your heart beating Boom…Boom…Boom…
The worried part of yourself asks, how are you going to do? Are you going to win first place?
Will you slip on the block? The pitter-patters of the water echoes the brick walls and blasts into your ears.
Warmups, people in the stands watching your every move. Your mind is overflowing with cheerful and worried thoughts.
You get out of the water "gosh that water was cold," as you reach for your warm and fuzzy towel.
A short time passes and you are up for your race.
Step up…Take your mark…BEEP!
Your heart jumps out of your chest.
Boom, you dive into the water so gracefully.
Splash…Splash…Splash…Your hand hits the water so fast you cannot even keep a steady beat.
Buzz! Cheering! You have won your race!

Eleni Sophocles, Grade 7
Strath Haven Middle School

All About Me

Gloria
Friendly, caring, quiet, and peaceful,
Sister of Jabree, Clayton, and Stephon,
Lover of animals, long-lasting friendships, and listening to music,
Who feels happiness when listening to music,
Nervousness when meeting new people, and mad when you don't get your way,
Who needs cell phones, summer time, and friends,
Who gives laughs, help, and encouragement,
Who fears the coming school year, the end of a great summer, and a quiz you didn't study for,
Who would like to see good homes for abused animals, education to children that can't afford it, and peace to the world,
Who lives in a small red house in Pennsylvania

Gloria Newman, Grade 8
Chichester Middle School

Nighttime

When darkness falls and eve approaches,
I see the faces on the white clouds fade.
I see the moon's smile light up the world,
While people make wishes on the stars that flicker in the night sky.
I see the families go inside their houses, and the street lights come on.
I see the building lights shut down, and people drive away.
When darkness falls and eve approaches, I see the back of my eyelids, and a dream cloud above my head.
That is what I see when darkness falls and eve approaches.

Carley Nodis, Grade 9
Chichester Sr High School

Music

Catchy beat that sticks in your head
Rhythm and rhyme
Better left unsaid
Let it flow across your
mind   without a thought,
Of wasting time
Finger snapping remedy
Toe-tapping melody
Lyrics feeding your imagination
What a wonderful, new
creation.

Alicia Huot, Grade 7
Armstrong Middle School

10 Years

10 years since the plane crashed
10 years since those screams rang out for help
10 years of silence
10 years of sadness
10 years of mourning
10 years of repairing
10 years of broken hearts
10 years since those 2, 751 lives were lost
10 years since 3000 children lost their parents
10 years since 9/11
That day will never be forgotten

Renee King, Grade 8
Chichester Middle School

Parasailing

I was up high
Almost touching the sheep-white clouds
It was so unreal...
I was parasailing
The view was amazing to see
It seemed the mountains and lake went on forever
It was so peaceful and serene
The only noise was the rippling sky-blue water below
The wind on my face was cool and smooth
I felt like I was flying, free as a bird
Never wanting to come down

Courtney Keating, Grade 7
Holicong Middle School

Meaningless Deaths

Deaths of thousands, families terrorized,
Building collapses with hundreds of people.
No one satisfied but one man. Hearts are broken,
People's legs and arms are broken, but why?
For power, you won't receive power, only fear.
The only thing you will gain is the pain of thousands.
Some celebrated others were not happy when that
Man died. There is no way to take away or change
What that man did on that exact day, 9/11/01.

Cory Massanet, Grade 7
Armstrong Middle School

Fall

As the leaves start to fall to the ground,
When I stop to listen there is not a single sound.

I can see all the bees flying away,
This is no longer a summer day.

Fall is the time when kids play,
By jumping in leaves till the end of the day.

Red, brown, and yellow,
As you can see fall colors are very mellow.

When the temperature starts to get colder,
I realize that summer colors were a lot bolder.

Leaves are blown everywhere,
When the wind flows through the air.

As each day passes by,
The sun sets earlier in the sky.

Now that summer has faded away,
It has turned into a fall day.

While the trees sway through the air,
The colorful leaves blow here and there.

As all the flowers are starting to die,
To their color and beauty I say goodbye.

Alex West, Grade 7
Landisville Middle School

Slow-Cooked Meat

I want to kiss you like slow-cooked meat;
kiss you strong, kiss you spiced
kiss you tender.
I want to mark you.
To leave lipstick, sweet as honeysuckle,
somewhere in the vacant expression of your heart.
I want to kiss you like slow-cooked meat.
To mold to your lips.
To melt on your tongue. To flutter in your stomach
like butterflies darting free of the net.
I want you to kiss me like it's your last breath
and you want it to mean something.
I want you to kiss me with all the passion
of a red-faced baby crying.
The furious beat of a love made bed.
The childish delight of laughter —
the kind that makes your stomach hurt.
I want to kiss you like slow — cooked meat.
To relish you. To take you in.
To dine on each flaw like
I'm falling in love.

Mollie March-Steinman, Grade 9
Pittsburgh CAPA 6-12 School

Giants Pride

Roses are red, and the Giants are blue
Ahmad Bradshaw will run all over you
And if you're a quarterback, you better watch out
Because Justin Tuck is going to make the crowd shout
When he tackles you, sacks you, and makes you fumble the ball
Michael Boley picks it up and goes for it all
He gets the touchdown, now put six on the board
Lawrence Tynes will kick it in to add one more
Eli Manning takes the snap and he's in the pocket
He sees his receiver and he throws a real rocket
Right to Hakeem Nicks, he catches it and jukes
A 50-yard reception, now that's no fluke
Brandon Jacobs gets the ball and runs it up the gut
If you're defending in his way prepare to get trucked
Nothing is more solid than the Giant's O-line
Never letting up a sack when it's Go-Time
How about the coach, you can't call plays without him
Even though he's 65 he's always up and at 'em
The Giants are the dream team they've proved it many times
So look out all you other teams, it's our time to shine

Elijah Caldwell, Grade 8
Paxon Hollow Middle School

The Spider

It's an eight-legged fly-eater.
Some of its web is no longer than a meter.

With two fangs that pack-a-punch,
Spiders eat interesting insects for lunch.

A spider can have numerous colors and shapes,
And with its silky web it tapes;

On its back, a poisonous spider looks like it has an hourglass.
And the male gets eaten by his lass.

Their children then balloon away,
Taking special care not to sway.

These spiders are silent like the dead.
Seeing super spiders like these that some people dread.

It's the best feeling because they're so unique;
Each one of them has a special technique.

Garrett E. Notz, Grade 8
Faith Tabernacle School

Night

The moonlight dances across the spacious lawn.
The stars brighten the dark, solemn, lonely sky.
A starry curtain closes around the earth.
Leaves rustle in the thick, damp, strong air.
Nature talks in peaceful simple patterns.
A calm silence is touched by a busy world.

Elizabeth Labows, Grade 7
Strath Haven Middle School

Science Class

I see beakers in the see-through cabinets
The smart board in the corner with its knotty wires
Rocks in the back looking jagged and rigid

The glowing smart board projecting notes that I need
The light shining dimly above me

I hear the teacher spewing dreadful facts about the atmosphere
Outrageous facts about wind patterns being said everywhere

I feel the facts all distorted in my head,
Making chaos in my brain
My hand taking insufferable notes,
That the teacher insists we need

Will I ever get out of this class?
Will I ever go to lunch?
Will these facts ever make sense?

Science class
Science class
Science class

Sean Duffy, Grade 8
Saucon Valley Middle School

Letter to Juliet

Dearest love; presence brighter than the moon
our affection fiercer than the sun
perhaps our love is, my fear, just too soon
All that's happened, oh, wish fate could be done
If I had known all order would collapse
Before, I need not learn the consequence
Now I ponder better times to relapse
it is far too late, they ask for vengeance
Young was I, I dreamed success, our tale
Unfortunately, I had a fool's hand
Yet I hear only dreadful cries and wails
tragic, Destiny's ship I did not man
It is redundant that I repeat, miss
you, my heart contracts my love, don't assist.

Christine Phan, Grade 9
Central High School

Myself

Does it shine through you like the rays of a sun?
Or is it locked inside like a prisoner that can't escape
I might be as silent as a rabbit passing by
While you are seen by everyone like a post online
You may be as bright as a flashlight
Or dark and dangerous like the night clawing at you
We are all like our fingerprints
No one is exactly alike
But when I'm with you
I am myself

Cindy Nguyen, Grade 7
Holicong Middle School

Christmas Morning

Children are up early
Trying to wake their parents
On a bright Sunday morning
Snowflakes are falling
All different shapes and sizes
Children open their presents
And find sweet surprises
They see the cookies and carrots gone
Knowing Santa had come
With a cup of milk half full
They knew he had a long ride home
Then family comes
From all over
To help celebrate the Christmas cheer
As everyone plays in the snow
A snowman is made
And there are snowball fights
All through the day
For the children Christmas is never boring
But nothing brings more fun
Than the joy on Christmas morning
Lynnea Johnson, Grade 7
Armstrong Middle School

Coca Cola

I pick up the Coke bottle
And a new cold rushes through me
That is not the winter chill
It is early winter and I sit on my step
Just returning from the corner store
With a new bottle of Coke in my hand
I take the cap off
And as my lips touch the soda,
It is not early winter
But the Fourth of July
And the fireworks are just going off
A whole crowd is gathered
In one spot
While in the center, a man
With long stringy hair
And a baseball cap
Is setting them off
My imagination blurs
And I am brought back
To reality as
I swallow the rest of my Coca Cola
Carmen Sylvester, Grade 7
William M Meredith School

The Moon's Grass

Blades of grass shining,
pointing upward at the moon.
Stubby, rough, and stiff.
Gregory Coffey, Grade 7
J R Fugett Middle School

Whales

Big and blue
Small and black

Eating shrimp and squid,
Krill and fish

High in the Arctic,
Or low in Mexico

Deep in the ocean,
Or at the surface

Flying out of the water,
Or in the deep, whales are amazing.
Thomas Wolf, Grade 7
Greencastle-Antrim Middle School

Grandmother

We were always together
Never apart
She was my mom-mom
Very close to my heart.

She lived with me, cared for me
Every single day
When I was sad
She would always know what to say.

We called her Dee-Dee
She was a big part of me
Letting her go
Was hard to see.
Natalie Magee, Grade 7
Strath Haven Middle School

Boom! Flash!

Boom! Flash!
10 seconds to go.
Let's make it count.
No time for being slow.

Catch the ball and go
Drive down the lane.
Break the defender's ankles;
I cannot be contained

Dribble it out.
Pop a shot.
It's a three.
Durantula cannot be stopped!
Nolan Bishop, Grade 8
Southern Lehigh Middle School

Soccer Tournament

All day, 8:50 to 5,
I see green
Shamrock-green soccer fields
And emerald-green jerseys
A star-patched soccer ball
That soars into netted goals
First silence
Then ear-piercing cheering
An overjoyed team
A grassy soccer field
And sweaty soccer gear
Trophies in hand
Shiny and smooth
Wanted and received
17 ecstatic smiles across faces
Now time for the picture
Click!
Anna Genus, Grade 7
Holicong Middle School

The Sound

I woke with a start,
The pounding in my heart.

A sound of a crack,
Just behind my back.

I crept into the hall,
Right against the wall.

I quickly dart,
Down the stairs not too smart.

From on the stairs I hear a hack,
All around was pitch black.

And thinking I saw it crawl,
I realized it was nothing at all.
Madeline Ciarallo, Grade 8
St James School

Goodbye Grandpa

I remember when I was young
I was about three
Every time we came to see you,
You were happy
We played rugby
We watched TV
But I still remember the night you died
It was on the news
They announced your death
A crash in the night.
Goodbye,
Grandpa
Talha Mahmud, Grade 7
Armstrong Middle School

Firework

Shining in the night
With sparks of light.
Flying through the air
And going everywhere.

Fireworks bring joy
To a little girl and boy.
They sparkle like glistening stars
While people watch the from their cars.

Rachel Busler, Grade 7
St Joseph School

Bravest Man

A brave man
The bravest I had ever seen
in the Army
Fought in World War II
Had lung cancer
But he faced it head on
God took his life away
He is in a happy place now
He was the bravest man I had ever seen

Starleen Correa, Grade 7
Armstrong Middle School

Bird Bomb

At the beach,
the birds are at watch.
They see us eat,
All of the birds want a treat.
We try to hide.
They all start to whine.
We know its time
For the birds to dive
in for the food.

Matt Brown, Grade 7
Southern Lehigh Middle School

Friends

F riendships that last a lifetime
R emain with you forever
I nterests are shared with one another
E verybody needs someone to love
N o one should be left alone
D evastating times become easier
S upporting and loving each other forever

Shaela Marsh, Grade 7
Moravian Academy Middle School

My Dream: Photography

I'm snapping pictures
Traveling around the world
Following my dreams

Arianna Gavatorta, Grade 7
Burgettstown Jr/Sr High School

Where I'm From

I am from grass, from the tool shed and the back patio.
I am from my mom's butterfly bush. (Purple, tall, it tasted like candy)
I am from the garden's flowers, my backyard tree
where leaves fall from it's branches as if they were ready to leave.

I'm from the TV and my soft bed,
from Robin and Mike.
I'm from never giving up and never stop trying,
from nothing to fear, but fear itself.
I'm from the Holy Ghost, who clears me from bad thoughts
and the Bible that I read from.

I'm from Kay and Chuck, cooked ham and cold ice cream,
from the Alzheimer's disease my grandfather is plagued with,
the life of my great grandmother, as if she was immortal.
Inside my heart is a locked door holding onto precious memories,
with good and bad times, most of them to be unseen by human eyes.

I am from those moments —
my older relatives — lost —
but life is to be everlasting in a family tree.

Ean McCloud, Grade 7
Whitehall-Coplay Middle School

My Favorite Things from Christmas

My favorite part of Christmas is looking at the lights,
Watching them twinkle on a cold winter's night

Thinking of Christmas and all that it brings like family, friends, and presents;
All of my favorite things.

I'm hoping for an iPod, a cell phone, some Aeropostale clothes,
Or maybe some Ugg boots to warm up my toes.

But whatever Santa decides to bring
I'm sure it will be some of my favorite things

Allison Geere, Grade 7
Armstrong Middle School

What Is a Friend

Friends are people who show love and compassion when you're feeling blue.
They take that sorrow and those tears away from you.

His smiling face always brightens my day.
His humility and patience is so grand I could never repay.

Our laughter and joyfulness bring us closer together,
and our favorite memories always last forever.

Jumping over puddles, playing games,
and always calling each other funny names.

This faithful friend is a strong bond that never severs.
I know I can count on his steady presence forever.

Melanie Marcano, Grade 8
St Peter School

A Day at the Beach

Lying in the soft sand
While trying to get a dark tan
Nothing is on my mind
Not even worried about the time
Sharp seashells by my feet
Oh, how I admire the heat
The waves are going up so high
Sadly, it's time to say goodbye
Tianna Boccuti, Grade 7
William M Meredith School

Christmas

Christmas time is near…
Presents and a stocking await me…
I'm so ecstatic for the snow…
Building a snowman…
Drinking hot chocolate in the cold…
The smell of Christmas trees…
Decorating the tree as a family…
Christmas is amazing…
Amber Hartner, Grade 7
Armstrong Middle School

Football

F ield goal
O ut of bounds
O ffensive line
T ouchdown
B oundaries
A ll cheer for their team
L oud cheering
L ots of running
Kyle Zgleszewski, Grade 8
Chichester Middle School

My Friend

I have found a friend
We tell each other secrets
Like friends would do
He may not be normal
He is good enough for me
We can play catch
He is so furry it sort of tickles
I have found a TRUE friend.
Kali Hawkes, Grade 7
Armstrong Middle School

Me

C razy
O utrageous
N ice
N ovember
O utgoing
R ocks
Connor Maggio, Grade 8
Chichester Middle School

Saturday Mornings

On Saturday mornings
I wake up around 8 o'clock
The alarm thankfully doesn't kick me out of bed at the crack of dawn
I go down the stairs quietly
My dog jumps up and greets me
On Saturday mornings
I say good morning to my parents
I eat a nice breakfast like eggs and bacon
It's nice to sit down and eat
On school days I rush out the door with a waffle in my hand to eat on the way
On Saturday mornings
I read the comics while sipping a glass of cold milk
They are really funny
Sometimes I laugh out loud at the jokes
On Saturday mornings
It's my relaxing time
No homework
No responsibilities
Saturday mornings is my favorite time of the week
Zoe Peeleman, Grade 7
Strath Haven Middle School

Saturday Night Dead

The full moon was out on Saturday night.
Its magnificent beauty was quite a sight.
As I stood in the graveyard, I contemplated how I got there.
But what I saw next gave me a scare.

Its wrinkly green skin covered it from head to knee.
Quickly, I became queasy.
Blood was dripping down its scruffy chin.
I prayed to the Lord to take away this horrific sin.

Within seconds there was millions more to come,
Some without limbs and some carrying bottles of rum.
Immediately, I turned on my heels and started to run
Through this endless graveyard hoping moon would turn to sun.

Unlike typical zombies, these ones were speedy.
They're catching up! Uh oh, there's that feeling again of being queasy.
Then I saw my dead grandma then a horrible light
As my eyes flickered open and I woke with a fright.
Steven Field, Grade 8
Sandy Run Middle School

What Are Friends?

Friends are people who change your life
They are like roses, with each petal, there is a different aspect that comes with it
Their seeds are just the beginning of happiness and trust, which take time to grow
You need to take care of them when they are hanging low
You have to watch out for the thorns, but they are your everything in life
They may lose a petal, but it will always grow back
You may not always see them, but they are always with you
They will grow into wonderful people that you will keep close to you forever
Marissa Lueddeke, Grade 7
St Thomas More School

Love

Love is hard to describe
I would run a mile for her
I look at her
and it makes me smile
She likes me as a friend
I like her more than that
She does not know
I am glad that she doesn't
I am scared she won't like me
She rocks my world
I love her.

Christian Porter, Grade 7
Armstrong Middle School

God's Wonderful Sea Animals

There are so many sea animals,
Big and small,
Some with long tails,
Some the size of a nail,
But God cares for them all.

Some sea creatures are fat; some are thin;
Some have short tails;
Some have long fins;
Some are little, and some are tall;
But God cares for them all.

Melissa D. Feaser, Grade 7
Faith Tabernacle School

My Favorite Sports

Soccer, basketball, football
I can't pick one I love them all
on streets, grass or sidewalk
we can never just sit and talk
shooting from the foul line
or running for a touchdown
whenever we play we never frown
we always have fun
and we always run
soccer, basketball, football
I love them all

Ricky Leitz, Grade 7
Armstrong Middle School

Ocean Predator

Down into the deep,
He waits with patience,
A fish swims across,
He rockets from the dark deep,
The fish gets away,
Waiting again,
Time passes by,
Waiting…waiting
In the deep dark ocean

Evan Wells, Grade 7
Armstrong Middle School

Where the Night Takes Me

I walked out to the quiet street and
As I wander, I hear trees whispering to each other.
The big, full moon pulled me into the forest and out.
The leaves raced down to the ground as the heavy wind blew.
I listen to the bushes yell to each other as I walk past them, into the foggy night.
I look back and see the world behind me sleeping deeper than ever.
And soon enough it starts to wake up.
Another day is another part of life.

Pankti Shah, Grade 7
Strath Haven Middle School

Winter

On an early winter morning there is magic in the air.
A cardinal sings a tune as it zips through the silence,
the delicate snowflakes gracefully dance to the ground,
safe and warm underneath the shining blanket of white snow.
The early morning sun glimmers through the snow-covered treetops,
the dark night is finally leaving,
the glowing moon is gone.
There is nothing like waking up in winter to a quiet and peaceful day.

Gabriella McGillin, Grade 7
Strath Haven Middle School

Box of Crayons

My family is like a box of crayons.
My mother red, the color mostly used, filling in the spots in the picture here and there.
My father blue, the fun color, but sometimes doesn't always make the picture.
My sister purple, an interesting color, sometimes useful, but grabs your attention.
Me pink, the party color, but may be a little too much at times.
A box of four crayons, sometimes they bring out the worst in each other, but in the end come together to make one beautiful picture.

Olivia Jacques, Grade 7
Strath Haven Middle School

The Five Senses of Love

Love acts like a hot blazing fire and a stormy soulless night
Love sounds like the voice of a white-winged smiling angel or a heartbroken sobbing girl
Love tastes like a heart-shaped sweet chocolate and a oval-like salty tear
Love smells like a honey-scented red rose or a medicine-aromatic perfume
Love looks like a sweet turtle dove yet a puppy's pleading eyes
But in the end, it makes me feel happy and warm inside
Love is the very glue that holds humanity together

Melissa Lu, Grade 7
Richboro Middle School

Zanzibar, Zanzibar

Zanzibar, Zanzibar in the tree.
Zanzibar, Zanzibar is a lonely man with a mane.
Zanzibar, Zanzibar is a protected child.
Zanzibar, Zanzibar is a fast lion.
Zanzibar, Zanzibar leaps off tree limbs so high you'd think it's a bird.
Zanzibar oh, poor Zanzibar you're almost gone.
Zanzibar, Zanzibar I hope you're not all done.

Kylie Sakraida, Grade 7
Greencastle-Antrim Middle School

Equestrian

Dawn. An echoing chorus of birds and earsplitting neighs.
In the stadium,
I force rubber footing out of their
Cozy piles into layers of dust-brown flooring.
Fancy riding shirts are sprinkled throughout.
Hanging arrays of disco ball-shiny ribbons
Reward impending excellence.
The distant pitter-patter of antsy hooves
Calm bulky bats swooping,
Into delicate butterflies fluttering.
As I plunge my hand into the soft, chalk-white fur of my partner,
I glue a confident disposition to myself.
As I prepare, I think;
Everything happens for a reason,
And I am here because I am an
Equestrian.

Rebecca Power, Grade 7
Holicong Middle School

My Village

I hear whispers coming up the stairs.
I hear winds swooshing in the air.
The top of my palace I am.
Watching the waves become stronger.
I am seeing a shadow form.
From the bottom of my heart I feel.
Something is coming.
Something that's big.
I hear a strike.
The screaming and yelling of my villagers is loud.
What could it be?
What do I see?
Another strike I hear.
I see the crumble.
My army is rushing to my side.
Attack!

Enissa Ramos, Grade 7
Landisville Middle School

Summer

Summer is cooling off on a 90 degree day.
It's going on vacation and not caring if you find your way.
Summer is barbecuing and having lots of fun.
It's going to the beach and soaking up the sun.
Summer is not going to school.
It's swimming in the pool, to try and keep cool.
Summer is going out to play with your friends.
It's being ready to take on whatever the weather sends.
Summer is waking up in the afternoon.
It's not caring about what day it is as long as school isn't soon.
Summer is going out with family.
It feels like running around happily.
Summer is truly the best.
It will always beat the rest.

Katherine Gana, Grade 7
St Anselm Elementary School

Me, Myself, and I

Joanna –
Talkative, loud, athletic, and honest,
Sister of PJ and Donald,
Lover of fall, changing leaves and the smell of fire,
Who feels joy when alone and with friends,
But nervousness when a needle is around,
Who needs friends, Friday nights, and bonfires,
Someone who gives their all, and tries their best,
Who fears rubber chickens and the dark,
Who tries to keep all A's,
Someone who lives in a small tan house down on Summit Ave.

Joanna McGinn, Grade 8
Chichester Middle School

Walking to Your Future

You are sleeping and you see your future
Your future wakes you up and takes you there
Your future tells you what your life is going to be like
Walking through the clouds of your future
You see that future ahead
You are touching your own future
Next thing you know you are right there
You are watching a sunset on the beach
Then the beautiful sunset is gone
Now you do not know what is next for you
Do not give up, you will always come back to see your future.

Andre Burch, Grade 7
Armstrong Middle School

Autumn

Autumn is the time when leaves start to fall.
Autumn is the time when all you can smell
Is that cool gush of wind coming your way.
Autumn is the time when you can taste that
Big turkey in the middle of your table.
Autumn is the time when you can feel leaves
In your hands.
Autumn is the time to spend time with your family
At the dinner table.
Autumn is the time to just have fun.

Chloe Blessington, Grade 7
Strath Haven Middle School

Christmas Night

As winter wonderland swirls through the air
Dreams of sugar run through my head
I wait for Saint Nicholas and the gifts he will bring
As the Christmas carolers sing
Magical memories floating around
I hear a thump and an unfamiliar sound
I wonder and wish, thinking it's him
I close my eyes as my thoughts dim
I lay my head down and go to sleep
For Santa doesn't give to kids who peek

Elisabeth Glasscott, Grade 7
J R Fugett Middle School

I Stand Alone

The world is engulfed in a cold night, and I stand alone
The wind blows the hair from my neck
The only light is from a street lamp
A figure dashes across the road
A stray cat, hungry and searching for food
I stand alone
Hands in my pockets
I listen as the chilling wind whispers
The cold seems like it will never end
I think of people whom I have loved and lost
I stand alone
I look at the stars twinkling without a care in the world
The moonlight casts a ghostly shadow
The trees are bare as the branches hit together
"Clack, clack, clack!"
I stand alone
The cold numbs my ears
Thoughts rush through my head
A car speeds by, and I'm interrupted
The world is engulfed in a cold night, and I stand alone

Rachel Smith, Grade 7
Armstrong Middle School

I Am

I am an adventurous boy who likes dogs.
I wonder what the world would be like at peace.
I hear no hatred but friendly words.
I see everyone helping others and no fighting.
I want the world to unite and give praise to God.
I am an adventurous boy who likes dogs.

I pretend that I can fly across the sky with ease.
I feel the wind rush across my face.
I touch the stars and feel the moon's craters.
I worry about all the war circling our lives.
I cry for a soldier's family who must live with him at battle.
I am an adventurous boy who likes dogs.

I understand that right now total peace exists only in heaven.
I say that you should "love your neighbor as yourself."
I dream of the future and what it might bring.
I try to be the best Catholic I can be.
I hope for world peace.
I am an adventurous boy who likes dogs.

Sean Ward, Grade 7
St Joseph Catholic School

Beneath the Steel

What lies beneath the steel? The rubble once stood tall
as a symbol for true liberty and justice for all.
Beneath that twisted metal, there are bodies buried deep.
Ashes hide their movements. Fire shields their pleas.
Beneath the burning embers, a man will give up soon.
Rescue will come shortly, but they've only got till noon.
The man lies still and silent, a prayer being lifted high.
After all that he has been though, it's time to say good-bye.
"I know I wasn't perfect, but I did my best. I tried.
Lord, it is finally finished." Just then, the trapped man cries.
"I've done some awful things and I've never let You know.
I want to get them off my chest before it's time to go."
Beneath the searching heroes, a silence is still heard.
The Lord is listening to a prayer and loving every word.
Beneath the broken steel where many souls are lost,
a miracle is lifted up—a twisted, metal cross.
The Lord heard many cries; He answered every one.
That cross had given hope in September 2001.
Across the mourning nation, it all seemed so unreal.
That ground is truly sacred; the ground beneath the steel.

Katelyn Fisher, Grade 9
Commonwealth Connections Academy

Forever

I thought you were mine, for forever and while,
I lived for the moments I could feel you smile.
"You are perfect for me, I am perfect for you,"
You used to say that, did you think it was true?
You walked so far, so far away,
All I wanted was for you to stay.
You helped my hopes to climb so high,
Only to see them crumble and die.
You knew how much you meant to me—
Do you know that I'm in misery?
You scared me, stained me, left me scarred,
But I'll forever still love you with all of my heart.
I wanted you then, I need you still,
Loved you forever, always will.
If you try to come back, I shouldn't forgive.
You've hurt me enough for as long as I live.
But I know one day you will be back
I will let you back in, that's a matter of fact.
And though I know it's not a good thing,
I'll love you forever, throughout everything.

Miranda Filak, Grade 8
Bellmar Middle School

Honesty

Honesty is as yellow as the sun on a summer afternoon.
It tastes like creamy milk chocolate.
It smells like the aromas of a pastry shop in a small town.
It reminds me of the chatter of the crowd at a sports event.
It sounds like a peaceful song at a memorial.
Honesty makes me feel like I'm being the best person I can be.

Ethan Everson, Grade 7
Schuylkill Valley Middle School

Five Senses

Love is pink and red.
It tastes like apple pie.
It sounds like classical music, specifically *"Ode to Joy."*
And it smells like fresh baked pastries, like tarts and strudel.
It looks like bright colors or a blurry rainbow.
It feels indescribably amazing and makes your stomach churn.

Kelly Ann Kiesewetter, Grade 7
Westmoreland Christian Academy

A Person Like No Other

Most people refer to the word "pop" as a
sound or soda. I'm referring it to my grandpa —
Grandpa DiNatale.

When Pop DiNatale saw someone in need,
he never said or thought, "Someone else will
help them." He was that someone else.

His face always lit up when we came to
visit him. He always enjoyed hearing Dad play
the piano as well as Reganne and me.

I rarely saw my Grandpa without a smile
on his face while we kids were around.
He was the best Grandpa I could ever ask for.

Even though I don't see him, he's still with
me. Soon I'll see him in a place called
Heaven where I'll always see him smiling.

Ronald E. Hiester, Grade 7
Faith Tabernacle School

Hockey

Hockey is a fast-paced sport,
You always protect your net, like a fort.
Skating up the ice with such a rush,
But you have to be careful not to get crushed.

The people from the stands shout,
As the other team gets scored on and pouts.
They interview players during intermission,
While the zamboni comes out to better the ice condition.

The coach gives the players a pep talk,
"Start to score, or take a walk!"
It's the second period and the puck drops,
The goalie makes a wonderful stop.

The players start getting tired; the period drags on,
The second intermission is far along.
It's the third period, time to do or die,
If we win the game, we will fly so high.

Jason Bias, Grade 8
Chichester Middle School

Brave

Brave is the color of the ocean's foam rippling to shore,
It sounds like the lone seagull's wings flapping at night
And tastes like the bold zest of island citrus
It smells like the salty sea air,
It looks like a Frisbee being flung
It makes me feel fearless.

Brave is the boost of confidence that only one who tries can reach.

Sabrina Dobron, Grade 7
Richboro Middle School

Philadelphia Car Show

Riding Septa
Rumble Rumble
"Control that crying baby!"
The Convention Center
"Could this escalator be anymore cramped?!"
First room
"Do we have to look at the Fiat?"
Luxury cars (more my speed) pun very much intended
"Whoa Lamborghini"
Lunch time
"Cheese steak please"
On the road again
"Thanks for taking me Dad"

Colin Kase, Grade 7
Holicong Middle School

My Twin

She looks like me — how could it be?
We came one after another, four minutes apart,
and the love we share comes from the heart.
She's always there for me in times of trouble,
and when people look at us, they see double.
Our life experiences we share together.
We know our friendship will last forever.
We smile, we laugh, we even cry,
but the love between us will never die.
I look back and regret the times we fight,
but guess what! I love my sister with all my heart.
We will never grow apart
because we were born together from the start!

Geminii Cabrera, Grade 8
St Peter School

Why I Like Fall the Best

Do you know what I really like about the fall,
Besides jumping in leaves and playing football,
I love walking with a chill in the air,
And the wind blowing in my hair.

I love all of the colors the leaves are turning,
I even love the smell of them when they're burning.
The best thing I like about the shorter days,
Is knowing soon are coming the holidays.

Billy Lemke, Grade 8
Chichester Middle School

Winter

I hear the wood cracking in my fireplace
I taste the hot cocoa in my mouth
I feel the cold frosty snow spitting at my face
I smell the frosty blizzard as it gives me chills all through my body
I see the brown crystalized fish coming up through the frozen ice,
and the water swishing as he floats out of the frozen river,
coldness hitting my face as I reel him in.

Will Carey, Grade 7
Strath Haven Middle School

Baseball

Heart pounds
As I step up to the plate
Waiting for the pitch
The ball comes in at an incredible speed
I get tense so I swing
CRACK! The ball blasted away
I jogged away I knew
Today was my time to shine

Kyle Goodwin, Grade 7
Armstrong Middle School

Coming Together

Everything will come together
And make sense
One day
For now
Just smile at the confusions
And keep thinking
That everything happens
For a reason!!!

Mariah Serrano, Grade 7
Armstrong Middle School

Soccer

It's the big game
The crowd cheers
Eager for us to score
Cheering when we score
Two minutes left with a dead tie
There is silence for the shoot out
Happy when we win the game
Can't wait for the championships!

Dawson Black, Grade 7
Armstrong Middle School

Mirrored Clouds

All I could see through my mirror
Were the clouds growing nearer.
Bursts of the thunder,
Make me wonder
Will the storm ever clear?
Then sun rays reflect off my tear.
Breaking through gates of black,
Finally the sun has come back.

Claire Adams, Grade 7
Holicong Middle School

Halloween

The crisp air sending chills
All up my spine…
Darkness creeping around…
Unrecognizable faces everywhere you turn,
Trying to give you a fright,
On this Halloween night.

Christina Semeraro, Grade 7
Strath Haven Middle School

Staying: The Holocaust

I close my eyes, walk through the door, and stay a while
Mom and I are shopping, bright packages catch my nine year old eyes
We go to the market, Abraham the butcher's shop is closed
"Why?" I ask, but Mom just shakes her head and
Stares at the foreign letters
We go home, we stay, then we go away
"Are we going on holiday?" I ask
Mom just shakes her head and
Stares at the foreign soldiers
We arrive, it's dirty there, it's full of
People in striped pajamas, people with shaved heads,
People in clean uniforms, People.
We stay for a month, two
You lose track of time there
One day, the soldiers come to me
"Will you come with us?" they ask
They ask, though I have no choice
And Mom behind me, crying
I close my eyes, walk through the door
It's dark and full of other people
The nozzles turn on, and I stay a while

Alexis Buncich, Grade 7
Conemaugh Township School

Dangers Facing Worms

Worms have many wonderful worldly dangers to face
If they are at my place:
The moles, the voles, the snakes, the rakes, the mice, the lice.
And worst of all, my ferocious dog, Sierra!

She will dig; she will fight;
She will dig a dirt mound ten feet in height!
The worst part about that is that if someone picks up a large piece of plywood,
Sierra will get the largest worm,
Just like the rats, and moles, and voles, and birds, and mice, and lice.

Wesley M. Ritrievi, Grade 7
Faith Tabernacle School

The Little Yellow Ball

The little yellow ball, sitting against the wall,
appears lonely and sad while the others play with all but him.

The ball, hiding in the dark, lurks in waters as a shark but shall never attack.
The ball, timid and tame, is mistaken
to be helpless and lame while the others play with all but him.

The sunshine, not dubious to shine: true.
But the little yellow ball manifests to be blue.
As the sunshine shares the glorious, perky rays,
they cheer all but the little yellow ball while the others play with all but him.

Depressed you may say, only of all hours of the day,
as the little yellow ball, hiding against the wall,
appears lonely and sad while the others play with all but him.

Anthony Vecchio, Grade 9
Hempfield Area High School

The Sims 3 World

Blue, green, red, and tan
Pick a sim and make a plan.
Small cars, big cars? You get to decide;
Humble Sims, crazy Sims, some full of pride.

Tall white buildings to small red diners,
Fishing at the beach and installing pool liners.
Cooking and writing are some abilities;
Buying groceries and books are some activities.

Soft dogs or rough-haired dogs? I doesn't matter
As long as you keep down the little bird's chatter.

"Click click," your fingers push the buttons.
A couple of Sims years have gone by.
Now one hour of playing passed as if five minutes.
Now I must take a break and come back to reality.

Julia G. Shreiner, Grade 9
Faith Tabernacle School

Silence

Speak its name, and it's broken;
It's words and ideas never spoken.

Silence is dead and cold;
When speech comes, it's suddenly sold.

In silence you're alone,
So you're on your own.

In silence you have no guide.
Speech comes, and silence scrambles to hides.

Silence is like a cold, dark cave
From where you seek to be saved.

Silence is something you cannot bare,
So speak if you dare.

Sara M. Nellis, Grade 8
Faith Tabernacle School

Friends

A person who helps you when you're down.
A person who makes you smile rather than frown.
A person who listens instead of speaks.
A person who doesn't judge who you are.
A person who respects your ideas.
A person who agrees with what you say.
A person who texts you just to say, "Hey."
A person who treats you the right way.
A person who does not make fun of you.
A person who really cares and wants the best for you.
That is the right friend for you.

Jason Husar, Grade 7
Armstrong Middle School

Motionless in Grains

Morning,
Blueberry-blue skies hover over the golden sand
The ocean waves splash as I lay in my soon-to-be casket
Sand hammers down on my motionless body
Splish splash as water pours over me
The taste of seawater covers my face
They keep pounding and pounding
Hoping to finish before it's all gone
They call others to help
Splashing and pounding
Splashing and pounding
Finally I lay there
Like a mannequin poised in one position
I am
Motionless In Grains

Ryan Brown, Grade 7
Holicong Middle School

Friendship

Friendships are meant forever
You will always be together
No matter how far apart we are
You will always be in their heart.

The day that we met we will never forget
Every time we argue I always regret
The past is the past like an old test
Every time we are together we have a blast
Some people like to hate because their friendships don't last.

Friends come and go
And friendships end
There will always be that one friendship
That will never meet its quotient.

Jorden King, Grade 8
Valley Middle School

Summer Memories

With thick stick in hand, and hat backwards,
I wandered to the back woods.
There, all is easy to imagine.
So my mind goes drifting, drifting away…
I dream of the old days full of laughter and fun,
And of getting wet in a rain storm.
I look back now and I laugh out loud
At a little girl who loved to jump in mud puddles.
Who loved to stay by her father's side
And cried in her most depressing moments.
That little girl has grown out of her childish ways
But that girl still loves to do one thing,
Wander to the back woods, with stick in hand,
And imagination drifting, drifting away
With the clouds on a summer day.

Amy L. Fogelsanger, Grade 9
Faith Tabernacle School

Me, Myself, and I
Richie
Brave, athletic, competitive, creative
Brother of Dustin and Justine
Lover of sports, food and family
Who feels happy when he plays sports, alive when he hits someone in football or ice hockey, and
Frustrated when people lie
Who needs more money, more time to play sports, and needs less school
Who fears clowns, stalkers, and becoming ineligible
Who gives time to his coaches, gives his best in school, and who gives love to his family
Who would like to see Canada, Rome, and Australia
Resident of Bernville
Spatz

Richie Spatz, Grade 7
Schuylkill Valley Middle School

Mt. Washington
Dread poured into my body like blood as we slowly progressed up the steep elevation.
The upside for going so high is the beautiful grass-green mountains that went farther than infinite, I convinced myself.
But, as we climbed higher, my eyes became cantaloupes as I noticed the steep drop-off far below mocking me.
Soon nature's natural tree scent filled the car and hugged my nose with affection.
The subtle song of the birds flowed in my ears effortlessly cheering me up.
Accomplishment and happiness delighted me as the mountain top approached and greeted me.
I almost fell out; almost wanting to hug the ground.
Although the crisp cold air pounded my face like a drum, I was still joyous.
I proudly stood next to the sign marking the great mount and smiled to the flash catching my appearance.
A grin was on my face as we descended ignoring the treacherous "what ifs" of what could happen.
This feeling didn't stop.
Always remembering, always feeling accomplished, always smiling longer than time.

Michael Mills, Grade 7
Holicong Middle School

The Wonders of Autumn
Fresh, crisp, cool air smelling like Orbit mint gum,
Thin, wavy, magenta, burnt orange and russet leaves floating through the air,
Drifting wind making the surrounding landscape turn into a beach with the surf lapping up against the shore,
Colorful, lightweight leaves landing on a soft mattress of avocado green grass,
"CRACK!" Hearing the thick, bulky, decayed branch smashing into a million pieces,
The whoosh of the magenta, fire-yellow leaves shooting up and around like a windstorm,
Rickety leaves laying down, decaying with every second,
Rough and rugged leaves flaking off as you rub them between your hands,
Veins on the leaf are like a never ending maze your finger tries to complete,
Shriveled up in a cocoon, all russet and dull, at the end of its life,
breathing its final breath.

Dylan Derstine, Grade 7
Indian Valley Middle School

Grief
Grief is the dark, blurred gray of a stormy sky, obscuring all other importance.
It sounds like horrible gasping sobs, and tastes of salty tears, smarting in your mouth.
Grief is the smell of a dead rose, it's crisp petals wilted and weakened.
Grief looks like crying people, mourning the loss of a beautiful brown-haired girl.
Grief makes me feel helpless, and exhausted.
Grief is a malicious snake, winding its way into one's life, and injecting you with the poison of unbearable sadness.

Cecilia Rabayda, Grade 7
Richboro Middle School

Cupcake

You can be as sweet as a cupcake
As sour as a grapefruit
As sweet as sprinkles
Or as bitter as lemon heads
But that does not matter
All that matters is
You are you
Be yourself
Don't worry about what others say
YOU ARE YOU!

Rebecca Finsel, Grade 7
Armstrong Middle School

My Best Friends

My best friends are the ones I love
They love me too and I feel like one
They are a part of me in a way
They always get me through the day
Through thick and thin I always know
What they do to let their care show
How sincere they can be
They show all their affection, and all to me
What it takes to be a best friend
Only I could imagine

Lindsay Palma, Grade 7
Armstrong Middle School

My Best Family Ever

I have the best family ever
I have a family of four
My sister
My mom
And dad
I also have a cat and dog
Who loves me very much
I have the best family ever
And I love them
I have the best family ever

Tyler Magazzu, Grade 7
Armstrong Middle School

Dreams

Dreams
They dance around me
As I fall asleep
Dreams
They sing to me
As I count my sheep
Dreams
They whisper to me
The thoughts that I can keep
Dreaming

Danielle Mervine, Grade 7
Strath Haven Middle School

No Longer Me

As I looked into the mirror, I see an unfamiliar face; it's no longer me.
Tears stream down my face,
Eyeliner and mascara smear,
I only wear it to impress you.
I choke out a couple swear words,
That I'd never say,
At least before I met you.
You've drank before,
You've done things you regret,
Will I be next?
As the tears keep coming,
My best friends come to mind.
Would they like this?
What would my parents say?
I no longer care,
Because I am no longer me.
Your hands have sculpted me,
Changing my imperfections,
I am no longer me,
But I am you.

Hannah Degler, Grade 7
Schuylkill Valley Middle School

The Jellyfish

The bright sun warms the sand underneath your feet.
It is so fine; it is a cushion, squeaking as you walk.
The ocean stretches out before you, calm, despite the oncoming tide.
You reach the end of the warm, pleasant sand.
It is hard-packed and cool underneath your feet.
The soothing ocean breeze becomes more prominent, offering relief from the heat.
For a moment, you admire the deep blues and sea-greens of the water.
The water is so clear; you see tiny fish darting about the shallows.
Tentatively, you reach your toe into the surf.
The cold water surges around your foot; you are shocked from the cold.
You determine the sensation delightful, and wade in deeper.
A small wave is coming, you duck underwater.
You feel the tugging of the current on your face, pulling you toward shore.
Through closed lids, you imagine the tiny fish examining this new intruder.
Suddenly, a fierce stinging sensation erupts in your arm.
You shoot out of the water like a rocket, and notice a globular mass floating nearby.
The sound of your cussing travels easily across the beach.
From the cooler, you pull out a bottle of vinegar and soak your arm with it.
The place has lost its peaceful charm; and another day has been ruined.
As you pack up to leave, you wonder why you bother with beach vacations.

Vivian Cirilano, Grade 7
St James School

Sunshine Features

My smile is like a happy child with a loving toy.
My eyes are like acorns captured by scurrying squirrels.
My ears are as soft as a baby's skin.
My hair is as wavy as a riptide coming to shore.
My heart holds love, care, and sunshine that is brighter than a sunflower's petal.
I live in a school and eat pencils and books.

Thoneca Akhter, Grade 7
Schuylkill Valley Middle School

Ode to Fallingwater

Fallingwater,
The residence of the Kaufmanns
An arts man
The originator
Frank Lloyd Wright

A daughter, I am,
Being attracted to the sight
Fortunate having the might
A longing for this desire
To see the most legendary creation by the designer

A hike within a forest and farm fields
Of twists and turns
A forest we pass, on the way to the art work
And then I bring to a halt.
The beauty had blinded me,
Creating me to stop.
The concrete is skin, beige, smooth and real
The sun is a lamp shining through the many clear glass windows
Throughout the tour, I had failed to speak.
Awe had seeped in my brain.

Diane Harris, Grade 7
Richboro Middle School

Super Soccer

I step up and send a shot toward the net.
To the right just inside the far post I aim.
All the pressure's so much, that it takes its toll,
And the ball hits the goalie, the "man-made" wall.

The defender just kicks the ball far upfield.
Our midfielder is able to make the trap
And then passes the ball to the left-hand wing.
To the right goes the wing, dribbles left, then SNAP!

The wing aims and fires — a terrific shot.
There's the goalie; he bobbles the ball away.
An improbable angle but still I shoot,
And this time's a fail…by the "man-made" wall.

Josiah Wells, Grade 9
The American Academy

Hedgehog

A hedgehog walking
The spines on its back relaxed
Its small body squeezing into tiny places
When the cry of an owl approaches
The hedgehog hides, covered in quills
The owl comes near but soon goes away
And the hedgehog lives to see another day
Thanks to its quills it has survived
The hedgehog listens for danger and hears none
So it gets up and walks away

Emma Hohl, Grade 7
Greencastle-Antrim Middle School

Someone

Before you were born, you were someone.
Someone with an unknown life ahead,
in the shadows of being discovered.

Someone who manages to have a normal life,
without a worry in site.
While others are walking on the edge,
between death and life.

Many questions with no answers,
and someone trying to find them.
Someone giving up everything,
just for someone else.

Small, large.
Skinny, fat.
Short, tall.
She, he.

Be yourself,
you are someone.

Andria Fahringer, Grade 9
Danville Area Sr High School

Friends

Friends are someone   you can count on.
They will always be there for you to laugh and to share.
They will always have your back, as long as you have theirs.
They will make you happy and cheer you up when you are down.
They are someone you can count and depend on for being there.
They are someone you can always trust with all of your secrets.
They will lead you to do the right things, not into trouble.
They are there to give you a shoulder to cry on.
They make everlasting memories.
They are one of a kind.
They are a friend.
This is what I
like to call a
Friend.

Payton Whyne, Grade 7
Good Shepherd School

Star

They are like candles lighting up the room
The stars are just glistering in the dark night,
Sparkling like glitter
Swoosh!
I can feel the shooting stars dancing all around me,
Holding me together.
Swimming in the sea of the night,
Sitting on the clouds,
Just waiting to slowly and silently sink into the still night.
They sparkle and glow
As one by one have to let go.

Siri Blomberg, Grade 7
Charles F Patton Middle School

A World of Illusions

The whole world was transformed from where I sit.
The cafeteria was a village.
Up front, there were guards, each with a different way of
Making sure that we couldn't escape.
The one in the middle of the threesome was in charge.
There was a policeman was next to him,
I saw him patrol the aisles.
The principal walked by,
He was the Ruler of the Land.

At my table,
There was a queen.
There was also a mirror,
A messenger, a fox, a fish, a friend,
And an empty seat where I once sat.
I could feel their flaming glares and their dagger eyes,
Both coming towards me at full speed, but nothing more than that.
I wasn't hurt, for I had a shield.
I sat with her instead of them, only she could protect me.

This is the world I left behind.
I'm looking for something new.

Emily Liu, Grade 8
J R Fugett Middle School

Christmas Time

The smell of hot chocolate is in the air,
Winter is here the trees are all bare.

Except for the fir trees, they are a beautiful blue or green,
Soon in my living room there will be one to view.

So many decorations to display,
Even an angel on top with her hands formed to pray.

My favorite decoration of all,
Is a large, shiny, crystal clear ball.

The tree is lit with many colored lights.
They shine through this season, what a beautiful sight!

Sarita Kunde, Grade 7
St James School

Exploring the Ship

Summer
Arrived at final boarding
Found myself staring at a ship carving
Docked in the sky-blue water
Trying to zone out the obnoxious motor
Liberty of the Seas
Cheetah-brown rash guards
Sun blaze-yellow bathing suits
Glass-clear pools waiting for a swimmer
Cold, metal bars lead upon the staircase to this great, massive ship

Jamie Karol, Grade 7
Holicong Middle School

York, Maine

Noon,
Shoreline flooded with people from all over.
Colorful beach towels coat the sand,
Umbrellas provide relief from the sun.
Kids retrieve their warm, suntanned towels,
While slippery seaweed hugs their wet legs.
Sapphire waves grasp at the shore,
Laughter filling the air.
The grainy taste of saltwater fills my mouth,
I swim out into mysterious water.
Night.
Waves regrouping,
The night is still and motionless.
The sun is being swallowed by darkness,
With it goes laughter and enjoyment from the day.
As the waves finally become silent,
They prepare for tomorrow.

Abigail Rose Brown, Grade 7
Holicong Middle School

The Tailgating Party

The afternoon,
Driving down Miller Parkway.
Stiff, rock-hard forest-green seats.
Stranger dropped muddy baseball,
My cousin triumphantly caught it.
The crowd anticipating a win,
Cheery tunes between plays,
4th row in Miller Park Stadium.
Tripped and my spoon hopped along the cold, hard ground,
So I slurped the Dippin' Dots.
Junky disposable grill caused
Greasy, oil-soaked hot dogs.
Waiting in the parking lot,
Crazy dances with my cousin.
The night ended late,
But it was as fun as I had hoped.
Brewers win!

Shelby Henn, Grade 7
Holicong Middle School

Ocean City

Hot glowing sun beats down
As I walk in the soft sand
I see the ocean sparkling from far way
Shells of all sorts are scattered around
Salty cold water tickles my toes
My feet sink in the sand
As the waves pass by
Waves licking the sand like lollipops
Lunch comes around and I take a bite of my sandwich
Cloud-gray seagulls beg for a bite
Then comes night
The glowing sun goes away and so do I.

Colleen Myers, Grade 7
Holicong Middle School

This Is Just Your Car

I am sorry
that I
have wrecked
your car

and which
was
the coolest
car ever

Forgive me
I got a ticket
Michael Papiernik, Grade 7
Charles F Patton Middle School

American Flag

Red
White
Blue
Fifty stars
Fifty states
Thirteen stripes
Thirteen colonies
Waves high in the sky
Shows love
Shows pride
Shows freedom
Ariana Seman, Grade 8
Bellmar Middle School

I Am

I am athletic and hardworking.
I wonder about sharks.
I hear humming in my head.
I see me eating frosted flakes in a bowl.
I want to be in the MLB.
I am athletic and hardworking.
I pretend to hit a home run.
I feel happy when I play baseball.
I worry the world will end soon.
I wish I had 1 trillion dollars.
I am athletic and hardworking.
Solomon Bayuk, Grade 7
Strath Haven Middle School

Falling Leaves

Leaves are falling on the ground.
Red and yellow, orange and brown.
I rake them up in a pile,
And they sit there for a while.
Then I jump and scatter them all,
It's only another sign of fall.
Then the trees have no more leaves,
Now I am waiting for a winter breeze.
Hannah Day, Grade 7
Bellmar Middle School

Jungle Birds

Squawking through the trees
calling out the daily news.
Brightly colored birds.
Abby Faust, Grade 7
Trinity Middle School

Snow

snow is falling down
coming slowly from the sky
making white blankets
Tyler Parsons, Grade 7
Charles F Patton Middle School

Grades 4-5-6
Top Ten Winners

List of Top Ten Winners for Grades 4-6; listed alphabetically

AbdurRahman Bhatti, Grade 5
Cambridge Friends School, MA

Katie Dominguez, Grade 4
St Joseph School, PA

Avery Fletcher, Grade 5
Balmoral Hall School, MB

Foxx Hart, Grade 4
F L Olmsted School, MA

Maximiliana Heller, Grade 5
Stanley Clark School, IN

Sarah Kim, Grade 5
Avery Coonley School, IL

Grace Lemersal, Grade 6
Meadowbrook Middle School, CA

Julia Peters, Grade 4
Toll Gate Grammar School, NJ

Lucas Tong, Grade 6
Chinese American International School, CA

Mallory S. Wolfe, Grade 5
North Knox West Intermediate/Elementary School, IN

All Top Ten Poems can be read at www.poeticpower.com

Note: The Top Ten poems were finalized through an online voting system. Creative Communication's judges first picked out the top poems. These poems were then posted online. The final step involved thousands of students and teachers who registered as the online judges and voted for the Top Ten poems. We hope you enjoy these selections.

The Crossing Guard

As I stare out the classroom window
my eye immediately focuses on
the neon-yellow vest worn
by the crossing guard.
She sits on the concrete entrance steps that lead
to an old apartment building.
Her big red hand-held stop sign
somewhat swaying back and forth.
She waits for the bell and the kids to come
running her way.
Up she goes into the street.
Holding the sign, she blows her whistle.
"Cross!" She yells in a sweet voice.
"Thank you," the kids say running across.
She heads back over to her step to rest up
for the rest of the kids heading her way.

Phoebe Connell, Grade 5
Lincoln Elementary School

Winter

December sprinkles snow;
It leaves a blanket on your lawn.
You get your sleds and winter clothes out to get ready for the cold.
The next day the snow stops and kids are running all around,
Making snowballs and snowmen and having snowball fights.

January gets frost bite.
You slide down the hill with the wind in your face;
Your toes and your fingers get really cold.
You ask your mom for hot cocoa.

February freezes up what's left of January.
The roads get covered in ice and cars aren't allowed on them;
Sidewalks get sheets of ice on them and it's hard to walk.
Icicles hang from the edge of your roof;
Lakes start freezing up, and people start to ice skate on them.

Billy Allison, Grade 4
Aston Elementary School

Life

Life is beautiful
Life is the grass brushing against my feet as I'm racing the wind
Life is watching the swishing sand on the beach
Life is as cool as a refreshing splash of water
Life is the dew on the grass on a foggy morning
Life is as bright as the gleaming sun
Life is the sparkling sea on a hot summer day
Life is having frozen frost on my window
Life is the most valuable and extensive gift God gave us
Life is being loved and saved by Jesus
Life is a flurry of flickering fireflies flying by
Life is flying free like a bird in the sky
Life is good
Enjoy it

Briana van Vianen, Grade 6
Linville Hill Mennonite School

My Vacation

On vacation I used my imagination
I saw Devils Tower, Mount Rushmore,
That was really fun for sure.
Budweiser tour was kind of a bore.

I missed my dog and two cats,
I really couldn't deal with that.

My dad said he would rather take a plane than a train.
Every day I would write letters to my best friend, Emma,
About my trip and how it couldn't be better.

Brooke Vebelun, Grade 5
Burgettstown Elementary Center

Hibiscus

Trumpet shaped like a horn
Speckled with dew in the morn

Her delicate petals are paper thin
They emerge from the bud within

She grows in a tropical paradise
Where the aroma is so nice

You can catch her dancing with the wind
When a warm breeze flows through the island

Mackenzie DeLawter, Grade 6
Pennridge North Middle School

Welcome

The first moment I laid eyes on him
I thought he was a stuffed animal.
He was so perfect.
Then, he made a noise.
It wasn't a bark or a growl,
It was a squeak.
I immediately held him in my arms.
His cries stopped.
Later that night, we found out that his favorite food
Was bacon and muenster cheese.
We named him Buddy.

Lydia Nusbaum, Grade 5
Lincoln Elementary School

The Beatitudes

B lessed are those who do what God wants
E ach and every day we look up to them.
A ll of the time we try to help somebody.
T o make good choices that God wants us to do.
I llness is something we have to cure
T ry to do one of the Beatitudes every day.
U se anger in a good way
D o not hurt others if they hurt you.
E very person who does it right will have a good time in heaven

Ashley Guava and Tracy Le, Grade 4
St John Vianney Regional School

Storms

Drip drop, hear the rain plop.
Click clash, hear thunder crash.
Zip zight, see stripes of light.
There's zuddles and duddles of seeable puddles.
In four minutes or under,
the storm is down yonder.
Then the next day,
the children all play,
in the remains of the storm,
that will come again someday.

Kelsey Davis, Grade 6
Ross Elementary School

White Gold

As I glide down the hill with the wind in my face
My sled glides with such wonderful grace!
I scream and I shout
I scream and I shout as my sled comes to a halt.

All my friends come
But I know the fun just begun!

We play and we play
Just to do it again the next day.

Hunter Kurdilla, Grade 6
Bellmar Middle School

Steelers

Steelers, Steelers you know them all
They can run, catch, and throw the ball
Our defense hits really hard
I hope they at least get the wild card
The Steelers can do all kind of things
And they also have six Super Bowl rings
Thank you Steelers for all you did
I know you will get a playoff bid
You better win the Super Bowl
And you better not make yourself look like a fool

Jacob Rathway, Grade 6
Bellmar Middle School

Remember

Remember the days when Hitler came around
Remember the cries that came out with no sound
Remember the Jews scared that they will be put in the ground
Or thrown in the gas chambers being drowned
Remember the soldiers who looked at you with a frown
Remember the people being thrown in the fire,
Being laughed at until you were gone
Waiting, hoping, until someone stepped up and Hitler backed down
Always remember the Holocaust!

Kayleigh Lahr, Grade 6
Nazareth Area Intermediate School

A Colorful Summer Painting

Blue for the sky so bright and new,
Yellow for the sun that's so bright too,
Green for the grass where children lay,
Red for the ball with which kids play,

Orange for the orange the picnic holds,
Purple for the book where a story is told,
White for the cloth the picnic is on,
Pink for the flowers which live near the pond,

Upon my paper I swirl and dab,
With orange and yellow I make a small crab,
I look at my painting and what do I see,
A colorful summer is all around me.

Katie Dominguez, Grade 4
St Joseph School

Rainbow

The rain falls from the clouds on gloomy days,
The water soaks into the ground and plants are raised.

The sun shines and gives a gleaming light,
A rainbow forms and it looks so bright.

From the rainbow appears brilliant colors,
No color is any less magnificent than the others.

A wondrous feeling comes from that rainbow,
It's like no other, that glorious glow.

It's a glow that stays with you, forever and ever,
There's not a second it's gone, never, never.

Karissa Heinrich, Grade 6
Commonwealth Connections Academy

Fall

Fall is cool
When you start school.
I have soccer games.
I have homework.
I see moving trucks.
I see trick-or-treaters too.
The leaves are changing.
The temperature's lowering.
Say goodbye to warmth,
And hello to coolness.
Sweaters and pants,
Instead of tube tops and shorts.
Fall is here to stay,
Until winter comes, of course!

Shayna McNamee, Grade 6
St John Neumann Regional Academy - Elementary Campus

Airsoft

The thrill of running for your life.
The silence of searching through the woods.
The beauty of looking at the scenery,
at the top of a tree.
The fun hanging out with friends.
The pain of pulling muscles in the winter,
and the happiness of running in the summer.
The sorrow for losing, and the right to brag about winning.
All in the fun glorious day
of an Airsoft War.

Evan Kerin, Grade 6
Ross Elementary School

Fall

Fall is wonderful fall is colorful,
with leaves dressed head to toe with red, yellow, and brown
I can't even see the ground.
As I jump into the leaves
I wear long sleeves
because of the cold fall breeze.
I woke up next morning got dressed again
went outside then did it all over again.
I can't wait until
when fall comes again.

Hayden Gerver, Grade 5
Newberry Elementary School

There She Goes, There She Goes

I have a cat and nobody knows
Where in the world that putty cat goes
She's here in the morning, she's here at night
But right around lunch the cat's out of sight
The cat's always happy, never in a bad mood
She only comes back to munch on some food
Sometimes it's dark and I begin to worry
So I yell out her name and she comes home in a hurry
With a swoosh of her tail and a flick of her nose
The cat runs off there she goes, there she goes

Corey Quaste, Grade 6
Pennridge North Middle School

Divorce

Once in a while something like this occurs, your
parents split up. It doesn't happen to everyone,
but it happened to me. Though I am at ease, I
am still full of sadness. My life is just pure
madness. I lay down sadly every day and
imagine them together, but, now I finally realize
it's not going to happen. I look up on my dresser
and see all of the wonderful pictures of them. I
love them so much and now I know my life is
great and that is my fate.

Jacob Horton, Grade 4
Jefferson Elementary School

Winter

Winter throws fall away when it's December.
Hot chocolate warms people after the cold day.
Tomorrow will have
Christmas joy.
When it's December,
twinkling snow falls down on the ground.
The sparkling snow covers the trees.
In January, the twinkling and sparkling snow of December
is disappearing, so say good bye.
No one wants it to end.

Bradly Wiest, Grade 4
Aston Elementary School

The Forest

The trees are bare covered with snow.
The frost covers them so the branches don't show.
The trees are perfect, all covered in white.
The sparkling snow is such a great sight.
The snow is shining while the moonlight is shone.
It gives the snow a sparkling tone.
The dazzling flakes fall from the sky.
An icy breeze carries them by.
The forest is still while the animals sleep.
The forest is still, without a single peep.

Mikayla Jennewine, Grade 6
Bellmar Middle School

What I Love About Winter

Winter is as cold as an ice cube.
Winter snow is as white as paper.
Snow in winter falls as fast as a race car.
Winter is as snowy as a snow globe.
The snow is as sparkly as glitter.
Sleds are as fast as a rocket.
The mountain is as steep as a hole in the earth.
Winter is as fun as Christmas.
Winter is as chilly as a refrigerator.
Winter is as awesome as me, John Machado.

John Machado, Grade 4
Wickersham Elementary School

All About Me

I'm smart caring and creative
I have 3 brothers and 1 aunt!
I love television dogs and ice cream
I feel excited at times and sad sometimes too
I need food shelter family and school
I give smiles love and care!
I would like to see my sister in California
I dream of money trees in my backyard
I am a student of Ms. Tadlock's 4th grade class
My nickname is Lovey!

Olivia Rueppel, Grade 4
Wickersham Elementary School

Trees of Our Lives

Majestic as the sunset
Color like rust
Texture like sandpaper
Tall as buildings
Quiet as a whisper yet loud as an orchestra
Won the hearts of animals
And have stood the test of time
Sturdy as a rock yet fragile as glass
Important as humans, but destroyed by us
Taken down for our own strange uses
But forever they will stay beside us
They are trees and they are everywhere
They grow in the soil of our own Mother Earth
They grow from the U.S.A. to China
Green, brown, white, black, trees of all different colors
And there's no stopping them

Jacob Dumaine-Schutz, Grade 5
Winchester-Thurston School

It's Not Fair

It's not fair
I really don't get it
Why I can't have ice cream for breakfast, lunch, dinner, and dessert
Why I can't live in an ice cream bed
Why I can't always have chocolate in my head
How I can deny ice cream and get pie
I wish I could live in an ice cream house, world, and universe
It's not fair that I can't have an ice cream maid
An ice cream tree
An ice cream bed
Have my own ice cream company
Have free ice cream everywhere
Why can't I have an ice cream paradise
Why can't I have an ice cream farm
With an ice cream ground
Why can't I live in an ice cream paradise

Christopher Wilkinson, Grade 4
St Alexis School

Winter

As the snow falls from the sky,
Every snowflake catches my eye.
The smell of pine and the cold winter air,
Passes through the trees and blows through my hair.
We decorate the house and tree,
There's so many ornaments for you and me.
Christmas is coming near,
I can't wait it's almost here.
It's Christmas Eve and the family's here,
Christmas is tomorrow let's sing and cheer.
It's Christmas and look at my cool toy.
It's so much fun, I'm full of joy.
Christmas is over, it's no longer here,
But we can't wait for the New Year!

Gina Ivan, Grade 6
Bellmar Middle School

Summer

Sunny, cheery, relaxing, pleasant
Sibling of the seasons
Lover of…
Children tubing in the river,
Colorful umbrellas on the beach,
Neighborhoods having barbecues
Who feels…
Sad when kids stay inside playing video games,
Unhappy when children go back to school,
Joyful when June comes again
Who fears…
Everyone's memories of summer will fade away,
Cold, chilly winds,
Approaching snowfalls
Who would like to see…
Many more kids playing sports,
More flowers blooming,
Less trash on the beach
Resident of the world

Summer

Camryn Carter, Grade 5
Pocopson Elementary School

Fall

September is fun!
Jumping in leaves, how much softer could it be?
Getting ready to catch the bus,
Leaves are falling
Trees are sleeping with a quilt of leaves in the September night.
September trees falling down,
Leaves are crumbling, covering broken branches,
Playing hockey in the street.

October is getting scarier, still getting colder through night,
The round, orange pumpkins getting scarier in the October night,
October days get shorter every night
October disappears as the days go on,
Ghosts are scaring you; skeletons pat you on the back.

November feasts,
Picking crops for the winter,
Getting colder as November goes on.
November holidays,
Packing up for the winter
Getting out all the food for Thanksgiving.

Bryce Craft, Grade 4
Aston Elementary School

My Grandparents Are…

The best grandparents in the world.
Those who represent happiness when I see them.
The feeling inside me when I spend the day with them.
Folks that I love so much.

Matt Kalamar, Grade 6
Moravian Academy Middle School

Here Is Fall
Different kinds of shapes of leaves
Different colors like yellow, orange, red and brown
I feel a cold breeze in my face
I hear the crunch of leaves under my feet
I taste yummy thanksgiving food, pumpkin pie with whipped cream
I smell fires in the air making me hungry
I feel that Summer ends
Fall comes then fall goes away

Victoria An, Grade 4
Worcester Elementary School

Fish
There is a fish living in me.
With scales like big slimy worms, and it has fins like very thin paper.
It gurgles like popping bubbles on a hot sidewalk.
It swims like little minnows.
It lives in my heart and makes me feel happy.
I wish I had thin fins like it has.
It makes me want to swim in competitions.
It makes me feel like a good person.

Madelyn Niss, Grade 5
Indian Lane Elementary School

The Battle Between Me and Myself
There's been a battle raging for eleven years
In somewhere no one would dare go
The battles of "What if?" or "What could happen?"
Boom, boom, boom goes the pounding
I feel the creeping of depression
The battle is inside me
And it will never stop
This is the battle between me and myself

Cheyenne Jones, Grade 6
Bellmar Middle School

Zoey
She has floppy ears,
And a brown nose.
Her hair is soft and shaggy.
Her tail is always wagging.
When she looks at me with that troubled look,
Her eyes glisten.
Even though she doesn't always listen,
To me my puppy Zoey is dear.

Kaitlynn Melvin, Grade 6
Bellmar Middle School

It's Fall
Fall is colorful red, yellow, orange and brown leaves.
Bake fresh cookies and eat them.
Drink hot cocoa.
Having fun on Halloween.
Eat turkey on Thanksgiving.
Smell the beautiful trees.

Jessica Kaur, Grade 4
Worcester Elementary School

Regrets in Time
Why does time have to fly by
as fast as it does each day?
I would like to slow it down
or maybe turn it around,
so I can change the mishaps I've made.
But time will not stop for anyone
at least nobody I ever met.
Now I will have to put those times behind me
and not repeat the actions I regret.

Carinna Lapson, Grade 6
Hopewell Memorial Jr High School

An Autumn Breeze
Birds gleefully chirp while soaring through the sky,
Mocking the sun, for it cannot fly.
Hovering above the colorful trees,
Then drifting away on a strong autumn breeze.

A faint breeze, just a wisp, passes through still air,
A cool taste of autumn combing through my hair.
Fresh and dewy rolling green slopes,
My mind fills with autumn hopes.

Jillian Lunoe, Grade 6
Pennridge North Middle School

Octopus
There is an octopus in me,
with sticky tar-like arms, like slithering
snakes, and a huge head like a bowling ball.
It pops like a bubble, it tiptoes on rocks like an eel.
It lives in my fingers and makes me want
to climb.
I wish I could have eight hands.
It makes me feel like an octopus.

Brendon Stocku, Grade 5
Indian Lane Elementary School

Monkey in Me
There is a monkey in me.
With fur like a bean bag, and hands like a gymnast.
It talks like cicadas and it wiggles like a caterpillar.
It lives in my soul, and makes me climb like a chimp.
I wish it made me jump.
It makes me want to flip in the air.
It makes me feel like a plane.

Connor Elliott, Grade 5
Indian Lane Elementary School

Time
In time I'll write the words that someday will be famous
And on that day I'll see a sign on something rare
And every time I see that thing and be talking leisurely
I'll be reminded of that day and share
That experience created a memory for me, for a life eternity

Kaylee Davis, Grade 6
Moravian Academy Middle School

My Dragon

I have a pet, that not many people have.
She likes crickets, worms, and carrots.
I have a bearded dragon,
And her name is Lily.
I take care of her all by myself.
She jumps all around,
And she likes it when I stroke her gently.
Every time I get ready to feed her,
She jumps off the back wall,
And comes to the front of her cage.
She is still just a juvenile,
But she is growing fast!
She greets me warmly when I come home from school.
I love it when she waves her front hand at me,
As if she's saying "Hello!"
Lily is the best!
She is just so special.
I wouldn't trade her for the world,
Because I love her so much!

Kaylene Chavez, Grade 6
Bellmar Middle School

Truth

Truth is a variable in an experiment of morals
Truth is an unclear reflection
It's a mystery of personalities
Truth is an unwanted answer
Truth is an unsolvable question
A fantasy of your conscience
Truth is an emotional hardship, an undeniable need
Truth is the deepest well of infinite possibilities
Truth can be your enemy in disguise
Truth is tethered to you; it will follow you
It haunts your shadow
Truth itself is silent but at times when you are
Tenuous truth will be thunderous
Truth can be the tears of the past
Truth is time it goes fast
Truth is pain
Pain can kill you
Truth is an alternative yet it's chosen last
Truth is the undiscovered virtue of mankind…

Mina Dragani, Grade 6
Springside Chestnut Hill Academy

The Hideous Elephant, Ernie

His parents called him ugly, and his friends did too.
He never really noticed, but it was all terribly totally true.
His hair was a mess and his trunk was too small.
His eyes were so squinty and he was way too tall.
Days went by without a whisper, wink, or word from Ernie.
He was on a brand new journey.
He was determined to find where he belonged.
He hoped his happiness wouldn't be prolonged.

Katelyn Patton, Grade 6
Interboro GATE Program

Basset Hounds Playing in the Park

In the middle of Pittsburgh
Lies the dogs with the biggest ears
With names like: Flash, Jake, Roscoe, Rufus, Dumbo, and Dash
All playing around until the dark of night
Listening to music
Watching TV
The Bassets prepare to party the night away
Drinking butter-flavored milkshakes
And sleeping in lazy basset piles
Daddies loving their baby bassets
Ears flopping in the breeze
Eating butter burgers
Watching birds fly

Liam Wheeler, Grade 6
Ross Elementary School

If Fall Could Be

If fall could be a color,
it would be as blue as my eyes as they sparkle.
If fall could be a taste,
it would taste just like pumpkin pie.
If fall could be a smell,
it would smell like cinnamon.
If fall could be a sound,
it would be crisp.
If fall could be a feeling,
it would be cozy.
If fall could be an animal,
it would be a deer running through the forest.
That is what fall would be.

Alexis Yeakel, Grade 5
Clearview Elementary School

The First Snow

The first snow of winter is cold and windy,
It is wonderful
I wake up and look up and all I see is white.
I touch the window, pull away because it is too cold
I tell my mom I'm going outside,
I grab my scarf, mittens, and coat
I walk outside and when I breathe I see my breath in the air
I stick out my tongue and feel a cold snowflake land on it
I think in my mind this is why I love winter's first snow

Katie Prentice, Grade 6
Hopewell Memorial Jr High School

Lemon

You look like a bouncy ball that has been stretched out to a point.
You feel like a rough road on a highway at night.
When I slice you, you sound like foam being ruffled in a box,
Like someone cutting wood with a saw.
Inside you feel like the wet bottom of a boat in the middle of a lake.
You taste like a sour, oozy geyser in the middle of a candy land.
Tell me, why do you have a point?

Thomas Fischer, Grade 5
Reiffton School

A Memorable Moment

The freshly emerging green leaves far below my feet were like a bowl of green apples. The animals hidden amongst the trees howled like the wind in my face. I was a bird learning to fly and the wind whispered courage in my ear. I flew through the air like the bird inside me while the wind painted my face with encouragement. In the green wilderness behind me, my mom's cheering voice gave me a push to get to the other side. As I clutched the slippery rope, the humidity floated under my nose, then it drifted away. Finally, I reached the other side. I never forgot zip lining in Costa Rica.

Savannah Schiebel, Grade 4
The Ellis School

Bentley

I got a new puppy he likes to run around he is the cutest thing I ever found
I got him a sweater for when it gets cold and I'll never sell him for he is worth a pot of gold
I'll take care of him from dawn to dusk for I will keep that promise I have to, I must
For Bentley my puppy he is very fluffy I saw him from the start and loved him from the bottom of my heart.

Danielle Giovinco, Grade 6
Pennridge North Middle School

Fall Dilemmas

I can hear the crunch of the leaves, as I step on orange, yellow and red beautiful ones.
The feel of Wind blowing in my hair, the chill up my sleeve, a bunch of leaves are falling off the old tree.
I see scarecrows hovering over the dead garden as if a deer mother watching over her young.
When I cover my eyes, the blast of cold air lingering around my face, as I am approaching the door.

Caroline Beljan, Grade 6
Pennridge North Middle School

Fluttering Free

The butterfly is a beautiful princess of air,
Delicate creature roams the sky without care.

Gracefully gliding o'er gorgeous fields,
Swoosh, whoosh, around the turn quickly yields.

Wandering wearily over wondrous rivers,
Plummets toward the water and everyone shivers.

Lands in a garden to take a rest,
Then flaps to the ground and decides on a flower that tastes best.

The appetizing aroma of astonishing flowers draws it in,
The tasty, terrific, leafy towers are what it shall eat for din.

Then flapping furiously with wings almost overlapping,
Gaining altitude starts to soar and quits flapping.

It dodges trees, a swift fox of the sky,
Keen and committed as it does fly.

Strong as a lion, delicate as a flower,
Fluttering freely with so much power.

As the sun fades and the air grows cool,
With what's left of the light, it's hard to see its beauty in full.

Quickly fading, it feels me with woe,
Fluttering freely into the sunset aglow.
Grace McFarland, Grade 6
Linville Hill Mennonite School

What Beauty Is to Me

Beauty is so many things, so many things to me,
here are some things I want you to see.

Beauty is a rose that blooms,
a sky of blue, the shining moon.

Beauty is the ocean waves, to hear the ocean roar,
jellyfish and my footprints on the shore.

Beauty is the stars that twinkle,
candy canes and ice-cream sprinkles.

Beauty is the trees that grow,
the autumn leaves and how they blow.

Beauty is the sun that shines,
how it sets to say good night.

Beauty is a smiling face,
a giggle, a hug, or a warm embrace.

Beauty is an eagle soaring through the sky,
to look at him gives us pride.

Beauty is my family around me,
the love we have will always be.

They say beauty is in the eye of the beholder,
beauty is everything to me, it seems, as I get older.
Kiera E. Feeley, Grade 6
Heights Terrace Elementary/Middle School

I Am From

I am from Rita, my dog, who fills my world with kisses as I slump my backpack from a long day away at school.
I am from Pisces, my frog, and Shelby, my turtle, who look at me with bright eyes.
I am from the running, freezing brook which is full of fish and mystery.
I am from the autumn fields full of wheat and corn as the farmers work.
I am from the lush forest of fern and trees with trails to hike and sites to camp.
I am from the frozen winter, the snow, the ice, and the cold.
I am from summer when heat dazzles me and I can splash through the pool.
I am from the shining lake where I can swim and let my mind blow.
I am from the sun that scars over the earth and fills my world with light.
I am from my family who will care for me when I need it most.

Jack Ochoa-Andersen, Grade 4
State College Friends School

I Am From

I am from Orvieto where cobblestones are the road and where the Duomo is covered in gold.
I am from my fat gray cat, Hanover who sometimes acts like a dog.
I am from my neighbors, Abi and Norah, who I share gooey warm s'mores with.
I am from long boring bus rides which smell of rotten eggs.
I am from New York with high buildings and bustling streets which helped me get over my fear of kidnappers.
I am from making Zwieback, stacking 20 balls of dough instead of 2 with my Oma.
I am from my best friend Katie who at the Chinese restaurant spills her rice all over the floor every time.
I am from my aunt and uncle Tip and Sharon's farm where sheep graze on the hills and where I am always welcome.
I am from my friends Alex, June, Katie L., and Lydia. My friends from school are always there for me.
I am from my family who helps me when I need it most.

Amelia Kasdorf, Grade 4
State College Friends School

I Am From

I am from my funny bunny brother that is always with me when I need him.
I am from the black and yellow uniformed Oregon Ducks that win almost every game they play!
I am from my sweet stuffed animals who I really like to sleep with.
I am from my dad's yummy-in-my-tummy pizza that I love to eat.
I am from my house where I love to live inside.
I am from my loving parents who will take care of me wherever we are.
I am from my Legos that I make creations with.
I am from my dogs, friendly, fuzzy, funny, fury, fur balls that always make me happy,
I am from football games where the cool uniformed players run across the field as my body shivers from excitement.
I am from the Percy Jackson books that are very adventurous!

Walter Geiger, Grade 4
State College Friends School

The Bad Day

Today was a really bad day.
In a super really sad way.
I was really not very gay,
On my super bad not-good day.

First I cut my classmate's hair,
Then at recess I would not share,
Next I told someone no one cares,
And now I'm in time out which isn't fair!

On my way home I got run over by a cat,
Next I got hit by a baseball bat,
When I got to my house I tripped over our mat,
So then in a chair I madly sat

So today was a horrible day.
Things didn't really go my way.
And now that it's done I'm gonna say,
Thank goodness I'm through with this horrible day!

Bridget Day, Grade 5
St Genevieve School

If Fall Could Be…

If fall could be a color,
it would be orange;
as orange as pumpkins.
If fall could be a taste,
it would taste just like pumpkin pie.
If fall could be a smell,
it would smell like fresh baked banana bread.
If fall could be a sound,
it would sound like leaves rustling.
If fall could be a feeling,
it would feel like a cozy house.
If fall could be an animal,
it would be a dog.

Colby Robertson, Grade 5
Clearview Elementary School

Who Am I?

I am the bursting, and blinding color yellow,
Always happy and cheerful.
I am the round shape of a sphere,
With no beginning and no end.
I'm the warm and soft texture of a just baked cookie,

Sensitive to the touch.
I am the sweet flavor of an orange,
Always "squirting" out fresh ideas.
I am the rushing of a river flowing
With my soothing voice.
Me and only me,
I am who I am.

Bailey Harper, Grade 6
Good Hope Middle School

Green Beans

You know what's greater than a forest?
A forest made of green beans.
Now you're probably thinking, whoa what is this??
But think again.
Broccoli trees, fallen moss-covered logs a.k.a. green beans.
Do things live in these logs?
Sure!
Animals make their homes inside them
Like peas in a pod.

Patrick Costa, Grade 5
Winchester-Thurston School

Jake

One that is very big,
He is always hyper and hungry for food.
One that's always excited,
And can be very destructive.
One that is very lovable,
And always happy.
This animal is not just any animal he is my dog.

Bradley Kennedy, Grade 6
Bellmar Middle School

Winter

December brings the first gift of snow,
And also the sleds from the sheds.
December makes footprints in the snow,
So detectives know where to go
And shouts with winter break,
And lets all the children play and sled.
December is a month of joy.

January brings the New Year,
With shouts and pans banging together,
But when they go out they'll be shivering cold.
January is a month of goals,
People set them high and low,
But like to have fun, will they last?

February starts to clean up the snow.
And bring back Jack Frost, to do his work,
February slips up the roads,
And loves to hear the sound of crash.
I wake up in the morning to white frost sitting on the grass,
And I hate to watch the winter go.

Sean Guinan, Grade 4
Aston Elementary School

Italian Vacation

My family and I, we took a vacation.
To a condo in Italy, with spacious rooms and ventilation.
On our way there, we stopped at a diner.
Outside the door, there was a shoe shiner.
The menu looked great.
From page one to page eight.
Pizza, spaghetti, ravioli, and more.
But the other food looked like it rolled off the floor.
Star shaped pasta with corn sauce.
Some weird, green, goo that looked like moss.
Mango chips with salami dip.
Extra hot tobasco sauce they burned my upper lip.
Tomatoes covered in cold Swiss cheese.
The stinger, antenna, and legs of bumble bees.
Hard, crumbly, tubes that tried to pass for noodles.
I was really surprised that they actually served poodles.
We didn't believe what our eyes had seen.
I'm pretty sure their hands weren't clean.
So when the waiter came I said.
Really, I would rather eat lead.

Matthias Holbert, Grade 6
Hopewell Memorial Jr High School

Hate

H is for Holocaust a word for fire
A is for Adolf Hitler a big, evil liar
T is for Tolerance what people desire
E is for Equality a thing that should not be divided
   by barbed wire

Pyeatt Hitchcock, Grade 6
Nazareth Area Intermediate School

Wouldn't It Be Funny

Now wouldn't it be funny if the creatures of the zoo
Took over the universe and in the cage was you

Now wouldn't it be funny if they put us in the cages
Fed us popcorn and paid us the lowest of wages

Now wouldn't it be funny if we had to work in the circus
Fly through rings of fire and maybe even tire

Now wouldn't it be funny if a smelly hippopotamus
Was appalled by our cute and quirky scents

Now wouldn't it be funny if we had to roar
Be like the lions and even sleep and snore

Now wouldn't it be funny if the animals ran at me
But I have to agree it was a fine, fun dream

Keara Golden, Grade 6
Eden Hall Upper Elementary School

War

I want to enlist in the army
But sometimes I feel bad
To leave my family and friends sad
Once I'm older of course
'Cause right now I'm only nine

And sometimes it kills me inside
To think of the others
Who haven't all made it
Or survivor's guilt
Where they're the only one who made it in their unit

And the children ask on Christmas
All they want is their parents
To come home from wherever
And to share their love
And that's about it till their days are over

Gabe Roteman, Grade 4
Jefferson Elementary School

The Sounds and Smells of Thanksgiving

You smell from the moment you wake,
The turkey being roasted,
its smell rising throughout the house.
You smell the scent of baking pie,
with apples stacked a mile high.

You can hear all day long,
The turkey sizzling in the oven,
The potatoes being mashed,
The preparing of the green bean casserole,
The pie being made,
And the whoop of football being played.

Emmy Hsiung, Grade 5
Falk Laboratory School

Forgiveness

I walk into the chapel room. I feel
something faint tap me on the shoulder. Then
I notice it feels different here than out
at the mall, or out at school.

I sit down in one of the many
aisles and that faint noise becomes a little
louder. While the priest is talking I do
not listen because with every word this faint
noise becomes less of a whisper and more
of a shout.

As it becomes louder and louder
my heart is racing inside me. I feel like
I am going to burst! But then, it stops.

I feel changed, but it does not hurt. I
know what to do. I listen to the priest intently.

I walk out of the chapel with a
smile on my face. For I know what has
changed me. The forgiveness of God.

Jacob Vito, Grade 4
Jefferson Elementary School

John Morton

His wife was Anna Justis
He died of tuberculosis
His stepfather was a surveyor
And he was a well-educated farmer
The presiding judge of the Court of Common Pleas
But tragically died at age 53
He signed the declaration
Also a good politician
Friends with Ben Franklin
And also James Wilson
Born in 1724
His accomplishments were galore

Talitha Kyle, Grade 4
Interboro GATE Program

USA Flag

We all love the red, white, and blue.
The flag waves so freely and true.
The flag up so high.
Like a bird up in the sky.
Even if it's not there.
You can feel it in the air.
Like the birds and the bees.
You can see it in the trees.
Our flag will talk to you when no one is around.
The flag can sing a beautiful sound.
Our freedom is so dear and true.
It's all because of the red, white, and blue.

Jacob Davis, Grade 6
Bellmar Middle School

America the Powerful

America, a powerful nation,
cut like a human body,
the terrible events of 9/11,
both Twin Towers obliterated.

The shock I felt at 8:58 am,
when the North tower was hit,
I could feel it shake and later fall,
beneath my feet.

Devastation and sorrow,
filled my coworkers' hearts,
while anger and terror,
towards whoever had done this filled mine.

Although New York City,
suffered many losses,
the United States of America,
has built back an even taller World Trade Center.

Ben Forster, Grade 6
Southern Lehigh Intermediate School

The Egg

An egg was on the dunes of the lovely beaches of St. June's.
One fine day the egg had split, a tiny beak popped out a bit,
Out came a little gull, of which species, I can't recall.
Covered with fluff, not very tough,
The chick was rather pathetic.
Feathers bold, feathers long, the mother was firm and strong,
And to the most extent, athletic.

As the years passed, the chick grew too.
The sun at full blast, he flew and flew.
He flew and flew where blue met blue.
Salt whipping at his face,
He raced and raced and raced and raced.
The beautiful gull had crossed the sea
And found a spot beneath a tree.
He got a mate, not a second late,
On the lovely beaches of Regg.
They dug a ditch, the female flinched.
And then she laid an egg.

Aidan Bodeo-Lomicky, Grade 6
East Hills Middle School

Hitler

H is for Hitler, the man with hate for Jews.
I is for inside the deadly gas chambers.
T is for terrible conditions they were put in.
L is for love that was trapped or consumed.
E is for equality the Jews got with freedom.
R is for remembering the ones that died
   and that we still love today, and hate is gone,
   and so is Hitler, and he means nothing to us anymore.

Avery Petrozelli, Grade 6
Nazareth Area Intermediate School

Heroes in Uniform

Courageous men who left their homes
Willing to risk it all
Marching out onto the battlefields
Winter, spring, summer and fall

Patriotic women with mud on their souls
Fighting day and night
Going to combat in blasting heat
And sometimes under starlight

From us here at home
Thinking about the special men and women
We know it can be tough
Being put in this position

All are different, but similar
On how each one performs
But they can all be named,
"Heroes in Uniform"

Emma Duane, Grade 6
Joseph P. Liberati Intermediate School

Christmas at My Grandmother's House

Waking up on Christmas morning
tiptoeing through Grandma's big house
finger tips tingling with anticipation
everybody else is asleep
dreaming
waiting for the first loud clear notes
of the piano playing "Joy to the World"
and then they come
they come as my dad strikes the piano
as I sing the notes loud and clear
"Joy to the world, the Lord has come"
as aunts and uncles, cousins and babies
come down the stairs
I know those are the truest words I've ever sung
with cookies, toast and eggs for breakfast
followed by stockings and presents and love
Christmas at my grandmother's house
my favorite time of year

Thea Risher, Grade 4
Wissahickon Charter School

Winter

Winter is as cold as ice.
The snow is as white as a polar bear.
A Christmas tree is as beautiful as a newborn baby.
Snowmen are as creative as art.
Christmas is as fun as presents.
Ornaments are decorative like a Christmas tree.
Snow angels are like real angels on a cloud.
Santa Claus is as nice as my family.
He is a gift giver to everyone around the world.

Khristian Moise, Grade 4
Wickersham Elementary School

My Worst Nightmare

You can hear and see them
thrashing through the water
you can hear their jaws snap
you can see their blue fins chasing after you
after a while you finally realize
you've been attacked
you hear yourself screaming without even trying
you look down and see all the blood
the next thing you know
you're safe and sound in bed
your baby brother's crying woke you up at night

Alana Gould, Grade 6
Hopewell Memorial Jr High School

The Holocaust

The time of the Holocaust was a very terrible thing,
When Hitler put hate upon the Jews,
And their families.
Many people died for no apparent reason,
Lots of people cried in this horrid situation.
He brainwashed others to join this murderous gang.
Now it seemed nothing could stop Hitler,
It came to the final event...

We remember the Holocaust...

Grace Karch, Grade 6
Nazareth Area Intermediate School

Mostly Me

One girl who loves to learn.
Two eyes that only let me see good things.
Three other people in my family that care for me.
Four nice friends that support me.
Five letters to make my name.
Six amazing years in church.
Seven is my lucky number.
Eight teachers that I really like.
Nine outfits that I love.
Ten fingers to do most of the things I choose.

Leean Andino, Grade 5
Clearview Elementary School

Edward H. White — An Explorer

He was born November 4, 1930.
He upgraded space crafts and made them sturdy.
He worked at the NASA spaceport.
This career was his kind of sort.
Edward was the first to walk in space,
Using jet propulsion, it looked like a race.
He won a lot of awards, almost ten.
He earned more achievements than most men.
A space fire killed him and his crew,
We remember him in our hearts, so bold, so true.

Joseph M. Pugh, Grade 5
Interboro GATE Program

The Field of Fun

Where the grasses would blow
Blown by imagination
Where the trees would gather
To watch us play our games

Games of laughs and games of love
And games of creativity
Where our minds would soar

Wind was our restaurant
It was chill cement brick
Mossy rocks were the tables
Velvet table cloths await

Let us dine there
Just think, pinecones and leaves on an earthy plate
They taste of our dreams

A cloud of exhaust passed by, a cloud of lost joy
The car drove on in to the house next door
We must keep this place, our favorite toy

So we tried our luck,
The answer was sad, "Get out of my yard!"
Our place of enjoyment was gone.

Hannah Jones, Grade 5
Foster Elementary School

Apples and Toad and Frogs, Oh My!

Here we are on beautiful day,
At our Uncle Andy's to come and play.
"Apple picking; let's hit the road."
Then we see two frogs and a toad.

The toad was fat, the frogs were thin,
Then we named them in a bin.
Apple picking— here we soar,
About twelve dozen or maybe more.

We found Sirjumpsalot under a car.
He had the spotlight like a star.
Then comes Argus; he's cute and fat
He's not gray and he's not black.

Apple picking, we cross the log,
Then Mom spots a little frog.
Her name is Cara; she's cute and thin,
With the three others she went in the bin.

The day is gone we're sorry to say,
Then our Uncle said take them home and play!
We played and laughed and had lots of fun
But let them go to hop and jump in the sun.

Jacqui Hofstetter, Grade 5
The American Academy

Favorites

Green like a fresh lime.
My grandma, because she is a great cook.
Sweet mashed potatoes with brown sugar,
Are yummy to eat with turkey.
Silly because I am happy.
My cousins I visit whenever I can.
Skunks because they are cute and fat.
Swimming... I swim with Alex on the swim team.

Gabrielle Haring, Grade 4
St John Vianney Regional School

Ancient Paths

If you follow the ancient paths,
You will find sugar cane sand upon an ocean
With the strong smell of salt in the mist,
It blows on you gently.
You'll also find the morning roses get watered
By the spring rain.
You will only find the wonders of the world,
If you follow the ancient paths.

Molly Smith, Grade 4
Lincoln Elementary School

Family

F orever they will be
A lways by your side
M ake you feel good if you have a bad day
I rritating at sometimes
L oyal they try not to lie
Y ou always know they love you even if they die
    they will be there for you standing by your side
    for the rest of your life

Alexis Armstrong, Grade 5
Newberry Elementary School

Worry

Worry is like your worst enemy that won't go away,
It smells like a room full of skunks,
It tastes like a bitter medicine that your mom forces on you,
It sounds like an angry sergeant yelling instructions,
It feels like 1,000 pounds on your back,
It lives in every 6th Grader's home!

Yoseph Bere, Grade 6
St. Jude School

Color

Yellow is...
As smooth as a rock on a beach.
As tough as a skier flying through moguls.
As cool as a winter breeze.
As vast as the western plains.

Jack Casturo, Grade 4
Jefferson Elementary School

Roy G. Biv

The colors. The wonders. Rainbows.
    After its show I say "Bravo."

    Rain and sun
    Join together to make one,

The giant colorful slide in the sky
    The makes me want to cry.

Rainbows are just such a sight,
    They're more than all right.

The colors just go with the flow,
    Unicorns can't say no,

To that splash of color in the sky that is so fun,
    To everyone, in the sun.

    When I stand by
    The wonders of the sky,

    I feel delight
    To see that sight.

    The stripe of joy
    That I enjoy,

    Is a rainbow.
    Go Rainbows!!!

Kelsey Gruber, Grade 6
Eden Hall Upper Elementary School

The Ocean Blue

Down by the sea
The wind blows strong
And there I stood
For what seemed very long
I looked out upon the deep ocean blue
The boats, the people
The dolphins and sharks
Why a bite from that creature would sure leave a mark
The salty air
Would make some choke
But not to me
"Invincible" people would joke
The sand around
Was flaming hot
People were still buried in it
They seemed ready to rot
And still I look
At that seashore
A beautiful heaven
I want to keep
Forever more

Brian Gallagher, Grade 6
Assumption BVM School

Halloween

H oping no one's behind you.
A lways knocking from door to door.
L aughing at the scary stuff.
L oving everyone's costumes.
O ver your bedtime.
W alking down the streets.
E ating Halloween candy.
E erie sight for you and me.
N ever tired of candy.

Douglas Noriega, Grade 5
Clearview Elementary School

Halloween

H ow scary it is on October 31st.
A lot of people go house to house.
L ooking like creatures of the night.
L ots of candy being passed out.
O h how fun Halloween is!
W itches flying in the air.
E verywhere I see scary costumes.
E very piece of candy needs to be checked.
N ever eat a lot of candy.

Mikayla Rowe, Grade 5
Clearview Elementary School

Holocaust

H itler
O utrageous
L abor
O pinion
C oncentration camp
A ryan
U nited
S ynagogue
T orah

Zealand Torres, Grade 6
Nazareth Area Intermediate School

Basketball

basketball
fun, irresistible
dribbling, shouting, sweating
I made a foul shot, "Yay"
defense defense!

Marlaina Bozek, Grade 4
Trinity East Elementary School

Summer

Summer is pink and blue.
It tastes like chocolate ice cream.
It sounds like laughter through children.
And it smells like apple pie.
It looks like the sun's shadow.
It makes you feel joyful!

Chaelyn Charles, Grade 5
Westmoreland Christian Academy

Pittsburgh

Pittsburgh, the best city in the world.
The Steelers have six Lombardi trophies.
The Penguins have Stanley cups.
The Pirates, they are good too.
The Panthers are victorious.
The city where all the people are loyal,
To all their sports teams, good or bad.
The food is great, too.
Where the greatest rappers have been born.
From Polamalu to Crosby.
From Ray Graham and Ashton Gibbs at Pitt.
Anywhere in this great city.
I will always have fun.

Griffin LaCarte, Grade 6
Bellmar Middle School

The Perfect Place

I need to find a place
Where everything is right

I need to find a place
Where no one gets into fights

I need to find a place
Where people never die
Where I can drift off and fly

I need to find a place
That's everything I love
A place that fits like a glove

Will Sulahian, Grade 6
Pennridge North Middle School

I Am Special

I am a daughter.
I am 9 years old.
I am the middle child.
I am cute.
I am fun.
I am funny.
I am a New York Yankee's fan.
I am a Wii player.
I am great at playing.
I am a superior friend.
I am a fantastic sister.
I am Kassy.

Kasandra Montalvo, Grade 4
Wickersham Elementary School

Snowflakes

Light and fluffy
Sparkling and glistening
Every one has a different shape
Softness

Mollie Dean, Grade 4
Fairview Elementary School

Beauty in Fall

Mosaics of red,
Yellow, orange, maroon.
It holds power in my head,
Makes me feel as bright as the moon.

Cool air flowing a silent sound
Just enough to make you shake.
Breaking twigs on the ground.
My heart and mind fall will take.

Katie Stutzman, Grade 6
Pennridge North Middle School

A Sign of Fall

Wind whips through the almost bare trees.
Not a calm wind, not just a breeze.
Enough to give you the chills.
As it dances through the grassy hills.

It makes the animals shiver.
Even the flowers quiver.
This is a sure sign for all.
That it is not summer, now it is fall.

Jacqueline Benamati, Grade 6
Pennridge North Middle School

Cars

I love the zooming
and the booming
of cars.
I love the running
and the gliding
and the dollars
I pay to be
in one of those machines
I love cars.

Liam Schenk, Grade 5
Winchester-Thurston School

The Color Purple

Purple looks like a grape,
Purple sounds like night winds,
Purple feels like a plum,
Purple smells like wine,
Purple tastes like grapefruit.

Paul Jensen, Grade 5
Clearview Elementary School

Hitler!

H olocaust
I ndifferent
T orah
L abor camp
E thnocentrism
R esistance

Jahan Dotson, Grade 6
Nazareth Area Intermediate School

I Am From

I am from Curtis and Edme, my black and white fantastic furry 5 month old kittens!
I am from the bus, where I sit and watch wonderful sights out my window.
I am from my trampoline, which with every step I take lifts me high into the deep blue sky.
I am from Legos, the colorful building blocks that make their way into many wonderful contraptions of greatness.
I am from math, the world of numbers and problems that you must solve to move on.
I am from baseball, the sport of experts, where every swing of the bat is a masterpiece.
I am from my friend, Marcus, who has been with me for many years and has always been my companion.
I am from building, where you sit down and concoct creations of excellence.
I am from reading, the wonderful place where every page you turn is an adventure.

Alex Mullen, Grade 4
State College Friends School

Fall Is Wonderful

The warmth of the sun wrapped around me like a blanket, but the cool wind played a prank and snatched it away.
Observing all the white and pink wild flowers dancing in the gentle wind.
Freshly mowed grass filled my nose while walking under the falling leaves.
I wish the fall would stay, but winter and ice will come and fall would slip away, oh just for another day.

The sky is blue the leaves are becoming few with colors of yellow, orange, and red flying through the air.
Sitting on my outdoor step watching the scarecrow scaring the crows away.
Off in the distance I hear the wind blowing and see the trees swaying.
Saying good-bye to fall even though I had a ball, winter has to gave its share just because it is fair.

Jordan Gustovich, Grade 6
Pennridge North Middle School

Adolf Hitler

The Holocaust was destruction of Jews by Nazis. Millions died because of a mean man named Adolf Hitler. Hitler had a plan, a plan to kill every Jew because of their beliefs. Nazis came and grabbed Jews from their homes, taking them to different camps, never to see their families again. They were put into gas chambers and tortured till their death. Starved, not cared for, and killed because of one man, Adolf Hitler. His heart was cold and filled with hate. Adolf Hitler embarrassed them and made them feel insecure. Feeling like animals and losing all hope. Jewish families in hiding, innocent people killed because of their religion. Why did he care? Were they really hurting anyone? No. Adolf was just a hater of all people's happiness. If he didn't like the way you looked, or how you talked, or our beliefs, you were dead to him. Literally. He made the Jews feel horrible, unloved, ashamed, and humiliated. Jews were ignored by bystanders and the Jews' friends who weren't Jewish, were turned against them all because of one man named Adolf Hitler, who had a plan.

Karlie McCrone, Grade 6
Nazareth Area Intermediate School

I Am From

I am from school with the knowledge trickling into my brain.
I am from playing with my friends, laughing and cheering.
I am from go-carts, the blowing wind in my face, dodging and swerving in and out to the finish.
I am from my grandpa and grandma's deep but soft laughs that make me giggle inside.
I am from my family laughing and the smell of fresh dumplings coming out of the oven.
I am from science, bubbling and fizzing, booming and snapping. Burning hot liquids and freezing cold liquids.

Christopher Fletcher, Grade 4
State College Friends School

Holocaust

There once was a group named the Jews who were hurt and harmed; many got shot by a firearm.
The Jews were brought to concentration camps to die because Hitler told a very bad lie.
The Nazis starved and burned men, women, and kids. They even sought the Jews that hid.
The Holocaust was a very sad time in history.
And why the Nazis did these terrible things will remain a mystery.

Noah Dutzer, Grade 6
Nazareth Area Intermediate School

Candy Colors

If I were brown,
I would be chocolate melting in your mouth.
If I were red,
I would be a Twizzler waiting to be taken out of the package.
If I were green,
I would be sour apple Fun Dip being licked off the stick.
If I were orange,
I would be a Cry Baby in your mouth while you were in tears.
If I were yellow
I would be candy corn at Halloween.
If I were purple,
I would be a grape-flavored lollipop.
If I were white,
I would be a mint-flavored Life Savor.
If I were blue,
I would be a blue raspberry Airhead Extreme.

Gianna Anthony, Grade 5
Holy Child Academy

Winter

Winter means snow and ice
And lots of school delays
Winter is when family comes home for the holidays.

Winter means sledding
Winter means fun.
Winter means snow instead of sun.

Winter means Christmas
Winter means leafless trees
Winter means cold toes and cold knees.

Winter means the days are short
And no more short sleeves.
Winter means celebrating
A Happy New Year's Eve.

Bella Pykosh, Grade 4
St Joseph School

Noah's Ark

God told Noah to build an ark,
There were hens and wrens and sparrows and larks.
Ponies and dogs and cats were there and,
Donkeys and chickens and one man.

Left that day for an adventure,
It was a dangerous and risky venture.
The waves were high, the sea tossed,
Noah feared all would be lost.

Yes, they went through a rough ride,
But, they got there safely and with pride.
They all came off the ark two by two,
In the sky was a rainbow of many hues.

Cameron Boon, Grade 6
Holy Child Academy

Halloween

I sit on my deck. watch the geese fly by
While I tug on my shirt.
I ride in my dad's truck
Watching people rake their lawns from leaves.

Kids are starting to wear jackets to school
While it gets colder outside
Leaves start to fall, grass turns brown
Parents are stocking up on candy, here comes Halloween!

People buying candy for the children
A long night for the little kids while they run and scream
Going house to house yelling "Trick or Treat."

Going to haunted houses,
Haunted hay rides and corn mazes
Apple cider… "mmmm is that good!"

During the Halloween parades
There are always mints that they throw to you
They are not great
But are pretty broken up when you get them.

So I tell you
Watch for the changes
Halloween is coming!

Anthony Leo, Grade 6
Assumption BVM School

The Beach

I walk through the burning hot sand
grains sinking between my toes,
the warm glow of the gleaming sun,
like a heat lamp on my face.

I look ahead and see
the beautiful turquoise ocean in front of me.
I put the coconut-smelling lotion on myself
and dash towards the ocean.

Before I dive in
I let the water tickle my toes.
"Wow, God, such a wonderful place
You've created for us to enjoy."

Then I finally jump into the water.
SPLASH!!
Oh my, it's so refreshing!
The water is as clear as a newly cleaned window.

I float peacefully over the calm waves.
As I look up at the clouds,
I whisper aloud,
"Thank you, God, for making this beautiful beach."

Mariana Stoltzfus, Grade 6
Linville Hill Mennonite School

All Alone

Putt…Putt…Boom!
The time has come,
My boat has gone.

I am as cold as ten blocks of ice.
Freezing as I sit for hours.

For what started out as a fishing trip,
Was more like an ugly slip.

My trusty ship has shut down,
Now my engine makes no sound.

I am locked in a box,
Until someone shall find the key.
Even though it looks like no one is coming for me,

I lay and I wait,
I lay and I wait,
I lay and I wait,

Should I swim,
Should I stay,
Should I swim,
Should I stay,

But there is no way,
I am all alone.

Emma Boback, Grade 6
Eden Hall Upper Elementary School

The Sun

The sun is words.
A gleaming shining ball lighting our lives inside and out.
Humiliatingly bright, it casts a shadow above us.
But it embraces us, shines down on us, puts words in our mouth:
shining gleaming dreamy golden bright
We live in its warmth, we are equals to it. In that way,
the sun does not shine above us but upon us.

The sun is colors.
Vibrant blues and yellows and neons
and pinks and grays and purples.
It explains things to us with color, loves us with color,
embraces us with color.
Old colors, new colors, and yet-to-be-discovered colors.

The sun is life.
As I walk along a sun-kissed earth, the sun sets,
closer, closer
until I can smell it, until I can feel it brush across my cheek.
And then it is gone.
It leaves a small trace of light as if to say:
another day my friend, another day.

Dominic Skeele, Grade 6
Slippery Rock Area Middle School

World War II

World War II with the sounds of explosions,
On the beach of Normandy and its erosions.

With a boom here and a bang there,
There is obviously action everywhere.

There were a lot of humiliations,
Because of most of the opponent's operations.

Every soldier was a hero,
No matter if their kill count was zero.

They strongly kept fighting,
Praying to see the next day's lighting.

Yes, they fought for me and you,
During the battle of World War II.

Andy Aubrey, Grade 6
St James School

November

I see colors changing,
Leaves falling to the ground;
When I walk, I hear crunchy sounds.
Days getting shorter, nights getting longer,
Breezes bringing winter to the ground.
Bare trees with only a few leaves,
November brings many good things to a start:
Breezy days, cool nights,
What a beautiful sight!
Weather changing from warm to cool,
From bright sky to blue,
From shorts and tees,
To pants and sleeves.
Perfect month for apple-picking,
Lots of birthdays soon to come,
Animals to be seen gathering food so soon,
November is a month to remember.

Erin Billigmeier, Grade 4
Aston Elementary School

The Turtle

I saw a turtle one spring day;
It looked as if it wanted to play.
I picked it up and rubbed its shell;
But when it bit me I yelled and yelled.
I scolded my turtle, but a smile had shown;
For the turtle that bit me was too cute to be thrown.
I carried my turtle all the way home;
But when my mother saw it, she made me write this poem.
I had learned my lesson indeed, indeed;
Never let a turtle make you bleed.
But that day I had learned another lesson;
Don't bring a turtle home as a present.

Emma Uffelman, Grade 5
Foster Elementary School

Anubis

My cat is black and he has short hair,
When he is in hiding you need to beware.

He likes to jump right out of the blue,
So be careful whatever you do.

He is still a kitten only six months old,
I try to teach him and he does mostly what he is told.

My kitten loves to lay and roll on the floor,
He is so sweet and cute it is him I adore.

He sleeps quite often and I hold him as he purrs,
Curling up on my lap this ball full of fur.

Anubis is his name and he is so special to me,
To my heart he holds the key.

Daijah Josey, Grade 6
St James School

What Makes Me Feel Afraid

What makes me afraid?
The swooping squealing black-as-night bats
Things that go bump in the night
And my sister's hair in the morning
That's what makes me afraid.

What makes me quiver and quake?
A rattlesnake's evil eyes staring me in the face
And black fuzzy spiders crawling up the wall
The thought of zombies giving chase
That's what makes me quiver and quake.

What makes me shiver and shake?
Hairy, scary wolves howling at the moon
Rumbling, tumbling thunder that comes crashing down
Vampires with sharp, pointy teeth
That makes me shiver and shake.

Sophia White, Grade 4
St Alexis School

Seasonal Scenes

All the leaves will soon die
yellows, reds, and browns falling from the sky
covering the ground like a blanket of colors.

Now the trees are bare
waiting with despair
for the next spring when everything will grow again.

Soon a snowy world will appear
a white powdery cushion year after year.
When the snow melts, all the waiting seeds will sprout up,
revealing a world of green.

Matteo Sanchez-Dahl, Grade 5
Falk Laboratory School

The Thrill of Tumbling

I can hear the screaming of the crowd.
Even though I do feel proud.

The routines not over yet,
And the thing I dread the most is next.

We start to move to our spots.
My stomach is in a knot.
I can hear my coach yelling "five, six, seven, eight."
As I stand in the corner hoping my tumbling will be first-rate.

I can hear the sounds of the girl's feet echo in the room,
Ba bum, ba bum, boom.

The girl in front of me just went,
Oh how I wish I could just be absent.

With the music and cheering of the audience.
It sounds like there is an avalanche.
I hope that mat doesn't trip me.
For when I land my tumbling it will be complete.

It feels like I've been standing here for a million years.
And now the mat is clear.

I go for the first flip, it was as fast as a whip.
Then my feet landed on the floor, and I'm not nervous anymore.
Now finally it has ended, and I think it was splendid.

Emma Whitford, Grade 6
Eden Hall Upper Elementary School

The Phillies

F antastic playing all year
O ffense ignite every single game
U tley hustles every time
R adical dazzling plays all game

A ll star players abound
C arlos Ruiz is the best catcher for all four
E xceptional fans
S weeping away every single team each series

A ll year round great games
R yan Howard always has power surges
E lectrical fans

T urning double plays to perfection
H unter Pence always doing his best
E xtraordinary fans

B est team in MLB
E astern division champions four years in a row
S hane Victorino as fast as a lightning bolt
T he four aces dominate, major leagues best!

Brandon Zook, Grade 6
Linville Hill Mennonite School

Winter

A blanket of white,
In the sun's bright rays.
In the gloom,
Of the moon.
The animals crawl into their dens,
And pets might have to go into their pens.
They will have to wait until spring,
When the birds will start to sing.

David Clarke, Grade 4
Ithan Elementary School

Toys

When Santa gave me a toy
I ran with great joy
I was so glad
That I was a good lad
I played and played
All day
Then I went and down I laid
That was a good day.

Joshua Neary, Grade 4
Middle Smithfield Elementary School

At War

I can't even lie,
The way time goes by,
My comrades might die,
This is for a reason,
We fight for our country's freedom,
So that our enemies go to treason,
So I must say goodbye
To those who might die.

Ayden S. McCabe, Grade 4
Middle Smithfield Elementary School

Paradise

Lying at the shore,
My feet dig in the sand
Watch the water flow,
Sun shines on me,
Watch the birds fly by,
Silence in the air,
Sitting in the sun,
My paradise is here.

Gabby Herring, Grade 5
Foster Elementary School

Apples

A wesome source of fiber
P erfect seedy core
P erfectly shiny juice
L uscious smooth cider
E xcellent cinnamon dumpling
S avory sweet pies

Bobbie Lee Martin, Grade 4
Fairview Elementary School

Colors of the Wind

Summer
Sunny, fun
Swimming, laughing, playing
Sun beaming down, snow falling
Sledding, laughing, sipping
Cold, crisp
Winter

Phoebe Day, Grade 4
Erdenheim Campus Elementary School

Earth and Life

Earth
Peaceful, wonderful
Calming, caring, loving
Together with earth and life; it's awesome
Helping, laughing, playing
Cool, special
Life

Christian Mexquititla, Grade 4
Erdenheim Campus Elementary School

Space

Stars
Glittery, shiny
Looking, wishing, watching
Shining in the night
Shimmering, smiling, amazing
Craters, space
Moon

Maheen Asif, Grade 4
Erdenheim Campus Elementary School

Puppy

puppy
playful eyes
loves his treats
running, jumping, doing tricks
crawls into my
warm bed
snuggling

Brianna Dinch, Grade 5
Trinity West Elementary School

Kitten

kitten
small, blind
mews a lot
follows its mom everywhere
eats a lot
tiny, adorable
cute

Carmen Hill, Grade 4
Trinity South Elementary School

Steelers

The Steelers are the best football team
With their black and gold and white.
It is every game that it seems
That they come in ready to fight.
They can punt and pass and kick,
And that's why they are my pick.
They will win the Super Bowl this year,
So that all of their fans may cheer.
They are the best.
It's no contest.
They will go all the way,
So that their dreams will not stray.

Matt Wobrak, Grade 6
Bellmar Middle School

Books

I love to read books,
  with different styles and looks.
Flipping through the pages,
Chapter after chapter,
I cannot wait for the end!
I anxiously read,
And imagine in my head,
The picture the story tells.
When I finish the last word,
I close the book,
And gently place it down,
  excited to read another.

Sarah Palli, Grade 6
Bellmar Middle School

The Holocaust

The Holocaust was filled with bad,
It made a lot of people more than just sad,
Bystanders just standing there,
Do they even care?
The police were even on Hitler's side,
You just have to realize that he lied,
Taking loved ones away from their families,
Hitler was doing stuff so badly,
He did stuff we would not even think of,
He had no love,
We will always remember that day,
When Hitler took all our loved ones away.

Hannah Jones, Grade 6
Nazareth Area Intermediate School

Apples

A wesome tangy cider
P erfect ripe juice
P leasant private food
L ovely interesting crisp taste
E xcellent smooth skin
S pecial sticky caramel topping

Damien Gailey, Grade 4
Fairview Elementary School

Gray

Gray is the color of sky
when it is drizzling
But it gets darker and darker
like black
I feel scared
when I look out the window
it is raining really hard
I rush upstairs and hide
under my mom's bed

Shaila Green, Grade 4
Wissahickon Charter School

Flippity Flap

Flippity Flippity Flap
Ploppity Ploppity Clap
Tweedledy Tweedledy Yum
Boingity Boingity Woo
Tappity Tappity Boo
Packity Packity Me
Dappity Dappity Bee
Stompy Stompy Gourd
This is the sound I make when I'm bored

Ty Augenstein, Grade 5
Foster Elementary School

Roller Coaster

I'm standing in line
waiting, waiting, waiting
finally I get on!
We go all the way up
all the way down
first a hoop
then a loop
we went really fast
I had a blast!!

Hannah Kline, Grade 5
St Theresa School

Ocean

Ocean
Warm, blue
Rising, falling, flowing
Always gets me excited
Pacific.

Sierra Hermann, Grade 6
Trinity Middle School

Winter

W hite snow falls gently on your head
I cicles glittering in the sunshine
N ight comes too quickly
T he fire warms every heart
E xcitement fills the air
R emembering the winter with delight

Olivia Marsh, Grade 5
Moravian Academy Lower School

Twin Towers

So tall and elegant,
Standing up in the big city.
Close to a church and tumbling down.
Whoever did take the towers away didn't take our pride and glory
for this country.
We still honor these towers on 9/11,
We still remember the people of 9/11.
The people's names are engraved on the metal bars around the fountains
where the towers once stood.
So stand and sing the National Anthem for these towers and people on 9/11.

Matthew Ford, Grade 4
Jefferson Elementary School

The Game Time Butterflies

You wake up early in the morning.
When you get to the stadium you meet with your friends and watch the little kids.
Once all the little kids' games are over that's when the butterflies start.
You warm up trying to hide this from friends.
When there's 15 minutes to games you all gear up and have a prayer.
The coin toss comes around and the pep talks everyone pumps up.
At kickoff the first butterflies all go away.
Once you get a taste of things all the butterflies go away
That is the same thing with life.

Frankie Veri, Grade 6
Hopewell Memorial Jr High School

I Am From

I am from Legos, billions of bricks — red, blue, green. What will I make next?
I am from the beach where I ride the waves in.
I am from family dog walks where my brother and I scooter and do tricks.
I am from roller coasters — up, down, spin around, loopdy-loop.
I am from chess. Little figurines fight for you.
I am from water, a nice drink and a cool pool.
I am from Mastermind, a guessing game Mom and I play.
I am from the Washington Museum of Art — pictures, sculptures, and more!
I am from Halloween, where I dress up as Mafia with my fedora.

Finan Turnage-Barney, Grade 4
State College Friends School

Lime

You're green as grass on a summer day.
You taste as if you've been soaking in bubbles in the sunlight.
On the inside you look like a 19th century horse wagon wheel.
You smell like a leather jacket hanging in the store.
On the inside you feel like a slimy, wet board sitting at the bottom of the creek.
When you're sliced you sound like a saw going through a dry piece of wood.
On the outside you feel like a scaly lizard sitting on a branch.
So please lime tell me, are you horrified of something?
Is that why you're bumpy?

Michael Haas, Grade 5
Reiffton School

Turkey Thanksgiving

Turkey, turkey grow
Grow your feathers bright and nice
Oh, walk your way home.
Grace Dingas, Grade 4
St Anselm Elementary School

How I Love Flowers

Flowers are pretty
They are white, orange, and pink
They smell very sweet.
Olivia Gribley, Grade 4
St Anselm Elementary School

Squirrels

Squirrels are so cute
They are very sensitive
They are just like me.
Giavonna Maio, Grade 4
St Anselm Elementary School

Kittens

Explorers, hunters, curious balls of fur,
One day she brought back a mouse,
I was so proud of her!
Mia Agostinelli, Grade 5
Foster Elementary School

Fall

Bare trees, falling leaves
Gusts of wind blowing around
Amazing colors
Sophia Conrad, Grade 4
St Joseph School

The Moon

The moon is shining
It is very bright tonight
You can see a man
Lucas Eberly, Grade 4
Erdenheim Campus Elementary School

Baleen Whale

Swims in the water
Breaching, spyhopping, hopping
Migrates north and south.
Jeff Ecker, Grade 6
Trinity Middle School

Fire

It consumes life itself
A spark, some heat and there it is
The monster that is calamitous
Sam Safferstein, Grade 5
Foster Elementary School

A Soldier's Last Story

He can hear the roaring of the enemy plane overhead
And he can see bombs like rain drops falling from the sky
Oh how many will be dead

With grenades being thrown
And bullets hurdling through the air, he is in a deadly war zone

As he thinks of the low survival rate and moves from place to place
His heart is in a race as the commander starts to berate

Unaware of what lies ahead, he jumps into the fight feeling a fright
And for those who die he feels contrite

As he moves forward into enemy zones
He feels the pressure build as he tried to fix the many atones

Then in one big flash his life was taken
By an enemy sniper leaving those he left behind sadly shaken

As she opened the door on that cool day in fall
Her fears came alive, two uniformed soldiers standing tall

Her eyes fill with an ocean of tears
As she heard the soldier's words, not knowing how to get through the coming years

Saddened by the fact that he had to depart
Giving his life for ours but proud knowing he earned a purple heart
Sarah Metzmaier, Grade 6
Eden Hall Upper Elementary School

Sports

Soccer, football, and baseball are major sports.
Soccer is my favorite sport.
They have many leagues, kids, middle school, high school, college, and professional.
You can start soccer at age four.
They have World Cups for professional teams have a tournament.
Do you have a favorite player?
My favorite player is Cristiano Ronaldo also called Ronaldo.
In England soccer is called football.

Football is a contact sport.
Football is known as NFL.
NFL stands for national football league in the United States.
Many teams play for the NFL.
The Steelers is a team in the NFL.

Baseball is a multitasking sport.
There are nine players on a baseball field.
There are three bases.
There is a pitcher, basemen, outfield men, catcher, and short stop.
There's a batter on the other team.
The pitcher can throw a fast ball.
If you hit the ball far you get a home run.
People enjoy major sports like soccer, football, and baseball.
Joshua Martin, Grade 6
Bellmar Middle School

Copies and Homework and Tests, Oh My!

School's not my favorite place to be
By the end of the day I'm quite drowsy.
In Latin I want to fall asleep
And on my desk I lie in a heap.

The punishment for lying on the table?
To coy quotes just for dreaming a fable.
In math I look down at the book
And at the problems that so long I took

In physical science we learn about heat,
About temperature and what to eat.
in English, what a grand delight
To have time to read books and to write.

And vocabulary is actually fun
With sweet rewards when we are done.
Then recess comes; we take a break.
Then lunch I eat what my mom makes.

At the end of school I shout for joy:
Time to go home and read and play.
The only thing that sorrows my heart:
The homework I have to do today!

David Matej, Grade 6
The American Academy

Mom's Home Cooking

My mom is really an excellent cook
And she doesn't need to use a cookbook.
The food my mom cooks is from Korea
I think it's better than any tortilla.

She packs me lunches that are delicious
My mom's food is very nutritious.
My friends try my food and think it is great;
To try tomorrow's food they can hardly wait.

Every night she makes me something good
I would eat three helpings if I could.
My favorite food is Ja Jang Myon.
I invite my friends to my house, "C'mon."

In every bite the noodles soften.
I'm so glad my mom makes them often.
When my dad's at home we eat together
He comes home late when there's bad weather.

My mom has chopsticks (Jo Ka Lak)
She uses them to cook friend rice in a Wok.
I live in America; their food is great.
but my mom's Korean food is what I like on my plate!

Samuel Chang, Grade 5
The American Academy

Happy Marriage

Your marriage was out of this world.
Through tough and weak,
snow and sun,
your love just gets higher and higher,
higher and higher.
Your life together has just begun,
your love has touched the sun.
Your love song is the best in the world.
There might be an end,
but right now your love song has just begun.

Isaiah Wenrick, Grade 4
Trevorton Elementary School

Wonderful Me

To you I'm just a person,
An ant in the middle of New York,
Not special, not different, just normal.
But I know who I am
And someday you will know too.
When you're working in a grocery store,
And I am a super model you will know
Because I know if I want something I will work toward it,
So one day you can think about me and say,
That girl is amazing, and I wanna be just like her.

Marta Walewska, Grade 6
Glenolden School

Cat in Me

There is a cat in me.
With fur as soft as a blanket,
and teeth like needles,
but won't bite.
It hisses like a snake when someone bothers it.
It snuggles like a baby when it's happy.
It lives in my heart,
I wish I could see it.
It makes me want to sleep.
It makes me feel like doing nothing all day.

Carly D'Ambrosio, Grade 5
Indian Lane Elementary School

Cheetah

There is a cheetah in me.
With sharp claws like needles,
and long legs like a tree.
It roars like a father lion protecting its family,
It creeps like a wild rat.
It lives in my legs,
and makes me fast like the blowing wind.
I wish I had soft hair like its fur.
It makes me want to run freely.
It makes me feel awesome!

Margaret Howe-Consiglio, Grade 5
Indian Lane Elementary School

Leaves in the Fall

L eaping into piles of leaves
E ating leaves when you jump
A t my friend's house
V ery cold fall
E xtra laughter
S nowflakes are just starting to dangle from the sky.

Justin Dougherty, Grade 4
Erdenheim Campus Elementary School

Fall

Fall always reminds me of cool air, colorful leaves
Pumpkins, Halloween, Thanksgiving
Squawking geese flying gracefully away
Fall is a time of festivity
A time of thanks
A time of a life.

Maxwell Yorgey, Grade 4
Worcester Elementary School

Winter Season

Winter is as sparkly as glitter.
Winter is like cotton balls falling from the sky.
Hot chocolate is as creamy as marshmallows.
Giving stuff is as fun as going shopping for other people.
Baking cookies is as fun as eating them.
Being with my family is as fun as building a snowman.

Ty'lia Stewart, Grade 4
Wickersham Elementary School

Grandparents Are:

The people you can go to if you need a buck or two.
The people who look after you when your parents are away.
The people you can go to if you need advice.
The parents of your parents.
The people that love me.

Brian Dadio, Grade 6
Moravian Academy Middle School

Stars

Shine all day and night,
Takes all the people's eyes when they look up,
Art is the same thing when you look up,
Runs all day and night,
Starts catching on fire at night.

Steven Passodelis, Grade 5
Foster Elementary School

Music

Music is like peace that you hear,
It smells like flowers,
It tastes like a devilishly, chocolate cake,
It sounds like birds in spring,
It feels like butterflies in your stomach
It lives everywhere!

Gabbi Frask, Grade 6
St Jude School

From the View of Summer

Summer
Green, orange, hot, peaceful
Sibling of the moon and stars

Lover of…
People surfing at the beach,
Kids tubing in the river,
Ice pops melting in the sun

Who feels…
Energetic in June,
Lonely when summer comes to an end,
Sorrowful in September

Who fears…
Temperatures dropping,
Leaves changing colors,
Summer time passing by

Who would like to see…
More beach balls in the air,
More kids at amusement parks,
More bright stars at night

Resident of the seasons
Summer

Samantha Ciccarelli, Grade 5
Pocopson Elementary School

The Beautiful Sun

That wonderful light,
It shines on me so bright.
The watcher of the world,
The amazing magnificent pearl!

The guide shines in my eyes
Like a flashlight in disguise.
The earth needs its light,
Bright giver, show your might!

Tell your story
About the days you were in your glory.
Tell about the beginning of time.
When you, the sun, were in your prime.

Share your happiness
Share your gladness
And share your light throughout the world!
To every boy and every girl!

The new world wants your shine.
Make it bright and make it mine!
Make the earth know you are here,
For every generation, you will appear!

Victoria Michalenko, Grade 6
St James School

The Sandy Beach

Sprinkle, squish between my toes,
The smell of the ocean to my nose.
I can feel each grain of sand,
It falls from air to my hand.
The shells I find close to shore,
Picked up by birds that fly and soar.
I walk all the way to the end of the land,
The land that holds the beautiful sand.

Katlyn Kossar, Grade 6
Bellmar Middle School

It's Winter

Snow on the buildings
Snow on the trees
It's winter! It's winter!
There is a cold breeze
The sky is blue
What will we do?
Make snowballs or sled
Oh, what will we do?

Diederik Schlingemann, Grade 4
Falk Laboratory School

I'll Be Back

It is now the season of Christmas
I hope you will miss us
I won't be here on Christmas day
'Cause I'll be celebrating it far away
So please don't cry
I'll be back on time
And I won't leave
When it's New Year's Eve

Alayne Ann Canezal, Grade 4
Middle Smithfield Elementary School

Bright

Stars so bright, twinkle in the night
The full moon so bright
The sun rose brighter than the moon
The sunset is coming soon
My mom's eyes remind me of stars
Thunder lights the sky with blue
The lights in my house are bright
Which reminds me of the moon.

Justin Benjamin, Grade 4
Middle Smithfield Elementary School

Apples

A mazing smooth sphere
P erfect tasty butter
P lump pie in the oven
L ots of sweet cider
E xcellent dumplings
S weet and crisp

Leah Gahles, Grade 4
Fairview Elementary School

The Amazing Athlete

Lake Effect pranced into the ring
The crowd clapped, clapped and clapped
As soon as they heard the bell ding
It got extremely quiet

Under the fluorescent bright lights
All you can see is the graceful athlete
Galloping to the first jump in the night
You could hear his hooves lifting from the sand (whoosh whoosh)

Then you see the gray horse
Jumping over a huge six foot jump, then continuing around the course
Soaring over each jump with his knees tight

He flew over the last jump like a kite flying through the sky
When he landed the crowd roared in applause — In the middle of July
He won the biggest show ever

As Lake Effect came back in for the prize
The crowd screamed in excitement, everyone was so surprised
That the trophy was fifty-feet tall

When he started the victory gallop
The crown clapped, clapped, clapped
He was saying thank you
By lifting his ears and watching the crowd

Lili Milano, Grade 6
Eden Hall Upper Elementary School

Winter

December brings snow
That settles on the ground
In piles that grow and grow each day.
December brings smiles
And presents for kids
And heavy coats.
January brings snowmen and igloos
Snowball fights, sledding down steep hills,
Fun and joy;
The sound of kids laughing,
A fluffy, white blanket covering the ground
Until the kids come out to play in the snow
But when it turns to night, a blanket of white snow
Covers the Earth.
Each day that blanket gets bigger.
The thing you see most are people shoveling the snow to make a snow hill.
If you look very closely you can see snowflakes falling from the sky.
February: the snow might melt;
Snowflakes don't fall as much
Because it's getting farther from Christmas,
but it is still very cold outside.

Jacob Strehle, Grade 4
Aston Elementary School

School

School is not a jail cell, it is a place where children learn
You wait until you're called on, so you can have a turn
Many peers surround you saying, "Hi" and "How do you do?"
There are some that are different, and some are very much like you
You read chapter books and novels
Filled with mystery and suspense
You write in 99 cent note books, creating paragraphs so intense
You visit the library with thousands of books on shelves
In art class you make sculptures of creatures and yourself
In math class you stare at the clock as time goes by
Solving equation after equation some involving the math term pi
At the end of the day you aboard your bus
Wondering why in the morning you made such a big, long fuss!

Lauren Kaminski, Grade 6
Hopewell Memorial Jr High School

Summer

Days get longer as patience gets shorter.
The school year is coming to an end.
Finally, yo soy libre!
You can do what ever you want!
You can go to the park or the pool.
But when it's too hot, you've got to stay cool.
The heat is so intense!
But wait, it's getting cooler.
What once was wonderful is now boring.
There is nothing to do.
Finally, school begins.
But the cycle will soon start again!

Logan Gutchess, Grade 6
Ross Elementary School

The Holocaust

It was a terrible time when Jewish people
died all because of one guy named Hitler.
He made everyone hate the Jews.
The Nazis sent Jews to camps
that they said were fun but they lied.
Some got poison gas poured on them,
others were starved.
Some hid and lived.
Others hid but got caught and died.
For the Jews that lived they finally got saved,
but we'll never forget
the Holocaust.

Arielle Cornelius, Grade 6
Nazareth Area Intermediate School

Grandma Is...

The best gingerbread cookie maker in the world.
The best chicken owner.
The person who gets a lot of DVDs for me.
The person who took me to Valley Forge.
One of the hosts of *Edstock*.

Clayton Sanborn, Grade 6
Moravian Academy Middle School

Imagine

As I walk by the river,
Hearing it grieve.
As the world turns slowly,
Slowly as can be.
I never thought that rivers could talk,
At least not in the human language,
It makes you think and daydream of things
That can never be...

Sophie Wirfel, Grade 5
Foster Elementary School

The Holidays

I see a man buying fancy attire,
Stockings are hung above us while we sit by the fire.
I feel the heat as I drink my hot cocoa,
It is so good; I think I'll go loco.
The snow outside is a glistening white,
While the moon is shining all over the night.
The wreath is hung on the door,
I wish this night could go on much more.

Jamey Napoleon, Grade 5
Foster Elementary School

Weekdays

Sunday is when the sun shines bright.
Monday is when the clouds are pearl white.
Tuesday is when it pours down rain.
Wednesday is when sadness flows down the drain.
Thursday is when happiness blooms like a bouquet.
Friday is when students shout hooray.
Saturday is when kids have fun.
My telling of the weekdays, is done.

Shania Lipinski, Grade 6
Bellmar Middle School

Winter

Winter time is almost here,
It is my favorite time of year.
There is snow all around,
Just lying still on the ground.
Water freezing into ice,
Outside looks like a snowy paradise.
Snowflakes dance at a cool breeze blow,
The sun shines on them for a bright snowy glow.

Samuel McCreary, Grade 6
Bellmar Middle School

Time

As I look at the clock it goes tick tock,
I wait and wait for that annoying sound to stop.
But then I realize time keeps going and going,
Even if I feel like slowing.
Now the sound begins to feel soothing,
And I finally concentrate on what I am doing.

Alexandra Trimber, Grade 6
Hopewell Memorial Jr High School

Rough Tough Guy

There once was a guy that was tough.
He always liked to play rough.
He got in trouble,
So he ran double,
His hands ended up in a cuff!

Nora Kogan, Grade 5
Foster Elementary School

Holiday

The night that Hanukkah started
And the presents were being guarded
We play the dradle
That was at the table
And after the night we parted

Jack Weiner, Grade 6
Moravian Academy Middle School

Christmas Cookies

Christmas cookies are so sweet
They're not hard for us to eat.
To choose a few
Is hard to do
Especially when they're such a treat.

Henry Vorosmarti, Grade 6
Moravian Academy Middle School

Santa

His suit is made of red fluff,
He could really use some earmuffs.
Santa is here,
But I have a fear
Of fat guys giving me stuff.

Sarah Kudzin, Grade 6
Moravian Academy Middle School

Snowflakes

Snowflakes
Winter wonder
Dancing and twirling
White as a feather floating down
Crystals

Luke Ippolito, Grade 4
Fairview Elementary School

Grandparents Are

A loving comfort at the end of the day.
The smell of cookies fresh baked.
Nice, caring, awesome, and amazing.
The feeling of warmth in my heart.
The best in the world.

Lauren Gerber, Grade 6
Moravian Academy Middle School

Jacques Yves Cousteau

Jacques Cousteau was on the cover of *Time* magazine
For being the National Geographic Nominee.
He was born in 1910 and died in '97
The last year of his life was his 87th
Invented an underwater breathing devised he called the Aqua-Lung.
Oh, it was so much fun.
He had so many titles for his name,
A French naval officer, innovator, scientist and much the same.
Helped remove mines from the Red Sea after the war.
Sailed a ship named "Calypso" from the shore.
Was a gunnery officer in WWII
This means heavy guns, Pew Pew!
He was a sickly child
His change of being healthy was more than a mile
Although expelled once from school for being misbehaved
It didn't stop him from addressing the first World Oceanic Congress before his grave.

Chase Sakers, Grade 5
Interboro GATE Program

Rainbow of Nature

If I were blue,
I would be the calm peaceful ocean in the warm summer day.
If I were green,
I would be the color-changing leaves in the fall.
If I were red,
I would be an apple on a tree waiting for fall to come so I can be picked.
If I were white,
I would be the snow falling from the clouds.
If I were purple,
I would be lavender growing in the grass.
If I were pink,
I would be a tulip blooming in the spring.
If I were black,
I would be the blacktop sizzling in the hot sun.
If I were orange,
I would be a leaf falling from the tree.

Juliana Ehnot, Grade 5
Holy Child Academy

Sammy the Seahorse

Sammy the Seahorse was king of the sea.
He ruled all the fishes in the deep blue sea.
One day came swimming a little sea star.
He said to Sammy, "Hey, you over there, come see my all stars."

The little sea star took him through the coral.
Then they came through the doors into a room filled with floral.
There in the corner were five little fishes,
And they played their horns like nobody's business.

Sammy the Seahorse now loves jazz music.
"Thanks, sea star," said Sammy. "Call me and we'll picnic."
They got together the following week
"Thanks, Little sea star." "You're welcome, Sammy, but call me Zeke."

Megan Rager, Grade 4
St Andrew's School

Jeffrey the Dragon
Jeffrey, the dragon was running around
In the field just chasing a butterfly.
When he heard a buzzing sound,
Then he suddenly made a loud cry!

The dragon's breath was hot.
It burned down a parking lot!
I wonder what the cause might be.
Jeffrey was stung by bumblebees!
Jon Catarroja, Grade 4
Middle Smithfield Elementary School

I See a Heart
I see a heart
with my mom and my dad on it.
And the heart is
pushing them together.
I hope they get married again
so I can have some food and cake
at the wedding
because they are not living together
because they got into an argument.
Semaj Edwards, Grade 4
Wissahickon Charter School

Dreams
Although some are scary
Dreams will never break me
They're like a million streams singing
Or butterflies skipping over the water
My dreams will make me sway
And dance on the treetops
I love the night
Because my dreams come alive
With miraculous joy
Keeley Maloney, Grade 6
Bellmar Middle School

Times Square/New York
Times Square
crowded, impressive
breathtaking, fascinating, interesting
go there!
New York
Opemipo Esan, Grade 5
Trinity East Elementary School

My Grandparents Are
Family Christmas Eve hosts.
Always having me over.
Glad when they watch me play tennis.
Always making me laugh.
Kind to everyone they know.
Two of my best friends.
Bailey Hancharik, Grade 6
Moravian Academy Middle School

Thanking
On one day
out of all the days
in the year,
we celebrate Thanksgiving.
We thank this country
for giving us a chance
at a better life.
We thank each other.
We laugh, we talk.
We reminisce.
Jack Girel Mats, Grade 5
Falk Laboratory School

Me!
Arabella
In am funny, pretty, talkative
I am daughter of Linda and Douglas
I love movies, Justin Bieber, singing
I feel relaxed about summer
Who needs food, cell phone, and a car
Who gives, love, care, handshakes
Who'd like to see Justin Bieber
A student of Miss. Tadlock
Bella boo
Arabella Albino, Grade 4
Wickersham Elementary School

That Feeling
I feel drops down my cheeks
As I try to wipe them away with my hand
But more is coming I feel it again
All the feelings are going through my head
As I put it on my dad's shoulder
He squeezes me tight
Says, "It's all right."
But I feel my heart sink down to my belly
As I sit down and say, "It's okay."
I just hate that feeling.
Sarah Bolt, Grade 4
Jefferson Elementary School

All About Me!
Smart, loud, nice
Sister of Savanna
Who loves my mom, sister, and dad
Who needs food, friends, and family
Who gives hugs, smiles, and high fives
Who feels happy about Christmas
Who'd like to see Paris, and Disneyland
Who dreams of becoming a baker
A student of Miss Tadlock
Serenity Milner
Serenity Milner, Grade 4
Wickersham Elementary School

Vacation Sensation
Lake Placid's the place to be
Whenever on vacation.
My family rents an island
That's like a new creation.

We all get together,
Mostly from Dad's side.
We'll stay with one another,
And at the end, divide.

We all unpack our things,
And put them in a boat,
A boat too small for everything,
But okay for three trips afloat.

We step onto the island,
And I breathe the freshest air.
I run up to the rented house,
And choose my room, fair and square.

This vacation's already over,
And I'm bummed, I won't deny.
Stepping sadly off the island
I look back and say, "Goodbye."
Hannah Master, Grade 5
The American Academy

Ripples, Ripples
Ripples, ripples in the pond,
And the frogs croak all day long,
This sound of which I am so fond,
Hear all of nature sing its song.

Birdies, birdies, in the trees,
Baby chipmunks by my feet,
Buzzing little yellow bees
Geese flying by in a v-shaped fleet.

Oak tree, oak tree, strong and tall,
Growing high touching the sky.
Home to animals, big and small
Helping all to live their life.

Happy, happy life is here,
Bright, beautiful colors all around.
Life is always free of fear
And you are free to run, leap and bound.

Ripples, ripples in the pond,
And the frogs croak all day long.
This sound of which I am so fond,
Hear all of nature sing its song.
Lucy Stone, Grade 6
Dorseyville Middle School

Football

Here in Pittsburgh it's a bright and sunny day,
And our favorite football team is here to play.

At the snap of the ball,
Here comes the defense they're like a brick wall.

When the third down comes on the football lawn,
Our offense keeps the chains moving on.

With all my heart I love my Steelers nation,
Just sitting in the stands what a wonderful sensation.

Warm or cold the fans are here ready to cheer,
In hopes of another Super Bowl year.

Anthony Guy, Grade 6
St James School

Friday Night

You can hear the cheers from the fans on Friday night
You see passes thrown from left to right
The coaches barking plays
The feeling of being hype all day
Hearing that crushing hit
Then at half time listening to the band play the last bit
The referees throwing the yellow flags
Or throwing those blue bags
The scoring of a long touchdown
The cleats tearing up the muddy ground
The home team couldn't win
Time to throw the playoffs into the bin
Then you think what just happened today
Friday night is the best time to play.

Marcus Tigner, Grade 6
Hopewell Memorial Jr High School

If I Were a Color...

If I were red,
I would be a beautiful rose,
If I were blue,
I would be a sky with a breathtaking sunset.
If I were green,
I would be a tree blowing in the wind.
If I were gray,
I would be a little squirrel scurrying around looking for acorns.
If I were brown,
I would be the soil on the ground for you to walk on.
If I were orange,
I would be the leaves changing colors.
If I were pink,
I would be a pretty little flower being picked.

Cartier Thomas, Grade 5
Holy Child Academy

Snoopy

You are my favorite cartoon,
You always come on at noon.
You are one of a kind,
And hard to find.
Your name is Snoopy,
You are very loud and whoopee.
Snoopy is funny and always happy.
If he gets mad he is a little snappy.
He lives in a little red house,
And is as nice as a mouse.
Snoopy is black and white.
Who never likes to fight.
His owner is Charlie Brown.
When Snoopy sees him he jumps up and down.

Caitlyn Trombley, Grade 6
Bellmar Middle School

War

Destroying land, breaking families,
Touching, murdering, sacrificing
Everyone is sad, everyone is scared,
Then hope arises, across the air,
BOOM! Shot down, people cry,
They are just trying to help!
BOOM! It comes down again, people go down,
CRASH! Planes go down; no one makes it out,
Soldiers are going down like marionettes,
It is a disaster, everyone cries,
People visit the graveyard,
They load it with bright flowers,
Tears streak down everyone's faces,
This is war to me.

Faith Kisker, Grade 5
Foster Elementary School

Fall

Children gathering candy
Well isn't that dandy
Halloween
I like that stuff

Hearing the leaves crunch under your feet
Then hearing someone call out and say, "it's time to eat"
Autumn
I like that stuff

People carving pumpkins
People dressing up as country bumpkins
Halloween
I like that stuff

Mark Duttenhofer, Grade 5
Pocopson Elementary School

Too Beautiful
We struggled out of the car,
after a long, long trip.
I got a glass of water,
and took a long, long sip.

We dashed to the elegant hotel,
with chandeliers as big as my body.
I grabbed my suitcase,
and sprinted out of the lobby.

We skedaddled to the elevator,
with an oversized grin on my face.
I pressed the up button on the wall,
to take us to our fancy place.

We took off when we reached our stop,
and we all ran to the right door.
I paused to look out the window,
to see a sight I could not ignore.

It was too beautiful.
Kanon Ciarrocchi, Grade 4
Ithan Elementary School

Friends
I don't have many friends
Instead I'm alone all day
I'm alone January to December
I do have one friend
But I cannot see him
For he is only imaginary
I go to a boring school
Where they all make fun of me
I went home crying
But my friend comforts me
I fought dragons and monsters with him
I went to the arcade with him
I did almost everything with him
I had a snowball fight with him
We watched movies
He was always there for me
But now I'm older
I have tons of friends
So I don't need him anymore
But I miss him
I wish he was still here.
Ian McGough, Grade 5
Winchester-Thurston School

Snowflakes
Wintery scene
Dancing in the cold wind
Twirling gently in the night sky
Freezing
Eden Roush, Grade 4
Fairview Elementary School

Christmas
Santa is coming
With lots of cheer
He will bring presents
So forget the tears

Christmas is a time to have fun
With family and friends
Memories to last a lifetime
I never want it to end
Victoria Perez, Grade 4
Middle Smithfield Elementary School

Halloween Party
Jack o lanterns gleaming bright
People laughing all the night
Mice began to scurry for fun
Then black cats started to run

Pumpkins smiling as people are carving
Boy I am starving
Witches and their brooms alight
For it's no longer Halloween Night
Emily Whyte, Grade 4
Burgettstown Elementary Center

Christmas
I like the upcoming holiday,
my grandma will come and stay.
She will bring some Dutch food,
which puts me in a good mood.

The snow is white,
we go for a sleigh ride.
The Christmas tree is green,
it is the finest I have ever seen.
Angus R. Vandersluis, Grade 4
Middle Smithfield Elementary School

Beautiful Sea
The sea glistening
in the early morning sun.
The sound of whale song
fills the sea with harmony.
Tide breaks — morning turns to night.
Jordan Barnett, Grade 6
Trinity Middle School

Apples
A mazing tasty sauce
P erfectly produced butter
P ies puffed perfectly
L ots of toppings
E xcellent fruit to eat
S tars included
McKenna Wass, Grade 4
Fairview Elementary School

His Family Is Gone
On a boat
A gloomy night
The other boat was out of sight
He and his sister start to fight
The father was distracted
It was too late when he saw the light
The boat came out of nowhere
They all froze in fear
Knowing the end was near
Their life flashed before their eyes
And no one could hear their cries
When he awoke he was all alone
Without a family or a home
Neil Hews, Grade 6
Interboro GATE Program

Grandpa Alexander
Grandpa Alexander
Every time
I hear a sad song
I think of you
I wish you were still alive
You did not get to see
my little sister Samia
she's 4 years old
she's getting tall
she wants to see
you for the first time
and I
want to see you again.
Rashard Douglas, Grade 4
Wissahickon Charter School

Snow
A bright white color
coming from the sky
and when it falls
on your hand
it is as light as air

The snow is falling
everywhere
making
people happy
every year
every month
every day
Arielle Kirkland, Grade 4
Wissahickon Charter School

My Puppies
My puppies go free
In the heavy summer rain,
Now they're filled with glee!
Madison Tournay, Grade 5
Burgettstown Elementary Center

Bald Eagles

Bald eagles are awesome!
They're fast, they're smart.
Every time I see one it looks like a dart.

Bald eagles are spectacular!
They're powerful and strong.
A bald eagle's wingspan is as
wide as a whale is long.

Bald eagles are majestic, marvelous,
and mighty.
Their eyesight is so keen
they can see a rabbit
three miles in the woods.

Whoosh! Bang! Slam!
The eagle sweeps down for its
favorite meal.
Ryan Stoltzfus, Grade 6
Linville Hill Mennonite School

Basketball

It's about shooting balls in to the hoop
taking the ball to the other side
taking the ball from the other team

It's about drinking water on the side
having a fun time
never giving up

It's about working together
having sportsmanship
to see if the ball will go in the hoop

It's about trying really hard to win
thinking of the game plan
to get very exiting

It's about competing with other teams
Basketball
Satvik Garapati, Grade 5
Pocopson Elementary School

Numerous Numbers

One of me
Two parents who love me
Three cats in the living room
Four pets in the house
Five fingers and toes on my body
Six jewelry boxes in my bedroom
Seven pairs of shoes sitting in my closet
Eight or more best friends
Nine windows around the house
Ten teachers throughout my grades
Ashley Hercik, Grade 5
Clearview Elementary School

Sports

Trying to get a first down
Then I get a touchdown
Football
I like that stuff

Aiming for the hole
Next thing I get a goal
Lacrosse
I like that stuff

Bam
I get a grand slam
Baseball
I like that stuff

Going to the hoop
Next thing I get a swoop
Basketball
I like that stuff

Skating down the rink
I need to think
Hockey
I like that stuff
Christian Garrison, Grade 5
Pocopson Elementary School

I'm No Monkey!

I thought I was a monkey,
Swinging from the trees,
Hanging from the branches,
Swaying in the breeze.

So I tried a tricky stunt:
Swinging to the ground.
But my monkey ways had left me
When I landed; that I found.

I fell hard on my left arm.
I screamed and then I howled.
I wished I were a monkey then.
I yelled and yelled out loud.

Friends helped me to the step
And tied a sling on me
That's when I realized, then and there,
I'd never a monkey be.

My words go out to monkeys,
Who like to swirl and twirl:
Maybe you're not a monkey,
But just a little girl.
Lena Harnish, Grade 5
The American Academy

Pat the Parrot

Pat the Parrot
Peeked outside
He is very truthful
He has never lied.
He told me there
Was something out there,
But when I looked,
Everything was bare.

That sneaky little squirrel
Was taunting him so,
That little squirrel
Was so low.
Then as he laughed
He ran away.
Pat never saw him
Until the next day.
Cody Shorts, Grade 4
St Andrew's School

Mike the Monkey

Mike the Monkey
Likes to climb trees
In the wild jungle
Where there are many bees.
Mike the Monkey
Bumped a bird's nest.
They both fell in the water,
And he belly-flopped on his chest.

Mike the Monkey
Came to a waterfall.
With the bee's nest on top of him,
He felt tall.
Mike grabbed the bird's nest
And held it tightly.
An elephant on the bank
Rescued them from the deep sea.
Hans Esteban, Grade 4
St Andrew's School

Tasteful Music

As I taste the music I hear…
Sweet b flats
Taste as if they are gumdrops covered in
Sugar
High pitch notes are as if they were
Caramel balls
Melting in your mouth
Sharps are as if they are
Kisses cut up
Low notes slowly dancing
On your tongue
I taste this music and I love it!
Madison Erin Bartone, Grade 5
Lincoln Elementary School

Guinea Pig

Sharp nails scratch the hardwood floors.
Sweat drips out of the tiny pores.

Moving slowly,
He catches the mini soccer ball with his paws.

He pushes it back.
It goes into the Dixie cup,
And he scores!

The stuffed animals silently go wild.

And he's back in the game.
He kicks and aims,
And it hits the post.

But then, his paw hits the ball,
Strait towards the Dixie cup,
And he adds one to the score paper!

And the stuffing filled animals stare in awe.

And that wins the game.
The ball bursts into a striking flame.
There is confetti everywhere.
The championships have been won!

He comes home with ten-inch tall trophy.
It is as high as a sky scraper.

Maddi Malik, Grade 6
Eden Hall Upper Elementary School

Diabetes

When I was a baby, very, very little,
I ended up at the hospital with quite a riddle.
They looked me over, ran some tests,
They said there were no pests.
My mom wouldn't give them a rest
Until she knew they were doing their best.
From their detection,
I had an infection.
For this was not true,
They did not have a clue.
When they figured it out,
My parents were sure to pout,
That I do not doubt.
I have diabetes,
It is not a breeze,
It's a chronic disease,
But I handle it with ease.
It is a blessing from above,
Made of love.
It taught me responsibility,
Not fragility

Courtney Vitale, Grade 6
Bellmar Middle School

Thanksgiving

Turkey, gravy, stuffing galore
I can't take waiting anymore!
The yummy foods from end to end
Seeming to make the table bend,
Is anywhere an end!
The family gathering makes me happy
I choose to sit next to my pappy
We laugh at jokes people are telling,
It seems to me everyone's yelling!
Thanksgiving is such a nice thing
That everyone starts to sing
The evening ends and everyone's gone home
I start to feel a little alone
But everything's all right
So I'm going to bed goodnight!

Haley Gault, Grade 6
Hopewell Memorial Jr High School

George

A mouse, a mouse is running my house
Chasing me around my room
I hate this mouse
It chews my clothes,
It gnaws my shoes,
And leaves little surprises all around my room.
It's driving me nuts!
Call the exterminator!
Get out the mouse traps!
Now I have to disinfect my room!
But when I look again,
He's rather cute
I think I'll keep him as a pet
And guess what?
His new name is George!

Layla Denny, Grade 6
Hopewell Memorial Jr High School

Never Forgotten*

We cry, we laugh, but we never forget,
The things we remember are always legit,
Even though we say every day, it's great,
It's not when you have a secret fate,
When it's a rainy day, I think of you,
Even when the sky is gray, I'll think it's blue,
I've never seen you mad,
So it makes me glad,
Though it is a glum day,
I will think of you in a happy way,
His family tries their best,
Without crying to take the ultimate test,
As you can see it's a hard time for this family,
You will always be in our hearts Lee!

Shannon Beech, Grade 6
Hopewell Memorial Jr High School
In loving memory of Lee Marki

Grandparents Are

A bowl of warm popcorn.
Newly mowed grass.
A brightly colored painting.
The kitchen smell of silver-dollar pancakes.
Some freshly baked apple pie.
Leah Bruckno, Grade 6
Moravian Academy Middle School

Bravery

As I slowly walk to the light
That God is guiding me to heaven
It is just so bright, but I am brave
To leave my home forever.
Katie Pituch, Grade 4
Jefferson Elementary School

Song

A song glides softly through the breeze,
Rustling about, in the trees.
Leaves fall down, with great ease.
The song is coming from birds and bees.
Zoë Thorpe, Grade 4
Jefferson Elementary School

Wind

Wind blowing softly
How curiously it goes
Searching
for a home.
Nicholas Kramer, Grade 4
Jefferson Elementary School

Night Sky

The night sky is not just a thing.
It's a desire, a light, a question.
A symbol to be free.
It shows life!
Isabella Friedrich, Grade 4
Jefferson Elementary School

Snowflakes

Bursting with joy
Fluttering and spinning
Freezing and wonderfully white
Crystals
R. J. Groscost, Grade 4
Fairview Elementary School

Periwinkle

Periwinkle is…
As pale as the sky
Is paler than a flower
As light as a cloud
Rose Genstein, Grade 4
Jefferson Elementary School

What a Dream

As I lay in bed, all tired and gloomy, I hear a loud crash outside
I look out my window to see what I hear, and then comes a big water tide

I run to my basement to get all the supplies
As a giant monster tree falls before my eyes

My basement is ruined, I'm a watery mess
I'd better hurry before my mom gets upset

I run outside before I get killed and notice high MPH winds
People are running and screaming real loud, like a vampire is coming up from behind

The trees start to tumble all over the ground
The waves all crashing is a very piercing sound

I run to my neighbors before the storm gets worse
But when I trip and fall there's no doctor or nurse

My neighbor is already in her hurricane den
I crawl in with them before all happens again

The waves are so big they're laughing at us
Because we're all scared, they think we're putting on a fuss

The lightning strikes, BOOM, leaving a big crack
It ended in silence as the sky turned black

My eyes open up — I'm in my room
What just happened…I guess it was a dream, I assume
Maddie Hudak, Grade 6
Eden Hall Upper Elementary School

I Am From

I am from my family that I love and adore.
I am from science, fishing, and more.
I am from my dogs who run around and swim all day.
And they're always ready to go out and play.
I am from my cat who loves me and begs me for food.
I love her even if she's in a bad mood.
I am from the beach where the sand is hot.
I catch hermit crabs. I catch a lot!
I am from Legos where I build every day.
It is fun because you can build any way.
I am from soccer where I run through the fresh cut grass.
Even though it is fun you may get a scratch.
I am from golf when I hit the ball with a lot of power.
I want to play good in only an hour.
I am from friends that are very kind and fun.
We always like to play and run.
I am from animals, like hedgehogs that are small.
I even like animals that are big and tall.
I am from Harry Potter when they got to Hogwarts and learn to teleport.
And vanquish Lord Voldemort.
I am from writing books that hook people on. When I write I try to make it fun!
Alex Voight-Shelley, Grade 4
State College Friends School

Snowflakes

Gorgeous blankets
Twisting and twirling
As light as a feather
Freezing
Bryttany Miles, Grade 4
Fairview Elementary School

Snowflakes

So beautiful
Twirling in the night sky
Dancing in the whispering wind
White lace
Kailee Lucas, Grade 4
Fairview Elementary School

Snowflakes

Different shapes
Bursting with happiness
Making the bare trees beautiful
White dream
Brianna Pardini, Grade 4
Fairview Elementary School

Snowflakes

Winter wonder
Catching them on my tongue
Light as a feather floating down
Crystals
Zachary Altenbaugh, Grade 4
Fairview Elementary School

Snowflakes

So beautiful
Dancing in the cold wind
Delicate as a spring flower
Freezing
James Sellers, Grade 4
Fairview Elementary School

Snowflakes

Gorgeous bushes
White as a silver bell
Dancing with the whispering wind
Freezing
Harley Varavette, Grade 4
Fairview Elementary School

Winter

Winter is coming,
Leaves on the ground,
Animals humming,
Storing food all around.
Carly Koppenhaver, Grade 4
St Joseph School

Red

Red is the liquid that comes out of your body when you get a cut,
Red is fierce, painful and gets what it wants,
Red never gives up because it is strong and never backs down from a fight
Red is the smell of apple pie when it comes out of the oven,
Red is the cinnamon that is baked in all those delicious baked goods
Red is the smell of the apple cider cookies
that are fresh from the kitchen, crunch, crunch, crunch
Red are the sirens you hear when cars slide off the road
Red is the voice of a tasty candy cane calling your name,
saying come eat me I'm sugary sweet
please come eat me.
Red is the is the footsteps you hear when you're sleeping
Red is the sound of Ho, ho, ho!
James Mack, Grade 4
Aston Elementary School

The Sky

You're beautiful like an ocean in the air.
When I look at you I feel love.
I see you and it's heart-warming like watching a sunset on an ice cold day.
You're so pretty I think of birds hopping through the flowers.
You open me up to a bright new world.
It's amazing, creative, and fun as friends, but you're the only friend I have now.
I think of you as enchanted, a miracle of God.
I think I know you but really you're mysterious.
When I'm indoors I sob because I can't see you and I'm lonely.
Sometimes I wonder if you're looking at me when I'm looking at you.
You're the coolest person I know, but you're not really a person.
You're the sky.
Trevor Leong, Grade 5
Winchester-Thurston School

Feeding the Homeless

Why are there so many people
homeless and hungry in the world?
Feeding the homeless makes you feel great.
It is very sad because of all the people who are hungry and cold.
When you're feeding the homeless you get to see the smiles on their faces.
Feeding the homeless makes you feel good about what you're doing for them.
The homeless appreciate getting fed.
I am very grateful for the homeless getting to eat.
There are many people in the world who are homeless.
It makes me feel bad to see all of their sad faces.
Feeding the homeless is a very sad thing
Taylor Cooper, Grade 6
Bellmar Middle School

If Fall Could Be

If fall could be a color, it would be orange, as orange as a big round pumpkin.
If fall could be a taste, it would taste just like Thanksgiving turkey.
If fall could be a smell, it would smell just like pumpkin pie.
If fall could be a sound, it would be people laughing.
If fall could be a feeling, it would be warm or calm.
If fall could be an animal, it would be a deer.
Keri Kern, Grade 5
Clearview Elementary School

The Four Seasons

Fall is one of the brisk seasons
Much shorter are the days
Why do I love this season?
It holds my birthday.
Winter has the most holidays
So cold and long are the nights
The snow is as still as paper
Except when we have snowball fights.
Spring is the season I regret
For I am allergic to pollen
And there is so much rain
For winter harmony has fallen.
Summer is the season of fun
Camp, no school, and pools
But don't get used to it;
Next is the season of ghouls
These are the four seasons
Winter, spring, summer, and fall
And all these seasons are bound
To an eternal ball.

Andrew Fingeret, Grade 5
Winchester-Thurston School

Friendship

Friendship—
It can rust without hope,
Or even trust.
Friendship—
Best friend,
Hopefully till the end.
Friendship—
Great memories,
Bad fight.
Now again we are tight.
This has happened before,
But now once more.
Friendship—
As it begins,
Again, again.
I hope it will last,
Again like in the past.
Friendship—
It shall begin
Again, again.

Jenna Kutcy, Grade 6
Bellmar Middle School

School

S chool offers opportunities to
C hildren of all ages.
H elping children learn is
O ne thing schools do well.
O ptimistic teachers help kids
L ove to learn.

Connor Coyle, Grade 4
St Joseph School

The Winter Secret

Footprints lead
to a snowbank
where children laugh and play.
As the winter mist blows in their faces
they don't mind one bit
because
they are too focused on their creation.
As they build and build
the project just stays as still as a rock.
Once the creation is done,
they jump with excitement.
After that they get a little chilly.
They go inside.
They look out the window.
"There it is," they say.
"This was an awesome day."

Meg Brennan, Grade 4
Cynwyd School

Young Man

The young man goes to school every day,
Completing his childhood.
He's unaware he'll have to pay
Nothing ahead looks good.

The young man waits at home all the time
For his parents to return.
He's patient for the bells to chime
What is ahead is a permanent burn.

The young man seeks an occupation
Looking around the town
He realizes people's generation
He takes a turn from his frown.
He realizes happiness and joy
He has transformed into a new boy.

Cole Hebert, Grade 6
Interboro GATE Program

Turkey

Turkey! That enticing aroma
when it's cooking that makes
you lick your
lips and
can't
wait to
eat it,
that juicy, buttery, wonderful
taste that leaves you wanting
more and more
of the
tender, moist,
glistening food
called Turkey.

Jessica Axelson, Grade 5
Falk Laboratory School

Petey

As I threw the stick
For him to go and fetch,
His eyes gleamed with hope
To show he did his best.
As he ran away,
His fur like a field of wheat,
He ran gracefully
Like a gazelle, eyes elite.
His eyes were like chocolate truffles
As I watched, all else was muffled.
All his glory glistened,
I will always miss him.

Charlie Tiberio, Grade 5
Winchester-Thurston School

The Joy of the New Year

Bottles popping on the night
of the New Year.

Purple grapes snap in my mouth.
Confetti booming all around the room.

Sparkling cider sizzles
in its glass.

The wonderful celebration
comes to an end when
the clock strikes twelve.

Madeline Reisinger, Grade 4
Lincoln Elementary School

The Falcon

Searching for its prey.
Sitting silently;
Eyes alert, and keen
Feathers are ruffled,
In the quiet breeze
Perched atop the grand oak tree.
Waiting;
And waiting.
Then suddenly it cries out!
Lifts its mighty wings and flies away:
Talons glistening in the sunlight;
Sparkling with each flap of its wings.

Grace LaCarte, Grade 6
Bellmar Middle School

Apples

A dmired pies I love
P erfect juice
P leasing butter
L ingering aroma
E xcellent cinnamon dumplings
S weet and tangy cider

Amber Reese, Grade 4
Fairview Elementary School

Swimming

Goggles, diving, jumping
Breaststroke, freestyle, butterfly, backstroke
Relay, meets, flip turns and streamline
Timers, stopwatches, splashes
Chlorine, water, Speedo
Swim caps, lane ropes, splashes
1st place, 2nd place, 3rd place
Hand league, head league, hand league to head league
Cheering, touchpad, flags
Ribbons, trophies, medals
Splashing, starter, bubbles
Diving board, benches
Kicking, strokes, learning
Pushing, grabbing, touching
Breathing, moving, starting

Blake Camerlin, Grade 4
St Alexis School

Being a Great Dancer

Jumping, tiptoeing, and even tapping.
Sliding oh how much fun dancing is!
You do all those things in dance.
There is ballet, tap, baton, hip-hop, tumbling, and jazz.
There are so many things to do.
There are so many things to choose.
I like dancing and you will too.
You can go to shows.
You can show your family.
You can show your friends.
You can show anyone you know.
When you do baton you can get hurt.
When you do tap you can slip.
When you do ballet you can get a cramp.
But you always know you have dance.

Catherine Cieszynski, Grade 4
St Alexis School

Kittens

Kittens are cute and playful,
jumpy and exciting!
I've never seen kittens with mittens,
but we've all been with kittens smitten!
Furry, fluffy, kittens full of love
as they meow and purr!
One minute they're as fierce as black thunder,
the next they're as sweet as cotton candy!
They're just too cute as they sleep in the sun
and tumble around in the grass.
The mother cat washes each tiny face.
I run towards the playful kittens.
I tumble down with them on the ground
and hold them tightly in my lap
and then freely let them go.

Brooklyn Stoltzfus, Grade 6
Linville Hill Mennonite School

Sweet Sweet, Treat Treat

Friday I went to a candy store.
There were gummies, sours and sweets galore!
I wandered down the fragrant rows.
There were lots of presents tied with bows.

I whizzed right past the sugar-free aisle;
Those candies really are not worthwhile.
Slowly I walked through the gummy section,
Wanting a collection of my favorite confection.

When I saw a fifty-dollar, chocolate turkey,
I told my mom, "Thanksgiving would be more perky."
As I ambled through the candy store,
I wanted all the candy—and then some more.

I thought I heard the back door close.
Would I have to stay all night and doze?
The lights went dim—
Was I locked in?

That's okay, more candy for me,
Locked in a candy store, what a place to be.
My mom tapped my shoulder, "It's time to go."
My dream over, all I could do was scream, "No!"

Laura Null, Grade 4
The American Academy

Noah's Grand Ark

There once was a man,
Noah was his name.
He brought lots of animals,
Two were the same.

He made the big ship by hand
With some wood and bark.
He saved all animals
And named the ship "Noah's Ark."

There were bunnies, puppies, and kittens,
There were roosters that cock-a-doodle-doo.
There were lions that ruled the jungle;
There were hamsters, guinea pigs, and gnus.

Frightful animals such as snakes, tigers, and bats
Along with scary squirrels and crocodiles
Massive spiders and dirty roaches,
There were freaky animals for miles and miles

God told Noah to build the ark.
You'll never forget the story.
When Noah saved all the animals
With all his bravery and glory.

Mia Anthony, Grade 6
Holy Child Academy

Sadness

Sadness is an illness
that cannot be cured
by a doctor.

It is a bully.
To scare the bully
of sadness away,

you have to punch it,
push it, and turn it away —
Yell. Scream. Hit.

Sadness is a sweet, sweet dragon —
Pulp and seeds.
Horns and teeth.

Talons and beaks.
He spits and gnaws
at your happiness, and

hides in the part of your heart
called its throat.
Jaelyn Wingard, Grade 6
Springside Chestnut Hill Academy

Roller Coasters

Roller coasters are fast
I rode on a bunch
some go fast like a cheetah
chasing its mid day lunch
some are old and slow
and make a "crunch" noise
as you go up the giant
hill of the roller coaster you
can see the metal rail at
the top laughing at you
some are for little kids
that go slow and are silly for small kids
some go so fast it feels like
you are going 1 million miles per hour
some spin and make you
feel like you are going
to throw up your lunch
roller coasters are dark
and you do not know where you are going
I like roller coasters
there are so many different kinds
Ben Salas, Grade 6
Eden Hall Upper Elementary School

Pumpkins

Pumpkins are bright orange
They sit lonely in the grass
They are fat and round
Paul Fulciniti, Grade 5
Burgettstown Elementary Center

Glue

I twist the cap.
I flip it over.
I squeeze it.
squeeze only air,
only air, only air.
I flip it up.
I look in the hole
is it clogged?…No.
I flip it back over
I shake I squeeze
over and over
one last squeeze
sigh finally!
slowly but surely
it comes out…
paper white
sap sticky
it oozes out
onto my paper.
Madison Stonebraker, Grade 6
Hopewell Memorial Jr High School

Swimming

I am on the block,
as happy as can be,
Like I am about to dive,
in the deep blue sea

I hear the whistle
so clear as I dive,
Off the block with,
every sort of glee

I swim and I swim,
and I try not to grin,
As I did the freestyle back,
with an easy first place lead,

I was so proud
I felt ten feet tall,
My parents knew that I would succeed,
that I'd win it all.
Kathryn Tague, Grade 4
Ithan Elementary School

Fall Is Here

Leaves are orange and red,
Some big wild flowers too,
I walk on the tracks full of leaves,
Following the big green trees,
I see many parts of yellow grass,
In the fields with many tracks,
The cold air starts to come,
Now I know that I must now run.
Shane Smykal, Grade 6
Pennridge North Middle School

Disney World

I went to Disney World
To all four parks.
We came at midnight
On the map we made a lot of marks.

I saw the castle
In line was such a hassle.
Then I saw Mickey Mouse,
So we went to his house.

I went to animal kingdom tree,
I felt so happy.
Saw lot of animals
Why aren't there any camels?

My family went to Epcot
We parked in the lot.
I saw the Epcot ball
I want to see it all.
Elisabeth De la Cruz, Grade 4
Middle Smithfield Elementary School

The Foul Shot

She stood there waiting,
the ball in her hand.
She had practiced this shot,
it should work like she planned.

But this was different,
it was the moment of fame.
She had only one chance,
to win the big game.

The score was tied,
time had run out.
This was the moment,
that practice was all about.

The crowd rose to their feet,
No one wanted to blink,
She released the ball,
And…what do you think?
Jacqueline Slinkard, Grade 4
Ithan Elementary School

Children

C hildren are always:
H appy
I maginative
L oving
D reaming
R unning and playing
E nergetic
N ice to everyone they meet
Haley Salus, Grade 4
St Joseph School

Misfortune

Stricken, battered, sad,
The big game you didn't win,
A second place race.
Everything feels empty, yet,
It will be all right again.

Gianna Vitelli, Grade 6
Sacred Heart School

Pen

pen
permanent, black
writing, sketching, drying
my teachers don't approve
ink

Sam Halulko, Grade 5
Trinity East Elementary School

White

White looks like cream.
White sounds like white sharks.
White feels like thin paper.
White tastes like the white milk I drink.
White smells like vanilla.

Devon West, Grade 5
Clearview Elementary School

Dog

There once was a dog
who loved to sit on a log.
The log got damp,
so the dog got a lamp
and then he started to blog.

Emily Nolen, Grade 5
Indian Lane Elementary School

Sick

There once was a girl named Jill
One day she found she was ill
She sat in her bed
With ice packs on her head
And to get better she took a pill

Erick Wade, Grade 5
Indian Lane Elementary School

Best Friends

There once was a girl named Tori
She played with her best friend Lori
They laid on the grass
Till it made a rash
And that's the end of my story

Phoebe Vella, Grade 5
Nether Providence Elementary School

The Experience of the Hurtful Tornado

Playing with my friends is the best of times.
We decided to play a game that was about making rhymes.
Then we saw a cloud, that was big and black and scary,
it reminded me of a big scary fairy.

The sky turned green, like the color of the grass,
pretty soon our windows would be shattered glass.
My mom called us in, before it was too late, even though it was already past eight.

I looked outside and saw a funnel falling form the sky,
now it would be easy for baby birds to fly.
The funnel started to touch the ground, the big clouds were turning all around.

It seemed as the funnel was saying, "I am big and scary,"
It's possible the funnel's name was Scary.
The winds blew really hard, making trees fall, now there is danger to all.

Now the funnel turned into a hurtful twister,
it reminded me of my screaming sister.
I heard loud bangs outside of my house, BANG!
It looked as if the tornado had fangs.

The winds started to calm, like flags flapping in the breeze,
now we are all very pleased.
The deep, dreadful, danger is gone,
Now the tornado is probably in Tucson.

Molly Kane, Grade 6
Eden Hall Upper Elementary School

Football

The quarterback says, "Hike" and I run for the football — we are at the 5-yard line
Linebacker sacked the quarterback, I go past the defensemen
I go past the linebacker, the quarterback runs 15-yards
We are down at the 20-yard line
The quarterback throws the ball and it was an incomplete pass
It is 4th down — we are in trouble
The quarterback throws the ball and I miss it
I'm running as fast as a cheetah —
The defensemen is right on my tail
I sack off the defensemen and I try to catch the ball
The defensemen tackles me before I can catch it
The ref calls a penalty on the defensemen
It is 1st down — Our team cheers
The ref told our coach "That's a warning"
The quarterback says, "Hike" and I run as hard as I possibly can
The quarterback throws it up and I catch it
I run for a touchdown — I go past everyone in my way
When I got my touchdown I did my victory dance
The crowd was so happy and amazed
It was such an awesome catch — our team was so happy
We won 49 to 28

Tyler Elliott, Grade 6
Eden Hall Upper Elementary School

Basketball

Basketball is really fun
But you'll surely have to run
So come on, I will tell you where
And show up – if you dare.
Taylor Hans, Grade 5
Burgettstown Elementary Center

Ghosts!

Ghosts fly in the sky.
They fly very high!
The ghosts say "Boo!!"
When they are coming after you.
Athena Mariano, Grade 4
Burgettstown Elementary Center

Frost

Frost covers the grass
Like a twinkling carpet,
Crunching as I stroll.
Scott Ferris, Grade 5
Burgettstown Elementary Center

Cold Fall Winds

Leaves swirling gently
around and around again.
Cold fall winds are here.
Emma Gragan, Grade 5
Burgettstown Elementary Center

Window

Dark nights, sunny days
I see everything through you
Clear pane in a frame.
Tesla Nicodem, Grade 6
Latrobe Elementary School

Sports Rule

Soccer is awesome!
Baseball and basketball rule!
Football is cool too!
Victoria Vieira, Grade 5
Nether Providence Elementary School

Fall Is Here

Air getting colder
leaves changing colors, pretty
leaves fall, trees are bare
Ally Nadzam, Grade 4
St Joseph School

All About Animals

Animals are cute
Sometimes they can be wild
They are furry, too!
Kylie O'Mara, Grade 4
St Anselm Elementary School

Gold

Gold is knock, knock, knocking on your door. You will soon discover that gold is
Cheerful, loud, and fierce; lucky like a leprechaun.
Gold is like a nonstop bowling ball: it climbs trees and races around the block.
In fall, gold is warm cheesecake and sticky honey buns.
In the camp, I smell the bonfire a mile away
I see gold trophies on the shelf.
In the winter it is a brand new sleigh. I sled down the hill with joy, faster than lightning.
Jingle, jingle I hear Santa's golden bells and his eight tiny reindeer,
Five golden rings from a friend I wear on the school bus,
"I'm the mother of yellow, the cousin of silver; we do everything together."
Golden sunshine shining in the spring morning makes your garden bloom just right
Golden birds are near, so are bees making honey; butterflies are dancing around the garden.
In summer, gold is blinking fireflies, flying and fluttering in the moonlight sky,
A shiny golden new ride at the amusement park,
White sugar on top of a golden funnel cake and crunchy fries a seagull takes,
A sandy beach and a wavy blue ocean,
A cool glass of lemonade you sold at the lemonade stand,
Kettle corn in a big, bad bag the size of a Ferris wheel.
Oh, I love gold.
Savannah McCoy, Grade 4
Aston Elementary School

Never Forget

The first day the Nazi soldiers took me, my mom, and my sister to the concentration camp.
Never forget.
When the Nazi soldiers were cruel to us when we got there.
Never forget.
When the Nazis took us to the death camp and we fought for our lives.
Never forget.
The day they killed my mom.
Never forget.
They day it was our turn to be sent to the showers.
Never forget.
When we were forced to go in that shower.
Never forget.
The day I got saved by the American soldiers.
Never forget.
The day I almost died.
Never forget the Holocaust.
Melissa Samson, Grade 6
Nazareth Area Intermediate School

I Survived

Life was normal until the dreadful morning
We looked outside and I saw the Nazis coming
They rounded us up and shipped us off without the simplest warning
They put us in camps, many were killed, only a few survived
Finally one day we were freed by the United States troops
But they were too late
Almost all of us were killed, three survived
After we were freed there was no place to go
Our homes had been destroyed
We could have prevented this all
If we would've stopped that man full of hate
Thomas Meeh, Grade 6
Nazareth Area Intermediate School

Butterfly

Wings so fragile
in patterns so neat
seeing you flying
is my special treat
bumble bees, ladybugs, caterpillars too
they all gape when they see you
I love you and you love me
butterfly, butterfly
so special to see!

Ayva Lacoco, Grade 5
St Theresa School

Best Friend

My friend, my friend;
she's so nice.
We love to play
and we both like rice.
We dance, sing, jump and laugh;
I will never forget her backyard path.
We have good times with each other.
She's just like her mother.
Both are nice and caring.

Meredith Kelly, Grade 5
St Theresa School

The Season of Fall

As I sped down the bustling hall,
I hurriedly slipped on my winter shawl.
Because it is my favorite season of all,
The chilly, colorful, wonderful fall.

Outside while we jump in the leaves,
We dance about the maple trees.
As I leap off a rock with ease,
I trip and skin both of my knees.

Shannon Glodowski, Grade 6
Pennridge North Middle School

My Family Loves Me

When I think of love,
I think of my family,
They love me so much,
And they mean the whole world to me,
And I will always love them.

Clare Marchese, Grade 6
Sacred Heart School

Christmas Lights

Christmas, Christmas, Christmas lights
Always such a beautiful sight!
Colorful lights red, blue, yellow, and green
Shine so bright upon the Christmas trees.
Glittering, glistening, dazzling lights,
Twinkling above on Christmas night.

Alex Bayer, Grade 4
Ithan Elementary School

Zucchini

You look like a house phone when it rings in the night.
On the inside you look like a tree stump when it's cut down with the pretty rings in and out.
When I peel you it sounds like me sliding down my hill on a snowy day.
When I chop you it sounds like a monkey banging a nail into a board.
You feel like soaking wet hair after coming out of the shower.
Or a slippery snail after it rains.
You smell like peppermint on Christmas morning.
Your taste is like steamed carrots coming out of the microwave on Thanksgiving.
Tell me, why do you trick us with your sneaky looks?

Karysa Karas, Grade 5
Reiffton School

Kiwi

On the outside, you look like a very hairy watermelon.
And you feel like a grown man's back before he shaves.
When I peel you, you sound like my pencil in a sharpener.
When I slice you, you sound like an apple getting squished by an angry baboon.
Inside, you look like a gleaming sun with seagulls in a green sky.
And you feel like my dog right when he comes out of the salty ocean.
You smell like an apple dancing with a cucumber on a rainy day.
You taste like a sour apple on a nice summer day.
Tell me, why are you as green as the fresh cut grass?

Jordan Groves, Grade 5
Reiffton School

Kiwi

You look like a hairy bouncy ball.
On the inside you look like a star shining at the night.
When I peel you, you sound like an apple being cut.
You smell like an old apple being made into applesauce on a hot day.
You are fuzzy like the hair that stands up on my arm after being shocked.
When I slice you, you sound like a silent night.
You taste like a lime on a boring day.
Tell me what season do you grow in?

Curtis Waltemyer, Grade 5
Reiffton School

Lemon

You look like a giant gum ball just waiting to be eaten by a little kid.
You feel like a bumpy road after a tornado.
When I slice you, you sound like a potato being ripped from the mud at the end of fall.
Inside you look like a watery reflection from the ocean on the first day of summer.
When I feel you, you feel like the bottom of a pool at the end of summer.
You smell like a sour patch kid in a crinkled bag.
You taste like a slimy slug coming out of the mud after it had rained.
Why are you so yellow like the sun after nighttime?

Chelsea Ramirez, Grade 5
Reiffton School

Snowflakes

So beautiful
Gleaming in the sky
Dancing in the whispering wind
Unique

Brennden Dixon, Grade 4
Fairview Elementary School

Layers

Above the rich leaves of autumn
buckwhite-colored snow lays
but below the leaves lie
the cool grass of summer

Samara Steinfeld, Grade 4
Lincoln Elementary School

Bowling

My favorite sport is bowling.
My Scooby Doo ball goes down the lane rolling.
It rolls and rolls
How many will fall?
Two, four, seven, or all?
The ball hits the pins; what did I get?
Oh, no! I get a baby split!
Next frame is better; I still have a pair.
I throw my ball and get a spare.
The next frame is the best,
And all the pins fall for me.
"A strike! A strike!" I'm so happy!
Now all ten frames are done.
That was so much fun!

Kyle Ferguson, Grade 4
St John Neumann Regional Academy - Elementary Campus

Christmas Tree

Christmas tree filled up with lights.
It brings happiness throughout the house.
Spinning in circles,
It reveals all the pretty ornaments.
Homemade ornaments and store bought ones are all around.
It has a beautiful skirt underneath.
Everyone stops to admire the pretty tree.
A star is on top shining so brightly.
All different kinds of ribbon fill up the branches.
It sits next to the fireplace with great joy.
The tree reminds everyone of Christmas time.
It sits sparkling with light and greatness.
The tree makes me happy.
I think it is a great symbol of Christmas.

Nina Jesko, Grade 6
Bellmar Middle School

School

School has just started and I am very sad,
It is time to get out pencil and pad.

My homework has already been turned in late,
If I keep this up my grades won't be great.

It is so low of them to make us study,
I wish I was sick and had an understudy.

Lunch seems to be the best part of my day,
I love the smell of delicious food on my lunch tray.

The bell soon rings and it is back to class,
It is time for a test, boy I hope I pass.

Michael DeFilippo, Grade 6
St James School

Hate

That four letter word was all that started it
The word that was heard all around started it
It started because of Hitler
All because of that old stickler
It was stuck in the children's minds
The people thought it was all just fine
The adults assumed it was good
To hate the Jewish, to give them no food
The Jewish people were killed in gas chambers
And making the others do impossible labors
While the survivors were beaten as they yelped
Then the Americans came and helped
But now the Holocaust is over
We are all glad it is over

Kara Carsey, Grade 6
Nazareth Area Intermediate School

Lemon

On the outside you look like a yellow baseball
ready to be thrown during a game.
You feel like a slippery water slide at a park.
When I slice you, you sound like a screechy cardboard box
being cut open by a knife.
Inside you look like
a bright yellow light that just got turned on,
like a slimy half-moon.
You feel like a slimy sponge that has just been used.
You smell like lemon Pledge
that has just been sprayed on a table.
You taste like bitter, sour, slimy glue.
Tell me lemon, why do you taste so bitter,
and why do you look like a slimy half moon?

Harrison Strunack, Grade 5
Reiffton School

Camps

People brought in by the thousands.
Tattered clothes no food or water.
Put to work the screams of pain.
Fear in faces all around.
Sweat and tears wet the ground.
People dying all around.
The only sound you hear and sight you'll see
is the plan of Hitler's perfect race.
Putting fear into the faces
of all the people in the Jewish race.
Gassing, starving, sickness too.
No one cared but everyone knew.
The victims did not know what do to.
Bystanders did but nothing too.

Ashley Borgo, Grade 6
Nazareth Area Intermediate School

Halloween

Creepy and cold
Spooky and sweet
Weird and wacky
Halloween
I like that stuff

Ghost and goblins
Witches and warlocks
Skeletons and scarecrows
Clowns and cats
Halloween costumes
I like that stuff

Sweet and sour
Hot and cold
Halloween candy
I like that stuff

Erin Towler, Grade 5
Pocopson Elementary School

Summer

Summer
Warm, exciting, special, and bright
Daughter of the sun
Lover of sandy beaches, smiles
Colorful kayaks
Who feels merry in May,
Awesome in August
Scared in September
Who fears falling leaves, being forgotten
Losing memories forever
Who would like to see…
More people having a good time
More sunny skies and
Lemonade stands
Resident of the Milky Way
Summer

Noa Driver, Grade 5
Pocopson Elementary School

If Fall Could

If fall could be a color
it would be yellow:
as bright as the sun.
If fall could be a taste
it would taste just like cinnamon buns.
If fall could be a smell,
it would smell like pumpkin pie.
If fall could be a sound
it would be a lullaby.
If fall could be a feeling
it would be slow
If fall could be an animal
it would be a doe.

Charles Szymanski III, Grade 5
Clearview Elementary School

Fall

I love fall!
The crisp cool air
Bright colorful leaves
Floating down from trees
Red, orange, brown
Leaves crunchy underfoot

Fall is awesome!
Thanksgiving arrives
Mom makes pleasant pumpkin pies
Outside you help pick
Perfect plump pumpkins

Fall is fabulous!
The puppies are as
playful as little colts
Frolicking in the leaves
Yip, yap, yowl

Fall is an amazing season
Created by God
Returning glory to the Creator

Katelyn Smoker, Grade 6
Linville Hill Mennonite School

Snow

Snow is falling from the sky.
My oh my
In the light it glistens,
Just listen.
Do you hear a peep?
Not me,
All I see,
Is winter creeping upon us.

Jordan Muirhead, Grade 6
Bellmar Middle School

Imagination

Knights and castles
aren't the only ones.
Soaring unicorns
get tossed in the air.
Tossed in a rainbow.
Escape from real.
No limits.
No boundaries.
Let your
imagination fly,
sugar smooth.
Go free.
Go far.
Just let go!
Taste it, smell it, see it.
Your imagination.

Camille Traczek, Grade 6
Ross Elementary School

Flowers Are Good Presents

Flowers smell so sweet.
On your birthday they're a lovely treat.
They come in all sorts of colors.
It's a very nice gift even for mothers.
They come in many sizes and scents,
They sometimes climb your fence.
They fill your heart with cheer.
They're something no one will fear.
Flowers make good presents.
They look nice in any residence.

Keelie Selvoski, Grade 6
Bellmar Middle School

Baking

Cookies, cakes, breads, pies
That's where my heart lies
Chocolate, vanilla, and marble cake
I can't pick my favorite to make!
The buzzer goes beep when it's done
Oh baking is so much fun!
Baking always makes me feel calm
I always bake with my mom
Baking is such a fun thing to do
I think you should try it too!

Rylie Campbell, Grade 6
Bellmar Middle School

Christmas in NYC

Looking at the gorgeous wreaths,
walking among crowded streets.
Central Park's gigantic tree,
gold garland just for me.
Towering buildings up above,
generous family that I love.
Sweet merry Christmas carols,
angels sing "Hark the Herald."
New York's amazing sights,
whizzing by on sleigh rides.

Lauren Gaertner, Grade 5
St. Sebastian Elementary School

The Theater

In the theater the lights go down
Everyone is quiet not making a sound
Drinks and popcorn by your side;
People whispering like telling lies
Everybody's waiting for the show;
Wondering how long before we go.
The movie starts to begin
Everyone smiling with a grin,
The movie projects on the screen,
Before you know it's time to leave!

Katelyn Benicky, Grade 6
Bellmar Middle School

Dance

It's about twisting and turning
stretching and bending
jumping and leaping

It's about long night hours
costumes with flowers
graceful with power

It's about stage lights shining
cheering and crying
feeling like flying

It's about ballet tap
jazz hip hop
modern and point

It's about feet and arms
happiness and charm
risk of harm

It's about dreaming and feeling
like no one is watching
wondering and thinking

It's about dance
Lilleth Snavely, Grade 5
Pocopson Elementary School

Hamsters

I love hamsters!
Hamsters are very small,
But it is good because
I wouldn't want mine tall.

Hamsters are
cuddly creatures,
and friendly, fuzzy
fur balls.

Hamsters are very busy.
They work and work
Until they get dizzy.

Screech! Screech!
Hamsters love to
run in their screechy wheel
because they
want to work off a
good meal.

Hamsters are the best pets
you can get!
I really like them
For my pet!
Kirsten Good, Grade 6
Linville Hill Mennonite School

All About Me

I'm cool, silly and bad
I have a sister
I'm a daughter
I love basketball, games, and math
I am funny
I need steak, ribs, and friends
I share food, toys, and games
I watch the regular show
I dream of basketball
My school's name is Wickersham
My nickname is Flacka
Liangelys Milanes, Grade 4
Wickersham Elementary School

Softball

Going up to bat,
My heart is racing.
Will I get a home run?
Gripping the bat,
My hands are sweaty,
As the ball is coming towards me
I hit it with a bang.
It flies through the air,
The crowd goes wild cheering my name.
It's a home run.
YES!!
Alexandria Sokol, Grade 6
Bellmar Middle School

Night

In the peaceful
darkness of the moonlight,
shadows walk upon
the grass.
Lights burn out,
candles shimmer as they
stand proudly to look
at the night sky which
will soon turn to
light and the candles
will burn out.
Annika Ohrman, Grade 4
Lincoln Elementary School

Pittsburgh Steelers

The Pittsburgh Steelers are seven and three.
They are the best team!!
They won eight AFC North games
They won Six Super Bowl games.
Their offense is incredible!
Their defense is unstoppable!
Big Ben is the best QB ever
Hines Ward is my favorite player
The Pittsburgh Steelers are unstoppable!!
Ashley Eley, Grade 6
Bellmar Middle School

White

White is
vanilla creamer and
icing that smells so, so good.
White tastes like eggnog,
And white chocolate
and tasty ice cream.
White looks like
rotted bones and
beautiful flowers that sing and
super stinky shoes that I need
to throw away.
White feels like
a soft, comfy pillow,
and a warm, fuzzy
blanket wrapped around you
and it is oh so cozy.
White looks like
ice that you slip, slide,
sadly across, then teases you.
White is when you are
so scared that you turn pale.
Joseph Shapiro, Grade 4
Aston Elementary School

Skateboard Riding

Skateboards have four wheels.
You fall down a lot.
It's hard on rocks.
You should wear a helmet.
It's hard the first time.
You can practice at skate parks.
There are different designs on them.
You can also have just colors.
It's a lot of fun.
You can wear special shoes.
They come in different sizes.
You can do jumps.
You can do flips.
You can go fast or slow.
You can get hurt.
You can't skate at the mall.
You can ride by yourself.
You can ride with friends.
You can ride on the sidewalk.
It's hard on grass.
Don't ride in the house.
Daniel Kilburg, Grade 4
St. Alexis School

Snowflakes

Melts in your hand
As soft as a sheep's wool
As white as a wedding dress
Gleeful
Tristan Pavkovich, Grade 4
Fairview Elementary School

Autumn

Leaves are crunching under foot
That is all I hear.
All the animals in the woods,
And all the pretty deer.

What a pleasant time
Is the autumn of twenty eleven.
It's not perfect . . .
But it's *almost* like heaven.

Fall is a time
When all the trees are dying.
But my mood is very happy
And I know that it's not lying.

Autumn is a sad time
For all the trees and plants.
But for humans it's a happy time
To celebrate and dance.

So what's my favorite season?
Spring, summer or winter? No, not at all!
It is beautiful, wonderful,
colorful Fall!
Christian Trowbridge, Grade 6
Assumption BVM School

Fall Fun!

The leaves are falling, the sun is
shining, fall is finally here!

Church bells are ringing, birds
are chirping, and kids are
singing their song.

Jumpin in leaves and climbing
trees till it's time for dinner.

Turkeys roasting, pie is baking
while we sip our hot cocoa
and chew our apples.

Festival is here, look a stuffed
bunny, playing and
winning games.

Holding bags filled with candy,
Snickers, Sweet Tarts
and more!

Fall is leaving
but it will be back next year.
Jocelyn Loehr, Grade 4
Worcester Elementary School

Peace, Love, and Happiness

If the world had peace,
The world would have no wars.
If the world had all love,
No guns would be fired
At brothers or sisters.
If the world had all happiness,
No one would ever despair,
Or feel sad.
If the world had peace,
Love and happiness,
Everything would be calm.
No one would fight,
Or feel worried about mothers or fathers,
Or brothers or sisters
Fighting for rights in a war.
Everyone would feel peaceful,
Loved and happy.
Madeleine Faure, Grade 5
Lincoln Elementary School

Cats

A cat is such a curious thing,
They treat themselves as if they're king.

Are you blowing me kisses when you blink?
I blow you kisses when I wink.

Why are your eyes always so intense?
Is it a sign of your defense?

You are always so cuddly and content,
Do you just love my wonderful scent?

Why do you always knead my bed?
Do you want to wreck the spread?

A cat is such a curious thing,
They treat themselves as if they're king.
Casey Steiner, Grade 5
Copper Beech Elementary School

Winter

December is ice hockey,
Snow,
Cold toes, and hands.
December is a white blanket of snow,
Snowboarding, and sledding.
January is hot chocolate
And warm blankets.
January is coldness — like ice —
And hibernation
February is the shortest month of the year.
February brings love,
Colds, and cards.
AJ Amicone, Grade 4
Aston Elementary School

Bullies

Bullies can be very cruel,
They act like they are super cool.
They do not listen to what teachers say,
They romp around the school hallway.

At first they tease,
And say mean things.
Then they punch, push
Kick, and shove.

Do not keep it all inside,
Do not run and try to hide.
Sit down on a bleacher,
And talk to a teacher.

Be nice,
Even though you'll never be friends.
Bullies are mean,
They are sick in the head.
Justin Cellucci, Grade 4
Ithan Elementary School

The Yankees Are Awesome!

The Yankees are awesome!
They're really fast.
No one can deny that
They last.

The Yankees are awesome!
Bang! Boom!
Around the bases,
They zoom.

The Yankees are awesome!
My favorite player is Jeter.
When he hits homers,
He's as hot as a heater.

The Yankees are awesome!
Granderson grabs a grand slam!
No one can stop him,
It's just the first pitch, BAM!
Colin King, Grade 6
Linville Hill Mennonite School

It All Started with One Man

It all started with one man
A man full of hatred
And just a four letter word
That four letter word started it all
That man's name is Adolf Hitler
That four letter word is hate
And Adolf Hitler is full of hate
He is the man who started the Holocaust
Mathew Sladek, Grade 6
Nazareth Area Intermediate School

Jane Swissvale

Born in Pittsburgh Dec. 6, 1815
And died in Swissvale, PA July 22, 1884
She encountered slavery
In Louisville, Kentucky
And wrote an autobiography called "Half a Century"
She wrote and spoke
On Lincoln's behalf
Believe me it doesn't make you laugh
She nursed over 182 wounded men
And they all lived and fought 'til the end
She moved to Minnesota
And then to Pennsylvania
Was strong-willed and fun
Her hair was long and so she wore it in a bun
She reigned as Saint Cloud's political boss
Wrote stories, poems, and articles about antislavery
For the Spirit of Liberty.

Kathryn Hickman, Grade 4
Interboro GATE Program

The Kiss

While our cheeks burn,
arms start to open, eyes shut, and lips meet
you kiss me or I kissed you
I don't know it happened so fast,
I didn't want it to end.
As the sunlight shines over the earth nothing matters
not even time
not even the air I breathe.
My heart starts pounding faster and faster by the minute.
I was made to kiss you.
My cheeks start to burn,
I open my eyes to get a quick glimpse at your cheeks,
they were red too.
Then it was over.
The kiss.
The kiss I have been waiting for all of my life.

Chyna Roger, Grade 6
Springside Chestnut Hill Academy

Cartoons

From the trouble caused by Bugs Bunny,
To Mr. Krabs' love for money,
Cartoons are not for buffoons,
From Tom and Jerry,
And a platypus named Perry,
Cartoons are also drawn,
The first cartoons were made in the 1920's
One of them was about a woodpecker named Woody,
Popeye will smoke his pipe,
While Bruce Wayne fights crime, known as The Dark Knight,
Then Superman will take flight,
Finn and Jake are also heroes, The Ice King is who they fight,
And now you know why cartoons are such a delight.

Jarrett Marks, Grade 5
Winchester-Thurston School

Been Gone too Long

He had left that one musky morning
I feared I would never hear from him
again He'd be in battle left to
right when snow would fall and Christmas
called all he would hear was bombs
ringing in his ears He knows that his little
daddy's girl was longing for someone to protect
her from the world but over seas and mountains
he was defending his own pride and joy his country
baked skin mighty thin is the way he called life for
twelve months He would be overjoyed to take a five
minute shower every three weeks short e-mails no
calls He mourned to see two tiny feet one day
the world changed when he walked off that plane

Lauren McCoy, Grade 6
Hopewell Memorial Jr High School

Unfortunate

On a gloomy, snowy night,
Spirits made a fright
They've come back to haunt people that knew the dead child
It wasn't because of him, but because of a driver who went wild

While walking, he went flying in the air
The careless driver just didn't even care
He was going to buy his mother a present
But it didn't end up to be that pleasant

While walking in the street
A speeding Volkswagen slipped on the sleet
Unfortunately killing the young kid
Only if the driver hadn't slid

Jacquelyn Dunleavy, Grade 6
Interboro GATE Program

My Fall Walk

The tiny bright flowers are in my sight.
I hear the birds "cheep, cheep" as they take flight.
As they get higher, higher and they gain height.
I think I have a poem set for the night.

As the sun's light hits my face.
I look around this beautiful place.
"Crunch, crunch" the leaves say as I pace.
As I pace away I see some birds in a race.

Garrett Larson, Grade 6
Pennridge North Middle School

Beach

B ig, beautiful waves
E ach day sunshine
A ll of the seagulls and sandpipers
C rabs scurrying in the sand
H ard shells carried in by the powerful waves

Blake Alexander, Grade 4
Burgettstown Elementary Center

A School Nurse Can Help You

A school nurse helps you when you are hurt. She'll bandage your knee if you fall in the dirt.
If you lose your tooth, she'll say, "Rinse your mouth out."
Because if you see blood, you are likely to shout.
Then, she'll give you a necklace or a case. It wouldn't be easy to take your tooth home in a vase.
She will be there most of time, unless she's eating her lunch.
But she'll come back fast if you need her a bunch.
If you cut yourself in art, she'll give you a Band Aid.
She'll get you back to class quickly so you can finish what you made.
If you get hurt in gym, she'll give you a pack of ice. You'll be back to see her if you have head lice.
If you fall on the playground and are scraped and bleeding, she'll bandage your knee.
You might even go see her if you get stung by a bee.
If your nose is bleeding, she'll tell you to squeeze at the top.
She'll also warn you not to run, jump, or hop.
She'll call your mom and you'll go home if you throw up in school.
I hope that doesn't happen because it's not cool.
Her job is to help kids if they get hurt, have a bad cough, or feel sick.
She helps you feel good and she tries to be quick.
She also checks your blood pressure, height, weight, and eyes.
She is always so sad when somebody cries.
She is nice, and I know that she cares. I can tell, because she shares.
Thank goodness we have a school nurse.

Katie Gant, Grade 6
Pennridge North Middle School

Holocaust

A simple life for a little Jewish girl, the parents' beaming eyes when she entered our scary world.
Little did they know that their happy life would change and maybe never be the same.
Years later, the girl barely even ten. She was taken away from her life and friends.
It was the day before the school play and she got the starring role.
She memorized her lines and was ready for the show.
But when she woke up the German soldiers were standing at her door.
They wanted to take her away from her safe, happy world.
"But tomorrow is the school play! I have to stay!"
"Pack one bag and we'll be on our way."
Tears rolling down her cheeks as she packed a bag.
Not knowing what would happen, she boarded a train.
As soon as she arrived she was thrown in a room.
No light, no food only the hope that she could go home.
They examined her two days later. They said she had lice and a disease called "typhus."
"I've never heard of typhus, what can I do?"
"Get in that shower and we'll get that lice off of you."
She died that day so did her family, it's sad to know that Hitler's plan went through.
You would just hope that people knew the right thing to do.

Mena Sawyer, Grade 6
Nazareth Area Intermediate School

I Am From

I am from the burning beach where sand sticks to the back of my shins
and I scratch for three days straight.
I am from my favorite cat Mia who snuggles with me when she knows I'm not feeling well.
I am from my home where I sip hot cider to warm me up during winter.
I am from my loving family who is always there when I need them.
I am from my adopted brother Jackson who my family took in from Haiti when he needed our help.
I am from my favorite holiday, Christmas, with a Christmas tree that has beautiful sparkling colors.

Lydia Crown, Grade 4
State College Friends School

The Present Mystery

The Christmas tree is up so high.
My mom says don't be shy.
Santa gives me a present.
The present will be pleasant.

I open the box.
What do I see?
A cute tiny elf.
Staring at me.
Miranda Ortega, Grade 4
Middle Smithfield Elementary School

Life

Life is like a game.
You have twist and turns,
Ups and downs.
Sometimes you have advantages.
Sometimes you run into problems.
We meet new people,
But they may not like us.
Live your life at your fullest.
As if you were to have it like you imagine.
Brooke Timko, Grade 6
Bellmar Middle School

Dark Cloud

I see the dark cloud
Way up in the sky very high
The birds aren't chirping
The trees are blowing
The park is empty
Here comes the rain
This weather is insane
The sun finally came out
Now no one can pout
Kinsey Johnston, Grade 6
Bellmar Middle School

I Love to Read

books
mysterious, unpredictable
interesting, exciting, fascinating
great covers pull you in
fiction
Ann Kozak, Grade 4
Trinity East Elementary School

A Whale with a Purpose

A whale swims throughout the sea
Visiting everyone mankind can see.
With a job he must do,
Discover oceans big and blue.
He will even visit me.
Must be a visionary.
Zachary Ecker, Grade 6
Trinity Middle School

Tomorrow Morning's Train*

I remember my friends, family all together
Our house filled with laughter
My life couldn't be any better
But now I'm sitting alone in a cold corner
On a train dreaming about where they're taking me
I hear huffing, puffing, chugging into camp
Then, I wake up to people being dragged out of the cattle cards
Loaded with people
Workers for the mills, Kapo for the ovens.
Holding on to their innocence
Embracing HOPE another 4-letter word.
Denying what is known,
Going right, left
Clinging to small hands.
Filling one upon another
Creeping forward
To an unknown fate, trembling, praying
The end will be soon.
Learning they will leave on
Tomorrow morning's train
Grasping at shallow hopes but tomorrow morning
Never comes for most people.
Luckily I got out, I was one of the few survivors of the Holocaust
But now all we can do is hope that more people lived through the Holocaust.
Ally Masel, Grade 6
Nazareth Area Intermediate School
A survivor's story!

Winter

December first brings the cold.
December sucks up all of the warmth and spreads the freezing cold weather to everybody.
December says to sit close to the fire; the furious wind whips you.
December brings Christmas, Santa, gifts, and presents.

December plays in snow, wearing mittens, heavy jackets, hats, and snow boots.
Many inches of snow touching your boots, feel your nose…cold.
See beautiful trees covered in snow, all white.

January, still wearing mittens and hats and everything to keep you warm.
January full of wonder, seeing all the cars covered in snow.
Sitting close to the fire so you are toasty warm.
Seeing kids playing in snow making snowmen.
Snowy days take school away.
Shouting kids yelling Yay!

February, still cold, but willing the warmness to come.
February now hearing the birds chirping, saying, "Welcome Back."
Trees bring their green leaves back, grass becoming green,
instead of brown and rough. Snow melting away.
February saying good bye to everything and see you next year!
Neeli Thakkar, Grade 4
Aston Elementary School

The Joy of Baseball
The yell of the crowd
The sound of the bat hitting the ball
A flat hit straight into the outfield
The crowd goes wild

The 7th inning stretch and the announcer is sketching
The batter is up and everything matters at this moment
The pitcher throws like he means it and
SMACK!

The crowd yells as the batter gets closer to home base
The catcher catches the ball and runs to the base
The batter slides and the catcher makes it to the base
The crowd goes silent and the umpire yells
SAFE!

The crowd went so wild that nobody could hear
The whole team came out and celebrated
Joy was going through the air like a windstorm
The other team was sad, but clapped for sportsmanship

Fireworks went off as a war
The grass of the field danced
The world was listening to everything
Max Campbell, Grade 6
Eden Hall Upper Elementary School

Dream Big
I trek a million miles up the fairway,
I thank the crowd for watching me at my side
I look at my ball 45 feet away in dismay,
I take my time.

I bend down and look at the break,
Over and over again and again
The sun setting at my back like in the morning when I awake,
I take my hat off to cool my head.

Every eye on me,
Watching my every move
My hand shacking and feet tingling because I'm tied for the lead,
I put the putter back and let it rip,

Clink!
The ball ran down the high hatred hill,
I look at the ball in admiration
It is on line with the cup like a board getting drilled,
It goes in?
I run to get the ball out of the cup with happiness
"Honey it is time to get up"
What?
Craig Kunkel, Grade 6
Eden Hall Upper Elementary School

Phillies
Doc Haliday does damage.
The fans are screaming,
As the ball park is gleaming.

Crack! Howard smashed that ball out of the park!
The homer was hit as far as a marathon.
The fans go racing to try to catch it.

The fans are waving their rally rags,
As Ryan Madson is closing it out.
Strike three! The batter is out like a light bulb.

The game is over. Time to celebrate!
The Phillies are going to the playoffs!
The Phillies are the best team ever!
Korey Stoltzfus, Grade 6
Linville Hill Mennonite School

The Lightbulb
When the sun sets in winter.
You flick a switch and there is immediate light.
It comes from the light bulb.
Created by Thomas Edison.
This is no small thing.
Glass.
Wire.
They are arranged perfectly.
Metal.
Conductor of electricity.
Lets the energy pass creating light.
This invention changed mankind.
It has been creating light for over 100 years.
Then you flick off the switch.
Jacob Lang, Grade 6
Bellmar Middle School

Soccer
It's half time and its five to five.
We walk onto the field to gain our positions.
The crowd is crazy but lazy too.
We have the ball in their zone like ice cream in its cone.

I took a shot that went high in the sky.
You hear the crowd quiet as a cricket.
You see the ball hit the net with seven seconds left.
My team was jumping everywhere like frogs in the air.

The coaches were screaming and my parents were beaming.
While we shouted the other team pouted.
We walked off the fields champions today.
I just hope next year won't delay.
Taylor Parrish, Grade 6
Hopewell Memorial Jr High School

Fluffy

I used to have a cute kitten named Fluffy.
She was my really cute, furry ball
with big, round eyes of ocean blue.
She left home, now I feel all alone.
She had a log home where she could always roam.
Fluffy always made cute little purrs and meows.
She slept soundly like a calm pond.
She was gray as a fierce thunderstorm.
Sometimes she was scared, sometimes playful.
I will never forget her sweet innocent face.
A cute ray of sunshine.
A cute little teddy bear.
Oh Fluffy, why did you leave me?

Amanda Zimmerman, Grade 6
Linville Hill Mennonite School

Seasons

Winter, spring, summer, fall
I think I like them all.
Winter cold with icy snow,
But I stay inside and warm my toes.
Spring is warm and sunny, too.
Birds chirp with the sky so blue.
Summer is warm yet fun.
With the everlasting sun.
Fall is when it starts to get cold,
And the chilly wind is getting bold.
So now you see why I like them all.
When we're done, the seasons start all over again
With winter, spring, summer, and fall

Danica Dong, Grade 6
Hopewell Memorial Jr High School

The Wind

Dancing gallantly through the barren trees,
Howling joyfully in such a ruckus,
The Wind arrives, and with it Fall,
All heralded by the small gentle breeze.

Darting like a bird, this way and that,
The frail woods are its plaything.
Rustling the colorful leaves and chilling our bones,
It strikes, as sudden as the midnight bat!

James Morrison, Grade 6
Pennridge North Middle School

Lemon

You are like a sun in the sky, all big and bright.
You feel like a bar of soap slipping and sliding around.
You sound like hard, crusty, baked bread being cut.
You look like a spider web on a wall.
You taste like a cry baby inside my mouth.
You smell like a scented candle that was just lit.
Why are you so sour?

Kaleen Borzillo, Grade 5
Reiffton School

Walking in a Winter Wonderland

I look out my window and think what is snow?
The way the wind makes it blow.
I always say I hate the cold.
I would rather play with a bowl of mold.
I do have to say the way the sun makes it shine.
The way it sparkles like the world is a crystal.
My friends make forts, snowballs, and more.
I would rather watch movies and eat popcorn galore.
I would drink my hot chocolate.
The warmth makes me enjoy it.
'Til my friends made me play.
It was only during the day.
We played games, made shapes, it was unique.
I was going crazy and acting like a freak!
I now love the cold snow.
The way it sparkles, the way it glows.
I was walking in a winter wonderland.

Maya Husni, Grade 5
Winchester-Thurston School

One Moment

I walk 80 miles after 7 days of torture,
bearing cuts and bruises from fighting to survive,
beneath a weeping willow, near a trickling stream I have arrived.
I quench my thirst
and soothe my wounds,
there is a meadow with a patch of flowers to relax in,
I feel a cool breeze draw near
as it whispers in my ear
the dreadful sound of anonymous fear.
This moment is okay,
this moment is all right,
then I feel a war coming near,
and I slip into the soil with one last tear.
On that day my soul was lifted,
on that day my soul was free,
but where this happened you cannot see,
for it was burned to ashes with war and agony.

Danika Moody, Grade 6
Neil Armstrong Middle School

Imagery of the Outside

What I am seeing is a flock of birds,
Suddenly on this fall day they multiply into thirds.
I can almost touch the balloons flying in the sky,
But yet I couldn't because they were far too high.
In this area I can absolutely taste the cool air,
I can taste it in this area almost everywhere.
Swoosh! Over there I can hear ducks floating upon the pond,
It attracted me to watch, the activity was fond.
Wow! I am smelling something almost like rain
I better get inside or it will be a pain.
Oh my, I used all my five senses today,
I will be in bed because it's the end of my day.

Molly Maley, Grade 6
Rice Elementary School

My Amazing and Slightly Historical U.S. Road Trip

On one amazing day I was born in Santiago,
then on another I moved to Omaha, then to Chicago
So it all started one day in Washington DC
Where Obama was standing there waiting for me.
Next, I walked the streets of beautiful Annapolis
Then I raced cars in Indianapolis
So after we head to Texas, from Dallas to Austin
and after we head north for baked beans in Boston
We hike through the cornfields of Des Moines, Iowa
and tanned at the sandy, hot beaches in Tampa Bay, Fla.
we visit the Statue of Liberty in gorgeous New York
where after we head to North Carolina to try some pulled pork
Then back to Florida, from Miami to Tallahassee
after a trip to Columbus, Albuquerque and Hawaii
Next to Mount Rushmore in South Dakota
then Minneapolis in beautiful Minnesota
From Phoenix to Detroit, to Memphis to Philadelphia
From Atlanta to Seattle, to Las Vegas to Louisiana
From Louisville to San Fran, from Denver to Alabama
From Houston to Salt Lake, I hope you liked all of my days
Though I loved St. Louis, I would marry LA.

Mark Kuzminski, Grade 6
Hopewell Memorial Jr High School

Green

Green is a young tree.
Green is the color of tomatoes when they are not yet ripe.
Green is a grasshopper.
Green is the color of many people's eyes.
Green is fresh summer grass.
Green is a Christmas color.
Green is the stem of a colorful flower.
Green is the smell of pine trees on the cool winter breeze.
Green is fresh cut grass and some leaves.
Green is the smell of fresh herbs being used in the kitchen.
Green is the smell of your mother cutting limes.
Green is a salad with ice cold lettuce.
Green is a juicy green apple.
Green is lime soda bubbling in your mouth.
Green is warm broccoli with a home cooked meal.
Green is a slimy slug on a mossy log.
Green is pointy cactus in the desert.
Green is how you feel when you're sick.
Green is running your fingers through a clover patch.
Green is thick, long crab grass stuck between your toes.
Green is the world.

Lindsay Ferguson, Grade 4
Aston Elementary School

Beautiful Snowflakes

There is a path of snowflakes left from the storm,
These beautiful snowflakes will leave when it's warm.
They're tiny and cute and they came from the sky,
Those beautiful snowflakes make me say "Oh my!"

Kaelyn McClain, Grade 4
Central Elementary School

Winter

Winter rides the sled down the big hill.
When he hits the bottom, Winter screams
Woo Hoo! That was awesome!!
Then Winter walks up the hill
and sees that the snow next to him is perfect.
Winter sees an ice rink;
Winter loves ice skating!
Winter sees kids and wants to play
Winter tries to talk to the kids,
but the kids can't hear;
All they can hear is the wind.
So the kids go sledding.
Icicles at the bottom of the hill
say "this is from Winter"
Then the kids heard Winter's voice
"It's Winter," he said.
The kids were amazed; they
told everyone they knew,
But the people did not believe them
So the kids took them to the place where Winter was.
Next thing you know, Winter blows away.

Johnny Eskridge, Grade 4
Aston Elementary School

Rip Curl

Thump, thump, thump
My heart beat quickens, as does my pace
I close my eyes for a second,
Letting the spray shower my face
And remember the shark as it came for me
Then I push up on my board
I ease my arm up for balance
A second later I am standing, letting pure joy evaporate my doubts
I snap the back of the board off my wave
And let the water enclose into a tunnel
This is what I want to be, this is what I want to feel,
Every day of my life
The light shines through the wave
I let my hand skim the surface of the wave
A gust of wind greets me as I explode from the rip curl
My family's smile blinds me
My best friend Alanna cheers with tearful happiness
I am Bethany Hamilton
I lost my arm to a shark,
But I wouldn't change what happened
Because I can surf again

Isabeau Newnam, Grade 5
Hillendale Elementary School

Nightfall

What are you supposed to do,
When you are being chased with a fright,
Whatever it is, it never leaves a clue.
There's no point in running, this is the dark of the night.

Nick DeEulio, Grade 5
Foster Elementary School

Christmas Morning

It's Christmas morning and I wake up in my bed.
I ran downstairs afraid that I would trip, fall, or hit my head.
There is so many presents that I'm excited,
I'm glad to see all of them I sighted.

I went to my mom and dad's room and jumped on their bed,
They woke up and whipped their head.
I opened my first present in a hurry,
My mom and dad went down in a scurry.

I opened my presents in a flash,
Clothes, shoes, and even cash.
I got movies, gift cards, CD's and more,
I got a lot of presents, that's for sure.

I was tired after opening all the presents,
But it was so pleasant.
As I still cheer,
It is the most wonderful time of the year.
Victoria Likovich, Grade 6
Hopewell Memorial Jr High School

It Rained for Forty Days and Nights

Ye Old Noah built an ark,
There were cats and rats and dogs — "bark bark!"
The animals came in twos,
Even the owls — "hoot hoot!"

It rained for forty days and nights,
Giving the small animals a little fright.
The animals came in all shapes and sizes,
It would be many days before the sun rises.

The ponies with their golden fur,
Wide open fields are what they prefer.
The unicorns were left behind,
But there were lions and tigers and bears — oh my!

God gave Noah a quest to complete,
He worked day and night with little sleep.
When Noah finally completed the quest,
Noah showed God his very best.
Maggie Browne, Grade 6
Holy Child Academy

Monsters

M any kids dress up as ugly monsters,
O n Halloween night you see a lot of ugly costumes,
N o one is at home,
S eeing everyone gives me ideas on what I'm going to be next year,
T reats are everywhere,
E ating treats is the best part of all,
R ed, orange and other colored trick or treat baskets,
S oon I will be eating candy.
Erica Hummel, Grade 5
Clearview Elementary School

Lacey's Dream

Hi, I'm Lacey! Who are you?
I love stories, you should too!

I'm having a dream that I want to come true,
Can you help me figure out what to do?

So when I dream here's what I see,
It's where ponies live and a princess with her king to be,

With chocolate covered mountains and vanilla ice cream,
Falling down rivers and though the streams,

Where I can be plain old me,
And every day I can sip some tea,

And know that you're still here with me,
And just with some sprinkles and chocolate ice cream,

That's how I have the perfect dream!
Karilyn Heinrich, Grade 4
Commonwealth Connections Academy

Noah's Zoo

The dam was about to break
All the animals were starting to wake.
Noah made an ark during light and dark
It turned out to be a huge ark.

Animals coming one by one
Making the journey under the sun.
Lions, tigers, and bears
Birds, monkeys, and hares.

Horses going "nay" and cows going "moo"
The ark is turning into a mad zoo.
From fish to birds
To elephants and buffalo herds.

The Earth was a mess
The ark turned out to be a huge success.
A lot happened that day
They were lucky Noah made the ark right away.
James Jardine, Grade 6
Holy Child Academy

Textbook

I open my book to thousands of words,
I think all this reading is kind of absurd.
The tests I'd stuffed in there were not my best,
Papers and papers along with the rest.
I start to think, "How important are books?"
I start to listen and take a look.
Learning about history, science, and math
They are all leading me down the right path.
Isabella Zuccaro, Grade 6
Hopewell Memorial Jr High School

Brother, Brother

Brother, brother you
are still
so little
so you won't understand
you are like a little angel
you talk like
a good boy and
you are my little
brother

That is not all
because you
are my baby of the world
That's the same thing my Mom
used to say to me
and you look just like me

You are still so little
you are like a little
strawberry covered
in chocolate

Basir Vann, Grade 4
Wissahickon Charter School

One Scary Night

It's a dark and scary night
and it's time for me to sleep,
but outside it seems so scary
I feel like I could weep;
I sit straight up in my bed
because I hear a sound,
I think it's getting closer
my heart begins to pound;
I hear a hoot, a snap, a creak,
I'm starting to get a fright,
I wish I hadn't grown up so fast
I would still have my night light;
I see a shadow of a hand
that's very long and thin,
It's beating on my window
and trying to get in;
I go to turn on the lights
and what do I see,
I was making all this fuss
over a stupid, little tree.

Hannah Barkman, Grade 6
Hopewell Memorial Jr High School

books

books
fun, exciting
laughing, gasping, staring
starting a new one
novels

Alison Spadaro, Grade 4
Trinity South Elementary School

Life

Life is good, life is bad
Life is happy, sometimes sad
Some people think life is short
Some people think life is long

But we are not sure
You can choose where to go
You can go up, or down
You have a choice what to do in life

You can be good, you can be bad
You can be happy, or sad
We are not sure that life will end tomorrow
But we are positive we will not last forever
But one thing will, our souls

Aaron Fry, Grade 4
Jefferson Elementary School

Rainbows

Rainbows
Fill us up with
Joy after the gray, sad,
Rain crashes down hard on the Earth.
Rainbows.

Rainbows
Help the clouds stop
Crying and fill the world up with
Color.

Rainbows
Fill up the world with warmth
After tears fill up the world with
Coldness.

Elena Lamberty, Grade 5
Falk Laboratory School

Football Is Fun

F ighting your way to the touchdown zone
O pen a space for you to run
O ne more touchdown and we are ahead
T ying the game 14 to 14
B ang! You get tackled!
A ll the people cheering you on
L eading the way
L ine backer scores a touchdown

I s that a touchdown? Yes, it is!
S ack the guy with the football

F un, we're winning the game!
U nknown who's going to win
N ow we celebrate! We won! We won!

Dustin Beiler, Grade 6
Linville Hill Mennonite School

Rain

Rain, the wonder of earth
It falls mercilessly
Never to say good-bye

It drips all along the cement
Placing a mystery for everyone
Day after day

Again, the wonders of the world
Falling from the sky
Leave us wondering
Wondering why

Kassidy Gibson, Grade 6
Hopewell Memorial Jr High School

Rascal

As fat he may seem
He is white in winter
And orange for Halloween
Can you guess it?
It's a cat
But he is much more than fat
He is lovable and friendly
But his name is not Henry
He is a seafood lover
And he loves one another
But he will learn that he is a rascal

Christopher Manko, Grade 6
Ross Elementary School

Fall

The leaves turn burgundy
Ash blonde and emerald
They tumble to the ground
In orderly fashion
Children in sweaters
Pants and sneakers
The days lack
The nights are lengthy
No longer warm
Fall is that time of year
When you wish for summer

Katie Reilly, Grade 6
Ross Elementary School

The Bus

Kids scream
others dream
The wheels screech
kids reach
The engine moans
a kid groans
Kids make paper planes
the bus roars across the plains

Mitchell Stry, Grade 6
Assumption BVM School

Ocean

I lay at the beach, with the wind in my hair reading a book without a care
I hear the wind calling my name, I sit there on the shore under a tree, as happy as can be.
I hear something, O how I wonder when I hear the thunder
I sit there thinking a storm is coming, I see an animal leap as I lay there on the beach
I feel the warm sand crumbling beneath my feet…as I hear a screech
It's coming closer, I can feel it now, and I see the dark thunder cloud
I run and hide without a thought, hoping I don't get lost
I trust my path without changing my mind, as I stop and look behind
I see a path, a place where I'd be safe…a little cave
I sit there for a million hours, waiting until the storms over…and then I see a lucky clover
I wish that the storm was over so I could get home and not be alone
And then it happened, my wish came true, I went somewhere I could not be blue, as the ocean

Breanna Maker, Grade 6
Eden Hall Upper Elementary School

I Am From

I am from my family where me and my cousins Adam, Danny, Paul, John, Leah, Kenny, Donny, and Lucy
run around and play, and Danny and I climb on climbing structures.
I am from my friends where me and Cole ice skate, make snow angels in our swimsuits,
and play with Nerf guns and laugh and laugh.
I am from my books that I read every day in the morning and the night, when it's dark and when it's light.
I am from my DSI, the toy I take on vacation, that I play and play until the power runs out.
Then I charge it up and play some more and you never will get bored.
I am from my hyped-up fur ball, Lance, the dog I like so much – in the summer.
he chases bubbles and in the winter it's snowballs, and that's what we do all year.
I am from sports, those miraculous sports, and my favorite one is baseball.
You swing and you hit or you swing and you miss, and if you hit you may get a base,
and that's why the game is called baseball.

Tim Durachko, Grade 4
State College Friends School

Day and Night

Day is when you hear the laughter of children playing on the gracious green grass.
Night is when the stars are all dancing gracefully in the mysterious star lit sky.
Day is when you hear the beautiful melody of birds singing in the sky while looking for food to feed on.
Night is when you see trees dancing in the crisp, cold wind.
Day is when clouds are as white as a ghost soaring in the luscious sky.
Night is when you smell the cool aroma of bonfires starting on the first day of winter.
Day is when the sun warms us with her delightful rays and beams.
Night is when the moon is peeking over the mountain, watching families laughing and having fun together on Christmas Eve.
Day is when people are watching the sun arise from her long evening nap.
Night is when you see nocturnal animals skittering through the forest for their harvest of food.
Day is when you hear the humming of bees sucking nectar from the beautifully colored flowers in a big spacious field of grass.
Night is when you hear the sound of coyotes talking to the moon in the booming wind.

Camryn Quaste, Grade 6
Pennridge North Middle School

We're All the Same

You know bad wars, fights, and so, but the worst one of all, it is so frightfully bad. When I explain, you will be so, so sad. The war started with a very bad man, he put together a very evil plan, because he wanted one race and would not understand that we were all the same. When you hear these words, you will be very sad, but not as sad as some people that were victims in camps. Because it all started with a very bad man that would not understand, that we were all the same. He didn't care about all of these people. He just sat in his chair, and looked at the screams of the soon to die people. He didn't care about other people's pain, he just wanted one race, because he was taught that they weren't the same, but they were.

Spencer Daugherty, Grade 6
Nazareth Area Intermediate School

Falling Leaves

Turn different colors,
Falling off different trees,
Raking them all up,
Fall off deciduous trees,
Brown, red, yellow, all colors.

Ally Kelly, Grade 6
Sacred Heart School

Gym

Gym
fun, exciting
tag, jumping, sports
happy, excited, cool, awesome
exercise

Jason James Salerno, Grade 4
Middle Smithfield Elementary School

America/USA

America
free, brave
voting, helping, learning
stars and stripes
U.S.A.

Trevor Filer, Grade 5
Trinity East Elementary School

Siamese Cats

cats
furry, funny
meowing, purring, sleeping
amazing majestic creatures
Siamese

Julia Faust, Grade 5
Trinity East Elementary School

Death

Last moments of life,
People will miss you when you're gone,
You are remembered,
Your spirit is with us all,
Sad, loving, joyful people.

Isabella Campbell, Grade 6
Sacred Heart School

Sledding

Going fast down slopes,
Racing over hills and mounds,
Sliding through the snow,
On a route in the forest,
With my sled underneath me.

Maria DiSanti, Grade 6
Sacred Heart School

Holocaust

Why? What's happening? What did the Jews do to go from,
Happiness to sadness, just in a blink of an eye,
You hear the screams for help,
The bystanders don't seem to care what was happening right in front of them,
Family members or friends, lost because of who they are,
They can't change that, no one can,
We could do them a favor and just respect their beliefs
I can't seem to understand why Hitler is trying so hard to take all of those poor lives out,
For what, hate, permanent memories, it's just not worth it
If Hitler experienced what the Jews experienced maybe he would have understood.

Ashley Omura, Grade 6
Nazareth Area Intermediate School

Holocaust

H ate The Holocaust was started because of this one word: Hate.
O utrage The Holocaust was an outrage to the Jewish people.
L ost A lot of Jewish people lost their lives and families in the Holocaust.
O bsessed Hitler was obsessed with killing the Jewish people.
C amps The Jewish people were put in really bad camps.
A dolf Hitler Adolf Hitler was the person that didn't like Jewish people.
U pset A lot of people were upset.
S cared Jewish people that got put into camps were very scared.
T errible It was terrible that Hitler was so mean and judged everyone
just because he had a bad experience with someone of that race.

Makenna Case, Grade 6
Nazareth Area Intermediate School

Holocaust

(Point of view by a 16 year old girl)
I don't remember much of my life because I have been here so long
But what I do remember is very little, I think of it very often
I remember my family and me playing
I remember my house full of laughter
But now that is all gone
I sit alone on a rock thinking about these things when I am not working in these camps
I feel tears running down my cheek
I will treasure these things until I die which may not be far away
I treasure these memories forever and forever may be closer than you think

Georgia Ferguson, Grade 6
Nazareth Area Intermediate School

Hockey

Hockey is a winter sport.
At the end of the season, the winner is presented with the Stanley Cup trophy.
Sometimes hockey is played outside.
My favorite player is Sidney Crosby, but sometimes he is called Sid the kid.
You play hockey with hockey sticks and a puck.
You will get a penalty for high sticking, tripping, slashing, and goalie interference.
If you get hurt, you will not be able to play for a while.
You can play with friends.
When you play hockey, you will fall down.
I like hockey.

Brandon Short, Grade 6
Bellmar Middle School

Mangoes!

Mad, mushy mangoes
A delicious orange ball
New mangoes as green as grass
Golden mangoes are the yummiest
Old mangoes as black as ashes
Eating them is as much fun as fishing
Super served mangoes

Sukhmani Kaur, Grade 6
Moravian Academy Middle School

Brownies and Milk

Brownies
Cakey, warm
Eating, laughing, sharing
Brownies go great with milk
Drinking, burping, slurping
Cold, refreshing
Milk

Rachel Marion, Grade 4
Erdenheim Elementary School

Seasons

Summer
Hot, shine
Swimming, running, sweating
Bright, sunny, numb, white
Shivering, skating, sledding
Cold, freezing
Winter

Jack Garlick, Grade 5
Foster Elementary School

Caroling on Christmas

Christmas
Cold, merry
Drinking, playing, talking
Getting ready to go out
Singing, asking, giving
Freezing, amazing
Caroling

Lucy Niemira, Grade 4
Erdenheim Elementary School

Dolphins

Dolphins play under the water all day.
They know under the sea is the place to be.
Watch out for sharks in the low reef parks.
Dolphins can breathe the water and the air,
They can breathe almost everywhere.
That's a dolphin's life
That's what they do almost every day.

Kelsey Geary, Grade 4
Grandview Elementary School

Music

Music can be quiet
Music can be upbeat
It can make you run away
And even move your feet

When you listen in the evening
Most people like it calming
When you listen in the day
It shouldn't make you yawning

There's rock-n-roll and pop and jazz
None of them have too much snazz
It can have lots of meaning
You can hear it when you're dreaming

But none of it is oh so bad
And it should never make you mad
When it's about nature
I think of a creature

When it's about machines
I think about them canning beans
Music is a wonderful thing
It can even make you sing

Nate Mosse', Grade 5
Winchester-Thurston School

My Neighborhood

Every morning I wake up
I can hear birds sing like
a great orchestra
and when the song ends
It starts over again
Then it stops for good
It was my alarm clock

I get up, get my school clothes on
And head downstairs
It was dark out
It was as dark as a cave

After breakfast I can see
my lovely street
my nice neighbors
and my great neighborhood with no graffiti
a lot of colors and me

When I walk to the bus stop
I look around and observe
each house, person, and animal
I think what a nice life I have

Judah Weekes, Grade 4
Wissahickon Charter School

Great Grandmom

I miss my great grandmom
She passed away when I was 4 years old
She had passed away
I miss my great grandmom
It was sad
because she had a heart attack in 2006
She had passed away
Everybody was crying at her funeral
I miss my great grandmom when she died
She was the best
great grandmom ever in
history.

Nasir Brown, Grade 4
Wissahickon Charter School

Hawks

I can see you from a mile away.
I can feel the wind's cold touch.
I fly hundreds of feet above the Earth.
I swoop down fast and grab my prey.
I watch as the mice scramble away.
I can outsmart the smartest.
I could catch a fast jackal if need be.
I can hear your every move.
I am stealthy as a sunset.
I can smell a rat from two forests away.
I am quick as a flash of lighting.
I am a hawk!

Jack Raymond, Grade 4
Cynwyd School

Pancakes

Pancakes so buttery and rich
taste better then IHOP
round and brown
and when you put them in your mouth
they melt
you can taste them on your taste buds
you taste the butter and syrup
my mom makes them
um I say
these are the best pancakes ever
you're right she says
we both laugh

Jordan Minor, Grade 4
Wissahickon Charter School

Hitler

H orrifying
I ntolerance
T errible
L ying
E vil
R epresents Nazis

Mason Hamilton, Grade 6
Nazareth Area Intermediate School

Rich and Poor

Rich
Snobby, Stuck-up
Winning, Ignoring, Complaining
Money, Greed, Problems, Sadness
Nothing, Crying, Wishing
Dirty, Broke
Poor

Eric Jazbinsek, Grade 6
Ross Elementary School

Hair Styles

Hair
Long, wavy
Flowing, unending, curling
Cap, braid, head, glow
Growing, shaving, rubbing
Smooth, shiny
Baldness

Jeremy Traini, Grade 6
Sacred Heart School

Marshmallows of the Air

Delicate, white, clouds,
Like a baby lamb's white fur,
Pictures in the sky,
Drifting very gradually,
Glimmering in the blue air.

Madeline Williams, Grade 6
Sacred Heart School

A Whale and Its Mother

There once was a whale in the sea.
It swam all over with glee.
Then came a diver
That drifted beside her
And the whale swam away quickly.

Will Edgar lll, Grade 6
Trinity Middle School

Birds

Beautiful, beautiful birds,
in the sky they fly,
'round the Earth they soar,
down to their nest they shall fly but,
soon they will soar again.

Sam Berdine, Grade 4
Burgettstown Elementary Center

God's Love for Us

Tender and Loving,
Receiving our attention,
Never-ending love,
Following us day by day,
We have everlasting life.

Jona Strauss, Grade 6
Sacred Heart School

What Mole?

I see an intruder in my small tunnel.
I can feel my tunnel's sides with my starry nose.
I may seem like a star-nosed nerd,
but I need these features or I cannot eat.

I swim through dirt or water.
I wave my 22 fingers to find my prey.
I use my nose for so much; no animal has a better sense of touch!

I cannot see you, but I can feel waves ripple with your movement.
I feel you look up with pleasure at the star-filled sky, but you don't look at me.
What am I not doing right?

I use my scaled paws to dig in snow, and swim in water, unlike some other mole.
I don't mind my icy stream, even if I don't see the faint sun's gleam.

I'm perfectly normal, why won't anyone look for me? I might be different but that's okay,
everything is different in some sort of way!

I am a star-nosed mole!

Moya Cleary, Grade 4
Cynwyd School

Yellow

Yellow is the bright sun that lets us enjoy the hot or cold days.
Yellow is a striped butterfly that flies to a colorful flower each day.
Yellow is the sweet, shiny, banana lollipop that is super sticky.
Yellow is the stars you see at night that twinkle in your eyes.
Yellow is the rustling leaves that fall off the tall, fat trees.
Yellow is a bright taxi beeping to people for money.
Yellow is creamy banana ice cream dripping in my mouth as smooth as silk.
Yellow is a bumble bee buzzing in my little ear.
Yellow is a yellow bird that is crashing into things.
Yellow is lemonade that is creamy and sour rushing in my mouth.
Yellow is a rubber duck in a bathtub, quacking and swimming back and forth.
Yellow is the yolk in the thin, round egg.
Yellow is a blanket that is as smooth as a cloud of cotton.
Yellow is lightning flashing in the sky: off, on, off, on.
Yellow is sand on a beach full of fun.
Yellow is a rug full of dirt that is dirty from shoes.
Yellow is a firefly looking for someone to tickle.
Yellow is highlighter, helping kids work.
Yellow is the sun getting ready to go to bed.

Jamie Horne, Grade 4
Aston Elementary School

I Am From

I am from my parakeet who sits and eats from my hand. It tickles but I dare not laugh.
I am from Daisy, my dog, where she begs and begs for a second dinner.
I am from Nina where we joke and joke until one of us explodes.
I am from go-carts where we race and race until bugs fly in my face.
I am from my mom where we hike and climb, get cuts and bruises.
I am from Lilli, where we act and write our own horror plays and movies.
I am from my dad where we read until the sun falls.

Nolan Wilson, Grade 4
State College Friends School

Cats

soft and cuddly
friendly and warm
I wish I had my own

black brown orange
white gray or almost blue
sleek and very beautiful
Madison O'Malley, Grade 5
Winchester-Thurston School

In Fall

In fall the trees are bare.
In fall the sweet scent of pie is in the air
In fall the leaves change color and
Halloween candy is everywhere!
In fall the heat from the fire fills the air.
In fall Thanksgiving turkey is so yummy!
Fall is the best season of all!
Josh Clark, Grade 4
Worcester Elementary School

A Child's Brain

A child's brain is different,
much more imaginative in thought.
A book could be a car,
a rock a speeding plane.
But there is one thing that we know,
nothing will be the same,
in a child's brain.
Maxim Vezenov, Grade 6
Southern Lehigh Intermediate School

My Cat

I have a cat and he is a foul beast
He scratches my mom's blinds
And huffs at me — a lion's roar.
I have a cat and he is a gentle boy.
He purrs and cuddles me
His name is Lavear
And he is my favorite pet
Amari Gilliard, Grade 4
Wissahickon Charter School

Red

Red is like red lipstick
that pretty girls like to wear
like me
like red high heels
and pretty red dresses.

Love red.
Amya Burton-Boulware, Grade 4
Wissahickon Charter School

The Journey

What is it about reading
that makes it so wonderful?
Like when you are three chapters deep
and just about to go into
this amazing journey
with elves, fairies, and giants,
or when you turn the page
and it makes that crinkling sound?
So what is reading?
Is it the book,
or is it the journey?
Sydney Cawley, Grade 5
Lincoln Elementary School

The Light

The light,
the light
it gives me fright
to see the light
always so bright
everyone knows
where it goes
except for me
for we
don't know
the light
Carleen Lenig, Grade 5
St Theresa School

Autumn Storm

In the pure light of crisp autumn,
children frolic on the rusted
metal poles of a playground.
A cool breeze blows.
Crows call the trees to erupt into color.
The clouds swarm the sun,
engulfing its rays and eating
its joy.
Lightning strikes, and the
children cry until the rain
settles and all is peaceful.
David O'Matz, Grade 5
Lincoln Elementary School

Soaring High

I was on the swings
I felt like I had wings
Flying up in the sky
I was going so high

I closed my eyes
But to my surprise
I hit a bump
It was a tree stump
Daniella Berrios, Grade 4
Middle Smithfield Elementary School

Halloween Night

H alloween can be scary,
A t night people trick or treat,
L ittle kids go with parents,
L ots and lots of candy,
O h, how people love candy,
W hy do we have to stop trick or treating?
E nergy is what kids have,
E arly to bed the next night,
N o I'm not going home.
Ashley Fallacaro, Grade 5
Clearview Elementary School

Horrible Hitler

H is for Horrible Hitler
O is for one man's destruction
L is for leaving your homes
O is for only the survivors saved at the end
C is for camps of death and labor
A is for Aryan, the Nazi name for the Jews
U is for unholy acts of Adolph Hitler
S is for stereotype
T is for terrible
Alexis Cole, Grade 6
Nazareth Area Intermediate School

First Things First

First the puppy and then the dog
First the rain and then the fog
First things first
First the kitten and then the cat
First the hair and then the hat
First things first
First the sugar and then the tea
That's the way it had to be
First things first
Saige Zullo, Grade 5
Claysville Elementary School

Holocaust Equals Darkness

Darkness came, covered the sky,
Made millions of those sadly die.
Lives and memories dreadfully shattered,
People thought it wouldn't matter.
Then they realized what they've done,
All those children had no one.
The sky was still black not blue,
And what they've done they'll surely rue.
Victoria Calzolari, Grade 6
Nazareth Area Intermediate School

Legos

Small little people
With heads like doorknob handles
And little box legs.
Bailey Sharp, Grade 5
Burgettstown Elementary Center

Rosey

Rosey is my wonderful dog
Her fur is as white as fog
I love her cute and cuddly face
In my heart she has a special place

She is growing day by day
She is like me in so many ways
Rosey is beautiful, kind, and sweet
Her licks are like yummy treats

Even though she chews all my stuff
Her fur is as soft as fluff
Rosey is my very special friend
And I will love her to the end

Jubilee Pons, Grade 4
Middle Smithfield Elementary School

Frogs

I am a quick leaping animal who lives in
almost all swamps, lakes, and rivers.

I love to eat crunchy, chewy insects
but really any insect is fine.

I blend in so well you could step on me!

I am part of an ecosystem with many
of my friends.

And I can warn and scare many
people and animals with my croak.

I am a frog.

Rowan Teran, Grade 4
Cynwyd School

The Air Show

The air show is
A fun place to go
If you go
You'll have a blast
The plane rumbles
As it takes off
They fly by
Like a roaring lion
I can hear
The blaring loud engine
One plane was as loud
As a train horn
That is why I like
The air show

Josh Zimmerman, Grade 6
Linville Hill Mennonite School

Happiness

Happiness
makes you feel up in the sky
when you feel it
it makes you want to fly
'cause the bright feeling
is the best thing ever
without happiness
it's that dark anger
lava filling up inside
no one likes it
it's not very good
violence that goes on in the world
but still there's life out there
even with the darkness that
builds up in the air.

Devin Valentine, Grade 4
Wissahickon Charter School

Paris

See the big Eiffel Tower standing high,
And the Rose Line, being religious
It's called the city of love,
Hello to Paris, France.

"Bon jour!" You may hear,
And smell the croissants,
Feel the warm air,
Hello to Paris, France.

In stripes and black, puffy hats
Surrounding people, in this place,
So kind and generous,
Hello to Paris, France.

Krysta Schrader, Grade 4
Middle Smithfield Elementary School

The Outdoors

I like the weather
  in autumn.
in the warmth of light,
the cool breeze of the dark,
as it rains all day,
there are starry clear nights,
with the moon high and bright.

I can rake big piles
  in autumn.
many different crunching sounds,
with leaves all around,
I rake all day
as the piling leaves
start to form big mounds.

Nadine Oury, Grade 5
Falk Laboratory School

Look at the Stars

Look at the stars
Shining so bright

Look at the stars
such a sweet sight

Look at the stars
they shine at night

Look at the stars
they are like a bright light

Emily Nase, Grade 6
Pennridge North Middle School

My Dog

My dog has the eyes
as blue as the sea
his personality
is brighter than the sun
he has a heart
as big as the world
when he cries
he melts my heart
he means more to me
than anything

Morgan Lynch, Grade 6
Hopewell Memorial Jr High School

The Confusing Night?

Why does the sun still shine?
When it's way past bedtime.
Why is he still so bright?
When it's half-past midnight.

He's kept everyone up too late,
And fooled them into thinking,
That it's still daytime, not yet night.
He's coaxed the owls back under cover,
And tricked wolves into giving out "Hoots!"

Paul Callahan, Grade 6
Pennridge North Middle School

Extraordinary

Some days are good
Some days are bad
This day is more than good
It's Extraordinary
Extraordinary is it
Not much more
Not much less
It's the most wonderful day
Without a delay
It's Christmas today!

Darby Matvey, Grade 5
St Sebastian Elementary School

Tree of Life

Tree of life stands up tall.
It's sagging branches touch the ground.
And give shade to everyone around.

It's apples are golden.
And its branches are beautiful.
Its leaves are like a burning fire.

If the sun hits it everything twinkles.
When the moon shines it sleeps.
But in the night it doesn't know
That people will cut it down.

I get up in the moonlight
To go to see the tree.
But when I get there, there is nothing to see.
I cry and cry until the sun comes up.

I see the stump where it once rises.
But I see a seed where the stump sits.
And I pick it up to plant another tree.
And every year I come back to see the tree.

Matthew Clevenger, Grade 4
Jefferson Elementary School

The Allergy Attack

Garbage cans full with Kleenexes to the top
I keep saying nose please stop
Runny nose, coughing, and mucus
I don't know how much longer I can take this
I think my nose is about to explode
All the way from head to toe
Twenty Kleenex boxes at my side
I really hope that they are two-ply
I hope these allergies go to the South
I can't take this nasty taste in my mouth
Goodnight sickness, good morning sunshine
All these allergies were a pain in my behind

Mara Gentile, Grade 6
Hopewell Memorial Jr High School

Cheetah

I am fierce.
I am very fast.
I use my speed to catch up to my prey.
When I see an animal I dash after it.
When I get my prey I quickly bite it so it does not escape.
I hear my prey.
I have spots.
I live in Asia.
I eat antelope and many other animals.
I go by myself when hunting for prey.
I am endangered.
I am a cheetah.

Adam Hetzelson, Grade 4
Cynwyd School

The Love

Pink the color
of love
Pink
the feeling
you get in your heart
Pink
the feeling you get in your heart when you meet a girl
Pink
the feeling of love
Pink
for Valentine's day
Pink
something
a girl would like
Pink
the emotion you get when somebody loves you
or when you love them right back

Jordan Norris, Grade 4
Wissahickon Charter School

Fall

September is red, yellow, brown leaves falling
From the trees like butterflies fluttering
in the spring.
School is coming when
It is cold,
And windy days grow shorter and
nights grow longer. Kids burst outdoors when
school is done.
October is Halloween candy and costumes,
jack-o'-lanterns staring in the deep, dark night,
waiting for you to come and trick-or-treat;
To walk up and look into their eyes.
November is Thanksgiving turkeys, gobbling
with their long brown necks,
eating all they can before Thanksgiving dinner.
Thanksgiving is not just the feast,
it's getting together with your loved ones.

Crystal Ambroselli, Grade 4
Aston Elementary School

Thanksgiving Dinner

T here it is it's Thanksgiving,
H ere it is, it's so soon,
A nd all the good foods,
N ow is the time,
K indness is always shared,
S o fun times to have,
G iving food to other people is so great to do, dig
I nto the food, have a
V ery nice meal, and share
I mportant memories from
N ovember and remember you are,
G oing to have the best Thanksgiving ever!

Elisa Torres, Grade 5
Clearview Elementary School

Bystanders

Adolf Hitler was a man full of hate
He made a plan to seal the Jews' fate
He sent them to camps, where they died
Their families sat at home and cried
Bystanders sat at home and hid, full of pity
Their families were being taken from the city
They feared that this would happen to them too
So nobody stood up, though, it was the right thing to do
Some of them realized, but it was too late
Hitler had won and we lost to his hate
Six billion Jews lost their lives in those days
All due to the actions of Hitler's cruel ways
And all those who witnessed these sick events knew
They could not let Hitler kill one more Jew
So we went to seek help and the Nazis soon fell
And peace was restored to all Jews who still dwelled
But there still were those few who stood by and hid
They did not try to stop him, but there were people who did
And honor those people as heroes we do
As they did before us, every last living Jew.

Serena Campanelli, Grade 6
Nazareth Area Intermediate School

Blue

Blue is the smell of blueberry pie, cake, and cupcakes,
The smell of fresh blue paint.
It's the sound of fire truck sirens, and
Big blue metal trains.
It looks like the shore with its
Blue ocean.
It's blue lakes and bursting fountains
Touching the big blue sky.
Blue feels like blue paint splattering on
Your hands,
That feeling you get coloring
With a blue marker,
Blue stars shining in the sky
Blue frosting on a cake,

Blue cars flying by me,
Blue stickers on my blue shirt,
Blue pants on my legs,
Blue paper on the wall,
Blue, blue everywhere!

Christopher Palmer, Grade 4
Aston Elementary School

I Am Nature

I am nature,
I am animals,
I am plants.
I hate pollution but I like sunshine and rain.
I provide shelter for animals and in return they do for me.
I am nature.

Colby Stanek, Grade 4
Lincoln Elementary School

A Walk in Autumn to Home

I slowly walk through the autumn forest
and feel the warm sun caress my skin.
I look forward and see colorful leaves,
magnificent trees and majestic mountains.

I smell the dried leaves,
and grab one to look at mother nature's art.
I look around me some more,
and notice the fragile elegance of this world.

I close my eyes and breathe once more,
then my soul is picked up by the wind
and carried back to home.
I open my eyes and there is no pain, no more sadness,
but complete joy.
I look down to see Earth,
then look up to my Heaven,
my timeless, joyful, and loving home.

Kaia Zorianna Bachman, Grade 5
Lincoln Elementary School

Kiwi

You are a ball blanketed in spikes,
A corrupted lemon overlaid in hair.
You feel like a squishy stress ball on a
guidance counselor's desk
just longing to be squeezed.
When you are peeled, you sound like
soft water ice just when you need it.
Inside you are a fancy sand dollar
lying on the beach hoping a new
journey is coming your way.
You feel slimy like my dog's ball when he's done playing.
You smell like grapes freshly picked from the orchard.
You taste like a tangle of grapes, lemons, and strawberries;
A fruit-lovers dream.
Tell me, kiwi, why do you let the
sourness over
power the sweetness?
Why don't you let the sweetness shine through?

Sydney Simpson, Grade 5
Reiffton School

Blue Bird

Blue bird, blue bird in a tree,
Blue bird, blue bird, now you're next to me,
Blue bird, blue bird, flying in the light,
Blue bird, blue bird, saying to you good night.
Blue bird, blue bird, sing with me.
Blue bird, blue bird, soaring near the sea,
Blue bird, blue bird, do not roam.
Blue bird, blue bird, it's time to go home.
Blue bird, blue bird, lying in your nest,
Blue bird, blue bird, now it's time to rest

Alexia Harrison, Grade 4
St John Neumann Regional Academy - Elementary Campus

A Zoo That Floats

There is a story called "Noah's Ark."
Who mainly made it with twigs and bark.
Two animals of each came that day.
Even the reindeer from Santa's sleigh.

The ark sailed for forty nights,
That had a sky with no lights.
It was dark; that's good for the bats,
But the thunder was too scary for the cats.

He sent a dove to find land,
The dove came back with nothing in hand,
Time went by and hope was none to be,
Until the dove returned with a branch from a tree.

The ark and the storm what a glorious fight,
But it was over when it was night.
The herbivores were happy; they did a little dance,
Except the carnivores who were in a hunger trance.

The animals were happy that they found shore,
Even the crocodiles, the snakes, and one big boar.
The kangaroos bounced and the zebras ran,
And one little lizard made a home in a can.

James Radomile, Grade 6
Holy Child Academy

Leopard

Leopard! Leopard! Spots dark as night,
Reeking beauty, strength, and fright,
What brain, what mind, what idea or thought,
Made a creature with such fury at heart?

How can something as great as you
Not be let free, but put in a zoo?
A horror, a hunter, a mother to your child,
How can you be these things, and yet be so wild?

Leopard, oh, Leopard, answer me this:
Do you have feelings, like love or sadness?
Creep, jump, and kill, is that all you do?
Do all other animals bow down to you?

As humans live, do you start to die?
Do you use what we use, like language and time?
And do you think? If so about what?
Do you think about what you're going to hunt?

Leopard! Leopard! Spots dark as night,
Reeking beauty, strength, and fright,
What brain, what mind, what idea or thought,
Made a creature with such fury at heart?

Amanda Carter, Grade 5
Copper Beech Elementary School

Spring

I can hear the bells ring
I can hear the birds sing
I can see the birds nesting
I can see the bears just awaking from resting
I can feel the warm air
I can feel the end near
I can smell the fresh flowers
I can count the last hours
Winter is over, spring is near
But by winter again, I'm out of here!

Carly Belich, Grade 6
Hopewell Memorial Jr High School

The Swim

You're waiting your turn to swim your event.
Your heart beats fast.
You walk up to the block, ready.
You get on the block in a ready stance and everybody chants.
It gets quiet then, BEEP, you're off.
Swimming as fast as you can you get to the flip.
Ready for another lap you gun it.
You're neck and neck with the guy beside you.
You slam the wall and you win.
Congratulations

Charles McClaine, Grade 6
Hopewell Memorial Jr High School

Holocaust

H is for hate, what was it worth.
O is for options, they had the option to help the victims.
L is for ludicrous, what Hitler did was ludicrous.
O is for observer, don't be a watcher.
C is for how cruel Hitler was.
A is for awful, what awful people the Nazis were.
U is for unnatural, the Americans thought nothing of it but
    the Jewish peoples' deaths were unnatural.
S is for shame, the Jewish people were covered in shame.
T is for time, something the Jewish did not have.

Nick Nolder, Grade 6
Nazareth Area Intermediate School

Jacques Piccard

Jacques Piccard was born on July 28th, 1922
Was a Swiss ocean explorer, a scientist who had a clue
To the Marianas Trench he dived, it's true!
Got people from the U.S. Navy to add more to his crew
He and his father built three submarines
They specially built them to survive the rough ocean terrain
The five-hour dive and 35,000 feet, so much to uncover
At the bottom now! A new shrimp species to discover
Jacques Piccard was great!
But died on November 1st, 2008

Francis Bosch, Grade 5
Interboro GATE Program

Jen

There once was a girl named Jen
Who liked a boy named Ben
They twirled and spun
Had lots of fun
Until Jen met a boy named Ken
Avery Lucas, Grade 5
Nether Providence Elementary School

Parrot Peyton

There once was a parrot named Peyton
Who fell in love with Heyton
Her hair stuck up
They broke up, yup
That was the romance of datin'
Isabella Hunter, Grade 5
Nether Providence Elementary School

Cloud Gazing

White, puffy pillows,
Different shapes and sizes,
Drifting in the sky,
Lazily floating figures,
Hiding the heavens on high!
Shannon Reilly, Grade 6
Sacred Heart School

A Grandmother Is

The warmth of a fire in the fireplace.
The person who makes the best cookies.
The person who is always in your heart.
Th. person you will never forget.
The greatness of a great person.
Taylor Hesse, Grade 6
Moravian Academy Middle School

Pickle

pickle
juicy, crisp
crunching, puckering, savoring
mm mm so good
dill
Ethan Newman, Grade 5
Trinity West Elementary School

The Flag

Sign of freedom
It waves with price
With fifty stars stitched behind
You may say who cares
But to me nothing compares!
Bryce Andra, Grade 4
Jefferson Elementary School

Lacrosse Goalie

I was the lacrosse goalie in the game
The routine was nothing but the same,

At last I could not bear to see
That the ball came flying to my knee

The ball hit with so much impact
That it came back almost exact

As if the ball was not done
Getting hit with the ball was never fun

Once again the ball came around
Before it came to me it went into the ground

I stuck out my stick when the ball hit with force
I deflected it to another source.

As if the ball were to whisper in my face,
When I deflected it the defender was on with another chase.

When he got the ball just like that
He threw it to me so I caught it and threw it with a loud WHACK!!

Then the other goalie caught it and the big bad ball came
Hurtling back to me as fast as a bull.

As the game drew to a close I thought to myself it did not matter win or lose,
I was not going to be in the blues.
Nicholas Jones, Grade 6
Eden Hall Upper Elementary School

The Wandering Jew

Hello, light, my only friend, take me far away, bring me home.
I must leave this awful place I've been here so long.
What's it like to be on the outside, not to be here?
I've forgotten what it's like, to see my mother's face,
my father's voice, and the name of my little brother.
I took all of it for granted, and now I may never see any of it again.
This life isn't right…Hello? Light? Where are you?
Now darkness covers what used to be my vision.
Black is all that I can see. That awful absence of color.
What is that, Mr. Soldier man? I must leave my home and all of my loved ones?
But why? And what exactly does happen at these alleged "camps?"
That is all that I remember of my old life, now here we are at this so-called *camp*.
I believe that it has been three days, maybe four.
I have been split from all of my friends and family.
My best friend lied to me. I don't know who to trust now.
Hitler thinks of so many ways to kill all of these people, all of these Jews, like me.
I can't take that thought, it's making me nauseous.
Oh, hello again, Mr. Soldier guy…What's that? I must disrobe? But why?
A shower? But why do I…All right, but…hey what's that coming through the ceiling?
Is that —
And that was *The Wandering Jew* —
Briana Campanelli, Grade 6
Nazareth Area Intermediate School

Time

Time.
Is it fast,
Or is it slow?
What does it mean?
If you're late
Or early
Or when it ends.
Is that it?
Can it tell us something else,
will time run out?
Will it ever ever end?
Can it end?
Or will we be here forever.

Time.
What is it?

Morgan Coccari, Grade 6
Bellmar Middle School

If I Were Your Blue Jay

If I were blue,
I'd be the sky protecting you.
If I were blue,
I'd be the tide rolling in.
If I were blue,
I'd be the water that keeps you hydrated.
If I were blue,
I'd be that sweet blueberry in your pie.
If I were blue,
I'd be the bluebell in the grass.
If I were blue,
I'd be a great blue whale in the ocean.
If I were blue,
I'd be that moldable clay in the ground.
If I were blue,
I'd be your Blue Jay.

Jonathan Williams, Grade 5
Holy Child Academy

Candy

Swirly lollipops
Tasty Tootsie Rolls
Joyful Jolly Ranchers
Perfect Hershey's
Oops my stomach really hurts
I ate way way too much
Next time let's just stick with
Swirly lollipops, no
Tasty Tootsie rolls, no
Joyful Jolly Ranchers, no
Perfect Hershey's, no
What to choose, what to choose
How about all of them
Here we go again

Emma Chothani, Grade 4
Jefferson Elementary School

Living on Wea-Land Farm

I love the farm!
Its beauty is magnificent!
The smell of the pine shavings
The gorgeous barn
There's nothing better
Than Wea-Land Farm!

As you shut the door,
You smell manure,
And see the cats
Chase critters and hiss.
There's nothing better
Than Wea-Land Farm!

You hear the heavy heifers.
They moo as loud as a motor
Since it's been so long since
They had their evening supper.
See the cows all sleeping like babies
Since they were so tired.
I love Wea-Land farm!

What land are we from? Wea-Land!!

Krista Weaver, Grade 6
Linville Hill Mennonite School

Poppies

In the Middle East, sandstorms blow
Iraqi children grow and grow
Paratroopers shouldn't be afraid of heights
Army wives say fight, fight, fight
Oh wouldn't that be so grand
To be back home
In the baseball stands
But today I am alone

The Major said
Wake up! Wake up! We've gone code red.
With a boom and a clap
I thought I'd never come back.
I was right.
What an ugly sight.
With all the blood and gore,
I wanted to scream,
"Mama I don't want to fight no more"

Poppies adorn the chests of our Veterans
We can all make the connection
that our Heroes are very tough
but they can never be thanked enough.

Will Schaninger, Grade 6
Southern Lehigh Intermediate School

Colors

The color red makes me
mad all the time
I don't know what to do
with myself.

The color orange makes me
happy and mad
at the same
time.

The color blue makes me
sad and shy.

Tyrell Martin, Grade 4
Wissahickon Charter School

Pigs in Blankets

All winter I was looking forward to this
A spring vacation just me and my sis.
We were going to Grandma's house to play!
Then I found out that we were going to stay
For two months and… three… weeks…
I thought it was going to be boring
But when we got there
All we heard were shrieks!
At first we were scared,
But when we walked into the living room
We actually saw REAL pigs in blankets!
So…wish us luck!

Erin Anderson, Grade 6
Hopewell Memorial Jr High School

Ellison Onizuka

June 24 the day of his birth
A lieutenant born to see the universe
A masters degree in engineering on his slate
The STS 51-C his first date
A candidate to be an astronaut
The shuttle Challenger he fought
A U.S. flight tester
An orbiting ship
The Challenger gone
Everyone dead including he
His body and homestead
In Kona Hawaii

Cody Capone, Grade 5
Interboro GATE Program

A Happy Treat

The lad asked.
The coins jingled.
The employee assembled.
The ice cream plopped.
The cone stood.
The boy licked.

Brianna Griswold, Grade 6
Lititz Elementary School

My Dream World

Anything I want can come alive,
Every wish I had right by my side.

The creativity, your own imagination.
We make what we want, no hesitation.

You can scream out,
Have no doubt.

Laugh and play,
Do what you say.

Let doves fly free,
Let me be me.

Everyone is appreciated; every soul alive,
From babies to people who realize.

Let my people celebrate, every single happy day,
Nothing bad will happen no matter what you say.

Please dream world, wait for me,
Mine, mine soon to be.

Camara Bey, Grade 6
St James School

Colors in Nature

If I were blue,
I would be a Blue Jay soaring through the sky.

If I were red,
I would be an apple falling from a tree.

If I were yellow,
I would be corn sitting in a field in the autumn.

If I were orange,
I would be a pumpkin growing bigger and bigger.

If I were brown,
I would be an owl hooting into the dark night.

If I were black,
I would be a crow sitting on a wood-peg fence.

If I were green,
I would be a goose floating on a lake.

If I were purple,
I would be a flower growing from the ground.

William Papoutsis, Grade 5
Holy Child Academy

Cars

When you turn on the engine it roars with excitement.
When you put it in drive the force pushes you back.
On the highway you get excited passing other cars.
The car is as fast as a lightning bolt, dodging one car to another.
The paint is as smooth as a baby's skin.
The leather is soft and smooth like a piece of animal skin.
When you hold the steering wheel you feel like you're in control.

Zachary Marzan, Grade 5
Winchester-Thurston School

School

Here I am once again with my friends.
Working hard to get my grades.
Sitting here for eight hours a day watching time pass my way.
Watching all the seasons and holidays fly by.
Waiting for June first to appear.
Finally it's here the day I have been waiting for all year.
The last day of school is finally here.

Jacob Jordan, Grade 6
Hopewell Memorial Jr High School

A Terrible Thing

An evil man once was here.
He caused every last tear.
Helpless people, treated like dirt.
They had no idea what they were in for.
Small spaces, shattered faces.
They were forced to go to these terrible places.
We will never forget the terrible actions of the Holocaust.

Hailey Durner, Grade 6
Nazareth Area Intermediate School

Being a Vampire

Wake up at night and sleep during the day
I cut you open and drink from your veins.
It does not hurt us immediately when we stand in sunlight
This is not referring to True Blood nor Twilight.
Our faces are pale our hearts are cold
We can live for hundreds of years which I guess is very old.

Christopher Dwyer, Grade 6
Hopewell Memorial Jr High School

One Day

One day you'll notice me
One day you'll say "Hi"
One day you'll care for me
One day you'll look me in the eyes
One day you'll have the feelings that I have for you
One day you'll love me and I'll love you too!

Anna Beno, Grade 6
Pennridge North Middle School

Call of Arms

As you gear up for a battle, and mount upon a saddle.
Nothing to loose but your life, with nothing but your trusty knife.

You turn to say good-bye, while you try not to cry.
Everything you love is lost, but you knew all along the cost.

As you turn to meet your unit, with a long path moonlit.
You don't know what's ahead, but there's nothing else to dread.

As you start your journey, you are a little squirmy.
You know what you are doing, there's nothing you are ruing.

To see if you can pass the test, you must find where the enemy rest.
When you find it you must fight, all the way through the night.

If you can pass the test, you'll be the very best.

Kevin Meurer, Grade 6
St James School

Champions

Butterflies in my stomach, as I await the start of the game
I'm informed by coach I will start the game pitching
Making the pressure worse
I hope I do good, but there is no guarantee
We start the game very even
The score 0-0
After my two innings of pitch
I'm moved to shortstop for the remainder of the game
It's finally the last inning
My team is winning
The score 5-0
My team awaits the final pitch
Down the middle
STRIKE THREE batter out
We are the champs

Tyler Pigoni, Grade 6
Hopewell Memorial Jr High School

What a Scary Night!

Walking home at night with my Dad by my side
Soon I hear police cars blaring
I stand stunned at the sight
Soon think what a scary night
The neighbor is shooting
I think of fleeting
Protecting me my father pushes me to the hillside
We lay there for hours
I look up and see policemen running, screaming, yelling
Finally a police car comes
I am saved at last
The worst is over for me
They take me to a safe place
I run inside and start to cry
What a scary night, what a scary night

Chloe Malloy, Grade 6
Hopewell Memorial Jr High School

Broken

Every night
I crawl into bed and bury myself under the covers
Until I can stand it no longer
When I must come up for air
I press my face against the window pane
That's when I find it
I find that star
And cling to it as the tears stream down my face
I stare into the darkness
The light from the star being the only one I see
I was once full of light and life and hope
I once had something in my life to pull me forward
I was once happy
But time and war and love tore me apart
I grasp my necklace and let the tears come
Silent and deadly
I am broken
And nothing in this world will make me whole again

Serena Woosley, Grade 6
Pennridge North Middle School

All God's Animals

As the slate gray squirrel scampers up a tree,
You can hear the buzz buzz of a bumblebee.

The little caterpillars are inching along,
As the royal Blue Jay sings a cheerful song.

There are furry bunnies bouncing on logs;
Down by the creek sits a little tree frog.

The tiny owls are hooting in the night,
As the raccoons fall asleep at first light.

The ladybug is like a swirling leaf.
But the beautiful butterflies give us much relief.

God made all the animals. They can be big or small.
None of them are the same, He just spoke and that's all.

Jalisa Yoder, Grade 6
Linville Hill Mennonite School

Remember Me

Remember me.
Remember me as a hero,
as a fighter.
I fought your battle for you when you were down.
I tried to fight but I tried too hard for you.
You did this.
This is your fault.
I loved you once, but now I'm gone.
Now it's time.
Time for you to finish.
Finish what I started.

Akua Wilson, Grade 6
Springside Chestnut Hill Academy

I Come From...

I come from watching the moon in bed and seeing the stars dance and wink
I come from playing in yellow spring flowers on warm afternoons
I come from drinking in scents of beef stew on cold winter days and the laughter of my sister in the summer
I come from drawing and art and doodle-scribble men
I come from my pencil dancing around my paper as words flow out
I come from turkeys and pumpkin pie at Thanksgiving and chocolate bunnies on Easter
I come from glowing sunrises and the dark flying away
I come from the words jumping off the page and flying around in my mind
I come from death and loss of loved ones
I come from soccer and blasting balls into the net
I come from New York and the Rockettes kicking down the moon
I come from sleep and undying laughter
I come from expectations and lost hopes
I come from tears spilling down my cheeks and a soft smile glancing off of my burned and scarred heart
I come from a comforting hand on my sad and sagging shoulder
I come from love and hate and hope
...I come from peace.

Morgan Miller, Grade 5
Friends School Haverford

Holocaust

H is for hate. The four letter word that started everything.

O is for obeying. The Germans had to obey Hitler or they would be punished or even killed.

L is for learning. Hitler made the kids learn about how Jews are bad people and they need to be dead in order to have a perfect world.

O is for operation. The Nazi's were sent on an operation to kill all of the Jews and bring them to the death camps.

C is for concentration camps. The concentration camp is also known as the death camp. This camp was for Jews that were sent there to be killed. They were held there for days, weeks, and even months

A is for awful. The Jews were put through awful things during their time at the concentration camps. Those who are still alive from surviving the Holocaust will remember this period of time for the rest of their lives.

U is for understood. We never understood why Hitler would do things like this to such innocent people, but later on we realized he was a mad man who thought life would be better off without a certain race or religion and that everyone would be better off without them.

S is for saved. One day when people thought their life was over they saw men in green camouflage uniforms and they said we're here to save you, you're free!

T is for terrible. The survivors will always remember this terrible event.

Emma Jorgensen, Grade 6
Nazareth Area Intermediate School

Senses of Nature

Look around, what do you see? Listen well, what do you hear?
Squirrels, soft as a teddy bear, claws sharp as thorns, silent as a still night.
Birds, feathers like rainbows, sounds like whistles in the clear morning sky.
A doe steps out, eyes big as teacups, fur like feathers, the ghost of the forest.
Grass waving 'round its hooves, pushed by a gentle breeze.
Crickets chirp, legs like sticks, small as a molecule, on a huge oak tree.
Bees buzz, covered in pollen, smelling of sweet honey.
Rabbits run, pelts like clouds, tails like snowballs, surrounded by flies, whose crystal wings were invisible.
Night has fallen, most asleep. But not all.
A skunk creeps out, stripe like the Milky Way, shining in the black night.
Fireflies twinkle, wings like glass, lights like stars in the darkness.
Dawn is coming, some animals waking, some crawling to their home for a well earned rest.
I must go back, my mother's home, then I will wait another whole week to appreciate the senses of nature.

Kayla Zemek, Grade 5
Winchester-Thurston School

My Brother!

I love my brother,
He loves me too,
We love each other,
Doesn't matter what we do.

We watch movies together,
Play video games too,
When he's with me I feel better,
Without him there's nothing to do.

He's 17 years old,
Going to college,
Leaving high school I'm told,
Getting more knowledge.

He'll be far away,
We'll be broken apart,
Even though I won't see him every day,
He'll still be in my heart.
Maryrose Ceccarelli, Grade 6
St James School

Hockey

Hockey is awesome!
I like all the teams.
All 30 of them.
My favorite is the Capitals.

Hockey is awesome!
I favor the food there.
My favorite is pizza.
People pay plenty for popcorn.

Hockey is awesome!
The sparkling, glimmering ice
The players skate as fast as cheetahs.
Whoosh! Zoom! That's the way I like it!

Hockey is awesome!
He's skating to the net.
He'll score, I bet!
Amazing! The Caps take the cup!
Christopher Petersheim, Grade 6
Linville Hill Mennonite School

The Holocaust

Adolf Hitler was the guy
Killing Jews he despised
Only blonde hair and blue eyes
Were the ones to survive
Otherwise you would die
In the day or the night
You'd be taken from your life
If you lived you now see a better light
Alyssa Zale, Grade 6
Nazareth Area Intermediate School

Tom the Tarantula

Tom the Tarantula
Was crawling all over.
The kids screamed when they saw
Tom was on a clover.
The kids picked him up.
Tom was terrified!
The kids threw him far
And Tom cried and cried.

Tom the Tarantula
Landed in Mexico.
Tom looked up
And saw a buffalo.
Tom the Tarantula
Was scared indeed.
He thought he would run,
So he took off full-speed.
Aidan Layton, Grade 4
St Andrew's School

Fly Away from Earth

When the sun does die,
Where shall we fly,
From Mother Earth?

To her child of birth,
The swirling sky,
Where icy life abounds,
Her descendant of blood,
Whose skin is sand and
Breath is the warm wind,
Child moons,
The home of the tiny strife of life,
To the farthest reaches of Chaos?

No matter where we go
We must hope for survival
As we have for millennia.
Daevan V. Mangalmurti, Grade 4
Falk Laboratory School

America

Our country stands in the clear.
The U.S. army protects us from fear.
The flag waves proudly in the air.
Anyone with a heart would truly care.
Each veteran risked their lives.
Some of their weapons were even knives.
Our country stands so strong.
Hopefully it will be around for long.
America is here to stay.
I would not have it any other way.
Red white and blue are the colors today.
We will always have rights our way.
Liam Budkey, Grade 6
St James School

Lucretia Mott

Fought for women's rights,
and got into lots of fights.
Born in Massachusetts, but grew up in PA,
she sheltered runaway slaves,
and made them behave.
She married James Mott,
he helped her a lot.
She believed in God,
some people thought that was odd.
Her child died at age five,
everyone liked it better when she was alive.
In 1868, her husband died,
everyone who knew him sighed and cried.
She died in 1880,
She was a courageous lady.
Kim Conmy, Grade 4
Interboro GATE Program

Strange Zoo

My friend took me to a place
where strange animals live
An eight-armed monkey
a seven-toed frog

We saw an elephant
as round as a log
a ten-headed lion
as fierce as a man

I saw a red bull
that chased itself
Then the land shook
as a colossal germ
sat and read a book
Richie Schwartz, Grade 6
Hopewell Memorial Jr High School

Can't Wait to See You

You have been gone too long
Wondering if there is something wrong
Yesterday seemed so far away
When I knew you weren't here to stay
Time came so fast with all the goodbyes
I held my tears in my eyes
Days pass so fast
You still weren't here
My only sister was nowhere near
Miles away so far
Wondering how you are
Hoping time would quickly pass
So I'd be with my sister at last
Happy now that you are here
My only sister here to stay
Amber Matthews, Grade 6
Hopewell Memorial Jr High School

My Dumbest Move
I was young
I was small
And I was 4
I jumped and jumped
All over my couch
Then I got on the arm of the couch
I jumped and...
I hit my eye on the iron lamp
My mom called 911
And said, "My child is hurt"
As soon as the guy came in
He asked, "what is the problem?"
Once I showed him my eye he left
And my mom took me to the hospital
They took me to the ER
To have my eye stitched
They put in medicine
To make it feel better
But, all it did was burn
When it was all over
I went home
Ansley Haught, Grade 4
St Alexis School

Lacrosse
It's about ruined grass
balls in the air
bodies slamming

It's about late day practices
early morning tournaments
cooly strong sticks

It's about sweaty bags of equipment
metal sticks
colorful gloves

It's about fights in the pros
fans in the stands
names being yelled

It's about paint on their faces
balls being shot
saves being made

It's in my blood
Evan Long, Grade 5
Pocopson Elementary School

Snowflakes
Gorgeous landscapes
White flutters everywhere
Light as a feather floating down
Brightness
Michael Doyle, Grade 4
Fairview Elementary School

Dog
dog
so fluffy
always playing around
so cute, so lovable
it likes cuddling
with its
master
Elizabeth Herrnberger, Grade 4
Trinity East Elementary School

Dreams or Nightmares
Dreams
Joyful, happy
Playing, biking, walking
All happens during your sleep
Running, scaring, freaking
Bad, scary
Nightmares
James Ogden, Grade 4
Erdenheim Campus Elementary School

Halloween and Christmas
Halloween
Creepy, scary
Running, screaming, laughing
First getting scared, then getting presents
Drinking, picture taking, sharing
Cold, funny
Christmas
Emma McCormick, Grade 4
Erdenheim Campus Elementary School

Cookies and Milk
Cookies
Chocolatey, warm
Tasting, soothing, craving
Always set them out for Santa
Pouring, sipping, smacking
Creamy, rich
Milk
Elena Hincapie, Grade 4
Erdenheim Campus Elementary School

Baseball and Football
Baseball
Fun, warm
Hitting, catching, throwing
Hitting a baseball, catching a football
Running, playing, passing
Rough, cold
Football
Anthony DiPietrantonio, Grade 4
Erdenheim Campus Elementary School

9/11
In the cool, crispy air
of September 11th,
the whole NYC woke
to two towers on fire.
The smell in the air was
like burnt plastic.
The sound on the ground
was a major crime scene.

At lunchtime
in Somerset County, PA
an explosion rocked the rural
town nearby. In the horrifying
scene of rubble and dust
the fuel tank exploded sending fire
through the clear morning sky...
KABOOOOOOOOOM!

People searching, some in tears
Families gather, the nation mourns
for all the people who lost their lives
on this the tragic day of 9/11.
Taylor Veisauyadra, Grade 6
Linville Hill Mennonite School

Gray
Shy is
all your feelings which don't
want to show
hiding you away
from
what every one else sees
so that they won't ever see
who you really are.
Dyneil Holden-Fobbs, Grade 4
Wissahickon Charter School

Tortoise
I move like a snail.
I have a big heavy shell on my back.

I sleep in a warm,
dark home of my own.
I feel the soft ground under my toes.

I eat fresh green leaves
and bright ripe vegetables.
I crunch on little critters.
I live a long life.
I am brownish-green.

I cool off in the shade
and let the breeze hit my face.
I am a big reptile that lays eggs.
Ethan Manin, Grade 4
Cynwyd School

The Beach

I love going to the beach.
The warm sand,
The relaxing sound of the ocean.
Everyone making sandcastles,
And swimming in the blue ocean.
But I only go once a year.
So I won't be going back,
Until next year

Samantha Richard, Grade 6
Bellmar Middle School

Cow My Dog

I have a dog.
Her name is cow.
She's fat like a log.
And as big as a plow.
When I'm sad
I'm never alone.
She makes me glad
That she lives in my home.

Josiah Wells, Grade 6
Bellmar Middle School

Snow

I woke up to a blast,
It was snowing at last.
A fluffy white layer of snow,
Was blanketing the ground very slowly.
Crisp little ivory flakes,
Were falling into the lake.
It was a wonderful sight,
Because it was all very bright.

Helen Hu, Grade 4
Ithan Elementary School

Day and Night

Day
Bright, Sunny
Playing, Driving, Climbing
Playmate, Partner, End, Dread
Sleeping, Snowing, Boring
Goth, Blanket
Night

Eli Hren, Grade 4
Jefferson Elementary School

Bread and Butter

Bread
Yummy, dry
Chewing, tasting, eating
Smooth like bread and butter
Spreading, melting, smiling
Smooth, creamy
Butter

Brennan Fluehr, Grade 4
Erdenheim Elementary School

Bad Morning

It was a cold stormy night,
I woke up in a jolt,
I saw a shadow lurking,
I followed it downstairs,
I heard a big bang and when I looked at the floor there was milk everywhere,
The refrigerator door was open,
I heard a little meow,
And I realized it was only my cat Zach.

Brandon Forte, Grade 6
Bellmar Middle School

I Am From

I am from marbles. When I look at them they take me into space.
I am from Mary. When I walk in, my dog Mary comes and rolls over to have a tummy rub.
I am from cacti that grow very slow. Some grow straight, round, and curved.
I am from the ocean where the crabs are scurrying in the sand.
I am from rides. I ride up, down, round and round.
I am from gems that sparkle and shine.
I am from cotton candy. When I eat it my hands and mouth get sticky.
I am from frogs—water frogs, tree frogs, colorful frogs, plain frogs…I like frogs.

Daniel Pacchioli, Grade 4
State College Friends School

The Dance

I am ready to dance, waiting for just the right time.
I glide onto the stage gracefully.
I feel the bass of my heart, my voice the melody.
Feeling the adrenaline pumping through my veins like a rushing river.
I have been waiting my whole life for this moment.
I am priding myself in this dance I have done.
I will remember this for the rest of my life.

Alexis Ozimok, Grade 6
Hopewell Memorial Jr High School

My Dad

My dad when I needed you you tended to my care.
When I was sick you'd pick me up and say it was okay.
Oh my dad I thank you for your wisdom, harmony, and love you've given me.
You're the reason I am who I am.
Now that you're gone I will cherish you for ever and ever.
I don't know how to thank you you've done so much for me.
All I can say is thank you and when I look up you're the light that shines on me.

Sylvan Rotuna, Grade 6
Hopewell Memorial Jr High School

Soldier

S oldiers are awesome because they go
O ut of the United States to protect us and
L eave their friends and family to go into
D anger,
I f I
E ver had to go into danger I would sacrifice myself because I would never
R un away because I would die proudly for my country.

Miles Hottenstein, Grade 5
Clearview Elementary School

Zucchini

You are the lime on a cool drink of water.
You feel like a ball with teeth marks of a dog.
When I peel you, you sound like the snake over wet sand and
Roller skates over the sidewalk on the 4th of July.
Inside you look like a flower with a bee drawing near.
Oh you smell like peppermint on Christmas Eve.
You taste like the dew in the valley.
You are the zucchini.
But tell me, why do you smell of peppermint?

Katrina Stump, Grade 5
Reiffton School

Fantastic Fun Fall

Everything silent except for cars rushing by.
Cool breeze nips my face.
Teeny yellow leaves surf the dark gray sky.
Last lonely monarch must make haste.

Aroma of pumpkin seeds cooking above the fire.
Trees shake releasing vibrant leaves.
Geese honking as they fly higher.
Orange, red, and yellow as far as the eye sees.

Raine Bedeaux, Grade 6
Pennridge North Middle School

Fall Festivals

The frozen outline of a deer, trapped in our gaze.
The roaring laughter hurts my head.
The blowing wind making me dread, getting out of bed.
I'm ever so anxious to be trapped in a cornstalk maze.

The turkey has a perfect glaze.
The leaves now beautiful shades of yellow, orange, brown and red.
The occasional "squawk" of geese flying overhead.
The festivals are all a haze.

Reena Sheppard, Grade 6
Pennridge North Middle School

Favorites

White, like a squishy marshmallow.
Jesus, because he saved us from sin.
Pierogies, yummy to eat whenever.
Happy, because it makes my family happy.
New Jersey, I visit two weeks before school.
Horses, because you can ride them.
Hide-and-seek in the dark, I play with my brothers and cousins.

Meghan Cowen, Grade 4
St John Vianney Regional School

Fall

F all is very cold,
A nd people wear coats,
L eaves fall off the tree,
L eaves crunch every time you step on them.

Samantha DeAngelis, Grade 5
Clearview Elementary School

Where Is the Love?

Where is the love?
I can see love in the world
But Hitler would never see love
Hitler wanted to believe in revenge
Oh Hitler, if you would only see
Don't judge a book by its cover
If you can see revenge
Why can't you see forgiveness?
You were a stereotype against the Jews
And convinced them that Jews were the enemy
When the real enemy was you
Your army was perpetrators
But some were against
If you would see what you were doing
Then you would see that they weren't the enemy
You would gas them, burn them, shave them, and torture them
Killing Jews isn't the answer
The answer is love and forgiveness
Where is the love that you have inside?

Thomas Le, Grade 6
Nazareth Area Intermediate School

Halloween

The witches come out on Halloween night,
The costumes give me such a fright.

Ghosts and goblins running about,
"Trick or treat" you will hear them all shout.

Bags and bags of candy as they go door to door,
Never getting enough and always wanting more.

Eating candy, laughing and having such fun,
But don't eat too much don't you want to save some.

People scaring you here and there,
I just want to give them a glare.

I go back to my house and dump it all out,
I go to bed, but I still hear them all shout…

"Trick or treat."

Elizabeth Padalino, Grade 6
St James School

Waffles

Waffles are fantastic.
Even the ones that are plastic.
The ample flavors make my belly thirst.
I think my taste buds might just burst!
Every time I see them it makes my mouth die.
And my eyes tear up and I wanna cry!
The flavorful butter drips down the side.
While my feelings for waffles I cannot hide!

Kiley Baldwin, Grade 6
Hopewell Memorial Jr High School

Christmas Morning

When I wake up on Christmas Morning
the feeling of that happiness
builds up some warmth in my body
me and my family
rush downstairs
and right there
under the beautiful Christmas tree
I see a whole bunch
of the perfect presents
All of the kids
rush to their presents
trying to find their name on it
It's so exciting
to see them

Paris Ford, Grade 4
Wissahickon Charter School

Sick

Runny nose, belly ache, and vomit, too
I don't know what to do.
I wish it was over
It feels like I got crushed by a Land Rover.
The sun is shining
But, I'm in bed watching the children play
It's been an awful day.
I can't breathe or eat
My breath smells like chicken feet.
I tried Advil, Aspirin, and many others
Now why would I bother?
I turned on the heater
But, I'm still cold
Once I'm healthy I'll be old!

Ava Grabowski, Grade 6
Hopewell Memorial Jr High School

Horses

Horses are the best
Out in the field
Running around
Saddles are on
The horses are ready to go
Eating their grains and apples
Stables have new fresh hay for them to eat

Alli Bagley, Grade 5
Nether Providence Elementary School

Summer to Winter

Summer
Hot, fun
Swimming, tanning, smiling
From warm to cold, here comes winter!
Singing, darkening, building
Cold, fun
Winter

Mae Sweeney, Grade 4
Erdenheim Campus Elementary School

Magic

It's all about the wishes and stars
sparks in the night
shinning so far

It's all about the invisibility
to keep it safe
so humans don't kidnap the key

It's all about the types of power
showering over you
at a certain hour

It's all about the dreams
the trust
the secret that hides in me

It's all about the caring
the part humans don't like
sharing

It's all about the secret
if you get it
you must learn to keep it

Magic!!

Sara Harkins, Grade 5
Pocopson Elementary School

It's About Halloween

It's about scary faces,
Boys being Frankenstein
Girls being Witches.

It's about ding dong ditches
Going to people's houses
Jumping out of bushes.

It's about saying trick or treat,
Give us treats
Or smell my feet.

It's about Dorney Park
Scary corn mazes,
Haunted houses

It's about the candy
The sweets
The sours

It's about finishing the candy
Craving more
Waiting for next year

It's the best holiday ever!

Daniel Dembek, Grade 5
Pocopson Elementary School

Snowy Day

Waking up so excited
When looking out at white.
Once I'm geared up
I'm ready to go.
The cold crisp,
White blanket
Covering my face.
I've waited a
Whole year,
To go down
What seems like
A mountain in my
Backyard.
The joyride
Was so fun.
I just wish it
Would go faster.
Then mom calls
I must go.

Emma DeBone, Grade 6
Bellmar Middle School

I Am

I am cool and collected
I wonder how it feels to run a mile
I hear people talking
I see a name tag
I want to become a football player
I am cool and collected

I pretend I am a football player
I feel happy
I worry about my family
I cry about pain
I am cool and collected

I understand math because it is fun
I say, "Try your best!"
I dream that I can walk on water
I hope everybody has fun
I am cool and collected

Nathaniel Vance, Grade 5
Nether Providence Elementary School

Popcorn!

Popcorn goes pop, pop, pop
a buttery and yummy bunch
I hope the popping will not stop
because I really love to munch!

Hot and tasty and salty too
I pop it in and eat
just add in a movie or two
and it makes my day complete.

Mia O'Brien, Grade 4
St Joseph School

Red

Red is like blood
but is not thicker
than water
red is sad
mixed with mad
and extreme anger
red makes you take a yard instead of an inch
when you are angry
when you are angry think of RED
Nadir Wardlaw, Grade 4
Wissahickon Charter School

Winter

snowflakes, wonderland
making snowmen, ice skating
drinking hot cocoa
Megan Gouldy, Grade 4
St Joseph School

Lake Erie

The liquid shifting
Below the beaming sunshine
Watch it as it goes
Carter Gannon, Grade 4
Jefferson Elementary School

Leaves

Leaves from the trees
Many different colors
Very beautiful
Giana Abbas, Grade 4
St. Joseph School

Winter Days

The white wintery snow
Ah, the freezing air
How I love that snow!!!

The melting icicles
Sometimes I eat them like popsicles
How I love that snow!!!

I imagine winter a big snow cone
As I'm climbing to the top
How I love that snow!!!

Whoosh, bang, shhh
That slippery sled slid again
How I love that snow!!!

The snow paints a magnificent picture
It makes me feel as happy as I could be
How I love that snow!!!
Allison Stoltzfus, Grade 6
Linville Hill Mennonite School

The Winter

The presents are as fun as a bounce house.
Winter is as fun as a game.
Winter is as cold as a freezer.
Sleds are as fast as rockets.
Winter is as fun as summer.
Dondre Tumblin, Grade 4
Wickersham Elementary School

Dancing Leaves

Oh, to see the leaves dancing
On the ground,
As the wind swirls them
All around.
The beauty I hope to remember
Of this sound,
Never to forget the peacefulness
That I have found.
Morgan Scott, Grade 6
Pennridge North Middle School

Blue is…

Blue is…
As wavy as the sea breaking
As still as water in a lake
As beautiful as the sky and…
As bold as the blue on our American flag!
Bella Pollice, Grade 4
Jefferson Elementary School

My Messy Room

Inside my messy room,
My mom says it's a garbage can
That just went through a tornado!
My sisters say it's indescribably icky,
Disgustingly disastrous,
But I think it's creative.
I release my backpack with a thud!
And see last week's spelling test —
It's just trying to find some peaceful rest.
I drop the two week old paper
that I was supposed to give to my mother,
But I tell you, I didn't meant to lose it!
My room is like a monster,
ready to devour anything within reach.
My mom threatens to get a sign that says,
"Crime Scene — Do Not Enter."
But honestly, I don't care.
I love my funky, junky,
messy room!
Mindy Beiler, Grade 6
Linville Hill Mennonite School

Violins

Violins bring love and peace to the world,
Violins are happy not sad.
They can be loud or soft.
They can be big or little.
Violin's music makes the world go round.
Ryan Kessler, Grade 4
Jefferson Elementary School

Sharks

Sharks
Giant fish
Chasing, killing, scaring
Wish I was one
Scary
John Lukas, Grade 6
Trinity Middle School

Leaf

Brown, green, purple, red, yellow
Falling on the ground
With no sound
And you'll feel mellow
Like a leaf
Danielle Richards, Grade 4
St Joseph School

Autumn

Leaves turn color now
Trees become bare, dull, and limp
Autumn is beauty
Jackson Fisher, Grade 4
St Joseph School

Index

Author Autograph Page

Author Autograph Page

Author Autograph Page

Author Autograph Page

Author Autograph Page

Author Autograph Page

Author Autograph Page

Author Autograph Page

Author Autograph Page

Author Autograph Page

Author Autograph Page

Author Autograph Page

Author Autograph Page

Author Autograph Page